Introduction *to* Public Librarianship

Kathleen de la Peña McCook

Neal-Schuman Publishers, Inc.

New York   London

Published by Neal-Schuman Publishers, Inc.
100 William Street, Suite 2004
New York, NY 10038

Printed and bound in the United States of America

The paper used in this publication meets the minimum requirements of American National Standard for Information Sciences—Permanence of Paper for Printed Library Materials. ANSI Z39.48-1992. ∞

Library of Congress Cataloging-in-Publication Data

McCook, Kathleen de la Peña.
  Introduction to public librarianship / Kathleen de la Pena McCook.
    p. cm.
  Includes bibliographical references (p.   ) and index.
  ISBN 1-55570-475-1 (alk. paper)
  1. Public libraries--United States. I. Title.
  Z731.M355 2004
  027.473--dc22

                                                        2004046012

Table of Contents

Figures

v

Foreword

For the past five years I have been teaching the public librarianship course at the University of Washington and have struggled to find the definitive text. Finally, that book is here. You are now holding a great overview of that fabulous invention and institution: the public library.

As I speak to librarians, library school students, and the broader community, I often say that in order for libraries to survive as an institution, we must hold onto our past, as we reach for the future. In other words, we must remember our roots. Of course, I do not mean blindly adhering to outdated formats, but rather that we remember and highly value our history and our roots, as we move wisely into the twenty-first century. The early chapters of *Introduction to Public Librarianship* clarify the social and political history that led to the founding and flowering of the public library movement, including the important role of women. The discussion of the role of philanthropy is an important reminder of our history, even calling to mind the conflict many felt over Andrew Carnegie's enormous gift to communities.

Later chapters emphasize truly how to "make the case" for strong, community-based, well-funded libraries. Through the explanation of the importance of standards, prioritization, role setting, and the complexities of governance, McCook sets the stage for a focus on funding, advocacy, and connections ("a place at the table"). This invaluable book includes topics of great importance to everyday library management; these range from unions, to staff development, to boards, and are covered with enough emphasis to give an excellent overview to a new librarian or student. A remarkable bibliography at the end of each chapter complements all of this information, with bibliographic citations gathered together in Appendix A: Selected Readings, at the end of the book.

Two excellent chapters—Chapter 9, "Youth Services," and Chapter 11, "Global Perspectives on Public Libraries"—were written by well-respected experts in their own fields: Linda Alexander and Barbara Immroth ("Youth Services"), and Barbara Ford ("Global Perspectives on Public Libraries"). Each chapter gives just the right emphasis for the nonspecialist public librarian and a great overview of the field.

The entire book provides the right amount of political sensitivity and activism that is so crucial for both understanding our history and shaping our future. As noted in the final words, "public libraries and the library workers who are committed to the continuation of this most democratic of all institutions face the future with the charge of maintaining a sense of place."

When I think of excellent libraries and what they can mean to a community, I remember a former mayor of mine, who always said, in reference to the library, "when a good community comes together good things happen." *Introduction to Public Librarianship* gives an overview and a blueprint of how to bring community together to make those good things happen.

Kathleen de la Peña McCook is an extraordinary thinker, writer, activist, teacher, and leader. Our profession is enriched by her passion. This book will become the standard text for those of us around the country committed to inspiring the next generation of librarians and library leaders. Additionally, it could be used to reinspire those of us well into our career, or as a primer for new library board trustees. However, for my purposes, I will finally have a textbook for my class! Now when I teach, I will enthusiastically assign this book, which helps remind all of us why public libraries are not only important to the progress of democracy, but why they are the most sacred institutions in our secular cities.

Deborah L. Jacobs
City Librarian
The Seattle Public Library
Seattle, Washington

Preface

As America's public libraries enter their third century of service, open to all who desire to use them, there is a need to introduce a new generation of professionals to public librarianship. The literature of public librarianship is extensive, but it is also dispersed among many subspecializations such as management, youth services, or community planning. In truth, public librarianship incorporates all of these specializations, just as public librarians work to serve all people—all colors, all ethnicities, all ages, all religions, all abilities, all economic means. This universality of mission and responsibilities presents a challenge. The public library of the twenty-first century is more complex than its nineteenth-century predecessor with multiple formats, remote access, and the mandate to provide equity of access to all. The larger community is made stronger by a vibrant public library and the library remains a positive indicator of the quality of life in any given community.

Purpose

Introduction to Public Librarianship provides the historical, sociological, and cultural background of the public library in the

United States. Such a full understanding is necessary for the future inheritors of our fundamental institution of democracy. This introductory volume is a guide to the extensive literature of the field's various areas of specialization. This book was written for students, new librarians, and librarians making their first foray into public librarianship, who wish to understand the historical and sociological foundations of different aspects of public librarianship. Readers of *Introduction to Public Librarianship* gain a greater understanding of seven key items:

1.   The history of public librarianship within the broader historical and cultural movements of the times

2.   The landmark literature of the field's development

3.   The evolution of standards and planning for public library service

4.   The role of the political process in the growth of libraries and library services

5.   Public libraries' adult and youth services as reflections of changing societal trends

6.   The current status of library services and the tools for evaluating and describing services

7.   The overarching ideas, principles, and goals that drive public librarianship and the necessity of continuing to work towards these goals

Organization

Each chapter provides a holistic approach to its subject. I have provided a historical background to the subject, an organizational context, and discussion about the development of public libraries. The chapters provide extensive endnotes and a thorough bibliography to help readers better understand the wealth of information available in public libraries and to help them explore topics in greater detail.

Chapter 1, "The Landscape of Public Libraries at the Beginning of the Twenty-First Century," provides readers with a context for understanding where we are today. The scope and range of public librarianship is defined and summarized. This chapter also includes background information about services to Native Americans and people of the First Nations, a population that is increasingly seeing new service. This understanding of the present situation will help readers understand the progress and development outlined in the rest of the book.

Chapter 2, "Brahmins, Bequests, and Determined Women: The Beginnings to 1918," reviews the historical antecedents and the legal basis for establishing tax-supported public libraries. It explores and discusses the fundamental *Report of the Trustees of the Public Library of the City of Boston, 1852,* one of the key documents of U.S. librarianship. This chapter pays special attention to the important role played by women in the establishment of service across the United States.

Chapter 3, "Public Library Growth and Values: 1918–2004," covers the history of public libraries from 1918 to the present. It focuses on efforts to equalize opportunity through the growing role assumed by the American Library Association (ALA), the enactment of federal legislation (LSA, LSCA, LSTA), and expanded scope of activity for the public library. It also discusses the work of national and state library associations and the role of state library agencies, as the growing voice of advocacy for libraries that resulted from these actions.

Chapter 4, "Statistics, Standards, Planning, and Results," explores public library statistics and reviews the development of standards for public library service. It analyzes the evolution of a planning process to replace standards and explores the role of the public library as a quality-of-life indicator in local communities.

Chapter 5, "Organization, Law, Funding, and Politics," reviews the political and economic context in which the public library functions. This chapter pays due attention to the organizational basis, legal basis, and funding basis of the public library, noting the parallels to municipal government structure and the move to larger units of service. We emphasize the importance of advocacy at all levels.

Chapter 6, "Administration and Staffing," surveys the structure of governance including model-enabling legislation. It presents the changing role of the library board over time, in addition to discussing the "Ethics Statement for Public Library Trustees." This chapter also introduces typical position descriptions.

Chapter 7, "Structure and Infrastructure," looks at the history of public library buildings (including the symbolism of the public library building), as well as the influence of the Library Services and Construction Act (LSCA) over construction during the last third of the twentieth century, and the shift in federal funding from construction (structure) to support for technology (infrastructure). This chapter also summarizes design standards including accessibility.

Chapters 8 and 9, "Adult Services" and "Youth Services," review the history and current status of these two distinct areas of service. In both chapters the service responses enumerated in the Public Library Association's *New Planning for Results* (Nelson, 2001) are reorganized under four categories to reflect a different way of looking at the public library's importance to its communities:

1. Public Sphere

2. Cultural Heritage

3. Education

4. Information

Chapter 9 is coauthored by Linda Alexander and Barbara Immroth, both professors of youth services, who also provide a list of recommended Web sites for libraries serving youth.

Chapter 10, "Connections," examines the importance of networking in public librarianship—the role of professional organizations, the work of state library agencies, and the growth of multitype library consortia. The boundary-spanning nature of public librarianship is defined and the importance of this to future development noted.

Barbara J. Ford, distinguished professor of international librarianship, wrote chapter 11, "Global Perspectives on Public Libraries." This chapter analyzes the importance of the *IFLA/UNESCO Public Library Manifesto* (1994), offers points of interest on public library development around the globe, and characterizes international library development initiatives.

Chapter 12, "Twenty-First Century Trends in Public Librarianship," examines four major factors that, I believe, will affect public library development in the first part of this century: (1) Sense of Place (SoP) in the Context of Regionalism; (2) Convergence of Cultural Heritage Institutions; (3) Inclusive Service Mandates and Social Justice Commitment; (4) Sustaining the Public Sphere.

Appendixes

There are two appendixes at the end of the book, both bibliographic in nature. Appendix A: Selected Readings, is an extensive list of readings, organized by topic, selected from 150 years of books, articles, and government reports, addressing topics related to the history and development of public libraries. Although I have also included Web sites, I have taken much care to review and assess salient items, especially those predating 1985. My rationale in this is gauged from a review of much current literature, which seems, increasingly, to rely upon bibliographic citations from online databases. It is my judgment that by providing this selected bibliography at the outset of the new century, I am helping to connect the public librarians of tomorrow with those from the past, who have written so much and so well for the good of librarianship.

The second appendix, Bibliography of National Statistics on Public Libraries, focuses more narrowly on efforts to gather statistical information pertinent to public libraries. Beginning with the first federal report on public libraries, completed in 1850, I present in chronological order the record of publications that track statistics about a wide array of aspects of public libraries, such as their numbers, activities, uses, physical features, management, programs, and holdings.

Public librarianship is one of the most rewarding areas of service within our profession. It is in many ways a practice that connects individuals with a rich history, one that mirrors our own national history. *Introduction to Public Librarianship* provides the essential information for future practitioners to go out and inherit the future of public libraries and continue to follow the ideas, principles, and goals, which have shaped over 150 years of public librarianship in the United States.

Kathleen de la Peña McCook
July, 2004

Acknowledgments

Special gratitude to Charles Harmon, director of publishing at Neal-Schuman, for patience and counsel, as I felt the need to read and review five times the number of items enumerated in Appendix A: Selected Readings, which added greatly to the length of time spent preparing this manuscript. Thanks to the great staff at Neal-Schuman. Special thanks to Michael Kelley, development and production editor, for watching over the final stages, and to Corrina Moss, publishing assistant, for her careful review of the manuscript. Thanks to the interlibrary loan service at the University of South Florida, Tampa campus library and to the dean, Derrie Perez, for her stewardship of a responsive academic library. Appreciation to Loriene Roy, professor at the University of Texas for her many helpful suggestions; Sara M. Taffae, director of computer services at the State Library of Louisiana for her observations on computing infrastructure; Gary O. Rolstad, formerly director of library development at the State Library of Louisiana for his wisdom on the role of trustees; Susan Dillinger, director of the New Port Richey Library for her thoughts on advocacy issues; and the RUSA Notable Books Council members, with whom I served from 2002–2004, for their insights on adult reading. I deeply appreciate the inspiration provided by

Kathleen Weibel, director of staff development at the Chicago Public Library, for her abiding practice of the library faith.

On a personal level, much deep gratitude and love to my husband Bill McCook for living through several years of my reading every scrap ever written about public libraries.

And to my daughter, Margaret Heim Christ, currently a doctoral student in accounting at the University of Texas-Austin, who helped me prepare the manuscript, I dedicate this book with much love and affection.

1

The Landscape of Public Libraries at the Beginning of the Twenty-First Century

Public Libraries Today

The public library in cities and towns and rural areas across the United States is a community center for books and information. In any community, the local public library provides a sense of place, a refuge and a still point; it is a commons, a vital part of the public sphere and a laboratory for ideas. The public library supports family literacy, fosters lifelong learning, helps immigrants find a place, and gives a place to those for whom there is no other place to be. The public library provides a wide-open door to knowledge and information to people of all ages, abilities, ethnicities, and economic status.

People who use the public library will fight to maintain it even in hard budget times. Even people who do not use the public library are fond of the idea of the public library. Individuals afraid of the influence of ideas may attack the public library. But, philanthropists and average citizens donate money to support the public library. Politicians make proclamations about the public library as the heart of the community. In the United States, the public library exists in cities and towns and rural counties due to many factors, many advocates, and many dreams.

1

Today throughout the United States, after over 150 years of tax-supported public library service, the variety of manifestations of the public library is astounding. Stand-alone libraries serve small towns, systems with dozens of branches meet the library needs of large cities, county libraries and multicounty systems reach even wider areas. The Peterborough Town Library, New Hampshire, is accorded the distinction of being the first public library to be established from the start as a publicly-supported institution in 1833. However, through an act of the Massachusetts General Court in 1848 the Boston Public Library was the first for which a state law authorized the establishment of a municipal public library.

If we look at three major assessments of the status of public libraries in the United States, conducted over the last 125 years we observe changing definitions of libraries. These three assessments were published in 1876, 1935, and 2003:

- U.S. Department of the Interior report, *Public Libraries in the United States of America* (1876)

- Carleton Bruns Joeckel's study, *The Government of the American Public Library* (1935)

- U.S. National Center for Education Statistics report, *Public Libraries in the United States: Fiscal Year 2001* (2003)

In the 1876 report, *Public Libraries in the United States of America*, the term "free public library" was used to describe tax-supported libraries, while the report covered and combined information on these, plus society libraries, historical societies, mercantile libraries, and government libraries. In 1935 Joeckel commented that definition of a "public library" is surprisingly difficult. He was referring to the varied methods of funding and governance that characterized libraries officially charged with the responsibility for providing free library service of a general nature to a particular community. Today, the 2003 report, *Public Libraries in the United States,* defines a public library more precisely:

> Public library (FSCS definition). A public library is an entity that is established under state enabling laws or regulations to serve a community, district, or region, and that provides at least the following: 1) An organized collection of printed or other library materials, or a combination thereof; 2) Paid staff; 3) An established schedule in which services of the staff are available to the public; 4) The facilities necessary to support

such a collection, staff, and schedule; and 5) Is supported in whole or in part with public funds (132).

Yet even with more precision in the definition that we use today, is there a typical public library in the United States? The answer is so complex that general characterization is practically impossible. Great urban libraries in New York, Chicago, and Los Angeles, serve millions of people in dozens of branches with many hundreds of librarians and library workers, and millions of books, while scattered rural libraries may stay open a few hours a week based on volunteer availability. Tax support, sometimes generous and sometimes modest, provides the glue that holds this continuum together, but from a belief in the "library faith" that this institution makes a difference in peoples' lives (Garceau, 1949: 50–52).

Today 9,129 public libraries (administrative entities) operate in the 50 states and the District of Columbia functioning with 16,421 service points. Public libraries in the United States have a combined operating income of $8.2 billion, spending an average $30.02 per capita. The nation's public library collection numbers 767.1 million books, 34.3 million audio materials, and 25.2 million video materials. These libraries require 133,000 staff to provides services. Circulation is 1.8 billion items, of which 653.9 million are to children. Patrons can access the Internet in 96 percent of public libraries (U.S. NCES, iii–vi). Each public library operates within the context of community norms and support—in a municipal, district, or county structure subject to local politics and the local economy. Figure 1.1 presents these factors.

Public librarians can use the Public Library Geographic Database to combine population characteristics from the U.S. Census to develop profiles of communities served.

For oversight and support, each state has a state library agency that distributes federal funds, which is charged by state law with the extension and development of public library services throughout the state. This agency should have adequate authority under state law to administer state plans in accordance with the provisions of the Library Services and Technology Act. Within the states about 400 cooperatives facilitate and promote library operations—often with a multitype focus. Additionally, regional cooperatives such as SOLINET, PALINET and BCR provide multistate services.

Librarians join together for continuing education and advocacy, through national associations such as the American Library Association, regional multistate associations such as the South

Figure 1.1: Number of Public Libraries, Population of Legal Service Area, Unduplicated Population of Legal Service Area, and Official State Population Estimate, by State: Fiscal Year 2001

State	Number of public libraries	Population of legal service area[1]		Unduplicated population of legal service area		Official state population estimate	
		Total (in thousands)	Response rate	Total (in thousands)	Response rate	Total (in thousands)	Response rate
50 States and DC[2]	9,129	278,830	98.5	273,921	98.5	281,098	98.0
Alabama	207	4,447	100.0	4,447	100.0	4,447	100.0
Alaska	86	627	100.0	627	100.0	627	100.0
Arizona	35	5,121	100.0	5,121	100.0	5,131	100.0
Arkansas	43	2,608	100.0	2,563	100.0	2,673	100.0
California	179	34,800	100.0	34,800	100.0	34,818	100.0
Colorado	116	4,241	100.0	4,187	100.0	4,301	100.0
Connecticut	194	4,163	100.0	3,406	100.0	3,406	100.0
Delaware	37	784	100.0	784	100.0	784	100.0
District of Columbia	1	572	100.0	572	100.0	572	100.0
Florida	72	16,552	100.0	16,307	100.0	16,332	100.0
Georgia	57	7,808	100.0	7,808	100.0	7,808	100.0
Hawaii	1	1,212	100.0	1,212	100.0	1,212	100.0
Idaho	106	1,136	100.0	1,136	100.0	1,321	100.0
Illinois	629	11,320	100.0	11,320	100.0	11,320	100.0
Indiana	239	5,796	100.0	5,675	100.0	6,080	100.0
Iowa	537	2,921	100.0	2,921	100.0	2,926	100.0
Kansas	321	2,239	100.0	2,234	100.0	2,688	100.0
Kentucky	116	4,005	100.0	4,005	100.0	4,042	100.0
Louisiana	65	4,477	100.0	4,469	100.0	4,469	100.0

State	Number of public libraries	Population of legal service area[1]		Unduplicated population of legal service area		Official state population estimate	
		Total (in thousands)	Response rate	Total (in thousands)	Response rate	Total (in thousands)	Response rate
Maine	273	1,178	100.0	1,178	100.0	1,275	100.0
Maryland	24	5,251	100.0	5,167	100.0	5,167	100.0
Massachusetts	371	6,348	100.0	6,348	100.0	6,349	100.0
Michigan	381	9,953	100.0	9,926	100.0	9,938	100.0
Minnesota3	140	5,760	0	4,919	0	4,919	0
Mississippi	49	2,789	100.0	2,787	100.0	2,787	100.0
Missouri	150	5,128	100.0	5,110	100.0	5,595	100.0
Montana	79	900	100.0	900	100.0	900	100.0
Nebraska	272	1,385	100.0	1,315	100.0	1,711	100.0
Nevada	23	2,001	100.0	1,998	100.0	1,998	100.0
New Hampshire	229	1,354	100.0	1,224	100.0	1,236	100.0
New Jersey	309	9,064	100.0	8,336	100.0	8,414	100.0
New Mexico	80	1,564	100.0	1,564	100.0	1,819	100.0
New York	750	18,913	100.0	17,700	100.0	18,976	100.0
North Carolina	76	8,086	100.0	8,085	100.0	8,085	100.0
North Dakota	82	551	100.0	551	100.0	642	100.0
Ohio	250	11,353	100.0	11,353	100.0	11,353	100.0
Oklahoma	115	2,858	100.0	2,828	100.0	3,451	100.0
Oregon	125	3,110	100.0	3,110	100.0	3,437	100.0
Pennsylvania	459	12,111	100.0	12,023	100.0	12,281	100.0
Rhode Island	48	1,286	100.0	1,048	100.0	1,048	100.0

Figure 1.1 continued. Number of Public Libraries and Population

State	Number of public libraries	Population of legal service area[1]		Unduplicated population of legal service area		Official state population estimate	
		Total (in thousands)	Response rate	Total (in thousands)	Response rate	Total (in thousands)	Response rate
South Carolina	41	4,035	100.0	4,012	100.0	4,012	100.0
South Dakota	126	605	100.0	595	100.0	755	100.0
Tennessee	184	5,559	100.0	5,484	100.0	5,556	100.0
Texas	540	19,355	100.0	19,355	100.0	20,852	100.0
Utah	70	2,233	100.0	2,233	100.0	2,233	100.0
Vermont	188	669	100.0	577	100.0	609	100.0
Virginia	90	7,074	100.0	7,074	100.0	7,079	100.0
Washington	65	5,842	100.0	5,842	100.0	5,975	100.0
West Virginia	97	1,794	100.0	1,793	100.0	1,793	100.0
Wisconsin	379	5,400	100.0	5,400	100.0	5,400	100.0
Wyoming	23	494	100.0	494	100.0	494	100.0
Outlying areas							
Guam	1	155	100.0	155	100.0	155	100.0
Virgin Islands	1	109	100.0	109	100.0	109	100.0

Figure 1.1 continued. Number of Public Libraries and Population

1 A state's total population of legal service area (defined in the glossary in appendix D) [in source document] may be more than the official state population estimate because, in some states, some public libraries have overlapping service areas.
2 50 States and DC totals exclude outlying areas.
3 Nonrespondent (all data are imputed).

NOTE: Detail may not sum to totals because of rounding. Response rate for population of legal service area is the percentage of libraries that reported the item. The other population items are single state-reported figures. Items with reponse rates below 100 percent include imputations for nonresponse. Data were not reported by the following outlying areas: American Samoa, Northern Marianas, Palau, and Puerto Rico.

SOURCE: U.S. Department of Education, National Center for Education Statistics, Federal-State Cooperative System (FSCS) for Public Library Data, Public Libraries Survey, Fiscal Year 2001.

Figure 1.1 continued. Number of Public Libraries and Population

Eastern Library Association or Pacific Northwest Library Association, state associations, as well as regional in-state associations, or even county or city associations. Each of these organizations and associations has contributed to the enhancement of library services through the development of guidelines, standards, benchmarks, and best practice.

Increasingly, public libraries work in partnership with other community agencies, such as museums, historical societies, botanical gardens, art centers, and social service agencies. These partnerships have increased since the creation of the Institute of Museum and Library Services in 1996, as the federal agency responsible for administering the Library Services and Technology Act. The ongoing development of active interaction with other cultural heritage institutions and social service agencies will transform the public library in the twenty-first century.

As an institution, the public library does not stand alone. This book situates the library within its historical context for each aspect of service. Throughout its history modern librarians must perceive the public library in connection with the print (or media) culture of its times, and in concert with broader social concerns, such as universal education and progressivism. Traditionally, the public has viewed libraries as broad collections of resources, but the process of selecting and gathering books has become a challenge with consolidation of media producers. Librarians today must develop an understanding of publishing and sources able to provide and build diverse collections. Additionally, the increase in multiple sources of media requires more attention to these issues, coupled with the challenges of providing electronic access. The "collection" has become dispersed, but the costs of items in the deep Internet still require review and evaluation for payment. Access to the free Web through portals and links and the creation of appropriate community-based ideas remains an important aspect of librarianship, and legal decisions about filtering and e-rate will make this access more complex.

Before turning to the history of the establishment of public libraries in the United States we should first ponder a very different type of library service—that of the people of the First Nations. When the National Museum of the American Indian opened in September 2004, a resource for the entire world to learn about Native American culture and life became available. That life and culture has been sustained by tribal community libraries. While it is outside the expertise of this author to address tribal community libraries, I have sought the wisdom of Professor Loriene Roy to provide a brief introduction.

First Nations: Tribal Community Libraries

This book does not address libraries for the First Peoples that reside on over 300 reservations within the United States. The First Peoples have a parallel history of knowledge and wisdom that must be considered in its own context. For a broader understanding of this alternative tradition, read *Tribal Libraries, Archives and Museums: Preserving our Language, Memory and Lifeways* (Roy, et al., 2005).

The United States government has addressed the heritage of "Knowledge Seekers" and "Wisdom Keepers," who live within Native American Tribes and maintain links with traditional tribal knowledge and history; see the official report *Pathways to Excellence*. Through the "Native American Library Services Program" the Institute of Museum and Library Services (IMLS) provides basic funds, assistance grants and enhancement grants to serve the range of needs of Indian tribes and Alaskan Native Villages. Loriene Roy (2000) has summarized these programs.

Research and projects such as TRAILS and Four Directions, conducted by Native American library scholars Lotsee Patterson and Loriene Roy, have supported tribal community libraries serving indigenous people. To understand the holistic approach to service development, you can review the papers presented at the International Indigenous Librarian's Forum (Roy and Smith, 2002), participate in meetings of the American Indian Library Association, and view work done at the National Museum of the American Indian. Roy (2000) makes the following observations about libraries serving American Indians:

> Indians are rediscovering or retaining their culture by establishing genealogy, reading and inventing literature, reclaiming their Native languages, and becoming involved with political and social issues such as natural resource management, reclamation and reburial of human remains, and protection of treaty rights. This renaissance is built partially by the work of the American Indian library community, which has labored for many years to find support for Native American educational needs.

Sources and Further Reading

American Library Association. American Indian Library Association (AILA). Available: www.nativeculture.com/lisamitten/aila.html.

Bill and Melinda Gates Foundation. Native American Access to
    Technology. Available: http://gatesfoundation.org/Libraries/
    NativeAmericanAccessTechnology.
Grounds, Richard A., et al. 2003. *Native Voices: American Indian
    Identity and Resistance.* Lawrence, KS: University Press of
    Kansas.
Hills, Gordon H. 1997. *Native Libraries: Cross-Cultural Conditions
    in the Circumpolar Countries.* Lanham, MD: Scarecrow
    Press.
Patterson, Lotsee. 2000. History and Status of Native Americans in
    Librarianship. *Library Trends* 49, no. 1 (Summer): 182–193.
Patterson, Lotsee. 2001. History and Development of Libraries on
    American Indian Reservations. In *International Indigenous
    Librarians' Forum Proceedings*, ed. Robert Sullivan, 38–44.
    Auckland, New Zealand: Te Ropu Whakahau.
Roy, Loriene. School of Information, University of Texas at Austin.
    If I Can Read, I Can Do Anything. Available: www.ischool
    .utexas.edu/~ifican.
Roy, Loriene. 2000. To Support and Model Native American
    Library Services. *Texas Library Journal* 76 (Spring): 32–35.
Roy, Loriene. 2003. Interviewed by Kathleen de la Peña McCook.
    December 2.
Roy, Loriene, and A. Arro Smith. 2002. Supporting, Documenting
    and Preserving Tribal Cultural Lifeways: Library Services
    for Tribal Communities in the United States. *World
    Libraries* 12 (Spring): 28–31.
Roy, Loriene, et al. 2005. *Tribal Libraries, Archives and Museums:
    Preserving our Language, Memory and Lifeways.* Lanham,
    MD: Scarecrow Press.
U.S. Institute of Museum and Library Services. Native American
    Library Services. Available: www.imls.gov/grants/library/
    lib_nat.asp#po. See also on this Web page the link to the
    Advisory Meeting on Native American Library Services
    (accessed January 13, 2000).
U.S. National Commission on Libraries and Information Science.
    1992. Pathways to Excellence: A Report on Improving
    Library and Information Services for Native American
    Peoples. Available: www.nclis.gov/libraries/nata.html.

References

Florida Resources and Environmental Analysis Center. *Public Library Geographic Database*. Available: www.geolib.org/PLGDB.cfm.

Garceau, Oliver. 1949. *The Public Library in the Political Process: A Report of the Public Library Inquiry*. New York: Columbia University Press.

Joeckel, Carleton B. 1935. *The Government of the American Public Library*. Chicago: University of Chicago Press.

Shera, Jesse H. 1949. *Foundations of the Public Library: The Origins of the Public Library Movement in New England, 1629–1855*. Chicago: University of Chicago Press. Repr., Hamden, CT: Shoestring Press, 1965.

U.S. Department of Education. National Center for Education Statistics. 2003. *Public Libraries in the United States. Fiscal Year 2001*. E.D. TABS, ed. Adrienne Chute, et al. Available: http://nces.ed.gov/pubsearch/pubsinfo.asp?pubid=2003399.

U.S. Department of the Interior. Bureau of Education. 1876. *Public Libraries in the United States of America: Their History, Condition, and Management. Special Report*. Washington, DC: U.S. Government Printing Office. Repr., as Monograph Series, no. 4, Champaign, IL: University of Illinois, Graduate School of Library Science.

2

Brahmins, Bequests, and Determined Women: The Beginnings to 1918

In public records and published books and articles, we often find the history of public libraries in the United States treated narrowly as the story of New England settlers bringing their values to bear on the development of a new kind of institution—tax-supported public libraries. Standard histories of libraries succinctly recount the received chronology of bookmen and Boston Brahmins. Likewise, readers can find consolidated versions of the comprehensive cultural and historical literature that we must survey to gain a broad picture of this history.

Parts played by men such as George Ticknor, Edward Everett, and Alexandre Vattemare contribute a great deal to our understanding what led to the establishment of the Boston Public Library. To further follow the mainstream development of public libraries in the United States, we must relate what happened in Boston, under the guidance of these men, to later history. However, at the very outset I want readers to note that women also expanded public library service throughout the nation.

Books were important to the development and stability of the seventeenth-century colonies, particularly in what would one day be Massachusetts, and were viewed as a means to provide a continuity of values. Many of the New England colonists had private libraries. Both men and women were readers. As Williams (1999: 2) points out:

> Europeans grasped the printed page as one of the surest ways to guarantee the safe transport of their ideas, knowledge and philosophies into the New World. As the carrier of inspiration, instructions, memories, and enjoyments, published material outlasted the long and dangerous voyage across the Atlantic to arrive unscathed on the other side. There was something concrete and unchanging about the printed word, and thus it was a rock in the courageous effort to carve out colonial Europe on the new continent. (2)

The most well-documented example of books brought to the New World as the "carrier of inspiration," is the effort of English Anglican clergyman, Thomas Bray, whose Society for Promoting Christian Knowledge established parish libraries along the eastern seaboard in Maryland, Virginia, and South Carolina between 1695 and 1704. Bray initiated three types of libraries: provincial, parochial, and layman's libraries. These also functioned as lending libraries for the public at large (Laugher, 1973). According to library historian Michael Harris, a few volumes from the original Bray libraries have survived in public or church collections, which serves as a reminder of a library venture that preceded the rise of the modern public library by two centuries (1995: 183).

The work of library historians reinforces the importance of New England in the development of tax-supported public libraries, because much of the synthetic literature about the founding of public libraries is based upon accounts written by New Englanders. Charles Coffin Jewett's *Notices of Public Libraries in the United States of America* (1851) provided the foundation for many later studies. Until 1876 the term, "public library," meant any library not privately owned, while the term "free public library" was used to indicate libraries that were most like the tax-supported "public library" of today. Yet in the years prior to laws enabling tax-supported public libraries in the mid-1800s, tens of thousands of libraries open to various publics were established in the United States. While New England's first colonists brought books with them in 1620, and Governor John Winthrop of Connecticut had over 1,000 volumes as early as 1640, the gradual acceptance and support of the tax-supported public library throughout the United States is far more complicated than the story of New England and its influence.

Print Culture and Precursors Influencing the Establishment of Tax-Supported Public Libraries

Ten Thousand Stories

During 1876, the centennial year marking the independence of the United States, the federal Office of Education issued the landmark report, *Public Libraries in the United States of America: Their History, Condition, and Management, Special Report.* It included the exhibit, "Table of Public Libraries Numbering 300 Volumes or Upwards," that was the catalyst for McMullen's (2000) study of the library past of the United States, *American Libraries Before 1876.* In his analysis, McMullen discusses over 80 types of libraries made available to various publics from the beginning of the colonial period to 1876. These included agricultural societies, apprentices' libraries, asylum libraries, athenaeums, church libraries, circulating libraries (commercial and society), government libraries, historical societies, ladies' libraries, lyceums, mechanics' libraries, mercantile libraries, social libraries, subscription libraries, and workingmen's libraries, as well as libraries affiliated with schools, seminaries, and colleges. McMullen's list calls to mind ten thousand stories that if known would help us to gain a fuller understanding of why communities throughout the United States organized and voted beginning in the mid-1850s to tax themselves to establish public libraries. Each collection helped to create the social and intellectual context that evoked a desire for books among its users.

Print Culture

Social historians help us trace the transformation of society into a widespread reading community.[1] To some degree the secularization of reading accounts for the diffusion of reading, but we should keep in mind that many types of reading—religious/devotional and secular—coexisted during the colonial period. People read out loud to each other, shared reading material, and read a variety of publications—devotional, secular, sensational, and serious. In the 250 or so years prior to the 1876 *Special Report*, reading and sharing books and other printed materials played a vital role in the lives of those living in the colonies and the new nation.

In the colonies, reading took place in quite diverse settings. When Benjamin Harris added a coffee shop to his Boston bookstore in 1690, the reading room in a coffeehouse became a happy consolidation that spread throughout the colonies—sometimes in connection with taverns and printers (Kaser, 1978). A variety of studies cover the world of reading in the colonies, examining religious reading, popular secular reading, the growing idea that reading was a necessity, and the development of the reading public.[2]

Reviewing the history of print culture during colonial times makes the backdrop against which the tax-supported public library was established and flourished more meaningful. But missionaries also viewed reading as a tool to convert Native Americans (Wyss, 2000), and we must remember that, in many parts of what would become the United States, African slaves were forbidden to read at all. In the antebellum South reading was seen as an act of defiance, and slaves were threatened with whipping or hanging for learning to read or write (Cornelius, 1991). By reviewing the growth of literacy and the role of reading in daily life, we come to understand more clearly the importance of the founding of the public library.

Difficult as it may be to fashion for ourselves an accurate sense of the scope of reading in the early days of the United States, taking the time to do so helps us to comprehend the social history that contributed to the eventual taxation of the community for this public good. After all, at the heart of the public library movement was an abiding belief that the provision of reading material was important to the progress of democracy.

The two major forerunners of the tax-supported public library were the *social library* and the *circulating library*. Early examples of each were in existence by the early 1700s. Social library collections emphasized literature, history, science, and theology, while circulating library collections reflected popular reading with an emphasis on fiction (as distinguished from literature). The discussions and debates about the book stock of each, almost from their beginnings, reflect the ongoing debates on book selection that persist today.

The Social Library

During the colonial period, the social library traces its roots to English gentlemen's libraries and book clubs of the early 1700s. The Library Company of Philadelphia, established in 1731 by Benjamin Franklin as a joint-stock company or proprietary library, was a type of organization that spread through the colonies and has long been deemed the best known of this early form of library. Further south, the establishment of the Charleston Library Society in South Carolina in 1748 demonstrates that the social library also existed outside of New England.

Social libraries were voluntary societies whose members owned books in common from pooled funds. These included athenaeums, mercantile libraries, and mechanics' and apprentices' libraries—mainly for young men. Each of these various social libraries involved the coming together of individuals to fund and develop collections based on their interests. Athenaeums emphasized more scholarly collections and cultural programs. Mercantile and mechanics' libraries, often supported by wealthy businessmen were intended to promote virtuous habits and diffuse knowledge among workers (Harris, 1995: 185–186).

While historians recount in their studies the story of some social libraries, enabling us to imagine the intellectual and pragmatic pursuits of members, we know of many others from the barest of records. Founding dates and locations of a sample provide an indication of the scope of social libraries prior to the advent of tax-supported public libraries. Mechanics' and Apprentices' libraries were established in Newport, Rhode Island (1791), Detroit, Michigan, and Portland, Maine (1820), Lowell, Massachusetts (1825), and thirty years later in San Francisco, California (1855). Athenaeums were founded in Boston (1807), Philadelphia (1814), Providence, Rhode Island (1836), Zanesville, Ohio (1828), and Minneapolis (1859). Mercantile libraries included Boston and New York (1820), Philadelphia (1822), Albany, New York, and Detroit (1833), Cincinnati (1835), St. Louis (1846), Milwaukee (1847), San Francisco (1853), Peoria, Illinois (1855), and Dubuque, Iowa (1866). These were not solely founded by those of British heritage, for newly emigrated Germans, as well, opened reading rooms as early as 1792 in Philadelphia.[3]

Studies of individual libraries and societies outside of New England, such as the Virginia Historical Society (Todd, 2001), or the St. Augustine, Florida, Library Association in the oldest city in the United States (Blazek, 1979) provide a clearer picture of particular places. Broader studies, such as "Women and the Founding of Social Libraries in California, 1859–1910" (Musmann, 1982), or Hoyt's *Libraries in the German-American Turner Movement* (1999), give us a more sweeping look at the growth of social libraries. From the beginning social libraries existed not only in New England, but also throughout the growing nation, with audiences that included women, new immigrants, and the other diverse publics.

The Circulating Library

Circulating libraries of popular books for rent were business enterprises that originated in Germany, France, and England in the mid-1700s. The first circulating library in the colonies was founded in 1762 in Annapolis, Maryland—an enterprise that failed, though it was copied in Boston in 1765 (where it also failed). The Boston Circulating Library, established in 1784, continued to 1787. Concurrently Benjamin Guild began a circulating library, in connection with the Boston Bookstore in 1785, which seems to have been profitable (Shera, 1949: 138–139).

Some circulating libraries were affiliated with bookstores, others with less likely enterprises such as millinery shops (catering mainly to women readers), and still others were freestanding enterprises. The institution spread through Massachusetts with circulating libraries established in Salem (1789) and Newburyport (ca. 1794) and elsewhere in New England: New London, Connecticut (1793); Keene, New Hampshire (1805); Providence, Rhode Island (1820); and Woodstock, Vermont (1821). Profits followed the fiction market and analyses of collections based on catalogs of the time show fiction dominating the holdings.

Meanwhile reading rooms continued to thrive in places like Lexington, Kentucky, described by a visitor in 1807 as subscribing to forty-two newspapers from all over the United States. Other locations were as different as a milliner's shop in Wadsworth, Ohio (1820), and rooms in manufacturing towns established for factory workers (1844) or New England mill girls (Kaser, 1978; 1980; McCauley, 1971). While the standard histories of the development of public libraries tend to leave women out, a fuller understanding is provided by Hildenbrand's monograph, *Reclaiming the American Library Past: Writing the Women In* (1996).

School District Libraries

School district libraries and arguments for their creation provided additional impetus for the foundation of tax-supported public libraries. The Common School movement of the 1830s that assured that every child would have a basic tax-supported education has been described as the product of social reform in an age of perceived social decline. Conceived as a bulwark of traditional values against the tide of immigrants, public schools with the addition of district libraries were viewed as the means to forge a new moral order by educating children properly (Fain, 1978). "The bridge between free schools and free libraries was omnipresent in the early documents of the public library movement," states Ditzion in his history of public libraries (1947: 22).

In 1812 New York's Governor addressed the legislature on the good that might come from providing books to the young; and shortly thereafter, in 1815, Jesse Torrey, a founder New York's Juvenile Society for the Acquisition of Knowledge, urged that governments use their money to establish free circulating libraries accessible to all classes and both sexes. Torrey was concerned that social libraries were too limited in their audience and did not provide for the education of women. His ideas—especially that the interdependence of public opinion and government demanded that all be educated, not just the privileged few—were used extensively as arguments for developing public libraries (Ditzion, 1940). The advocacy of New York Governor De Witt Clinton (1835) for collections attached to common schools as the basis of a tax on each district for a school library really marks the first state law for tax-supported (though school-based) free library service (Joeckel, 1935: 9).

The support for school district libraries must be reviewed in the context of the work of universal education advocates such as Horace Mann, leader of the common school movement and first Secretary of the Massachusetts Board of Education (1837), whose *Annual Reports* and other writings formed the intellectual basis for secular, universal education. Mann's efforts to provide access to education included strong pronouncements about the importance of books and reading.

By 1847 there were 8,070 school district libraries (Jewett, 1851: 104). Although the school district as a unit of governance was too small, staffing and location were volatile, and book procurement uneven, the significance to future public library development was of some consequence. The school district system did much to establish certain principles that formed the basis for public libraries, including taxation and state aid to libraries. Support for libraries affiliated with school districts was critical in recognizing the library as an educational agency, an extension of the system of public education beyond the formal instruction offered by schools (Joeckel, 1935: 12). The story of Harper and Brothers' development of collections for these libraries, as told by Freeman (2003), includes title lists that illustrate the scope of reading deemed appropriate for schools.

An account of the extent of school district libraries appeared in the U.S. Bureau of Education's *1876 Special Report* (1876: 38–69), which provides a summary of how far school district libraries had spread across the United States. Following the first such law enacted in New York in 1835, Massachusetts passed legislation providing for school district libraries in 1837, owed in large part to the eloquence and earnestness of Horace Mann. Eight other states enacted laws by

1848. Before the first law for tax-supported public libraries, ten states had already identified the importance of tax support for school district libraries. A study by Held of school district libraries in California notes, "Although generally unsuccessful, the attempt to organize popular library service upon the governmental basis of the school district played a distinct role in the evolution of American libraries" (1959: 79). Held's study gives a picture of early library development far away from the common patterns of New England.

Although most discussion of the history of public libraries include the school district library, many considerations of the development of libraries in the United States largely dismiss the school district library, because it was not particularly successful in actual delivery. However, the spread of this concept in connection with tax-supported schools across the nation certainly was a factor in creating a fertile opportunity for governments to establish public libraries in the following years.

Tax-Supported Public Libraries

Factors Leading to Their Establishment

The phrase, "free public library," as used by McMullen in his study of the library past of the United States most reflects the public library of today. McMullen identifies two types: (1) ordinary libraries established by local governments, and (2) township libraries established by state governments, but intended for at least partial support and control by local officials (2000: 121). Ordinary libraries resembled social libraries (and in fact were often converted from social libraries) in that support came from users in the form of taxes paid to the local government. Public libraries as tax-supported community agencies enabled by law have existed since the mid-nineteenth century. While by consensus, the establishment of the Boston Public Library (state law enacted in 1848; opened in 1854) marks the beginning of the public library movement, we can point to earlier examples of free public libraries, such as the Peterborough Town Library in New Hampshire, which was granted support in 1833 from a general state fund. Nevertheless, because of the well-documented discussions about its establishment, by-and-large most historians consider the Boston Public Library to be the wellspring from which the key principles for tax-supported public libraries flowed.

Historians have attempted to determine what social and economic factors came together in New England to create the proper context in which people could visualize the idea and gather support for public libraries. Shera's book, *Foundations of the Public Library*, provides a social history covering 1629–1855. He concludes that "Complex social agencies do not arise in response to a single influence; the dogma of simple causation is an easy and ever threatening fallacy. It cannot be said that the public library began on a specific date, at a certain town, as the result of a particular cause. A multiplicity of forces, accumulating over a long period of time, converged to shape this new library form" (1949: 200). In all, he identifies seven diverse factors that contributed to the emergence of tax-supported public libraries:

- Economic resources in the community
- Scholarship, historical research, and the urge for conservation
- Local pride
- Social importance of universal public education
- Self-education and the Lyceum movement
- Vocational influence
- Religion, morality and the church

Economic Resources

The personal philanthropy of wealthy individuals and the growing wealth of New England provided the financial basis for library development. Examples of the generosity of individuals toward the establishment of libraries abound. Caleb Bingham, a Boston publisher, donated books for a children's library to Salisbury, Connecticut, in 1803 and the town later supplemented this donation with tax monies. Francis Wayland, president of Brown University, donated $500 to the town of Wayland, Massachusetts, in 1847 to establish a public library providing the town matched the donation—a donation that, Ditzion notes, was instrumental in getting the principle of tax support under way (1947: 44). Contributors donated much larger amounts to establish the Boston Public Library, including $50,000 from Joshua Bates and $10,000 from Abbott Lawrence.

Scholarship

The inadequacy of libraries in the United States to support research and scholarship, and the desire to preserve the documents of the nation further motivated public funding of libraries. Various groups established historical societies and other social libraries devoted to history in the eighteenth century (e.g., Massachusetts Historical Society, 1791), and these organizations focused much attention on preserving and building scholarly collections. Throughout New England individuals expended a great deal of energy on building libraries out of private collections. Isaiah Thomas, founder of the American Antiquarian Society in 1812, donated his personal collection of 8,000 books and acquired the collection of 1400 books of Increase, Cotton, and Richard Mather for the society. The many other private libraries being gathered helped to enhance the idea of the need to develop scholarly resources and preserve the past.

Local Pride

The motivation of local pride came to the fore when Boston learned that John Jacob Astor had drawn up a will donating $400,000 to establish a public library in New York. The former Harvard professor and scholar, George Ticknor, one of the key supporters of the Boston Public Library and the primary author of the 1852 *Report of the Trustees of the Public Library to the City of Boston*, used the competition between the two cities as a factor to argue for a public library. Shera observes, "It is difficult to envision an agency more characteristic of this period [ca. 1800–1850] than the emerging public library. America, proud of her economic growth, but confronted by the ancient tradition of European culture, sought eagerly to demonstrate her awareness of the necessity for preserving her own heritage" (1949: 216).

Universal Education

The acceptance of universal education as a public responsibility was evidenced in taxation for schools and school district libraries. This concept added strength to the argument for a tax-supported public library. Edward Everett, former governor and Congressman of Massachusetts (and future Secretary of State and Senator) was, with Ticknor, a driving force in establishing the Boston public library. Everett had appointed Horace Mann as Secretary of the Massachusetts Board of Education and oversaw the improvement of common schools and the extension of education throughout the state. He argued for extending the process of education beyond formal education through a tax-supported public library. Ticknor, who felt that the preservation of the republic must be based on the foundation of an educated population, enforced Everett's arguments (Ditzion, 1947: 13–18).

Self-education

A fully developed plan for adult education through an educational society that would reach every part of the nation was set forth in 1826 by Josiah Holbrook of Derby, Connecticut. He based this plan on the idea of the lyceum, a local association formed for weekly lectures and discussion, which often included small libraries of books and periodicals. From the first lyceum in 1826 the idea expanded to over 3,000 in towns, counties, and states, by 1835. The National American Lyceum, an organization of individual lyceums, adopted as its purpose, "the advancement of education, especially in the common schools, and the general diffusion of knowledge" (Knowles, 1977: 16–18). The support and popularity for the lyceum idea provided additional receptivity to the support of agencies for self-improvement.

Vocational Influence

Education for the trades and vocational education in New England was a complex mixture of organizations and societies. The Mechanics Institute movement, which originated in England, grew in response to the industrial revolution and provided education and training to working men, often with support from manufacturers and factory owners. These institutes usually incorporated libraries to support the education of students. Mercantile libraries, initially a type of social library for men in business, also added lectures and courses. Of these institutions open to working people Shera remarks:

> If the working classes of the nineteenth century achieved only temporary success in founding libraries planned to meet their needs, the importance of the vocational motive in public library encouragement is not thereby discredited; for as the wage-earning portion of the population increased and it became correspondingly more difficult for the uneducated individual to compete successfully with his highly trained fellows, there developed an increasing pressure for any agency that would raise the apprentice out of the ranks of the day laborer and into the middle-class (1949: 237).

Religion and Morality

The religious tenor of New England was based on a high degree of reading widely. From the days of the parish libraries founded by Thomas Bray to the time of the establishment of the Boston Public Library, members of churches valued reading and relied upon parish libraries. The American Sunday School Union, founded in 1817, had as one of its goals to provide communities with libraries for religious instruction (Boylan, 1988).

Legislation

The various types of social libraries discussed above were entities with state charters and governance by trustees or boards of directors elected by shareholders. The trustees or directors were responsible for personnel, budgets, and drafting of rules of use. Thus long before the enactment of laws and legislation for tax-supported public libraries, models were in place for the oversight of library organizations. The steps to legislation that made it possible for communities to tax themselves for public library service are not unlike the process of policy development today. As we have seen, the spirit of the times established the intellectual and societal justification to tax people for universal education. New York enacted State law in 1835 providing for the funding of school district libraries. A year later, New York also offered matching grants to school districts for the support of libraries using federal monies from the Deposit Act of 1836. Similar laws in the states of New England resulted in library service based on school districts, especially through the efforts of Horace Mann in Massachusetts and Henry Barnard in Rhode Island.

But it is to New Hampshire that we owe the honor of being the first state to enact a law to provide for public libraries, in 1849—"An Act Providing for the Establishment of Public Libraries." Whether this was due to the successful town library in Peterborough (1833), funded initially from a state fund but continued by local monies, or perhaps the persuasion of French ventriloquist, M. Nicholas-Marie Alexandre Vattemare, who had addressed the New Hampshire state legislature the day before on the importance of international exchanges of books, the precise reasons for the introduction of the Act at this time we cannot deduce.[4] Nevertheless, this was the watershed event in U.S. public library history.

On Friday, June 28, 1849, Josiah C. Eastman introduced the Act Providing for the Establishment of Public Libraries, and the New

Hampshire legislature passed the Act into law on July 7, 1849. It provided:

1) that towns might appropriate funds for the establishment, housing and maintenance of libraries;
2) that such libraries would be free to all;
3) the town might receive, hold, and dispose of gifts or behests made to the library; and
4) that libraries established under the law would annually receive works published by the State (Shera, 1949: 186–189).

The Massachusetts law enacted in 1851 came about somewhat differently. Brown University President, Francis Wayland had long been a vocal advocate in favor of libraries as a means by which "the man denied the aristocracy of property, is welcomed into the prouder and nobler aristocracy of talent."[5] Wayland's donation in 1847 to the town of Wayland, Massachusetts, to establish a library came up against the dilemma that the town had no authority to contribute to the library's upkeep from municipal funds. Although the library was established in 1850, its right to operate without state authority was subject to some concern. The representative from Wayland to the Massachusetts legislature, Rev. John Burt Wight, eventually drafted a bill that authorized towns to establish libraries. His remarks to the House were published in Horace Mann's *Common School Journal* and are important as an early example of policy on public library objectives. Wight described the anticipated social benefits and emphasized the fact that the new law would inspire the establishment of libraries throughout Massachusetts. These libraries would supplement the public school system, provide utilitarian information, support moral and intellectual advance, preserve public documents, encourage creative writing, and increase the effectiveness of public instruction. After the Act passed, Wight sent a circular throughout Massachusetts to encourage the creation of town libraries. In the circular Wight noted, "The universal establishment of such libraries in this Commonwealth—and may I not say in the new England states, in the United States, and throughout the entire civilized world—is a question only of time."[6] Thus, Wayland's gift was the catalyst behind universal establishment.

The Boston Public Library

The Boston Public Library opened to readers on May 2, 1854. Although we have reviewed the New Hampshire and Massachusetts actions that preceded the Boston Public Library, the impetus to establish tax-supported public library service in the United States received its main fuel from this single event. The decision of a major city to enact taxes for the support of a public library was of tremendous import.

In addition to the general factors in New England that created the climate for acceptance of the idea of a tax-supported public library, specific factors in Boston fell in line. It was in Boston that the concentration of social libraries had created recognition of the value of library resources among those of influence in the city. It was at a meeting at the Boston Mercantile Library in 1841 that M. Nicholas-Marie Alexandre Vattemare had proposed the unification of Boston's major social libraries and a committee to investigate this idea appointed by the Mayor Josiah Quincy. Vattemare pursued the mayor with the idea and it continued as a front-burner concern for the city through the 1840s. As a city geared to oversee functions related to the community's well being (fire protection, education, health), Boston considered it to be a proper function of city government to support a public library; there was little question about the matter.

The authorization to establish the Boston Public Library predated the 1851 Massachusetts state law by three years. A Joint Special Committee of the City Council presented a proposal to the General Court of the state in 1848 that approved a special act permitting the city of Boston to establish a public library.[7] The special act is of great importance to the history of the public library in the United States, for it is the first legal recognition by a state of tax-supported municipal library service.

> The City of Boston is hereby authorized to establish and maintain a public library, for the use of the inhabitants of the said city: and the city council of the said city may, from time to time, make such rules and regulations, for the care and maintenance thereof, as they may deem proper; provided, however, that no such appropriation for the said library shall exceed the sum of five thousand dollars in any one year.
>
> — *Massachusetts Acts and Resolves*, 1848. Chapter 52. Passed by the General Court of Massachusetts.

In 1851 Mayor Benjamin Seaver declared that time had passed since the enactment of the act and that the city should hold an election to create a board of trustees to move the idea forward.

The trustees submitted the *Report of the Trustees of the Public Library to the City of Boston* in 1852, written by a subcommittee of trustees, mainly driven by George Ticknor and Edward Everett—a seminal document in the history of public librarianship in the United States.[8] *The Report of the Trustees* begins with a compelling justification for the library as an institution, describes how public education upon completion ends opportunity after schooling is complete, and notes that there is no provision to put books within the reach of young men and women. The report throws down the gauntlet in the form of a question, "Why should not this prosperous and liberal city extend some reasonable amount of aid to the foundation and support of a noble public library, to which the young of both sexes, when they leave the schools, can resort for those works which pertain to general culture, or which are needed for research into any branch of useful knowledge?" (Boston Public Library. *Report of the Trustees,* 8)

Tying the argument firmly to support of public education, the trustees summarize the current status of libraries in Boston (athenaeums, mercantile libraries, mechanics libraries, apprentices libraries, social libraries, circulating libraries, Sunday school libraries), which do not satisfy the demands for healthy, nourishing reading, "by the great masses of people, who cannot be expected to purchase such reading for themselves." The proposed library would fall into four classes: (1) books that cannot be taken out of the library; (2) books that few persons wish to read; (3) books that will be often asked for; and (4) periodical publication. The report goes on to lay out steps to establish the library, including a building and selection and accession of books that are wanted—trusting that, in the long run, the collection will include most books that could reasonably be wanted. The public library is conceived as the "crowning glory of our system of City schools."

A Boston city ordinance was passed in October 1852 stating that the method of governance was to be a board of trustees with the librarian to be appointed annually by the city council. The impact of this choice of structure laid the foundation for libraries throughout the United States to adopt the board plan of administrative management. So, in the course of the establishment of the Boston Public Library we find the basic structure of U.S. library governance (board plan), the justification for the establishment of tax-supported public libraries, and in its first years the selection of librarians, like Justin Winsor, who would become national leaders in the emergent profession of librarianship.[9]

Figure 2.1: Report of the Trustees of the Public Library of the City of Boston, 1852

City Document - No. 37.

REPORT

OF

THE TRUSTEES OF THE PUBLIC LIBRARY OF THE CITY OF BOSTON

JULY, 1852.

BOSTON:

1852.

J.H. EASTBURN, CITY PRINTER.

CITY OF BOSTON.

In Board of Mayor and Aldermen, June 30, 1852.

Ordered, That the Trustees of the City Library be requested to report to the City Council upon the objects to be attained by the establishment of a Public Library, and the best mode of effecting them; and that they be authorized to report in print.

Passed. Sent down for concurrence.

BENJAMIN SEAVER, Mayor.

In Common Council, July 1, 1852.

Concurred.

HENRY J. GARDNER, President.

A true Copy. Attest:

S. F. McCLEARY, JR., City Clerk.

REPORT.

The Trustees of the public library, in compliance with the order of the two branches of the City Council, submit the following report on the objects to be attained by the establishment of a public library and the best mode of effecting them : –

Of all human arts that of writing, as it was one of the earliest invented, is also one of the most important. Perhaps it would be safe to pronounce it, without exception the most useful and important. It is the great medium of communication between mind and mind, as respects different individuals, countries, and periods of time. We know from history that only those portions of the human family have made any considerable and permanent progress in civilization, which have possessed and used this great instrument of improvement.

It is principally in the form of books that the art of writing, though useful in many other ways, has exerted its influence on human progress. It is almost exclusively by books that a permanent record has been made of word and deed, of thought and feeling; that history, philosophy and poetry, that literature and science in their full comprehension, have been called into being, by the co-operation of intellects acting in concert with each other, though living in different countries and at different periods, and often using different languages.

Till the middle of the fifteenth century of our era, it was literally the art of writing by which these effects were produced. No means of multiplying books was known but the tedious process of transcription. This of course rendered them comparatively scarce and dear, and thus greatly limited their usefulness. It was a chief cause also of the loss of some of the most valuable literary productions. However much this loss may be regretted, we cannot but reflect with wonder and gratitude on the number of invaluable works which have been handed down to us from antiquity, notwithstanding the cost and labor attending their multiplication.

The same cause would necessarily operate to some extent against the formation of public and private libraries. Still however, valuable collections of books were made in all the cultivated states of antiquity, both by governments and individuals. The library formed by the Ptolemies at Alexandria in Egypt was probably the direct means by which the most valuable works of ancient literature have been preserved to us. At a later period, the collections of books in the religious houses contributed efficaciously toward the same end.

The invention of printing in the fifteenth century increased the efficiency of the art of writing, as the chief instrument of improvement, beyond all former example or conception. It became more than ever the great medium of communication and transmission. It immediately began to operate, in a thousand ways and with a power which it would be impossible to overstate, in producing the great intellectual revival of the modern world. One of the most obvious effects of the newly invented art was of course greatly to facilitate the formation of libraries.

An astonishing degree of excellence in the art of printing was reached at once. The typography of the first edition of the whole Bible is nearly equal to that of any subsequent edition. But the farther improvements which have taken place in four hundred years in cutting and casting types and solid pages, in the construction of presses and their movement by water, steam, and other power, in the manufacture of paper, and in the materials and mode of binding, have perhaps done as much to make books cheap and consequently abundant, as the art of printing as originally invented.

Figure 2.1 continued. Trustees Report, Boston Public Library, 1852

It is scarcely necessary to add that these causes have led to a great multiplication of libraries in Europe and America. In nearly all the capitals of Europe large collections of books have been made and supported at the public expense. They form a part of the apparatus of all the higher institutions for education, and latterly of many schools; they are found in most scientific and literary societies; and they are possessed by innumerable individuals in all countries.

In proportion as books have become more abundant, they have become the principal instrument of instruction in places of education. It may be doubted whether their employment for this purpose is not, particularly in this country, carried too far. The organization of modern schools, in which very large numbers of pupils are taught by a small number of instructors, tends to make the use of books, rather than the living voice of the teacher, the main dependence. Still however, this is but an abuse of that which in itself is not only useful but indispensable; and no one can doubt that books will ever continue to be, as they now are, the great vehicle of imparting and acquiring knowledge and carrying on the work of education. As far as instruction is concerned, it will no doubt ever continue to be, as it now is, the work of the teacher to direct, encourage, and aid the learner in the use of his books.

In this respect the system of public education in Boston may probably sustain a comparison with any in the world. Without asserting that the schools are perfect, it may truly be said that the general principle and plan on which they are founded, are as nearly so as the nature of the case admits. They compose a great system of instruction, administered in schools rising in gradation from the most elementary to those of a highly advanced character, open to the whole population, and supported by a most liberal public expenditure. The schools themselves may admit improvement, and the utmost care should be taken, that they keep pace with the progress of improvement in other things; but the system itself, in the great features just indicated, seems perfect; that is, in a word, to give a first rate school education, at the public expense, to the entire rising generation.

But when this object is attained, and it is certainly one of the highest importance, our system of public instruction stops. Although the school and even the college and the university are, as all thoughtful persons are well aware, but the first stages in education, the public makes no provision for carrying on the great work. It imparts, with a noble equality of privilege, a knowledge of the elements of learning to all its children, but it affords them no aid in going beyond the elements. It awakens a taste for reading, but it furnishes to the public nothing to be read. It conducts our young men and women to that point, where they are qualified to acquire from books the various knowledge in the arts and sciences which books contain; but it does nothing to put those books within their reach. As matters now stand, and speaking with general reference to the mass

Figure 2.1 continued. Trustees Report, Boston Public Library, 1852

of the community, the public makes no provision whatever, by which the hundreds of young persons annually educated, as far as the elements of learning are concerned, at the public expense, can carry on their education and bring it to practical results by private study.

We do not wish to exaggerate in either part of this statement, although we wish to call attention to the point as one of great importance and not yet, as we think, enough considered. We are far from intimating that school education is not important because it is elementary; it is, on the contrary, of the utmost value. Neither do we say, on the other hand, because there are no libraries which in the strict sense of the word are public, that therefore there is absolutely no way by which persons of limited means can get access to books. There are several libraries of the kind usually called public, belonging however to private corporations; and there are numerous private libraries from which books are liberally loaned to those wishing to borrow them.

It will however be readily conceded that this falls far short of the aid and encouragement which would be afforded to the reading community, (in which we include all persons desirous of obtaining knowledge or an agreeable employment of their time from the perusal of books), by a well supplied public library. If we had no free schools, we should not be a community without education. Large numbers of children would be educated at private schools at the expense of parents able to afford it, and considerable numbers in narrow circumstances would, by the aid of the affluent and liberal, obtain the same advantages. We all feel however that such a state of things would be a poor substitute for our system of public schools, of which it is the best feature that it is a public provision for all; affording equal advantages to poor and rich; furnishing at the public expense an education so good, as to make it an object with all classes to send their children to the public schools.

It needs no argument to prove that, in a republican government, these are features of the system, quite as valuable as the direct benefit of the instruction which it imparts. But it is plain that the same principles apply to the farther progress of education, in which each one must he mainly his own teacher. Why should not this prosperous and liberal city extend some reasonable amount of aid to the foundation and support of a noble public library, to which the young people of both sexes, when they leave the schools, can resort for those works which pertain to general culture, or which are needful for research into any branch of useful knowledge? At present, if the young machinist, engineer, architect, chemist, engraver, painter, instrument-maker, musician (or student of any branch of science or literature,) wishes to consult a valuable and especially a rare and costly work, he must buy it, often import it at an expense he can ill afford, or he must be indebted for its use to the liberality of private corporations

Figure 2.1 continued. Trustees Report, Boston Public Library, 1852

or individuals. The trustees submit, that all the reasons which exist for furnishing the means of elementary education, at the public expense, apply in an equal degree to a reasonable provision to aid and encourage the acquisition of the knowledge required to complete a preparation for active life or to perform its duties.

We are aware that it may be said and truly, that knowledge acquired under hardships is often more thorough, than that to which the learner is invited without effort on his part; that the studious young man who makes sacrifices and resorts to expedients to get books, values them the more and reads them to greater profit. This however is equally true of school education and of every other privilege in life. But the city of Boston has never deemed this a reason for withholding the most munificent appropriations for the public education. It has not forborne to support an expensive system of free schools, because without such a system a few individuals would have acquired an education for themselves, under every possible discouragement and disadvantage, and because knowledge so acquired is usually thorough, well-digested and available, beyond what is got in an easier way. The question is not what will be brought about by a few individuals of indomitable will and an ardent thirst for improvement, but what is most for the advantage of the mass of the community. In this point of view we consider that a large public library is of the utmost importance as the means of completing our system of public education.

There is another point of view in which the subject may be regarded, – a point of view, we mean, in which a free public library is not only seen to be demanded by the wants of the city at this time, but also seen to be the next natural step to be taken for the intellectual advancement of this whole community and for which this whole community is peculiarly fitted and prepared.

Libraries were originally intended for only a very small portion of the community in which they were established, because few persons could read, and fewer still desired to make inquires that involved the consultation of many books. Even for a long time after the invention of printing, they were anxiously shut up from general use; and, down to the present day, a large proportion of the best libraries in the world forbid anything like a free circulation of their books ; – many of them forbidding any circulation at all.

For all this, there were at first, good reasons, and for some of it good reasons exist still. When only manuscripts were known, those in public libraries were, no doubt, generally too precious to be trusted from their usual places of deposit; and the most remarkable, if not the most valuable, of all such collections now in existence – the Laurentian in Florence – still retains, and perhaps wisely, its eight or nine thousand manuscripts chained to the desks on which they lie. So too, when printed books first began to take the place of

Figure 2.1 continued. Trustees Report, Boston Public Library, 1852

manuscripts, the editions of them were small and their circulation limited. When, therefore, copies of such books now occur, they are often regarded rightfully as hardly less curious and valuable than manuscripts, and as demanding hardly less care in their preservation. And finally, even of books more recently published, some, – like Dictionaries and Cyclopædias, – are not intended for circulation by means of public libraries, and others are too large, too costly, or otherwise too important to be trusted abroad, except in rare cases.

But while there are some classes of books that should be kept within the precincts of a public library, there are others to which as wide a circulation as possible should be given; books which, in fact, are especially intended for it, and the end of whose existence is defeated, just in proportion as they are shut up and restrained from general use. It was, however, long after this class was known, before it became a large one, and still longer before means were found fitted to give to the community a tolerably free use of it. At first it consisted almost exclusively of practical, religious books. Gradually the more popular forms of history, books of travel, and books chiefly or entirely intended for enter-tainment followed. At last, these books became so numerous, and were in such demand, that the larger public libraries, – most of which had grown more or less out of the religious establishments of the middle ages, and had always regarded with little interest this more popular literature, – could not, it was plain, continue to be looked upon as the only or as the chief resource for those who were unable to buy for themselves the reading they wanted. Other resources and other modes of supply have, therefore, been at different times devised.

The first, as might naturally have been anticipated, was suggested by the personal interest of a sagacious individual. Allan Ramsay, who, after being bred a wig-maker, had become a poet of the people, and set up a small bookseller's shop, was led to eke out an income, too inconsiderable for the wants of his family, by lending his books on hire to those who were not able or not willing to buy them of him. This is the old-est of all the numberless " Circulating Libraries;" and it sprang up naturally in Edinburg, where in proportion to the population, it is believed there were then more readers than there were in any other city in the world. This was in 1725; and, twenty years ago, the same establishment was not only in existence – as it probably is still – but it was the largest and best of its class in all Scotland. The example was speed-ily followed. Such libraries were set up everywhere, or almost everywhere in Christendom, but especially in Germany and in Great Britain, where they are thus far more numerous than they are in any other countries; the most important being now in London, where (for at least one of them) from fifty to two hundred copies of every good new work, are purchased in order to satisfy the demands of its multitudinous subscribers and patrons.

All "Circulating Libraries," technically so called, are however, to be regarded as adventures and speculations for private profit. On this account, they were early

Figure 2.1 continued. Trustees Report, Boston Public Library, 1852

felt to be somewhat unsatisfactory in their very nature, and other libraries were contrived that were founded on the more generous principle of a mutual and common interest in those who wished to use the books they contained. This principle had, in fact, been recognized somewhat earlier than the time of Allan Ramsay, but for very limited purposes and not at all for the circulation of books. Thus the lawyers of Edinburg, London, and Paris, respectively had already been associated together for the purpose of collecting consulting Law Libraries for their own use, and so it is believed, had some other bodies, which had collected consulting libraries for their own exclusive especial purposes. But the first Social Library of common or popular books for popular use, in the sense we now give the appellation, was probably that of the "Library Company," as it was called, in Philadelphia, founded at the suggestion of Dr. Franklin in 1731, by the young mechanics of that city, where he was then a young printer. The idea was no doubt a fortunate one; particularly characteristic of Franklin's shrewd good sense, and adapted to the practical wants of our own country. The library of these young men, therefore, succeeded and was imitated in other places. Even before the Revolutionary war, such libraries were established elsewhere in the colonies, and, after its conclusion, many sprang up on all sides. New England, in this way, has come to possess a great number of them, and especially Massachusetts; two-thirds of whose towns are said at this time, to possess "Social Libraries," each owned by a moderate number of proprietors.

That these popular "Social Libraries" have done great good, and that many of them are still doing great good, cannot be reasonably doubted. But many of them, – perhaps the majority in this Commonwealth, – are now languishing. For this, there are two reasons. In the first place, such libraries are accessible only to their proprietors, who are not always the persons most anxious to use them, or, in some cases, but not many, they are accessible to other persons on payment of a small sum for each book borrowed. And, in the second place, they rarely contain more than one copy of a book, so that if it be a new book, or one in much demand, many are obliged to wait too long for their turn to read it; so long that their desire for the book is lost, and their interest in the library diminished. Efforts, therefore, have been for some time making, to remedy these deficiencies, and to render books of different kinds more accessible to all, whether they can pay for them or hire them, or not.

Thus, within thirty years, Sunday School Libraries have been everywhere established; but their influence – great and valuable as it is – does not extend much beyond the youngest portions of society and their particular religious teachers. And, within a shorter period than thirty years, District or Public School Libraries have been scattered all over the great State of New York, and all over New England, in such abundance, that five years ago, (1847) the aggregate number of their books in the State of New York was above a million

---

Figure 2.1 continued. Trustees Report, Boston Public Library, 1852

three hundred thousand volumes, and fast increasing; but neither do these school libraries generally contain more than one copy of any one book, nor is their character often such as to reach and satisfy the mass of adult readers.

Strong intimations, therefore, are already given, that ampler means and means better adapted to our peculiar condition and wants, are demanded, in order to diffuse through our society that knowledge without which we have no right to hope, that the condition of those who are to come after us will be as happy and prosperous as our own. The old roads, so to speak, are admitted to be no longer sufficient. Even the more modern turnpikes do not satisfy our wants. We ask for rail-cars and steamboats, in which many more persons – even multitudes – may advance together to the great end of life, and go faster, further and better, by the means thus furnished to them, than they have ever been able to do before.

Nowhere are the intimations of this demand more decisive than in our own city, nor, it is believed, is there any city of equal size in the world, where added means for general popular instruction and self-culture, – if wisely adapted to their great ends, – will be so promptly seized upon or so effectually used, as they will be here. One plain proof of this is, the large number of good libraries we already possess, which are constantly resorted to by those who have the right, and which yet – it is well known, – fail to supply the demand for popular reading. For we have respectable libraries of almost every class, beginning with those of the Athenæum, of the American Academy, of the Historical Society, and of the General Court, – the Social Library of 1792, the Mercantile Library, the Mechanics Apprentices' Library, the Libraries of the Natural History Society, of the Bar, of the Statistical Association, of the Genealogical Society, of the Medical Society, and of other collective and corporate bodies; and coming down to the "Circulating Libraries" strictly so called; the Sunday School Libraries, and the collections of children's books found occasionally in our Primary Schools. Now all these are important and excellent means for the diffusion of knowledge. They are felt to be such, and they are used as such, and the trustees would be especially careful not to diminish the resources or the influence of any one of them. They are sure that no public library can do it. But it is admitted, – or else another and more general library would not now be urged, – that these valuable libraries do not, either individually or in the aggregate, reach the great want of this city, considered as a body politic bound to train up its members in the knowledge which will best fit them for the positions in life to which they may have been born, or any others to which they may justly aspire through increased intelligence and personal worthiness. For multitudes among us have no right of access to any one of the more considerable and important of these libraries; and, except in rare instances, no library among us seeks to keep more than a single copy of any book on its shelves, so that no one of them, nor indeed, all of them taken together, can

---

Figure 2.1 continued. Trustees Report, Boston Public Library, 1852

do even a tolerable amount of what ought to be done towards satisfying the demands for healthy, nourishing reading made by the great masses of our people, who cannot be expected to purchase such reading for themselves.

And yet there can be no doubt that such reading ought to be furnished to all, as a matter of public policy and duty, on the same principle that we furnish free education, and in fact, as a part, and a most important part, of the education of all. For it has been rightly judged that, – under political, social and religious institutions like ours, – it is of paramount importance that the means of general information should be so diffused that the largest possible number of persons should be induced to read and understand questions going down to the very foundations of social order, which are constantly presenting themselves, and which we, as a people, are constantly required to decide, and do decide, either ignorantly or wisely. That this can be done, – that is, that such libraries can be collected, and that they will be used to a much wider extent than libraries have ever been used before, and with much more important results, there can be no doubt; and if it can be done anywhere, it can be done here in Boston; for no population of one hundred and fifty thousand souls, lying so compactly together as to be able, with tolerable convenience, to resort to one library, was ever before so well fitted to become a reading, self-cultivating population, as the population of our own city is at this moment.

To accomplish this object, however, – which has never yet been attempted, – we must use means which have never before been used; otherwise the library we propose to establish, will not be adjusted to its especial purposes. Above all, while the rightful claims of no class, – however highly educated already, – should be overlooked, the first regard should be shown, as in the case of our Free Schools, to the wants of those, who can, in no other way supply themselves with the interesting and healthy reading necessary for their farther education. What precise plan should be adopted for such a library, it is not, perhaps, possible to settle beforehand. It is a new thing, a new step forward in general education; and we must feel our way as we advance. Still, certain points seem to rise up with so much prominence, that without deciding on any formal arrangement, until experience shall show what is practically useful-we may perhaps foresee that such a library as is contemplated would naturally fall into four classes, viz:

I. Books that cannot be taken out of the Library, such as Cyclopædias, Dictionaries, important public documents, and books, which, from their rarity or costliness, cannot be easily replaced. Perhaps others should be specifically added to this list, but after all, the Trustees would be sorry to exclude any book whatever so absolutely from circulation that, by permission of the highest authority having control of the library, it could not, in special cases, and with sufficient pledges for its safe and proper return, be taken out. For a book, it

Figure 2.1 continued. Trustees Report, Boston Public Library, 1852

should be remembered, is never so much in the way of its duty as it is when it is in hand to be read or consulted.

II. Books that few persons will wish to read, and of which, therefore, only one copy will be kept, but which should be permitted to circulate freely, and if this copy should, contrary to expectation, be so often asked for, as to be rarely on the shelves, another copy should then be bought, – or if needful, more than one other copy, – so as to keep one generally at home, especially if it be such a book as is often wanted for use there.

III. Books that will be often asked for, (we mean, the more respectable of the popular books of the time,) of which copies should be provided in such numbers, that many persons, if they desire it, can be reading the same work at the same moment, and so render the pleasant and healthy literature of the day accessible to the whole people at the only time they care for it, – that is, when it is living, fresh and new. Additional copies, therefore, of any book of this class should continue to be bought almost as long as they are urgently demanded, and thus, by following the popular taste, – unless it should ask for something unhealthy, – we may hope to create a real desire for general reading; and, by permitting the freest circulation of the books that is consistent with their safety, cultivate this desire among the young, and in the families and at the firesides of the greatest possible number of persons in the city.

An appetite like this, when formed, will, we fully believe, provide wisely and well for its own wants. The popular, current literature of the day can occupy but a small portion of the leisure even of the more laborious parts of our population, provided there should exist among them a love for reading as great, for instance, as the love for public lecturing, or for the public schools; and when such a taste for books has once been formed by these lighter publications, then the older and more settled works in Biography, in History, and in the graver departments of knowledge will be demanded. That such a taste can be excited by such means, is proved from the course taken in obedience to the dictates of their own interests, by the publishers of the popular literature of the time during the last twenty or thirty years. The Harpers and others began chiefly with new novels and other books of little value. What they printed, however, was eagerly bought and read, because it was cheap and agreeable, if nothing else. A habit of reading was thus formed. Better books were soon demanded, and gradually the general taste has risen in its requisitions, until now the country abounds with respectable works of all sorts, – such as compose the three hundred volumes of the Harpers' School Library and the two hundred of their Family Library – which are read by great numbers of our people everywhere, especially in New England and in the Middle States. This taste, therefore, once excited will, we are persuaded, go on of itself from year to year, demanding better and better books, and, can as we believe, by a little

Figure 2.1 continued. Trustees Report, Boston Public Library, 1852

judicious help in the selections for a Free City Library, rather than by any direct control, restraint, or solicitation, be carried much higher than has been commonly deemed possible; preventing at the same time, a great deal of the mischievous, poor reading now indulged in, which is bought and paid for, by offering good reading, without pay, which will be attractive.

Nor would the process by which this result is to be reached a costly one; certainly not costly compared with its benefits. Nearly all the most popular books are, from the circumstance of their popularity, cheap, – most of them very cheap, – because large editions of them are printed that are suited to the wants of those who cannot afford to buy dear books. It may, indeed, sometimes be necessary to purchase many copies of one of these books, and so the first outlay, in some cases, may seem considerable. But such a passion for any given book does not last long, and, as it subsides, the extra copies may be sold for something, until only a few are left in the library, or perhaps, only a single one, while the money received from the sale of the rest, – which, at a reduced price, would, no doubt often be bought of the Librarian by those who had been most interested in reading them, – will serve to increase the general means for purchasing others of the same sort. The plan, therefore, it is believed, is a practicable one, so far as expense is concerned, and will, we think, be found on trial, much cheaper and much easier of execution than at the first suggestion, it may seem to be.

IV. The last class of books to be kept in such a library, consists, we suppose, of periodical publications, probably excluding newspapers, except such as may be given by their proprietors. Like the first class, they should not be taken out at all, or only in rare and peculiar cases, but they should be kept in a Reading Room accessible to everybody; open as many hours of the day as possible, and always in the evening; and in which all the books on the shelves of every part of the Library should be furnished for perusal or for consultation to all who may ask for them, except to such persons as may, from their disorderly conduct or unseemly condition, interfere with the occupations and comfort of others who may be in the room.

In the establishment of such a library, a beginning should be made, we think, without any sharply defined or settled plan, so as to be governed by circumstances as they may arise. The commencement should be made, of preference, in a very unpretending manner; erecting no new building and making no show; but spending such moneys as may be appropriated for the purpose, chiefly on books that are known to be really wanted, rather than on such as will make an imposing, a scientific or a learned collection; trusting, however, most confidently, that such a library, in the long run, will contain all that anybody can reasonably ask of it. For, to begin by making it a really useful library; by awakening a general interest in it as a City Institution, important to the whole people, a part of their education, and an element of their happiness and

Figure 2.1 continued. Trustees Report, Boston Public Library, 1852

prosperity, is the surest way to make it at last, a great and rich library for men of science, statesmen and scholars, as well as for the great body of the people, many of whom are always successfully struggling up to honorable distinctions and all of whom should be encouraged and helped to do it. Certainly this has proved to be the case with some of the best libraries yet formed in the United States, and especially with the Philadelphia Library, whose means were at first extremely humble and trifling, compared with those we can command at the outset. Such libraries have in fact enjoyed the public favor, and become large, learned, and scientific collections of books, exactly in proportion as they have been found generally useful.

As to the terms on which access should be had to a City Library, the Trustees can only say, that they would place no restrictions on its use, except such as the nature of individual books, or their safety may demand; regarding it as a great matter to carry as many of them as possible into the home of the young; into poor families; into cheap boarding houses; in short, wherever they will be most likely to affect life and raise personal character and condition. To many classes of persons the doors of such a library may, we conceive, be at once opened wide. All officers of the City Government, therefore, including the police, all clergymen settled among us, all city missionaries, all teachers of our public schools, all members of normal schools, all young persons who may have received medals or other honorary distinctions on leaving our Grammar and higher schools, and, in fact, as many classes, as can safely be entrusted with it as classes, might enjoy, on the mere names and personal responsibility of the individuals composing them, the right of taking out freely all books that are permitted to circulate, receiving one volume at a time. To all other persons, women as well as men – living in the City, the same privilege might be granted on depositing the value of the volume or of the set to which it may belong; believing that the pledge of a single dollar or even less, may thus insure pleasant and profitable reading to any family among us.

In this way the Trustees would endeavor to make the Public Library of the City, as far as possible, the crowning glory of our system of City Schools; or in other words, they would make it an institution, fitted to continue and increase the best effects of that system, by opening to all the means of self culture through books, for which these schools have been specially qualifying them.

Such are the views entertained by the Trustees, with reference to the objects to be attained by the foundation of a public library and the mode of effecting them.

It remains to be considered briefly what steps should be adopted toward the accomplishment of such a design.

If it were probable that the City Council would deem it expedient at once to make a large appropriation for the erection of a building and the purchase of

Figure 2.1 continued. Trustees Report, Boston Public Library, 1852

an ample library, and that the citizens at large would approve such an expenditure, the Trustees would of course feel great satisfaction in the prompt achievement of an object of such high public utility. But in the present state of the finances of the city, and in reference to an object on which the public mind is not yet enlightened by experience, the Trustees regard any such appropriation and expenditure as entirely out of the question. They conceive even that there are advantages in a more gradual course of measures. They look, therefore, only to the continuance of such moderate and frugal expenditure, on the part of the city, as has been already authorized and commenced, for the purchase of books and the compensation of the librarian; and for the assignment of a room or rooms in some one of the public buildings belonging to the city for the reception of the books already on hand, or which the Trustees have the means of procuring. With aid to this extent on the part of the city, the Trustees believe that all else may be left to the public spirit and liberality of individuals. They are inclined to think that, from time to time, considerable collections of books will be presented to the library by citizens of Boston, who will take pleasure in requiting in this way the advantages which they have received from its public institutions, or who for any other reason are desirous of increasing the means of public improvement. Besides the collections of magnitude and value, which can hardly fail in the lapse of years to be received in this way, it may with equal confidence be expected, that constant accessions will be made to the public library by the donation of single volumes or of small numbers of books, which, however inconsiderable in the single case, become in the course of time, an important source of increase to all public libraries. A free city library, being an object of interest to the entire population, would in this respect have an advantage over institutions which belong to private corporations. Authors and editors belonging to Boston would generally deem it a privilege to place a copy of their works on the shelves of a public library; and the liberal publishers of the city, to whose intelligence and enterprise the cause of literature and science has at all times owed so much, would unquestionably show themselves efficient friends and benefactors.

In fact, we know of no undertaking more likely, when once brought into promising operation, to enlist in its favor the whole strength of that feeling, which, in so eminent a degree, binds the citizens of Boston to the place of their birth or adoption. In particular the Trustees are disposed to think that there is not a parent in easy circumstances who has had a boy or a girl educated at a public school, nor an individual who has himself enjoyed that privilege, who will not regard it at once as a duty and a pleasure to do something, in this way, to render more complete the provision for public education.

In order to put the library into operation with the least possible delay, the Trustees would propose to the city government to appropriate for this purpose the ground floor of the Adams school house in Mason street. They are led to

Figure 2.1 continued. Trustees Report, Boston Public Library, 1852

believe that it will not be needed for the use of the Normal School proposed to be established in this building. It may be made, at a small expense, to afford ample accommodation for four or five thousand volumes, with an adjoining room for reading and consulting books, and it will admit of easy enlargement to twice its present dimensions. Such an apartment would enable the Trustees at once to open the library with five thousand volumes, a collection of sufficient magnitude to afford a fair specimen of the benefits of such an establishment to the city.

Should it win the public favor, as the Trustees cannot but anticipate, it will soon reach a size, which will require enlarged premises. These, as we have said, can be easily provided by the extension of the present room on the ground floor; and it will be time enough, when the space at command is filled up, to consider what further provision need be made for the accommodation of the library. Should the expectation of the Trustees be realized, and should it be found to supply an existing defect in our otherwise admirable system of public education, its future condition may be safely left to the judicious liberality of the city government and the public spirit of the community.

BENJAMIN SEAVER,
SAMPSON REED,
LYMAN PERRY,
JAMES LAWRENCE,
EDWARD S. ERVING,
JAMES B. ALLEN,
GEORGE W. WARREN,
GEORGE WILSON,
EDWARD EVERETT,
GEORGE TICKNOR,
JOHN P. BIGELOW,
NATHANIEL B. SHURTLEFF,
THOMAS G. APPLETON.

Boston, July 26, 1852.

At a meeting of the Trustees of the Public Library held on the 6th instant, the foregoing Report was submitted by a SubCommittee previously appointed for that purpose, consisting of EDWARD EVERETT, GEORGE TICKNOR, SAMPSON REED, and NATHANIEL B. SHURTLEFF, and was unanimously accepted and ordered to be printed.

GEORGE WILSON, Secretary.

Figure 2.1 continued. Trustees Report, Boston Public Library, 1852

Truth or Myth?

The rather detailed discussion thus far provides a narrative and chronology of the founding events in U.S. librarianship. In an interesting 1973 revisionist essay, Michael Harris looks at the events that lead to the founding of the Boston Public Library from a different perspective. He describes additional discussions held by the standing committee of the Boston Public Library not usually discussed in general histories, notably expressions of concern by committee members about the increase in foreign populations—generally viewed as unlettered and ignorant. Harris asserts that George Ticknor, the intellectual Boston Brahmin who was the main author of the *Report of the Trustees of the Public Library to the City of Boston*, was motivated to a large degree by the idea that in establishing a public library Boston would uplift the masses so they would be sober, righteous, conservative, and devout. To do this, Harris contends, the trustees selected to oversee the nation's libraries after the enactment of library legislation in the mid-1850s were drawn mainly from the white, male, Protestant, wealthy business, and professional class.

Extending the Harris thesis in her 1979 monograph, *Apostles of Culture: The Public Librarian and American Society, 1876–1920*, Garrison describes the first leaders of the American Library Association—Justin Winsor (Boston Public Library, Harvard); William Poole (Boston Athenaeum, Cincinnati Public Library, Chicago Public Library, Newberry Library); and Charles Ammi Cutter (Harvard, Boston Athenaeum)—as well as most others assuming positions of responsibility for libraries just after the initial enabling legislation, as from the gentry elite. These individuals placed great emphasis on moral norms as a way of shaping the moral values of a society. Their response to political upheaval and labor unrest after the Civil War was to impose on others their middle-class values of "thrift, self-reliance, industriousness, and sensual control" seeing themselves as the saviors of society.

Francis Miksa, writing in 1982, compared the standard histories of the development of librarianship in the United States—Shera's *Foundations of the Public Library* (1949) and Ditzion's *Arsenals of a Democratic Culture* (1947)—with Harris's and Garrison's revisionist views, and analyzed the challenges of writing library history. Miksa noted that Ditzion, Harris, and Garrison focused on the human element and that such efforts must be viewed as somewhat lacking in their extrapolation of the parts to the whole. Miksa suggests studies of individual librarians would do much to enhance our knowledge of public library history.

Because dominant groups manage memory and myths and because women have largely been invisible from membership, women have been written out of traditional public library history, as Suzanne Hildenbrand contends in her 1996 edited volume, *Reclaiming the Library Past: Writing the Women In.* Since 1982, the addition of research examining the importance of women in the founding and growth of the U.S. public library system has enhanced our understanding of public library history to a great degree.[10] The public librarian concerned to grasp history more completely will necessarily supplement the classic texts with this new knowledge.

Annus Mirabilis—1918

1876

The United States held its first World's Fair, popularly known as the Centennial Exhibition (formally titled the International Exhibition of Arts, Manufactures and Products of the Soil and Mine), during 1876 in Philadelphia's Fairmount Park overlooking the Schuylkill River. That same year Philadelphia was host to a conference of librarians in the *annus mirabilis* for U.S. librarianship.

Histories mark 1876 as the start of modern librarianship in the United States, because in that year:

- the American Library Association was founded;
- *Library Journal* (then the American Library Journal) began publication;
- Dewey's *A Classification and Subject Index, for Cataloguing and Arranging the Books and Pamphlets of a Library* (Decimal Classification) was published; and
- the first major government report on libraries, *Public Libraries in the United States of America: Their History, Condition, and Management, Special Report*, was issued.

The formation of the American Library Association gave a voice to those working in libraries, as well as a forum to discuss professional issues. Papers presented at early ALA meetings addressed the proper role of public libraries and the "fiction" question. Opinions ranged from a desire for the total exclusion of fiction, because of its dubious effect on readers, to a more liberal selection policy. Most librarians agreed that "the mass reading public was generally incapable of choosing its own reading material judiciously," [and that]

"Libraries should intervene for the benefit of society by acquiring and prescribing the best reading materials for the reading public's consumption" (Wiegand, 1986b: 9–10). Studying the journals and articles written during these formative years of public librarianship provides an understanding of the long distance librarians have come in developing a philosophy of service.

Years of Expansion

After 1876 the number of public libraries in the United States grew steadily, with states rapidly enacting library legislation and the formation of many state library commissions. By 1896 nearly 1,000 public libraries dotted the landscape. Each public library established in a town or county is a story in itself. Some of the stories are grand and well documented, while others will never be told.[11] Many factors account for the growth in the number of public libraries established between 1876 and World War I, but four bear special mention: (1) the contribution of women's organizations; (2) philanthropy; (3) the establishment of state commissions and traveling libraries; and (4) the professionalization of librarianship.

Women's Role in the Expansion of Public Libraries

Throughout the United States, as state and local bodies enacted laws enabling tax support for public libraries, women's efforts were central to the passage of these laws and the establishment of new libraries. The role of women in U.S. public library development is barely mentioned by twentieth-century library historians Shera and Ditzion, since women were usually written out of the received history of public library origins. Yet women's clubs that formed after the Civil War were a major force in the spread of libraries. Women's club history, including the growth of women's clubs for self-education and community service, bears review to gain understanding of the sociological context in which public libraries developed.

The General Federation of Women's Clubs notes in its chronology that by 1904 women's clubs had established 474 free libraries and 4,655 traveling libraries. Paula D. Watson has identified and summarized key work of women in organizing libraries throughout the United States. She observes that many women's clubs were organized expressly to found public libraries (see Watson, 1994; 1996; 2003).

The work of women in Michigan, preserved in *Historical Sketches of the Ladies' Libraries Associations of Michigan* (Bixby and

Howell, 1876) prepared for the 1876 Centennial Exhibition—the same event where the American Library Association was formed—is indicative of the grassroots efforts made by women throughout the nation to expand the limits of women's lives and open new possibilities. Children's services played a large role in many of these Michigan libraries long before the American Library Association addressed the issue. The case studies detailed by Watson (1994; 1996; 2003) provide on-the-ground accounts of women's contribution to the spread of public libraries throughout the period following 1876. In fact, women's efforts also figure prominently when we examine the remaining factors accounting for the growth of public libraries in general.

Philanthropy

Donations from individuals were often the impetus for the establishment of public libraries, not only as the means to purchase buildings and books, but also as an opportunity for the donor to express personal philosophies on the common good. By the mid-1800s the habit of philanthropy was deemed a proper manifestation of the stewardship of wealth.[12] Motivation for donations to libraries may have been a conservative defense by the wealthy to educate the population to be more orderly and submissive or "shrewd policy on the part of millionaires to expend a trifle of the gains which they made off the people in giving them public libraries" (Ditzion, 1947: 136–137). Then again, part of the motivation was likely the manifestation of the ideals of the social obligations of the wealthy.

After the Civil War, with no income tax or corporate tax, vast fortunes were accumulated by industrialists, merchants, and financiers. From 1880 to 1889 $36,000,000 was donated to libraries, including large donations by Astor, Lennox, and Tilden to New York. Smaller donations also made it possible for towns across the United States to establish libraries. However, no single donor made more of an impact on the development of U.S. public libraries than Andrew Carnegie.

Andrew Carnegie donated over $41,000,000 for the erection of 1,679 libraries in 1,412 communities across the United States between 1898 and 1919. Many of them were in the Classical Revival style and over time have become architectural landmarks. They are the largest single group of buildings nominated to the National Register of Historic Places. Much has been written about Carnegie, a poor boy from Scotland who became one of the most ruthless capitalists in the United States. His role in the Homestead Strike of June

1892 stands yet as one of the bloodiest incidents in U.S. labor history as Pinkerton guards sent to break the strike killed striking steel workers.

The motivation behind Carnegie's selection of libraries as a focus of his philanthropy has been variously discussed. His father, a weaver in Dunfermline, Scotland, had led his fellow-workers to pool their funds to purchase books for reading out loud—a fact Carnegie often mentioned. As a young clerk in Pittsburgh he had been allowed to use the workingman's library of a Colonel Anderson in Allegheny, which helped convince Carnegie of the importance of access to books to educate and inspire workers. Carnegie wrote essays on his philosophy of wealth and stewardship and made observations that wealthy men should live modestly and use their wealth to help those who would help themselves. He was a product of Scotch Presbyterianism and felt that the concentration of wealth in the hands of a few was a part of life described by evolution. The rich should act as trustees for the poor. Thus, felt Carnegie, the best focus of philanthropy would be universities, libraries, medical centers, public parks, meeting and concert halls, and churches. His philosophy is well known because of his writing (especially his famous essay, *Gospel of Wealth*, in which Carnegie described this philosophy).

Bobinski undertook a comprehensive study of the scope of Carnegie's library philanthropy, analyzing Carnegie's approach of giving funds for library building, but also requiring that the communities furnish the site and pledge to the ongoing support of the library. Although Carnegie initially (1886–1896) gave buildings with endowments—the "retail" period—to communities in which his industries were located, he changed to a "wholesale" approach from 1896–1919 requiring community support (Bobinski, 1969: 13–23).

Carnegie hired James Bertram as a private secretary to handle most of the correspondence relating to the library program, and grants were limited to English-speaking countries. Communities requesting a library were sent a short questionnaire (reproduced in Bobinski, 1969: 203–206). If their response was satisfactory they were asked to supply a letter describing the site and vouching that it was purchased and paid in full. Finally, each community was required to pledge at least ten percent of the amount of the grant for annual maintenance. In this way 1,679 communities from forty-six states were able to build libraries. Indiana received the most—164 in all—although the northeast received the most money due to large gifts to single cities (often for multiple branch libraries).

The first library to serve African Americans was the Western Branch Library in Louisville, which opened in 1905. Responding to the concerns of Albert Ernest Meyzeek, the plan for Carnegie to fund the public library system of Louisville included a branch for "colored" citizens. The Reverend Thomas Fountain Blue was appointed director—the first African American to head a public library.

The grants were generally well received and much sought after. Watson has detailed the efforts of women's clubs to organize for the purpose of obtaining Carnegie grants for their communities. She observes, "the awakening of public sentiment in favor of libraries was the chosen work of state federations of women's clubs and individual clubs throughout the United States" (1994: 262). The work of women in securing Carnegie libraries in western states has also been noted by Passet in *Cultural Crusaders: Women Librarians in the American West* (1994), and in Held's study of the rise of public libraries in California (1973).

However, some communities refused the money as "tainted" by Carnegie's repressive policies toward labor, while others could not meet the financial obligation of the annual pledge. In the volume, *Carnegie Denied* (1993), a number of scholars have analyzed those communities that applied for building grants, but which did not complete the project. In their study of Carnegie libraries in New York, Stielow and Corsaro (1993) examined the work of the Progressives, including Melvil Dewey, to promote the library cause, thus melding the pseudo-aristocratic robber barons with the ideals of a new social awareness.

Ditzion's assessment of Carnegie's contribution as a stimulant, not an initiator is astute. While the public library as an entity began on firm footing in New England, the growth might have been slowed as communities waited for big donors. Carnegie's great contribution to the idea of the public library was that it needed to be supported by the people of a community through taxation. "Popular initiative, participation and control were the desired aims" (Ditzion, 1947: 150). Philanthropy and the growing involvement of women in the political process were the fuel that moved the public library idea to catch fire.

State Library Commissions and Traveling Libraries

Another great impetus to the growth of public libraries occurred in 1890 with the passage of the Massachusetts Law creating a state Board of Library Commissioners charged to help communities establish and improve public libraries. The law included a grant of $100 to begin collections in towns where none existed. Elizabeth Putnam

Sohier, a driving force in the legislative process, was appointed to the first Massachusetts Free Library commission and is representative of the tenacity of women and women's clubs in the spread of library legislation (Watson, 2003: 75). The state soon became more than a passive agent vis-à-vis the development of public libraries. Similar laws were quickly passed in New York (1892), Maine, New Hampshire, and Connecticut (1893).

The New York state law, promoted by Melvil Dewey, accelerated the rate of public library development. Dewey devised a system of "traveling libraries" for New York in 1893 to provide one-hundred volume collections that were sent to areas of the state that had no access to a library. The "traveling library" idea was also put into action by women's clubs in Delaware and Maryland before those states established state library commissions. In 1901 a report by Dewey on traveling libraries gave prominent notice to the activities of women's clubs. The New York system worked closely with the state federation of women's clubs to establish libraries where none existed and to improve and encourage small libraries. A network of women workers was formed and assigned to specific areas of the state to encourage reading and library development (Watson, 1994: 238–241).

In some states women developed and supported traveling libraries for many years before the state provided support. In Illinois, between 1898 and 1905, three hundred traveling libraries were maintained before state legislation passed. By 1904 thirty-four states with women's federations were overseeing over 300,000 volumes in 4,655 traveling collections. Watson provides comparative data on the establishment of traveling libraries by state in her insightful article, "Valleys Without Sunsets: Women's Clubs and Traveling Libraries" (2003: 89–93). For an excellent case study of the influence of women and their work in traveling libraries see Christine Pawley's 2000 article, "Advocate of Access: Lutie Stearns and the Traveling Libraries of the Wisconsin Free Library Commission: 1895–1914."

The traveling library projects were closely tied to efforts across the country to establish state library commissions. Watson notes, "There is little doubt that the state federation of women's clubs can claim credit for the passage of legislation in many states to establish library commissions," and then details the efforts of women in Kentucky, Georgia, Illinois, Indiana, Maine, and Wisconsin (1994: 244). From this came appointment of women as commissioners or trustees to these commissions. In his assessment of library law and legislation, Alex Ladenson views the major expansion of public libraries after 1890 as attributable to the passage of legislation for the state library commissions (1982: 55–57).

The Professionalization of Librarianship

During the period 1876–1918 the founding and growth of the American Library Association plus the entry of women into the profession contributed to an increase in the number of public librarians, who in turn were active in helping to expand the numbers of libraries. The founders of the American Library Association are well known to us due to the thoughtful analyses by Wiegand in several studies, including *The Politics of an Emerging Profession*, which paints a picture of an organization led by a highly homogeneous group of men who, in the words of Wiegand, "shared a relatively closed definition of reality and believed a rational, informed electorate was essential to democracy" (1986b: 230). The ALA members developed recommended reading lists and collection guides so that libraries might support "best reading" that would induce society to reduce social conflict and insure social order. In Thomas Augst's opinion, "Just as the blighted social and economic landscape of industrial capitalism was putting the power of the individual in question, this liberal ideology was propagated with missionary zeal by a new cadre of professional librarians and educators. As they spread the gospel of public culture to small towns across the United States, public libraries would acquire the status as a public good, worthy of tax support" (2001: 12).

Public library historians of the 1940s, such as Shera (1949) and Ditzion (1947), failed to treat comprehensively the entry of women into librarianship as paid employees, and their role, as we see in their classic studies of the founding of U.S. public libraries. While the 1979 study by Garrison, *Apostles of Culture*, examined the entrance of women into the profession, it tended to view early women librarians as sustainers of the moral views of their male counterparts. Hildenbrand (2000) questions this view, seeking rather to argue for a history of librarianship that looks at the interrelatedness of socially constructed categories. Subsequent studies indicate that the addition of women to the ranks of the library profession may have been a strong factor in the shift from library service shaped for cultural uplift to one of community-based service. The shift included the opening of stacks, the foundation of youth services, and development of services to immigrants.

Progressive movement ideals after the 1890s were internalized in librarianship as the field was more open to women, and which occurred with the establishment of formal educational programs. The first education program, the School of Library Economy, opened by Melvil Dewey in 1886 at Columbia University included women as students and proved to be controversial as unauthorized coeducation. When Dewey moved to Albany as the secretary of the University of the State of New York and director of the state library in 1888, the program went with him. Programs began throughout the nation (some in large libraries, some affiliated with higher education, some as summer training programs) and the creation of these programs made it a profession more accessible to women.[13]

The American Library Association's practice of moving annual conferences about the nation stimulated interest in library matters. Certainly discussions and programs held by the Association made an impact on the way librarians thought about the services they were providing. By the early 1900s progressive library leader, John Cotton Dana, observed that the public could forge its own use of the library by using the library in the ways that it determined, an observation substantiated by the work of Lutie Stearns in Wisconsin for more democratic provision of library services (Mattson, 2000; Pawley, 2000).

As public libraries were established throughout the nation the attitude toward collection development and users gradually shifted. Wiegand points out that by the time of entry into World War I, the "reforming spirit of the Progressive era had identified the 'problem' groups in American society—the immigrants, the urban indigent, and criminal and insane, the remote rural dweller, the impressionable child, to name but a few—and the historical record shows that the ALA had sponsored some activity or group which sought to address the socialization needs of each" (1986b: 235). In Jones's study of libraries and the immigrant experience, he notes that the ALA Committee on Work with the Foreign-Born in the first quarter of the century had an effect on library service: "Ironically, then, as immigrants were being transformed into Americans, librarians were also being transformed through their contacts with immigrants....In the process they, too, were changed, metamorphosed into more tolerant Americanizers, more progressive citizens, and more responsive professionals" (1999: 30). From its founding to World War I the internal debates and personal beliefs of U.S. librarians within the American Library Association demonstrated a slow but concerted evolution toward a greater commitment to access as needs of immigrants, working people and children began to receive focus and attention.

World War I marked a turning point for librarians in the United States. In his study of librarians during World War I, *An Active Instrument for Propaganda*, Wiegand described the state of libraries prior to the War as consisting of thousands of local libraries scattered across the United States staffed by women and men who developed high quality collections but who longed for a consolidation of their position within the community. The entrance of the United States into World I gave these librarians the opportunity for connection to other community agencies through cooperation with the War effort—characterized by Wiegand as "an exhilarating experience that constituted a capstone to the public library movement in Progressive America" (1989: 133). Yet this experience was one of the most reprehensible periods of U.S. library history, inasmuch as public librarians put service to the state before democratic principles—censoring German-language material and pacifistic and antiwar literature.

At the close of the War the U.S. public library had achieved integration into the fabric of the life of the commonweal. The close association with the war effort both at the local level and through the American Library Association provided the profession with long sought after credibility. By 1918 public libraries were generally accepted as a standard component of municipal services. Yet in spite of the patriotic rush to a place on *Main Street*, progressive ideas and values were gaining strength among many librarians. In the next chapter we survey the continuing development of public librarianship in the United States as it moves toward greater acceptance and support as an institution, while struggling to define values beyond the mainstream of life in the United States.

Notes

1. See Hugh Amory and David D. Hall, eds., *A History of the Book in America*, vol. 1, *The Colonial Book in the Atlantic World* (Cambridge: Cambridge University Press, 2000). For background on the concept of the "reading revolution," see Reinhard Wittmann, "Was There a Reading Revolution at the End of the Eighteenth Century?" in *A History of Reading in the West*, ed. Guglielmo Cavallo and Roger Chartier, 284–312 (Amherst: University of Massachusetts Press, 1999).

2. Hellmutt Lehmann-Haut, et al., *The Book in America: A History of the Making and Selling of Books in the United States* (New York: R. R. Bowker, 1952); Richard D. Brown, *Knowledge Is Power: The Diffusion of Information in Early America, 1700–1865* (New

York: Oxford University Press, 1989); William J. Gilmore, *Reading Becomes a Necessity: Material and Cultural Life in Rural New England, 1780–1835* (Knoxville, TN: University of Tennessee Press, 1989); Isabel Lehuu, *Carnival on the Page: Popular Print Media in Antebellum America* (Chapel Hill, NC: University of North Carolina Press, 2000); Ronald J. Zboray, *A Fictive People: Antebellum Economic Development and the Reading Public* (New York: Oxford University Press, 1993); David D. Hall, *Worlds of Wonder, Days of Judgment: Popular Religious Belief in Early New England* (New York: Alfred A. Knopf, 1989).

3. The single most enlightening document on a variety of social libraries is the U.S. Bureau of Education's "Public Libraries of Ten Principal Cities," in *Public Libraries in the United States of America; their History, Condition, and Management. Special Report*, 837–1009 (Washington, DC: Government Printing Office, 1876). This article includes sketches on the founding and development of diverse social libraries such as the New York Historical Society Library (1804), Boston Athenaeum (1807), Cincinnati Circulating Library (1811), Apprentices' Library of Brooklyn (1823), Young Men's Association Library of Chicago (1841), Baltimore Mercantile Library Association (1842), Mercantile Library of San Francisco (1853), and Portland, Oregon Library Association (1864). Included for many of the libraries highlighted are membership rolls, budgets, and collection descriptions.

4. Think of Vattemare as Bono. French ventriloquist, M. Nicholas-Marie Alexandre Vattemare, is one of the most interesting personalities in U.S. library history. He was indefatigable in his efforts to establish an international system of exchanges of books and documents. From 1839–1849 he campaigned for this idea and was successful in creating an exchange system with the Library of Congress, as well as many states. We can only imagine, looking back, how much influence a persuasive idealist like Vattemare had on the public library idea. Sometimes a charismatic individual can escalate an ideal. In today's world we have Bono fighting to lessen the debt of poor nations. For background on the connections of ventriloquism and the ideas of the enlightenment see Leigh Eric Schmidt, "From Demon Possession to Magic Show: Ventriloquism, Religion, and the Enlightenment," *Church History* 67 (June 1998): 274–304 On the idea of International Exchanges, see E. M. Richards, "Alexandre

Vattemare and His System of International Exchanges." *Bulletin of the Medical Library Association* 32 (1940): 413–448.

    5. Francis Wayland, in his influential 1838 speech, *Discourse at the Opening of the Providence Athenaeum*, argues this point. Wayland had been arguing for an athenaeum that would be open to all. While this would not come about until the enactment of laws over a decade later, Wayland's discourse provides additional insight into the idea of a free public library. His donation to the town of Wayland was the catalyst that laid the groundwork for free public libraries throughout Massachusetts.

    6. Jesse H. Shera, *Foundations of the Public Library: The Origins of the Public Library Movement in New England, 1629–1855* (Chicago: University of Chicago Press, 1949; Repr. Hamden, CT: Shoestring Press, 1965), 199. Shera is quoting Wight's circular letter. The summary of the Massachusetts legislation is also in Shera (1949), 189–199. The full text of Wight's speech appeared as "Public Libraries" *Common School Journal* 13 (1851): 257–264.

    7. "The Report of the Joint Special Committee to the Boston City Council of December 6, 1847" is reprinted in Horace Greeley Wadlin, *The Public Library of the City of Boston: A History* (Boston: The Trustees, 1911), 8–9. See also Shera (1965), 170–181; Carleton Bruns Joeckel, *The Government of the American Public Library* (Chicago: University of Chicago Press, 1935), 18; Alex Ladenson, *Library Law and Legislation in the United States* (Metuchen, NJ: Scarecrow Press, 1982), 7–8; Ditzion (1947), 18–19.

    8. "Boston Public Library. Report of the Trustees of the Public Library to the City of Boston. 1852," reproduced in Shera (1965), 267–290. The specific steps that led to the establishment of the Boston Public Library, including the intriguing role of the French ventriloquist M. Nicholas-Marie Alexandre Vattemare, (see note 4 supra) whose 1841 presentation to Boston society of his plan for an international exchange of books caused recognition that Boston, at that time, had no great library to receive such an exchange, have been detailed in various histories of the library. For more extensive background see the 1876 U.S. Department of the Interior. Bureau of Education, Special Report (863–872); Shera (1965: 170–199), Ditzion (1947: 5–7), Joeckel (1935: 16–22), Ladenson (1982: 7–9), as well as many articles and books. See, for example: Wadlin (1911); Walter Muir Whitehill, *Boston Public Library; A Centennial History* (Cambridge, MA: Harvard University Press, 1956); Frances R. Knight, "A Palace for the

People: the Relationships that Built the Boston Public Library" (PhD diss., University of Oxford, 2000); Donald G. Davis, Jr., *Winsor, Dewey, and Putnam: the Boston Experience* (Champaign, IL: Graduate School of Library and Information Science, University of Illinois at Urbana-Champaign, 2002).

9. 1847, "Report of the Joint Special Committee to the Boston City Council" is reprinted in Wadlin (1911), 8–9; 1851, John B. Wight's speech to the Massachusetts Legislature is reprinted in "Public Libraries" *Common School Journal* 13 (1851): 257–264. The state law enacted in Massachusetts in 1851 resulted in the establishment of ten town libraries by 1854: New Bedford, Beverley, Winchendon, (1851); Fay Library in Southborough, (1852); Lenox (1853); and Newburyport, Framingham, Groton, Woburn, and West Springfield (1854). 1852, "Report of the Trustees of the Public Library to the City of Boston" is reproduced in Shera (1965), 267–290. Ditzion (1947: 19) adds several more early sources to this list, including an 1852 special library committee report to the trustees of Concord, New Hampshire; speeches delivered at the Librarians' Convention of 1853; speeches at the laying of the cornerstone of the Boston Public Library; and the Boston Public Library memorial to the philanthropist, Joshua Bates.

10. Women are largely ignored in Shera (1949), Ditzion (1947), and Harris (1995). Garrison's treatment of women (1979) was, as Francis Miksa (1982) demonstrates, somewhat speculative. For comprehensive bibliographic treatment see the following series: Kathleen Weibel, Kathleen de la Peña McCook (Heim) and Dianne J. Ellsworth, *The Status of Women in Librarianship, 1876–1976*, a Neal-Schuman Professional Book (Phoenix, AZ: Oryx Press, 1979); Kathleen de la Peña McCook and Katharine Phenix, *On Account of Sex: An Annotated Bibliography on the History of Women in Librarianship, 1977–1981* (Chicago: American Library Association, 1984); Katharine Phenix and Kathleen de la Peña McCook, *On Account of Sex: An Annotated Bibliography on the History of Women in Librarianship, 1982–1986* Chicago: American Library Association, 1989); later years by Lori A. Goetsch and Sarah B. Watstein, *On Account of Sex: An Annotated Bibliography on the History of Women in Librarianship, 1987–1992* (Metuchen, NJ: Scarecrow Press, 1993); Betsy Kruger and Catherine A. Larson, *On Account of Sex: An Annotated Bibliography on the History of Women in Librarianship, 1993–1997* (Lanham, MD: Scarecrow Press, 2000).

11. The grand include Phyllis P. Dain, *The New York Public Library: A History of Its Founding and Early Years* (New York: New York Public Library, 1972). Dozens of books, theses, journal articles, and celebratory histories for most states and a good many individual libraries are listed in Donald G. Davis, Jr., and John Mark Tucker, *American Library History: A Comprehensive Guide to the Literature* (Santa Barbara, CA: ABC-CLIO, 1989) and updated in the journal, *Libraries and Culture.*

12. The religious and moral underpinnings of library philanthropists may be of interest. Suggested background: John H. Hammer, "Money and the Moral Order in Late Nineteenth and Early-Twentieth Century American Capitalism." *Anthropological Quarterly* 71 (July 1998): 138–149; Alexis Tocqueville, *Democracy in America* (London: Oxford University Press, 1952); J. McNeil, *The History and Character of Calvinism* (Oxford: Oxford University Press, 1967); C. Howard Hopkins, *The Rise of the Social Gospel in American Protestantism, 1865–1915* (New Haven, CT: Yale University Press, 1940).

13. W. Boyd Rayward, "Melvil Dewey and Education for Librarianship," *Journal of Library History* 3 (1968): 297–313; Charles D. Churchwell, *The Shaping of American Library Education* (Chicago: American Library Association, 1975); Donald G. Davis, Jr., and Phyllis Dain, "History of Library and Information Science Education, Papers issued in advance of the Library Education, Centennial Symposium," special issue *Library Trends* 34 (Winter 1986); Laurel Ann Grotzinger, James Vinson Carmichael, and Mary Niles Maack, *Women's Work: Vision and Change in Librarianship* (Champaign, IL: University of Illinois, 1994).

References

Amory, Hugh, and David D. Hall, eds. 2000. *A History of the Book in America.* Vol. 1 of *The Colonial Book in the Atlantic World.* Cambridge, MA: Cambridge University Press.

Augst, Thomas. 2001. American Libraries and Agencies of Culture. *American Studies* 42 (Fall): 12.

Bixby, A. F., and A. Howell. 1876. *Historical Sketches of the Ladies' Library Associations of the State of Michigan, 1876.* Adrian, MI: Times and Expositor Steam Print. Reprinted in Kathleen Weibel, Kathleen Heim (de la Peña McCook), and Dianne J. Ellsworth. *The Status of Women in Librarianship, 1876–1976,* pp. 3–4. Phoenix, AZ: Oryx Press, a Neal-Schuman Professional Book, 1979.

Blazek, R. 1979. The Development of Library Service in the Nation's Oldest City: The St. Augustine Library Association, 1874–1880. *Journal of Library History* 14: 160–182.

Bobinski, George S. 1969. *Carnegie Libraries: Their History and Impact on American Library Development.* Chicago: American Library Association.

Boston Public Library. 1852. *Report of the Trustees of the Public Library to the City of Boston.* Reproduced in Jesse H. Shera, *Foundations of the Public Library: The Origins of the Public Library Movement in New England, 1629–1855* (Chicago: University of Chicago Press, 1949; Repr., Hamden, CT: Shoestring Press, 1965), 267–290.

Boylan, Anne M. 1988. *Sunday School: The Formation of an American Institution, 1790–1880.* New Haven, CT: Yale University Press.

Carnegie, Andrew. 1889. The Best Fields for Philanthropy. *North American Review* 149 (December). Also quoted in Bobinski, 1969: 11.

Carnegie, Andrew. 1900. *The Gospel of Wealth and Other Timely Essays.* New York: The Century Co. Repr. ed. Edward C. Kirkland. Cambridge, MA: Harvard University Press, 1962.

Churchwell, Charles D. 1975. *The Shaping of American Library Education.* Chicago: American Library Association.

Cornelius, Janet Duitsman. 1991. *When I Can Read My Title Clear: Literacy, Slavery and Religion in the Antebellum South.* Columbia, SC: University of South Carolina Press.

Dain, Phyllis P. 1972. *The New York Public Library: A History of Its Founding and Early Years.* New York: New York Public Library.

Davis, Donald G., Jr., and John Mark Tucker. 1989. *American Library History: A Comprehensive Guide to the Literature.* Santa Barbara, CA: ABC-CLIO.

Ditzion, Sidney H. 1940. The District School Library, 1835–1855. *Library Quarterly* 10: 545–547.

Ditzion, Sidney H. 1947. *Arsenals of a Democratic Culture: A Social History of the American Public Library Movement in New England and the Middle States from 1850–1900.* Chicago: American Library Association.

Fain, Elaine. 1978. The Library and American Education: Education Through Secondary School. *Library Trends* (Winter): 327–352.

Freeman, Robert S. 2003. Harper & Brothers' Family and School District Libraries, 1830–1846. In *Libraries to the People: Histories of Outreach*, ed. Robert S. Freeman and David M. Hovde. Jefferson, NC: McFarland and Co.

Garrison, Dee. 1979. *Apostles of Culture: The Public Librarian and American Society, 1876–1920.* New York: The Free Press.

Goetsch, Lori A., and Sarah B. Watstein. 1993. *On Account of Sex: An Annotated Bibliography on the History of Women in Librarianship, 1987–1992.* Metuchen, NJ: Scarecrow Press.

Hall, David D. 1994. Readers and Reading in America: Historical and Critical Perspectives. In *Proceedings of the American Antiquarian Society* 104: 337–357.

Harris, Michael H. 1973. The Purpose of the American Public Library: A Revisionist Interpretation of History. *Library Journal* 98 (September 15): 2509–2514.

Harris, Michael H. 1995. *History of Libraries in the Western World.* 4th ed. Lanham, MD: Scarecrow Press.

Hayes, Kevin J. 1996. *A Colonial Woman's Bookshelf.* Knoxville, TN: University of Tennessee Press.

Held, Ray E. 1959. The Early School District Library in California. *Library Quarterly* 29: 79.

Held, Ray E. 1973. *The Rise of the Public Library in California.* Chicago: American Library Association.

Hildenbrand, Suzanne. 2000. Library Feminism and Library Women's History: Activism and Scholarship: Equity and Culture. *Libraries and Culture* 35 (Winter): 51–63.

Hildenbrand, Suzanne, ed. 1996. *Reclaiming the American Library Past: Writing the Women In.* Norwood, NJ: Ablex.

Houlette, W. D. 1934. Parish Libraries and the Work of Rev. Thomas Bray. *Library Quarterly* 4: 588–609.

Hoyt, Dolores J. 1999. *A Strong Mind in a Strong Body: Libraries in the German-American Turner Movement.* New York: Peter Lang.

Jewett, Charles Coffin. 1851. Report on the Public Libraries of the United States of America, January 1, 1850. In *Report of the Board of Regents of the Smithsonian Institution.* Washington, DC: Smithsonian Institution.

Joeckel, Carleton Bruns. 1935. *The Government of the American Public Library.* Chicago: University of Chicago Press.

Jones, Plummer Alston, Jr. 1999. *Libraries, Immigrants, and the American Experience.* Westport, CT: Greenwood Press.

Kaser, David. 1978. Coffee House to Stock Exchange: A Natural History of the Reading Room. In *Milestones to the Present: Papers from Library History Seminar V,* ed. Harold Goldstein, 238–254. Syracuse NY: Gaylord Professional Publications.

Kaser, David. 1980. *A Book for a Six Pence: The Circulating Library in America.* Pittsburgh, PA: Beta Phi Mu.

Knowles, Malcolm S. 1977. *A History of the Adult Education Movement in the United States: includes Adult Education Institutions through 1976.* Huntington, NY: Robert E. Krieger Publishing Company.

Kruger, Betsy, and Catherine A. Larson. 2000. *On Account of Sex: An Annotated Bibliography on the History of Women in Librarianship, 1993–1997.* Lanham, MD: Scarecrow Press.

Ladenson, Alex. 1982. *Library Law and Legislation in the United States.* Metuchen, NJ: Scarecrow Press.

Laugher, C. T. 1973. *Thomas Bray's Grand Design.* Chicago: American Library Association.

Malone, Cheryl Knott. 2000a. Books for Black Children: Public Library Collections in Louisville and Nashville, 1915–1925. *Library Quarterly* 70 (April): 179–200.

Malone, Cheryl Knott. 2000b. Toward a Multicultural American Public Library History. *Libraries and Culture* 35 (Winter): 77–87.

Massachusetts, State of. *1848 Acts and Resolves, Chapter 52.* Boston: State of Massachusetts.

Mattson, Kevin. 2000. The Librarian as Secular Minister to Democracy: The Life and Ideas of John Cotton Dana. *Libraries and Culture* 35 (Fall): 514–534.

McCauley, Elfrieda B. 1971. The New England Mill Girls: Feminine Influence in the Development of Public libraries in New England, 1820–1860. Doctoral Thesis, Columbia University.

McCook, Kathleen de la Peña, and Katharine Phenix. 1984. *On Account of Sex: An Annotated Bibliography on the History of Women in Librarianship, 1977–1981.* Chicago: American Library Association.

McMullen, Haynes. 1985. The Very Slow Decline of the American Social Library. *Library Quarterly* 55: 207–225.

McMullen, Haynes. 2000. *American Libraries Before 1876.* Beta Phi Mu Monograph Series, no. 6. Westport, CT: Greenwood Press.

Miksa, Francis. 1982. The Interpretation of American Public Library History. In *Public Librarianship: A Reader,* ed. Jane Robbins-Carter, 73–90. Littleton, CO: Libraries Unlimited.

Musmann, V. K. 1982. Women and the Founding of Social Libraries in California, 1859–1910. PhD diss., University of Southern California.

Passet, Joanne E. 1994. *Cultural Crusaders; Women Librarians in the American West, 1900–1917.* Albuquerque NM: University of New Mexico Press.

Pawley, Christine. 2000. Advocate of Access: Lutie Stearns and the Traveling Libraries of the Wisconsin Free Library Commission: 1895–1914. *Libraries and Culture* 35 (Summer): 434–458.

Phenix, Katharine, and Kathleen de la Peña McCook. 1989. *On Account of Sex: An Annotated Bibliography on the History of Women in Librarianship, 1982–1986.* Chicago: American Library Association.

A Separate Flame Western Branch: The First African-American Public Library. Available: http://lfpl.org/western/htms/welcome.htm.

Shera, Jesse H. 1949. *Foundations of the Public Library: The Origins of the Public Library Movement in New England, 1629–1855.* Chicago: University of Chicago Press; Repr., Hamden, CT: Shoestring Press, 1965.

Stielow, Frederick J., and James Corsaro. 1993. The Carnegie Question and the Public Library Movement in Progressive Era New York. In *Carnegie Denied: Communities Rejecting Carnegie Library Construction Grants, 1898–1925,* ed. Robert Sidney Martin, 35–51. Westport, CT: Greenwood Press.

Todd, Emily B. 2001. Antebellum Libraries in Richmond and New Orleans and the Search for the Practices and Preferences of Real Readers. *American Studies* 42 (Fall): 195–209.

U.S. Department of the Interior. Bureau of Education. 1876. *Public Libraries in the United States of America: Their History, Condition, and Management. Special Report.* Washington, DC: U.S. Government Printing Office. Repr., as Monograph Series, no. 4, Champaign, IL: University of Illinois, Graduate School of Library Science.

Wadlin, Horace Greeley. 1911. *The Public Library of the City of Boston: A History.* Boston: The Trustees.

Watson, Paula D. 1994. Founding Mothers: The Contribution of Women's Organizations to Public Library Development in the United States. *Library Quarterly* 64 (July): 237.

Watson, Paula D. 1996. Carnegie Ladies, Lady Carnegies: Women and the Building of Libraries. *Libraries and Culture* 31 (Winter): 159–196.

Watson, Paula D. 2003. Valleys Without Sunsets: Women's Clubs and Traveling Libraries. In *Libraries to the People: Histories of Outreach*, ed. Robert S. Freeman and David M. Hovde, 73–95. Jefferson, NC: McFarland and Co.

Wayland, Francis. 1838. *Discourse at the Opening of the Providence Athenaeum*. Providence, RI: Knowles, Vose.

Wiegand, Wayne A. 1986a. The Historical Development of State Library Agencies. In *State Library Services and Issues: Facing Future Challenges*, ed. Charles R. McClure, 1–16. Norwood, NJ: Ablex.

Wiegand, Wayne A. 1986b. *The Politics of an Emerging Profession: The American Library Association, 1876–1917*. New York: Greenwood Press.

Wiegand, Wayne A. 1989. *An Active Instrument for Propaganda: The American Public Library During World War I*. Westport, CT: Greenwood Press.

Williams, Julie Hedgepeth. 1999. *The Significance of the Printed Word in Early America*. Westport, CT: Greenwood Press.

Wittmann, Reinhard. 1999. Was There a Reading Revolution at the End of the Eighteenth Century? In *A History of Reading in the West*, ed. Guglielmo Cavallo and Roger Chartier, 284–312. Amherst, MA: University of Massachusetts Press, 1999.

Wyss, Hilary E. 2000. *Writing Indians: Literacy, Christianity and Native Community in Early America*. Amherst, MA: University of Massachusetts Press.

Young, Arthur P. 1981. *Books for Sammies: The American Library Association and World War I*. Pittsburgh, PA: Beta Phi Mu.

3
Public Library Growth and Values: 1918–2004

From 1918 to the present, U.S. public libraries have continued to expand outlets, extend service areas, and define broad goals in the context of equity of access, lifelong learning, and intellectual freedom. This chapter summarizes the growth of the library idea from a largely state and local initiative to its acceptance by the nation as a vital and necessary community agency. Today 9,129 public libraries (administrative entities) serve communities in the 50 states and the District of Columbia with 16,421 points of service (e.g., central libraries, branches, bookmobiles). Also in this chapter, I delineate the role of librarians in developing a national planning initiative. Here readers can examine for themselves the changing philosophies regarding service to all patrons through lifelong learning, support for democracy, and intellectual freedom.

Equalizing Library Opportunity: Toward a National Role

During World War I librarians greatly expanded their scope of service and visibility by work on the home front and overseas. The American Library Association's Library War Service in training camps and Europe broadened the general public's appreciation for library service (Kelly, 2003). This active engagement positioned librarians as more active participants in their communities. Whether municipally or county-based, the establishment of state commissions that promoted the library idea coupled with the success of the library in the war effort ensured that in 1918 citizens widely embraced the public library as an appropriate community agency. After World War I the history of public libraries in the United States and the American Library Association as a factor in the development of public libraries became even more intertwined with the actions of local and state governments.

ALA historian Dennis Thomison has observed that ALA, enlivened by the success of its Library War Service, planned for an "Enlarged Program" that would include a fund raising campaign to "encourage and promote the development of library service for all Americans" (1978: 70–71). After much effort and discussion the "Enlarged Program" was dropped, but the planning and work that went into the program shaped the thinking of association leaders after 1918. In 1919 ALA supported the Smith-Towner bill that proposed federal funds to extend public libraries for educational purposes and a bureau of libraries at the federal level. Although the bill was not enacted, the idea to extend access with federal support was in the air (Molz, 1984: 75).

The ALA's "Enlarged Program" concept, the experience of a national role for libraries during World War I, and the ALA Council's ongoing discussion of federal support for libraries expanded the scope of discussion about the role of public libraries during the 1920s. Of special note were the association's focus on adult education and extension. The 1924 report to the Carnegie Corporation, *The American Public Library and the Diffusion of Knowledge,* included the observation that "the free public library is already an accepted and cherished figure in American intellectual life," and put forth the suggestion that the ALA should provide the support for the growth and expansion of smaller libraries (Learned, 1924: 75–80). In 1926 the ALA study, *Libraries and Adult Education,* was published and the association established the Board on Library and Adult Education (later the Adult Education Board) with reports in the *ALA Bulletin.*[1] The concept of the library as an agency of ongoing education for adults became firmly established in United States society.

It should be pointed out that library services for youth had been gaining acceptance as a specialization in U.S. libraries and this movement, enlivened by the efforts of Anne Carroll Moore of New

York Public Library (where she served from 1906–1941), created even more broad-based support for libraries in communities. As children's literature found a growing appreciative audience it followed that public libraries offering services for children would be viewed as important to community life (Fenwick, 1976; Jenkins, 2000).

The ALA Committee on Library Extension (established in 1925) worked to extend library services to unserved areas in the United States and appointed a regional field agent for the South, Tommie Dora Barker, with funding from a Carnegie Corporation Grant. The League of Library Commissions (established in 1904 and affiliated with ALA eventually becoming the State Library Agency of the Extension Division in 1942), worked on rural issues before and during the depression-era New Deal. The Citizens' Library Movement, especially in North Carolina, demonstrated a grassroots desire for library service (Library Projects, 1933). During the 1920s and 1930s ALA embraced the idea of libraries as a means to provide adult educational opportunities and combined this idea with many efforts to extend library service to unserved areas.[2]

Libraries at the Federal Level

The idea that there should be a federal role for libraries began under the aegis of Carl H. Milam, Executive Secretary of ALA from 1920–1948, with his 1929 memorandum to the ALA Council, "What Should be the Federal Government's Relation to Libraries?" (Sullivan, 1976: 165). Milam's service on the U.S. National Advisory Committee on Education provided him an opportunity to consider issues, such as federal aid to libraries, in the larger context of the reform ideals of Roosevelt's New Deal planning based in progressive era reform and policy development.

The ALA Executive Board appointed its own National Planning Committee in 1934, which developed a "National Plan" to examine the inequity of tax-support for public libraries and sought provision of financial support so that library materials might be available throughout the nation (Sullivan, 1976: 165; Milam 1934). The National Plan was discussed at ALA Council during the 1934 annual conference and while a sticking point was the locus of control (federal versus state and local), the committee made revisions affirming state and local responsibility and continuance and increase of local support. The National Plan was approved (A National Plan, 1935). Molz notes that, "the issuance of the *National Plan* was the first time that the Association itself entered the national political arena to state a plank as a public policy actor" (1984: 37).

The work done by ALA's Library Extension Board laid much groundwork for a national vision of library service driven by a clearer idea of equity of financial support. Beginning in 1929 the Library Extension Board's occasional mimeographed newsletter, *Library Extension News,* was subtitled, *Equalizing Library Opportunities.* The idea of equalization was clearly addressed in a 1936 ALA publication issued jointly by the Library Extension Board and the Committee on Planning, *The Equal Chance: Books Help to Make It.* Using line drawings and charts, *The Equal Chance* compared per capita income to public library availability and declared, "It is increasingly true in our modern world that knowledge is power and that the uninformed man not only is handicapped in making a living, but is a liability as a citizen, for whose ignorance we all pay" (1936: 15). This simple pamphlet urged people to get involved in state and national planning for library support to achieve "equalizing of library opportunity."

Due to the work of ALA leaders, the U.S. Department of Education authorized funds in 1937 for a Library Services Division. Of this, Joeckel (1938: 468) observed: "The creation in 1937 of a Library Service Division in the United States Office of Education was an event of great significance in the history of Federal relations to libraries....Prior to the establishment of this Division, there was no Federal office directly responsible for leadership in a Nation-wide program of library development. The new unit will serve as a Federal library headquarters and will provide a national focus for library interests."

Carlton B. Joeckel was appointed chair of a new ALA Committee on Post-Defense Planning (later changed to Post-War Planning) by the executive board in October 1941, which issued *Post-War Standards for Public Libraries* in 1943. Part of a national effort to help make the world a better place in which to live, the *Post-War Standards* asserted the importance of the public library and recommended that public library service should be universally available in the United States and its territories.[3]

A National Plan for Public Library Service was published in 1948 by the American Library Association. The chapter reporting an inventory and evaluation of service, noted:

- total national public library income is less than one-third of the amount required to provide minimum service;

- there are very great inequalities among the states in per capita expenditures;

- there are serious inequalities in library expenditures *within* each of the states; large proportions of the American public are served by libraries weak in total income or in income per capita (Joeckel and Winslow, 1948: 30–31).

Essential features of a national library plan were defined with the role of the state library agency delineated as central to achieving adequate, purposeful public library service. *A National Plan for Public Library Service* proposed "a nation-wide minimum standard of service and support below which no library should fall " (Joeckel and Winslow, 1948: 160). The *National Plan* included a strong call for equalization of financial support, "Very great inequalities among the states in per capita expenditures for public libraries are a dominant characteristic of American library development....Some degree of national equalization of these great differences between the states in library support must be a major concern in library planning" (Joeckel and Winslow, 1948: 30).

ALA established a Washington Office in 1945 to clarify the role of librarians in federal research programs, to form a closer relationship with the Office of Education and other library-related agencies, and to strengthen influence with Congress (Thomison, 1978: 162–164).

The Public Library in the Post-War World

Concurrent with the completion of *A National Plan for Public Library Service*, the ALA membership addressed the question of the role of the public library in the post-war world. The ALA leadership developed plans for a study "to define legitimate library activity by adapting the traditional educational purposes of libraries to new social conditions and the public's willingness to pay for such services" (Raber, 1997: 43). Robert D. Leigh of the University of Chicago was selected to carry out, between 1947 and 1952, the multipart project that would be called the *Public Library Inquiry*.

At a forum on the *Inquiry* held in 1949, Bernard Berelson, author of the *Inquiry* volume, *The Library's Public,* responded to concern about his findings that the library reached only a minority of the population—the better educated. He noted a split between the professed and practiced objectives for the public library. "Just as many lawyers will tell you that their objective is to see justice done, whereas they are actually out to win cases, so many librarians will tell you that education is their objective, when they are busy trying to increase circulation" (Asheim, 1950: 62). The *Inquiry* contributed to the reformulation of the public library's service mission during the 1950s by acting as one of many catalysts that stimulated the innovative outreach efforts of the late 1960s and early 1970s (Maack, 1994). Librarians worked with the new ALA Washington Office for national level legislation.

The passage of the Library Services Act (LSA) in 1956 was the result of 35 years of concerted effort on the part of the American Library Association. Designed to assist in the establishment of library service in areas unserved, especially in rural parts of the country, the LSA required that each state submit a plan for library development before it was eligible to receive federal aid (Casey, 1975). Although this chapter has not focused on the activities of state library agencies, we must note that the work of the state library agencies, usually in collaboration with the ALA state chapters, has been central to overall national public library development. The 1966 report, *The Library Functions of the States* (based on a 1960 survey), recognized the importance of state library agencies in their intermediary role between the federal government and local libraries, and recommended that state library agencies strengthen their role (Monypenny, 1966).

In 1964 the LSA was amended and expanded to include urban libraries and construction and retitled the Library Services and Construction Act (LSCA). In 1966 library cooperation was added to the scope of the LSCA, as well as services to the institutionalized, blind, and people with physical disabilities. The LSCA stimulated a wide variety of innovative library development. States were given considerable flexibility to adapt to state needs within federal priorities, which included: public library construction and renovation; interlibrary cooperation and resources sharing; adaptation of new technologies for library services; and outreach to special segments of the population—e.g., the disadvantaged, those with disabilities, the elderly and homebound, those in institutions, those with limited English-speaking ability, those who needed literacy services, those on Indian reservations, and innovative services at child-care centers and for latchkey children. (ALA, Washington Office).

Civil Rights and Public Libraries

General public library histories prior to Civil Rights legislation in the 1960s barely mention the "ugly side of librarianship"—the segregation that prevailed in libraries throughout much of the United States in the first 65 years of the twentieth century (Mussman, 1998; Cresswell, 1996). From *Plessy v. Ferguson* (1896) through *Brown v.*

Board of Education (1954), many public libraries had separate and unequal facilities for African Americans—if they had any at all. Eliza Atkins Gleason in *The Southern Negro and the Public Library* (1941) provides a careful history of the treatment of African Americans by libraries up to World War II. Writers such as E. J. Josey, Alma Dawson, John Mark Tucker, and Patterson Toby Graham have constructed histories on the manifestation of segregation in various states and regions. The 1963 ALA study, *Access to Public Libraries,* found direct discrimination (complete exclusion), but also "indirect" discrimination practiced by branch libraries in northern cities that were so differentiated in terms of quantity and quality that one group was more limited in its access to the library resources of a community than another. Of these findings, Virginia Lacy Jones commented, "No one should have been surprised that branch libraries discriminate against Negroes, since all public institutions in the United States had discrimination against Negroes built into them. This fact is well known in the South; it is time the North woke up to it" (1963: 744).

The Nation's Library Structure

In 1966 President Lyndon B. Johnson appointed a National Advisory Commission on Libraries (NACL) charged with the task of considering the nation's library structure, the nature of the present and wisest possible future of federal support in the development of national library and informational resources, and the most effective shaping of those resources to the nation's common need over the next decade (Knight and Nourse, 1969). Among the recommendations of the NACL was the establishment of the National Commission on Libraries and Information Science (NCLIS). At its initial meetings NCLIS developed the goal, "To eventually provide every individual in the United States with equal opportunity of access to that part of the total information resource which will satisfy the individual's educational, working, cultural and leisure-time needs and interests, regardless of the individual's location, social or physical condition of level of intellectual achievement" (U.S. NCLIS, 1975).

NCLIS released its action plan, *Toward a National Program for Library and Information Services: Goals for Action* in 1975. This program set forth eight program objectives:

1.   Ensure that basic minimums of library and information services adequate to meet the needs of all local communities are satisfied;

2. Provide adequate special services to special constituencies, including the underserved;

3. Strengthen existing statewide services and systems;

4. Ensure basic and continuing education of personnel essential to the implementation of a National Program;

5. Coordinate existing federal programs of library and information service;

6. Encourage the private sector (comprising organizations which are not directly tax-supported) to become an active partner in the development of the National Program;

7. Establish a locus of federal responsibility charged with implementing the national network and coordinating the National Program under the policy guidance of the National Commission;

8. Plan, develop, and implement a nationwide network of library and information service.

In one sense, as Molz (1984: 120) points out, the *National Program* was the "lineal descendent" of the *National Plan* of 1934. It was widely distributed and formed a critical part of the policy framework for thinking about national public library planning for the last quarter of the twentieth century.

During its initial years as a federal agency NCLIS prepared for the first White House Conference on Library and Information Services (WHCLIS) in November 1979, which was preceded by 57 pre-conferences in states and territories and 6 special national pre-conferences. The ALA, state chapters, and state library agencies collaborated intently on this national WHCLIS effort. Delegates approved resolutions urging an increased library role in literacy training, improved access to information for all, the free flow of information among nations, and the idea of a library as a total community information center and an independent learning center. Criticized by some for the unwieldy process, the WHCLIS nevertheless positioned libraries as of continuing importance to the nation's well-being. The sheer enormity of the pre-conference activity and post-conference publications gave librarians a broad visibility among policy makers.

The second White House Conference on Library and Information Services convened July 1991, with three conference themes: library and information services for literacy, democracy, and productivity. Following this second White House Conference, taskforces from ALA, the Urban Libraries Council (ULC), and Chief Officers of State

Library Agencies (COSLA), identified two major goals: improvement of information access through technology and the educational empowerment of those who still live outside the mainstream of quality library service (McCook, 1994). This thinking undergirded new library legislation in 1996, the Library Services and Technology Act (LSTA). The LSTA was a section of the Museum and Library Services Act (MLSA) that moved the administration of federal aid to public libraries from the Department of Education to a new agency, the Institute of Museum and Library Services. LSTA built on the strengths of previous federal library programs, but included some major differences. While it retained the state-based approach from previous legislation, it sharpened the focus to two key priorities for libraries—information access through technology and information empowerment through special services. By locating federal support for libraries within the Institute of Museum and Library Services, since 1996, the government emphasized the community-based role of libraries, and it included in the mission of the public library the range of lifelong learning. In this new agency, libraries and museums have converged as cultural heritage institutions with a renewed commitment to collaborative engagement within local and world communities (McCook and Jones, 2002).

The reauthorization of the Museum and Library Services Act (MLSA) in 2003 updated the LSTA to promote improvements in all types of libraries; to facilitate access to, and sharing of, resources; and to achieve economical and efficient delivery of service for the purpose of cultivating an educated and informed citizenry. The Act authorized a doubling of the minimum state allotment under the Grants to States Library Agencies program. It helps to coordinate statewide library services and supports a wide array of programs from family literacy to providing broad access to sophisticated databases. It also develops the role of libraries as "information brokers" helping to make resources and services, which are often prohibitively expensive, more readily available (IMLS, 1996).

Achievement of a national voice for public libraries resulted from ongoing collaboration among librarians organized in national and state library associations and through state library agencies. Advocacy for library support at local, state, and national levels throughout the twentieth century was orchestrated by the American Library Association and the National Commission on Libraries and Information Services, with countless hours contributed by members of associations.

The Evolution of the Public Library Message

Librarians worked to achieve federal support to provide for more equal public library service from World War I to the passage of the LSA in 1956. They continued this progress with the LSCA in 1964 and the LSTA in 1996 and 2003. While federal funding has yet to ensure that all people can experience equal access, it has done much to expand access to library services. We have seen how astute leaders connected library issues to federal programs during the New Deal to gain a place for libraries in post-war planning efforts. The library community continues to hold this place at the federal level with the evolution of funding, through a series of acts and legislation. What remains is to identify the overarching issues that librarians used to help shape public policy, which resulted in successful legislation.

Lifelong Learning and Literacy as Public Library Functions

The idea of lifelong learning provided much of the impetus throughout the 1920s and 1930s for librarians and communities to develop enthusiasm for the establishment of library service where none existed. In his history of the adult education movement in the United States, Malcolm S. Knowles observed that by the 1920s: "the library moved from the status of an adult education resource toward that of an adult education operating agency...it moved from perceiving its constituency as consisting of individuals toward perceiving it as a total community, and...it moved from regarding its function as custodial toward regarding it as educational" (1977: 115). In her historical review of libraries and adult education, Margaret E. Monroe identified a variety of library services to adults provided by libraries during the first half of the twentieth century that incorporated aspects of adult education (1963: 6). Librarians produced a steady thoughtful commentary on literacy, reading, and lifelong learning, developed programmatic responses and conducted research on these topics throughout the twentieth century. This work provides a robust history of librarians working with adult educators and financers to forge alliances to enhance the lives of adult learners and new readers, and it provided library advocates with a strong argument to take to sources of funding at local, state, and national levels (McCook and Barber, 2002).

Justifying Policy: Libraries as the Cornerstone of Democracy

Public libraries were characterized in founding documents as providing the resources for citizens to become informed about events and thus able to participate in the democratic process with greater knowledge. The Public Library Inquiry, carried out and published between 1947 and 1952 has been characterized by Raber (1997: 3) as a professional legitimating project that "constituted an exercise in identity creation that relied heavily on the role of the public library as a sustaining contributor to American democracy."[4] The concept of libraries as supporting the democratic process provided librarians with an ongoing rationale useful in promoting support for libraries and tied closely to the idea of adult lifelong learning. Much of the advocacy that provided input to policy makers for the passage of the LSA rested on these premises.

A structural change within the American Library Association occurred in 1950 when a merger of several ALA units took place (Division of Public Libraries, Library Extension Division, and the Trustees Division) creating the Public Library Division (changed in 1959 to the Public Library Association—PLA). The PLA began to assume increasing responsibility for setting public library standards issuing documents in 1956 and 1966. In the 1970s another shift took place from a national approach to standards to a local planning process (Pungitore, 1995: 71–74).

"The Public Library: Democracy's Resource, A Statement of Purpose," was issued amidst the adoption of the new Public Library Association planning process. This one-page document identified the public library as offering access freely to all members of the community "without regard to race, citizenship, age, education level, economic status, or any other qualification or condition."

When the Public Library Association began to move to a planning process in place of national standards, the effort to establish a national mission for public libraries was no longer part of the PLA agenda, although, as noted above, the 1979 *Mission Statement* and the 1982 "Democracy's Resource" statement surely represent such efforts. While the PLA pulled back from broad mission definition in the 1990s, the American Library Association and the National Commission on Libraries and Information Science continued to provide general statements of direction. In 1995 the ALA's journal, *American Libraries,* listed "12 Ways Libraries Are Good for the Country," which included the statement, "Libraries safeguard our freedom and keep democracy healthy." With a photograph of the Statue of Liberty in the background the first of the "12 Ways" listed was "to inform citizens," because democracy and libraries have a symbiotic relationship.

The 1999 ALA Council adopted the statement, "Libraries: An American Value," included it as an official public policy statement (Policy 53.8), and printed it on the cover of the Association's 1999–2000 *Handbook*. This statement noted, "we preserve our democratic society by making available the widest possible range of viewpoints, opinions and ideas." That same year the ALA sponsored a Congress on Professional Education that resulted in an effort to develop "A Statement on Core Values," and the National Commission on Libraries and Information Science passed a resolution adopting the *Principles for Public Library Service* based on the *UNESCO Public Library Manifesto*. These *Principles* include the key mission that the public library will be a "gateway to knowledge," and that "Freedom, Prosperity and the Development of Society and of individuals are fundamental human values. They will be attained through the ability of well-informed citizens to exercise their democratic rights and to play an active role in society" (U.S. NCLIS, 1999). The millennium president of ALA, Nancy Kranich, reaffirmed the commitment of libraries to the democratic process editing a monograph of essays on the role libraries play in democracy, *Libraries and Democracy: The Cornerstones of Liberty* (2001).

In a 2003 speech before UNESCO, IMLS Director, Robert Martin, made clear that support for libraries in the United States was based upon the recognition that democracy demands wisdom and vision in its citizens and that libraries will contribute to more than an information society. Libraries are the foundation of a learning society. The long identification of public libraries in the United States with the principles of a democratic government has been central to their support. Initially this support came as libraries characterized themselves as helping to maintain social order and education. Over time, however, the adherence to the ideals of intellectual freedom—sometimes at odds with the larger governmental actions during World War I, the Cold War, and the War on Terrorism—has come to define the core of the profession's ethical stance (Resolution on the USAPATRIOT Act, 2003: 93).

Public Librarians as Defenders of Intellectual Freedom

Today the defense of intellectual freedom is a central value of public librarians. This commitment to intellectual freedom went all the way to the Supreme Court in 2003 when the American Library Association challenged the Children's Internet Protection Act (CIPA).

CIPA places restrictions on funding available through the LSTA and the Universal Discount Rate by requiring filters or blocks on Internet access (Supreme Court Upholds CIPA, 2003).

How did U.S. public librarians move from their initial somewhat censorious stance of selecting and providing the "right books" and sometimes banning the "wrong ones" to become staunch defenders of the First Amendment and intellectual freedom today?

The involvement in censorship and book banning by public librarians at the end of World War I has been characterized in chilling terms: "Librarians willingly but quietly pulled from their shelves any title that might raise suspicions of disloyalty. Some librarians burned these titles, many of which were classic works of German philosophy, books advocating American pacifism, and simple German-language texts" (Wiegand, 1989: 6). Recognizing that it has been less than a century that brought librarians from participation in censorship to fighting it in the Supreme Court, we see that a change in philosophy regarding intellectual freedom between the end of the First World War and the years following the Second World War mark the growth of U.S. public librarianship as a profession (Robbins, 1996).

The public library gradually made a transition from an agent of social stability to one that supported all points of view. Geller (1984), in *Forbidden Books in American Public Libraries,* characterizes 1923–1930 as the period of a critical shift by public librarians toward a more expansive philosophy of collection development. In 1931 George F. Bowerman, director of the Washington, DC public library, addressed the issue of censorship and reminded librarians that classics like Eliot's *Adam Bede*, Hardy's *Jude the Obscure,* or Whitman's *Leaves of Grass* were once deemed worthy of condemnation. He characterized censorship as repugnant to public librarians and noted, the public library is "not an institution for the inculcation of standardized ideas....it stands for free opinion and to that end it supplies material on both or all sides of every controversial question of human interest" (1931: 5–6).

In his study of propaganda and the public library from the 1930s to World War II, Lincove describes discussions in the field that addressed fascist propaganda as a threat to democracy and capitalism. The core of debate was whether the library should censor based on moralism and control versus a philosophy that would provide access to mainstream and controversial ideas, especially foreign and domestic political propaganda.

The man who would later be named poet laureate of the United States, Stanley J. Kunitz, editor of the *Wilson Bulletin for Libraries* from 1928–1943, provided unyielding defense of the freedom to read. In his ongoing column, "The Roving Eye," Kunitz was critical of librarians who did nothing to oppose censorship. While cherishing democracy, Kunitz opposed the right wing with its intolerance, intellectual provincialism, and patriotism that cloaked an Americanism supporting merchants of death.

Kunitz' editorials are a legacy to the community of public libraries striving to define intellectual freedom as a professional ethic. The social control exercised by boards of trustees has been characterized as crucial in the debate over propaganda. Librarians became increasingly concerned that the oversight of boards created an atmosphere of censorship and caused librarians to select on the safe side. This seemed especially confounding as the library was coming to be viewed as an important vehicle for adult education.

After reading Bernard Berelson's 1938 essay, "The Myth of Library Impartiality" in the *Wilson Library Bulletin,* Forrest Spaulding, director at the public library of Des Moines Iowa, which had a strong adult education program, worked with his own board of trustees to develop a Library Bill of Rights. This was adapted and adopted by the ALA at the 1939 San Francisco conference. *The Grapes of Wrath*, by John Steinbeck was published in March 1939 and immediately banned at some libraries because of its social criticism (Lingo, 2003). After passage of the Library Bill of Rights, the ALA Adult Education Board distributed copies to help libraries fight against requests to censor. Because of the rash of banning across the nation, the ALA appointed a committee to study censorship and recommend policy. In 1940 that committee reported that intellectual freedom and professionalism were linked and recommended a permanent committee that was established as the Committee on Intellectual Freedom to Safeguard the Right of Library Users to Freedom of Inquiry (changed in 1947 to the Committee on Intellectual Freedom).

Following World War II the loyalty programs implemented by President Truman, the establishment of the House on Un-American Activities Committee, and the general cold war atmosphere presented new threats to intellectual freedom. Librarians responded with a renewed commitment to fight censorship activities. A revised Library Bill of Rights was issued in 1948 with a far stronger statement of the librarian's responsibility to defend the freedom of inquiry (Berninghausen, 1948). State intellectual freedom committees were formed, the "Statement on Labeling" was adopted (1951), and a national conference was held in 1952.[5] Events that brought about the

"Freedom to Read Statement" (1953) included the overseas library controversy and attacks on the International Information Administration's libraries. Robbins (2001) views the adoption of the "Freedom to Read Statement" and the ALA's commitment to overseas libraries as instrumental in the identification of librarians as defenders of intellectual freedom.

During the half century since the adoption of the "Freedom to Read Statement," the profession has continued to face and cope with many challenges. New interpretations of the Library Bill of Rights have been issued, including Access for Children and Young People to Videotapes and Other Nonprint Formats (1989); Access to Electronic Information Services and Networks (1996); and Access to Library Resources and Services regardless of Gender or Sexual Orientation (2000). These and other amplifications of the basic tenets of intellectual freedom define the "active advocacy" that librarians accept when they join the profession (Conable, 2002: 43).

The internalization by public librarians of the principle of defending intellectual freedom carried on through the Office of Intellectual Freedom and the Freedom to Read Foundation of the American Library Association has been fundamental in establishing librarians' "jurisdiction as providers of free access to diverse ideas to all" (Robbins, 1996: 163).

Facing the Twenty-First Century

As public librarians face the twenty-first century the profession can look back on a history based in commitment to democratic ideals, lifelong learning, and equal opportunity to the world's knowledge for all. Librarians have worked hard to establish the public library as an essential community service, sought local, state, and federal funds to implement and expand public library service, and defined and articulated an ethos that defends the ideals of free inquiry.

Notes

1. American Library Association, Commission on the Library and Adult Education, *Libraries and Adult Education* (Chicago: American Library Association, 1926). For additional background on the Adult Education Board meetings and minutes through its history, see archives of the American Library Association under Reference and User Services Association. 30/0/0. Available: www.library.uiuc.edu/ahx/ala/alacard.asp?RG=30&SG=0&RS=0 (accessed May 22, 2004).

2. National leaders, such as Louis R. Wilson based in North Carolina, were able to speak out for citizen involvement. Connected to ALA's Extension efforts, see Frank P. Graham, "Citizen's Library Movements," *Library Extension News* 14 (May, 1932), 2. For an overview of this effort in North Carolina, South Carolina, Georgia, Kentucky, Mississippi, Tennessee, and Virginia, see Mary Edna Anders, *The Development of Public Library Service in the Southeastern States, 1895–1950* (PhD diss., Columbia University, 1958), 69–80. For an in-depth study of the North Carolina Citizens' Library Movement, see William Eury, "The Citizens' Library Movement in North Carolina" (MA thesis, George Peabody College for Teachers, August, 1951).

3. Molz, 1984: 39–63. The role of Joeckel, the ALA Committee on Post-War Planning and the New Deal National Resources Planning Board, are viewed as laying the groundwork for federal legislation for library funding. Molz's characterization of Joeckel's rational planning approach and Milam's pragmatic incremental approach provide insight into the evolution of federal support (1984, pp. 95–96). See also Sullivan (1976: 135–140); records in the ALA Archives: Post-War Planning Committee File, 1941–1948, including correspondence, reports, drafts, minutes, budgets, statistics, surveys, lists, proposals and plans concerning a restatement of public library standards—*Post-War Standards for Public Libraries* (1943), undertaken by the ALA at the request of the National Resources Planning Board (NRPB); a comparison of existing library services with the standards; the formulation of the detailed *A National Plan for Public Library Service* (1948) including a Plan for Public Library Service in America; and post-war planning for school, college, and university libraries. Available: http://web.library.uiuc.edu/ahx/ala/alacard.asp? RG=93&SG=10&RS=6. Adequate provision for library service had been recognized in the *National Resources Development Report for 1943*, issued by the NRPB in the section, "Equal Access to Education."

4. Raber, "The Public Library and the Postwar World," 23–36, and "The Beginnings of the Public Library Inquiry," 37–49. The Public Library Inquiry consisted of seven volumes all published by Columbia University Press:

- Bernard Berelson, *The Library's Public* (1949);

- Alice I. Bryan, *The Public Librarian* (1952);

- Oliver Garceau, *The Public Library in the Political Process* (1949);

- Robert D. Leigh, *The Public Library in the United States*, 1950;

- James L. McCamy, *Government Publications for the Citizen* (1949);

- William Miller, *The Book Industry* (1949);

- Gloria Waldren, *The Information Film* (1949).

Supplementary reports were issued on library finance, public use of the library, and effects of the mass media, music materials, and work measurement. For complete list, see Raber (1997: 82).

5. Robbins, *Censorship and the American Library: The American Library Association's Response to Threats to Intellectual Freedom: 1939–1969,* Appendix C, "State Intellectual Freedom Committees" (Westport, CT: Greenwood Press, 1996), 181–183; American Library Association, Office for Intellectual Freedom, *Intellectual Freedom Manual,* 6th edition (Chicago: ALA, 2002), 186–192; William S. Dix and Paul Bixler, eds., *Freedom of Communications: Proceedings of the First Conference on Intellectual Freedom, New York City, June 28–29, 1952* (Chicago: American Library Association, 1954).

References

12 Ways Libraries are Good for the Country. 1995. *American Libraries* 26 (December): 1113–1119. Available: www.ala.org/ala/alonline/selectedarticles/12wayslibraries.htm.

ALA Responds to CIPA Decision. 2003. *Newsletter on Intellectual Freedom* (September): 175.

American Library Association. 1936. *The Equal Chance: Books Help to Make It.* Chicago: American Library Association.

American Library Association. Commission on the Library and Adult Education. 1926. *Libraries and Adult Education.* Chicago: American Library Association.

American Library Association. Office for Intellectual Freedom. 2002. *Intellectual Freedom Manual.* 6th ed. Chicago: American Library Association.

American Library Association. Washington Office. Historical Perspective on LSTA. Available: www.ala.org/ala/washoff/WOissues/federallibprog/lsta/lstahst.htm.

Asheim, Lester. 1950. *A Forum on the Public Library Inquiry.* New York: Columbia University Press. Repr., Westport, CT: Greenwood Press, 1970.

Barker, Tommie Dora. 1936. *Libraries of the South: A Report on Development.* Chicago: American Library Association.

Berelson, Bernard. 1938. The Myth of Library Impartiality. *Wilson Library Bulletin* 13 (October): 87–90.

Berninghausen, David K. 1948. Library Bill of Rights. *ALA Bulletin* 42 (July-August): 285.

Bowerman, George F. 1931. *Censorship and the Public Library.* New York: H. W. Wilson.

Casey, Genevieve M., ed. 1975. Federal Aid to Libraries: Its History, Impact, Future. Special issue, *Library Trends* 24 (July).

Conable, Gordon. 2002. Public Libraries and Intellectual Freedom. *Intellectual Freedom Manual.* 6th ed. Chicago: American Library Association.

Cresswell, Stephen. 1996. The Last Days of Jim Crow in Southern Libraries. *Libraries and Culture* 31 (Summer/Fall): 557–573.

Dawson, Alma. 2000. Celebrating African-American Librarians and Librarianship. *Library Trends* 49 (Summer): 49–87.

Ditzion, Sidney H. 1947. *Arsenals of a Democratic Culture: A Social History of the American Public Library Movement in New England and the Middle States from 1850–1900.* Chicago: American Library Association.

Dix, William S., and Paul Bixler. 1954. *Freedom of Communications: Proceedings of the First Conference on Intellectual freedom, New York City, June 28–29, 1952.* Chicago: American Library Association.

Du Mont, Rosemary Ruhig. 1986. Race in American Librarianship: Attitudes of the Library Profession. *Journal of Library History* 21 (Summer): 488–509.

Fenwick, Sara Innis. 1976. Library Services to Children and Young People. *Library Trends* 25: 329–360.

Geller, Evelyn. 1984. *Forbidden Books in American Public Libraries, 1876–1939: A Study in Cultural Change.* Westport, CT: Greenwood Press.

Gleason, Eliza Atkins. 1941. *The Southern Negro and the Public Library: A Study of Government and Administration of Public Library Service to Negroes in the South.* Chicago: University of Chicago Press.

Graham, Patterson Toby. 2002. *A Right to Read: Segregation and Civil Rights in Alabama's Public Libraries, 1900–1965.* Tuscaloosa, AL: University of Alabama Press.

Harris, Steven R. 2003. Civil Rights and the Louisiana Library Association. *Libraries and Culture* 38 (Fall): 322–350.

Institute of Museum and Library Services. 1996. Museum and Library Services Act of 1996. Available: www.imls.gov/about/abt_1996.htm.

Institute of Museum and Library Services. 2003. Highlights of the New Law (2003). Available: www.imls.gov/whatsnew/current/092503a.htm.

Jenkins, Christine. 2000. The History of Youth Services Librarianship: A Review of the Research Literature. *Libraries & Culture* 35 (Winter): 103–140.

Joeckel, Carleton Bruns. 1935. *The Government of the American Public Library.* Chicago: University of Chicago Press.

Joeckel, Carleton Bruns. 1938. *Library Service*, Staff Study 11 prepared for the U.S. Advisory Committee on Education. As quoted in "The United States Office of Education: Progress and Potentialities of Its Library Programs," ed. Douglas M. Knight and E. Shepley Nourse, in *Libraries at Large: Tradition, Innovation, and the National Interest*, ed. Douglas M. Knight and E. Shepley Nourse, 466–491. New York: R. R. Bowker.

Joeckel, Carleton Bruns. 1943. *Post-War Standards for Public Libraries*. Chicago: American Library Association.

Joeckel, Carleton B., and Amy Winslow. 1948. *A National Plan for Public Library Service*. Chicago: American Library Association.

Johnson, Alvin. 1938. *The Public Library—A People's University*. New York: American Association for Adult Education.

Jones, Virginia Lacy. 1963. The Access to Public Libraries Study. *ALA Bulletin* 57 (September): 742–745.

Josey, E. J. 1970. *The Black Librarian in America*. Metuchen, NJ: Scarecrow Press.

Kelly, Melody S. 2003. Revisiting C.H.Milam 's "What Libraries Learned from the War" and Rediscovering the Library Faith. *Libraries and Culture* 38 (Fall): 378–388.

Knight, Douglas M., and E. Shepley Nourse, eds. 1969. *Libraries at Large: Traditions, Innovations and the National Interest; The Resource Book Based on the Materials of the National Advisory Commission on Libraries*. New York: R. R. Bowker.

Knowles, Malcolm S. 1977. *A History of the Adult Education Movement in the United States: includes Adult Education Institutions through 1976*. Huntington, NY: Robert E. Krieger Publishing Company.

Kranich, Nancy, ed. 2001. *Libraries and Democracy: The Cornerstones of Liberty*. Chicago: American Library Association.

Kunitz, Stanley. 2000. The Layers. In *The Collected Poems*, 217–218. New York: W. W. Norton.

Learned, William S. 1924. *The American Public Library and the Diffusion of Knowledge*. New York: Harcourt.

Library Projects Under Public Works, Civil Works and Relief Administrations. 1933. *ALA Bulletin* 27 (December): 539.

Lincove, David A. 1994. Propaganda and the American Public Library from the 1930s to the Eve of World War II. *RQ* 33 (Summer): 510–523.

Lingo, Marci. 2003. Forbidden Fruit: The Banning of *The Grapes of Wrath* in the Kern County Free Library. *Libraries and Culture* 38 (Fall): 351–377.

Looking Toward National Planning. 1934. *ALA Bulletin* 28 (August): 453–460.

Maack, Mary Niles. 1994. Public Libraries in Transition: Ideals, Strategies and Research. *Libraries and Culture* 29 (Winter): 79.

Martin, Robert S. 2003. Cultural Policies in Knowledge Societies:the United States of America. Speech presented at UNESCO Ministerial Roundtable: Toward Knowledge Societies, UNESCO Headquarters, Paris, France, October 10, 2003. Available: www.imls.gov/whatsnew/current/sp101003.htm.

Marshall, A. P. 1976. Service to African-Americans. In *Century of Service: Librarianship in the United States and Canada,* ed. H. Jackson and E. J. Josey, 62–78. Chicago: American Library Association.

McCook, Kathleen de la Peña. 1994. *Toward a Just and Productive Society: An Analysis of the Recommendations of the White House Conference on Library and Information Services.* Washington, DC: National Commission on Libraries and Information Science.

McCook, Kathleen de la Peña, and Peggy Barber. 2002. Public Policy as a Factor Influencing Adult Lifelong Learning, Adult Literacy and Public Libraries. *Reference and User Services Quarterly* 42.1 (Fall): 66–75.

McCook, Kathleen de la Peña, and Maria A. Jones. 2002. Cultural Heritage Institutions and Community Building. *Reference and User Services Quarterly* 41 (Summer): 326–329.

McReynolds, Rosalee. 1990/1991. The Progressive Librarians Council and Its Founders. *Progressive Librarian* 2 (Winter): 23–29.

Milam, Carl H. 1934. National Planning for Libraries. *ALA Bulletin* 28 (February): 60–62.

Molz, Redmond Kathleen. 1984. *National Planning for Library Service: 1935–1975.* Chicago: American Library Association.

Monroe, Margaret E. 1963. *Library Adult Education: The Biography of an Idea.* New York: Scarecrow Press.

Monypenny, Phillip. 1966. *The Library Functions of the States.* Chicago: American Library Association.

Mussman, Klaus. 1998. The Ugly Side of Librarianship; Segregation in Library Services from 1900–1950. In *Untold Stories: Civil rights, Libraries and Black Librarianship,* 78–92. Champaign, IL: University of Illinois, Graduate School of Library and Information Science.

A National Plan for Libraries. 1935. *ALA Bulletin* 29 (February): 91–98.

A National Plan for Libraries. 1939. *ALA Bulletin* 33 (February): 136–150.

Public Library Association, Goals, Guidelines and Standards Committee. 1979. *The Public Library Mission Statement and Its Imperatives for Service.* Chicago: American Library Association.

Pungitore, Verna L. 1995. *Innovation and the Library: The Adoption of New Ideas in Public Libraries.* Westport, CT: Greenwood Press.

Raber, Douglas. 1997. *Librarianship and Legitimacy: The Ideology of the Public Library Inquiry.* Westport, CT: Greenwood Press.

Reagan, Patrick D. 2000. *Designing a New America: The Origins of New Deal Planning, 1890–1943.* Amherst MA: University of Massachusetts Press.

Resolution on the USAPATRIOT Act and Related Measures that Infringe on the Rights of Library Users. 2003. *Newsletter on Intellectual Freedom* 52 (May): 93.

Robbins, Louise S. 1996. *Censorship and the American Library: The American Library Association's Response to Threats to Intellectual Freedom: 1939–1969.* Westport, CT: Greenwood Press.

Robbins, Louise S. 2001. The Overseas Library Controversy and the Freedom To Read: U.S. Librarians and Publishers Confront Joseph McCarthy. *Libraries and Culture* 36 (Winter): 27–39.

Shera, Jesse H. 1949. *Foundations of the Public Library: The Origins of the Public Library Movement in New England, 1629–1855.* Chicago: University of Chicago Press. Repr., Hamden, CT: Shoestring Press, 1965.

Sullivan, Peggy. 1976. *Carl H. Milam and the American Library Association.* New York: H. W. Wilson Company.

Supreme Court Upholds CIPA. 2003. *Newsletter on Intellectual Freedom* 52 (September): 173, 187–191.

Thomison, Dennis. 1978. *A History of the American Library Association, 1876–1972.* Chicago: American Library Association.

Tucker, John M. 1998. *Untold Stories: Civil Rights, Libraries and Black Librarianship.* Champaign, IL: University of Illinois, Graduate School of Library and Information Science.

Tucker, Harold W. 1963. The Access to Public Libraries Study. *ALA Bulletin* 57 (September): 742–745.

U.S. National Commission on Libraries and Information Science (USNCLIS). 1975. *Toward a National Program for Library and Information Services: Goals for Action.* Washington, DC: U.S. Government Printing Office.

U.S. National Commission on Libraries and Information Science (USNCLIS). 1995. NCLIS at 25. Available: www.nclis.gov/about/25yrrpt.html.

U.S. National Commission on Libraries and Information Science (USNCLIS). 1999. NCLIS Adopts "Principles for Public Service." Available: www.nclis.gov/news/pressrelease/pr99/ppls99.html.

Van Fleet, Connie. 1990. Lifelong Learning Theory and the Provision of Adult Services. In *Adult Services: An Enduring Focus for Public Libraries*, ed. Kathleen M. Heim (de la Peña McCook) and Danny P. Wallace, 166–211. Chicago: American Library Association.

Wiegand, Wayne A. 1989. *An Active Instrument for Propaganda: The American Public Library During World War I.* Westport, CT: Greenwood Press.

4

Statistics, Standards, Planning, and Results

Making the Case: From Faith to Fact

Making the case for public library support persists as a central task of the library profession. The "library faith"—the belief that libraries support reading and the democratic process—grew and flourished as public libraries were founded throughout the United States (Garceau, 1949: 50–52). Once the idea of the public library as an agency worthy of community funding was broadly established during the nineteenth and early early-twentieth centuries, the profession sought ways to identify norms and guidelines that would ensure quality service.

Initially librarians relied upon statistics and checklists to establish models that could be used when defining local service. In 1933 the American Library Association developed and released the first "Standards for Public Libraries." They issued revised public library standards in 1943, 1956, and 1966, and all implied that meeting numerical goals would establish quality. After 1966 the Public Library Association changed its approach, no longer developing standards, and initiated a planning process that encouraged each library to develop its own goals to reflect community needs. At the state level, however, data and statistics have been used by many states to create state standards in collaboration with the planning process to establish the case for library support at the local level.

Some efforts have been attempted to link outcomes from library input data to demonstrate that libraries contribute to the quality of life in a community. The Office of Planning and Development in Hennepin County, Minnesota, uses public library circulation and reference transactions per capita as indicators to assess progress in the County's achievement of a healthy and sustainable community. Some argue that the community indicator movement has not provided a compelling argument, because causal explanations would be based on data that might have several interpretations (Heckman, 2000). Efforts to include libraries in the indicator movement will ensure that library-related outcomes will be viewed as key variables in future initiatives (McCook and Brand, 2001). Demonstrating in as compelling a way as possible that strong public libraries enhance the lives of people and their communities is essential to future funding, and the Institute of Museum and Library Services (IMLS) advocates this tack.

In this chapter we will summarize how public librarians attempt to measure services and their impact—the necessary prelude to inclusion as a key variable when quality of life studies and projects take place. We discuss library statistics and their standardization, the history of standards development in public libraries, the change from the use of national standards to a planning process noting the current status of state library standards and their articulation with the planning process, and the growing use of outcome measures to develop research that can be used by policy makers to advance library support.

Statistics for Public Libraries

Today most public libraries report statistics electronically to the data coordinator at their state library agency—a fairly straightforward activity using the Federal-State Cooperative System for Public Library Data. However, the current process required some determination, and overcoming various obstacles was not easily achieved. The history of public library statistics development falls into five periods: exploratory (1870–1937); developmental (1938–1956); broadening responsibility (1956–1965); diversified responsibility (1965–1989); and the current era, which began in 1989 when the National Center for Education Statistics (NCES) initiated a formal library statistics program (Schick, 1971; Chute, 2003). See Appendix

B for a bibliography of national statistics gathered and reported for U.S. public libraries from 1853 to the present.

It was not until 1968 that the gathering of public library statistics was codified. Standardization in the United States is coordinated by the American National Standards Institute (ANSI), founded in 1918 to promote and facilitate national consensus standards across all fields and occupations. ANSI's guiding principles are consensus, due process, and openness. There are over 175 entities accredited by ANSI, each issuing "American National Standards." (ANSs). The entity body most closely allied with libraries is the National Information Standards Organization (NISO), founded in 1939 and accredited by ANSI to identify, develop, maintain, and publish technical standards to manage information in the changing and ever-more digital environment. NISO standards apply both traditional and new technologies to the full range of information-related needs, including retrieval, repurposing, storage, metadata, and preservation. NISO has issued many ANSs, including *Guidelines for Abstracts, Printed Information on Spines, Permanence of Paper for Publications and Documents in Libraries and Archives, Durable Hardcover Binding for Books*, and, of most interest to this discussion, *Information Services and Use: Metrics and Statistics for Libraries and Information Providers—Data Dictionary* (Z39.7) formerly called *Library Statistics*.

The *Information Services and Use: Metrics and Statistics for Libraries and Information Providers—Data Dictionary* standard (Z39.7) identifies and defines the basic data collection categories used to collect library statistical data at the national level. It is intended to provide valid and comparable data on library services, staff, users, and collections. Initially published in 1968 as the *Library Statistics* standard, Z39.5 was affirmed in 1974, revised in 1983, revised in 1995, and has just undergone a new revision with the new name. NISO held a "Forum on Performance Measures and Statistics for Libraries" in 2001 that recommended moving beyond defining data elements to providing methodologies for qualitative and quantitative measures of library service. It was also recommended that NISO take a leadership role in supporting the development of surveys and measurements to gauge service quality and outcomes.

Information Services and Use: Metrics and Statistics for Libraries and Information Providers identifies categories for basic library statistical data at the national level, and provides associated definitions of terms. In doing so it deals with the following areas of library operation:

- Reporting unit and target population

- Human resources

- Collection resources

- Infrastructure

- Finances

- Services

The standard is not intended to be comprehensive in scope. Instead, it presents a framework for comparable library data by describing common elements pertaining to libraries of various types in the United States. It does not address detailed statistics for specific areas where it seems more appropriate for experts in those areas to make recommendations (e.g., music, government documents, maps). The standard also integrates metrics for electronic network use (e-metrics) into each section as appropriate.[1]

Today, under the mandate of the National Education Statistics Act of 1994, the National Center for Educational Statistics (NCES) collects descriptive public library statistics for over 9,000 libraries, as the "Library Statistics Cooperative Program." The "Public Libraries Survey," conducted annually beginning in 1988, collects data electronically using the Federal-State Cooperative System (FSCS) for Public Library Data.[2] Each state has a designated data coordinator to whom each library submits data using Bibliostat Collect.

The Oregon State Library provides an informative "behind the scenes" look at what happens to the data after they are submitted from the local library to the state data coordinator.

Through its Library Statistics Cooperative Program, the National Commission on Libraries and Information Science (NCLIS) serves as a liaison to the library community, organizes meetings and training workshops, organizes training and technical assistance, monitors trends, and advises NCES on policy matters. In addition to the national reports issued by NCES, many individual states have long published their own statistical series.[3] To facilitate the use of the revised standard, *Information Services and Use: Metrics and Statistics for Libraries and Information Providers,* the Institute of Museum and Library Services has funded a leadership grant in education and training to provide public librarians with multifaceted

---

Figure 4.1: Oregon State Library: Reporting Public Library Statistics

After statistics are turned into the State Library, they go through a detailed examination process. We examine data against previous years, looking for "outliers", that is, data values exceeding expected changes. We look particularly at staffing, income, and expenditures.

The State then electronically transmits all of the legally established public libraries' data to the U.S. Census Bureau at the request of the National Center for Educational Statistics (NCES) at the U.S. Department of Education. NCES works closely with COSLA (Chief Officers of State Library Agencies), the National Commission on Libraries and Information Science (NCLIS), the American Library Association (ALA), the Institute of Museum and Library Services (IMLS) and the U.S. Census Bureau (the data collection agent for NCES) to design and conduct the survey.

After the data has been transmitted, the Census compiles the data and checks it for values outside the "norm". When a figure is an outlier, outside of normal variance, the same edit checks that you see in Bibliostat Collect are raised. If there is no "federal" note attached to the data that verifies its accuracy, the Census contacts the State Data Coordinator to seek clarification. In the past, the Oregon State Library has been asked to verify branch library addresses, revenue, amount of children's programming and other information for many Oregon libraries.

After the Census has checked the data, the preliminary data file is sent to the NCES for review. The data is run again against statistical formulas to check for outliers. Census also delivers preliminary tables to the FSCS Steering Committee and NCES for review for data quality. Census contacts the State Data Coordinator for clarification of any questionable data and data corrections, if necessary, based on this review.

When the final data file is approved, the Census will go back and use standard formulas to "impute" data, that is, provide estimates for missing data. The preliminary imputed file is then sent to NCES for review. Approved data is then produced in the E. D. Tabs and the database is published. Shortly afterwards, it is available through Bibliostat Connect. This process takes at least seven months.

Source: Oregon State Library Web site, April 1, 2004

---

instruction regarding the usage of and uses for networked information resources (Information Management and Use Policy Institute).

To comprehend how statistics have been used to assist in the development of public libraries, readers must understand the adoption of library standards—a history that began during the exploratory period of library statistics development in the 1930s.

National Standards for Public Library Service: 1933–1966

As seen in Chapter 2, the move to develop public library standards in the 1930s occurred at the same time that the library profession began efforts to develop a national plan for public library service. The 1933 "Standards for Public Libraries" was a simple document with a short introduction defining the rationale for the public library: "in order that every man, woman and child may have the means of self-education and recreational reading." Recommended books for each public library collection per capita were:

- 3 for cities under 10,000
- 2 for cities of 10,000 to 200,000
- 1.5 for cities over 200,000

Recommended standards for lending and library registration were to be measured statistically:

- 50% percent registration and 10 books per capita for cities under 10,000
- 40% percent registration and 9 books per capita for cities 10,000 to 100,000
- 35% percent registration and 8 books per capita for cities 100,000 to 200,000
- 30% percent registration and 7 books per capita for cities 200,000 to 1,000,000
- 25% percent registration and 5 books per capita for cities over 1,000,000

Income was recommended at $1.00 per capita and at least $25,000 total, though it was recognized that smaller towns would usually need to spend more or enlarge the unit of service.

Much of the professional discussion in the 1930s focused on the size of the governmental unit required to support library service (Fair, 1934). This discussion was consolidated in Joeckel's seminal 1935 study, *The Government of the American Public Library,* which summarized the various types of county library systems and characterized them as predominantly emphasizing rural library service. Joeckel argued for larger units of library service—ideally regional— to sustain quality service. Many of the ideas he presented in his analysis have influenced cooperative library projects right to the present. The establishment of the Library Services Division in the U.S. Office of Education in 1938 provided a federal vantage point for national-level planning in collaboration with the National Resources Planning Board. The ALA, anticipating the post-war period in which public library service would be seen as a responsibility of democratic government, appointed Joeckel chair of its Committee on Postwar Planning to (1) oversee the development of post-war standards, (2) coordinate data collection on the status of the U.S. public library, and (3) develop a national plan for public library service.

The result was *Post-War Standards for Public Libraries*, issued in 1943, based on the assumption that "public library service should be available without exception to all people and in all political jurisdictions throughout the nation" (ALA, 1943: 15). The lengthy and detailed *Post-War Standards* document included discussion of the rationale for standards in eight areas: (1) Service; (2) Government and Administration; (3) Size and Area; (4) Finance; (5) Buildings; (6) Book Collection; (7) Personnel; and (8) Technical Processes. Covered were items such as recommended percentages of registered borrowers; number of books that should circulate each year for children and adults; hours of service; and collection size as a function of community served. Financial standards were addressed in terms of "limited," "reasonably good," and "superior" service with much attention to the need of a minimum of $25,000 to maintain basic service.

The second phase of the Post-war Planning Committee's work, the inventory and evaluation titled, "Taking Stock of the American Public Library" (1943), was used as the basis for the third phase: *A National Plan for Public Library Service*. At the close of World War II, national per capita public library support was $0.72; and 35 million people were still unserved by any library. The *National Plan for Public Library Service* is of particular importance in the discussion of standards, because it used the standards in place at the time to characterize library service in general as mediocre, and further, it provided a platform from which to argue for the strengthening of library services throughout the United States in support of the goal "to bring into the life of every American an adequate, purposeful public library....only to be achieved by the joint efforts of local, state and federal governments" (Joeckel and Winslow, 1948: 152).

Acceptance of the idea of larger units of service, support from the state, and even support from the federal government gained traction in discussions during the early 1950s. At the behest of the American Library Association, the Social Science Research Council carried out The Public Library Inquiry, "an appraisal in sociological, cultural and human terms of the extent to which librarians are achieving their objectives," and "an assessment of the public library's actual and potential contributions to American society." The Public Library Inquiry reports, especially Leigh's general report, *The Public Library in the United States* (1950), set forth much of the philosophical justification for developing standards in the context of systems.

Early in the 1950s the Public Library Division of the ALA was formed and immediately sought funding to revise and restate the 1943 standards. A Coordinating Committee on Revision of Public Library Standards was appointed and convened in 1954. By 1956, after several meetings and solicitation of profession-wide comment, the committee issued its recommendations, *Public Library Service: A Guide to Evaluation with Minimum Standards*. These 1956 *Standards* incorporated ideals from the 1943 *Post-War Standards* and the *National Plan,* but went further to emphasize the educational function of the public library, the quality of service, and the organization of service. The concept of library systems was defined taking note of the fact that while some large cities could provide excellent library services, smaller jurisdictions could not generate enough fiscal support to do so. Thus the 1956 *Standards* advocated that "libraries working together, sharing their services and materials, can meet the full needs of their users. *This co-operative approach on the part of libraries is the most important single recommendation of this document*" (ALA, Coordinating Committee, 1956: xv). Data on costs were issued as a supplement that was updated periodically.

Direct aid to public libraries in rural communities and small towns came with the passage of the Library Services Act (LSA) in 1956 and extended to urban areas and construction in 1964 (Library Services and Construction Act—LSCA). Other federal legislation, such as Operation Headstart, part of the Economic Opportunity Act, funded library projects in response to the War on Poverty of the 1960s. This federal aspect of funding for public libraries and recognition of the changing context of service was very much in the minds of the Standards Committee of the Public Library Association at the time of the issuance of the *Minimum Standards for Public Library Systems, 1966.*

The 1966 *Standards* built on the 1956 *Standards*, with the intent that the library profession would frequently revise its standards. An addenda of "Statistical Standards" identified quantitative statements such as hours of service; quantities of materials recommended by size of library; recommended salaries; and ratio of staff to population. Given how rapidly the United States was changing at the time, on its publication the 1966 *Standards* reflected the past instead of anticipating the future. In retrospect, these *Standards* themselves announced the end of the "standards" phase of U.S. librarianship, though none of those who worked on the 1966 document realized it at the time.

Planning for Public Library Service: 1966 to the Present

Planning and Role Setting for Public Libraries (PRSPL)

The 1966 *Standards* were issued at a time of great change both in the United States and within the American Library Association. The ALA received the results of the report, *Access to Public Libraries,* in 1964—a self audit on the restriction of freedom of access to public libraries based on race—and was digesting this report's implications at the time the 1966 *Standards* were released. The growing recognition that society in general was split into a nation of rich and poor, that there was indeed an "Other America," galvanized ALA members to establish the group that became the Social Responsibilities Round Table and to appoint a Coordinating Committee on Library Service to the Disadvantaged.[4]

It became clear that the 1966 *Standards* did not address the needs of all the people public libraries purported to serve; that is, all residents of the United States. The Public Library Association, concerned about a lack of momentum and clear sense of direction for the profession, launched a "Goals Feasibility Study," that resulted in the 1972 publication, *A Strategy for Public Library Change* (A. B. Martin, 1972). The ALA identified several responsibilities for public libraries, including supporting formal and continuing education, facilitating acceptance of a changing society, motivating the dispossessed and disorganized, and provision of service alternatives at the neighborhood level. The focus on community-based planning helped shift the profession's discourse to the idea of local planning models (Lynch, 1981).

Additionally, librarians increasingly recognized that the extant standards were not scientific and could not provide a basis for evaluating library service. The Standards Committee of the Public Library Association, which had already begun to consider revision of the 1966 *Standards,* decided to collaborate with Ernest R. De Prospo of Rutgers University to seek funding from the U.S. Office of Education for the study, "Measurement of the Effectiveness of Public Libraries," which was reported in the 1973 volume, *Performance Measures for Public Libraries.* Mary Jo Lynch of ALA's Office for Research characterized the study as focusing the library profession on output rather than input (Pungitore, 1995, 75–76).

In her analysis of the shift from standards to a planning model, *Innovation and the Library,* Verna L. Pungitore describes the profession's response to this move. Combined with working papers of the PLA's Goals, Guidelines, and Standards Committee (GGSC—a change from simply the "Standards Committee"), the goals feasibility and performance measures studies—caused some furor in the library press, arising from the notion of discontinuing standards in favor of community planning. The new direction, a "Design for Diversity," would focus on planning for the future, rather than reporting on the past, managing rather than comparing, and a new concern for output (Blasingame and Lynch, 1974). In 1975 the GGSC consolidated its working papers into "Goals and Guidelines for Community Library Service," to be used while the ALA developed new tools to enable librarians to analyze, set objectives, make decisions, and evaluate achievements.

In 1977, with funding from the U.S. Department of Education, the Public Library Association developed manuals for local planning, which resulted in the publication of *A Planning Process for Public Libraries* (Palmour, 1980). The *Planning Process*, a manual outlining methods for community analysis and planning for services, was the new innovation that replaced national public library standards. A companion volume, *Output Measures for Public Libraries,* describing data collection and the use of quantitative measures, was released in 1982 (Zweizig and Rodger).

Between the time when funding for the planning process was awarded and the manuals published, the Public Library Association issued one important document, *The Public Library Mission Statement and Its Imperatives for Service* (1979). The GGSC, chaired by Peter Hiatt, meant for this project to serve as an interim document or bridge, from the 1966 *Standards* to the 1975 "Goals and Guidelines for Community Library Service," as well as planning manuals scheduled for release in the early 1980s. However, the tone and spirit of the *Mission Statement* demonstrated that even as the planning model was in the works to replace a national standards model, many public librarians still hoped for the PLA to develop an overall statement of purpose for the U.S. public library. The *Mission Statement* identified factors in U.S. society that called for a radical shift in emphasis of the public library: runaway social change, exponential increase in the record, total egalitarianism, and depletion of natural resources. The report identified ten actions that public libraries would have to undertake to respond adequately to these factors:

1. Provide access to the human record through collections and networking

2. Organize the human record from a myriad of directions

3. Collect, translate, and organize the human record on all intellectual levels in print and nonprint packages

4. Dramatize the relevance of the human record with public information, guidance, and group activities

5. Develop policies for preserving the record

6. Take leadership in defining a new statement of ethics

7. Coordinate acquisition policies

8. Create a network for access to the record regardless of location

9. Develop procedures for all to use the record

10. Ensure that all will have access regardless of education, language, ethnic or cultural background, age, physical ability or apathy.

This *Mission Statement* focused on the entire community as the target audience for public library service. While tension would continue over the need for a broad mission for public libraries, the profession's move to a planning model and local definitions of service characterized public librarianship for the rest of the twentieth century (Pungitore, 1995: 92–94).

In 1981 the Public Library Association executive board endorsed the move from national standards to local community-based planning. The result, *Planning Process for Public Libraries,* was identified as a new strategy for enabling local libraries and library systems to determine their own goals. A series of programs and workshops sponsored by PLA took place in the early 1980s to disseminate the process. Consequently, the Public Library Association revised its "Statement of Principles" in 1982, with reference to planning. Inexorably the change in the way of developing goals and plans for libraries was moving from national standards to local planning.

The next stage in the move toward adoption of the planning model was the introduction of the Public Library Development Program (PLDP) announced in 1986 (Balcom, 1986). The initial component of

PLDP was *Planning and Role Setting for Public Libraries: A Manual of Options and Procedures* (McClure, 1987), which identified eight potential roles for public libraries and a choice of level of effort for the process; a revision of the output measures manual; and a data service. The eight roles selected formed the basis of much library planning that followed and reflected a range of library activities:

1. Community Activities Center

2. Community Information Center

3. Formal Education Support Center

4. Independent Learning Center

5. Popular Materials Library

6. Preschoolers Door to Learning

7. Reference Library

8. Research Center

The association launched the PLDP with plans for facilitating the adoption of the process, including a trainer's manual, output measures for children and young adults, and an annual data service report.[5] The broad acceptance among public librarians of the PLDP was reported in a 1993 survey of state agency use of the process (Smith, 1994). In a 1995 study of the profession's move from standards to the adoption of the PLDP, Pungitore (1995: 180) concluded that innovation can be facilitated and that public libraries can be "revitalized and reinvigorated" to assume a significant role.

New Planning for Results (NPFR)

The PLA evaluated the effectiveness of the PLDP in 1995 with a national survey, interviews, and an invitational conference, which concluded that the planning model was working and that its use had done much to include the community and staff in planning (Johnson, 1995). Refinements were suggested and to this end PLA appointed a ReVision Committee in 1996 to update *Planning and Role Setting for Public Libraries*. The outcome was the 1998 publication, *Planning for Results: A Public Library Transformation Process* issued in two parts: a guidebook and a "how-to-manual" (Himmel and Wilson, 1998). The eight roles for public libraries that had been identified in 1986 were expanded to thirteen "library responses" to community needs 10 years later:

1. Basic Literacy

2. Business and Career Information

3. Commons

4. Community Referral

5. Consumer Information

6. Cultural Awareness

7. Current Topics and Titles

8. Formal Learning Support

9. General Information

10. Government Information

11. Information Literacy

12. Lifelong Learning

13. Local History and Genealogy

Planning for Results also placed a greater focus on resource allocation. Training and workshops were held at state conferences and sponsored by state library agencies to assist in adoption of procedures. A companion volume, *Managing for Results,* was issued in 2000 to help turn plans into reality (Nelson, Altman, and Mayo, 2000).

Refining and modifying the planning process continues as a top priority for the Public Library Association. A streamlined approach to the planning process was published in 2001, *The New Planning for Results* (Nelson, 2001). Three assumptions guided the new tool: (1) Excellence must be defined locally—it results when library services match community needs, interests, and priorities; (2) Excellence is possible for both small and large libraries—it rests more on commitment than on unlimited resources; and (3) Excellence is a moving target—even when it is achieved, excellence must be continually maintained.

To support the implementation of the planning process the Public Library Association has launched a series of volumes, the *Results* series, offering a consistent set of themes.[6]

Today the Public Library Association makes a clear distinction between the first planning movement (which began about 1980 and continued until 1995)—the "Planning and Role Setting for Public Libraries" (PRSPL) model and the New Planning for Results (NPFR)

model now operative. The earlier approach separated the development of planning goals and service goals and indicated they could be
developed separately; today's NPFR approach is based on the prem-
ise that resource allocation decisions must be subordinate to and
driven by the library's service priorities as reflected in the service
goals and objectives. Additionally the PRSPL model was used as a
process to develop new services and programs with the assumption
that they would be funded with new resources. By way of contrast
NPFR makes the assumption that library planners will use the
NPFR process to identify library priorities and reallocate extant
resources to fund them. "At its core NPFR is about managing
change" (Public Library Association, 2003: 29–30).

State Standards, Ratings, and Peer Comparison

State Standards

The Public Library Association's decision to move away from the
model of national standards has not meant that the profession at
large has rejected the idea of standards for service. Although planning for results may be more effective for the actual development and
delivery of library service, pragmatism at the state and local level
has also necessitated that quantitative standards continue to be
developed. This is because librarians recognize that it is more compelling to make their case to city councils, county commissions, and
regional boards with quantitative standards in hand. Thus many
states have continued to develop and publish state-level standards
for public libraries. It should also be noted that actions of the Public
Library Association and the American Library Association which
tend to be the narrative thread that is followed in this discussion, are
by no means the entire story of the development of public library
mission and direction. State library agencies through their own long-
range planning, state library associations, federal entities such as
the Department of Education's Office of Library Programs, the
National Commission on Libraries and Information Science, and
today the Institute of Museum and Library Services, private foundations, multitype library consortia, library systems, and local libraries
and their boards are all participants in the constant process of delib-
erating on the goals and standards of public libraries.

Moorman has described the way that many states have developed their own quantitative measures of resource-based library effectiveness to use when building the case for library funding. A 2003

study by Hamilton-Pennell reviewed the standards of all fifty states and identified the key reasons that state level standards continue to be developed: (1) assist in planning efforts; (2) provide an evaluation and mechanism tool for public accountability; (3) provide a philosophical context for quality public library service; (4) serve as a library development tool by stimulating growth and development; (5) serve as a tool to identify strengths and select areas for improvement; (6) provide a shared vision for library service; (7) assist in determining whether resources are sufficient; and (8) set minimum guidelines for receipt of state aid.[3]

Ratings

Another method for comparing libraries has been developed by Thomas J. Hennen, Jr., who compiles Hennen's American Public Library Ratings (HAPLR) that appears annually in *American Libraries*. Hennen uses input and output measures to devise a weighted score for public libraries that he uses to rate library performance by population. In 2003 the following libraries (in the indicated population categories) received the highest ratings:

- Denver Public Library [over 500,000]

- Santa Clara County Public Library, CA [250,000–499,999]

- Naperville Public Library, IL [100,000–249,000]

- Lakewood Public Library, OH [50,000–99,999]

- Washington-Centerville Public Library, OH [25,000–49,999]

For some high scoring libraries the HAPLR ratings have been used in press releases and noted on library Web sites, but the methodology has been questioned by Lance and Cox, who use a bivariate correlation to demonstrate the lack of validity of the HAPLR. Nevertheless, the Hennen ratings get broad visibility and high ratings are often noted on library Web sites. He uses this approach in *Hennen's Public Library Planner*, which provides a structured tool for planning and policy development.

Peer Comparisons

The Public Library Peer Search page on the National Center for Education Statistics Web site provides access to FSCS data. Statistics on variables including income, operating expenditures, staffing, size of collection, and circulation, can be compared among libraries of similar size (Bassman, 1998). Bibliostat Connect also offers FSCS data, information from the Public Library Data Service, state, and other data to assess public library quality by conducting graphical peer comparisons using national (FSCS), proprietary (PLDS), and local (State) data sets. The peer comparison output helps libraries identify strengths and weaknesses. The New York State Library Web site provides a clear example of the way Bibliostat Connect can be configured for a state to provide easy access and manipulation of public library-specific data, quick creation of rank-order tables, averages, and percentiles. Data can be organized alphabetically, by peers and by benchmarking.

Yan and Zweizig (2000) surveyed public library directors to determine their use of statistics from the Public Library Data Service and the Federal-State Cooperative System for Public Library Data. Comparison ranked high among respondents' reasons for accessing peer data. As data reporting and gathering is refined and information used for peer comparison available more quickly, librarians will have another tool for decision making and policy making.

Public Libraries, Outcomes, and Quality of Life

Throughout the United States indicators are being used to determine quality of life. Georgia's Department of Community Affairs has developed a community indicators Web site for 450 communities. Library data are not included. Jacksonville, Florida, has a "Quality of Life Project" that represents an effort to monitor progress on an annual basis by means of selected representative quantitative indicators. Library circulation is used as an indicator.

The decision about which indicators to use to measure quality of life by a state or community is the result of neighborhood meetings or visioning processes that provides a consensus about important variables that contribute to that community's definition of well-being. There are a number of organizations that provide background on the use of community indicators, notably Redefining Progress, which recognizes the national movement to use community indicators to change community outcomes. Through their Community Indicators Project, existing and emerging initiatives using community indicators have been linked. Redefining Progress and the International Institute for Sustainable Development (IISD) merged their online databases on indicator initiatives as the *Compendium of Sustainable Development Indicator Initiatives*. The *Compendium* provides a comprehensive and up-to-date information base of sustainable development indicator initiatives being carried out at the international, national, and provincial/territorial/state levels. With a searchable source so at-the-ready it is fairly easy to assess which variables and values communities have selected to provide indicators of progress.

It is far more compelling, however, for library indicators—whether used by the profession or by larger quality of life initiatives—to be outcomes rather than inputs. Several recent research projects demonstrate this approach to the evaluation of public library services.

Joan Durrance and Karen Fisher-Pettigrew conducted a study of the role of the public library in helping citizens obtain community information over the Internet in 1998–2000. One important aspect of their work was the development of a toolkit to put outcome evaluation in context to determine the impact of library services.

The usefulness of the planning for results model in measuring the effect of library service on people's lives has been demonstrated using outcome based evaluation in the 2002 study, *Counting on Results* (Lance). Data from 45 public libraries in twenty states were collected and analyzed to demonstrate the importance of the library to the community. Six of the public library service responses from *Planning for Results* (basic literacy, business and career information, commons, general information, information literacy, and local history and genealogy) were used to standardize and simplify the collection of outcome data from library patrons (Steffen and Lance, 2002).

There are two main reasons for considering the importance of libraries in the context of community indicator development. The first is the most pragmatic. When public libraries are included as indicators contributing to a better "quality of life" for a community, they can attract better support and additional resources from funding entities. If the service is missing from the list of indicators a community has deemed important enough to rank, then the service is far less likely to gain adequate support to execute its mission and goals. Libraries are often included among services that community leaders suggest contribute to the quality of life of a community, but they are seldom identified as important enough to be included as an indicator.

The second reason that should compel librarians to strive to have their services counted as indicators of genuine progress has been explored in a *Public Libraries* "Perspectives" column on libraries and sustainability. Jeffrey L. Brown observes, "Libraries have a reputation as one of our society's most trusted institutions, librarians can offer their facilities as neutral ground where community or economic groups that have been in conflict can meet to mediate their differences" (24). It is Brown's characterization of the reputation of libraries that provides the strongest motivation for librarians to assert the importance of their work. What other agency has received such trust? By working to establish libraries and library services as vital community indicators librarians will broaden the influence of an important institution and in doing so strengthen the influence of a trusted institution.

Notes

1. NISO Z39.7–2002, "Draft Standard for Trial Use." *Information Services and Use: Metrics and Statistics for Libraries and Information Providers—Data Dictionary* (July 26, 2002–July 31, 2003). Available: www.niso.org/emetrics/index.cfm. See also reports of the Information Use Management and Policy Institute, Florida State University, including *Developing National Data Collection Models for Public Library Network Statistics and Performance Measures.* Available: www.ii.fsu.edu/getProjectDetail.cfm?pageID=9 &ProjectID=8.

2. The NCES data are listed in Appendix B: Bibliography of National Statistics on Public Libraries.

3. Although states submit data through the Federal-State Cooperative System (FSCS) for Public Library Data, many states continue to provide access to their own statistics continuing traditions of regular publication. For examples see the following state library Web sites:

- Alaska: www.library.state.ak.us/dev/plstats/plstats.html
- Connecticut: www.cslib.org/stats.htm
- Florida: www.flalib.org/publications/PLStandards2004.doc
- Illinois: http://lrc.lis.uiuc.edu/IPLAR/
- Maryland: www.sailor.lib.md.us/MD_topics/lib/_sta.html
- Massachusetts: http://mlin.lib.ma.us/mblc/sadac/aris_index.shtml
- Nebraska: www.nlc.state.ne.us/Statistics/statlist.html
- New Hampshire: www.state.nh.us/nhsl/ldss/stats.html
- Ohio: http://statserver.slonet.state.oh.us/libstats/html/toc.cfm
- Oregon: www.osl.state.or.us/home/libdev/publibstats.html
- South Carolina: www.state.sc.us/scsl/lib/stats/

- Texas: www.tsl.state.tx.us/ld/pubs/pls/index.html
- Utah: http://library.utah.gov/statisticspublib.html

4. Michael Harrington, *The Other America: Poverty in the United States* (New York: Macmillan, 1962); Toni Samek, *Intellectual Freedom and Social Responsibility in American Librarianship, 1967–1974* (Chicago: American Library Association, 2001); American Library Association, Committee on Economic Opportunity Programs, *Library Service to the Disadvantaged: A Study Based on Responses to Questionnaires from Public Libraries Serving Populations Over 15,000* (Chicago: American Library Association, 1969).

5. The Public Library Association, Public Library Development Program documents:

- Charles R. McClure, et al., *Planning and Role Setting for Public Libraries: A Manual of Options and Procedures* (Chicago: American Library Association, 1987).

- Nancy Van House, et al., *Output Measures for Public Libraries: A Manual of Standardized Procedures* (Chicago: American Library Association, 1987).

- Public Library Association, Public Library Data Service, *Statistical Report* (Chicago: Public Library Association, annual, 1992–present) continues *Public Library Data Service Statistical Report* (Chicago: Public Library Association, 1988–1991).

- Peggy O'Donnell, *Public Library Development Program: Manual for Trainers* (Chicago: American Library Association, 1988).

- Virginia A. Walter, *Output Measures for Public Library Service to Children: A Manual of Standardized Procedures* (Chicago: Association for Library Services to Children, Public Library Association, American Library Association, 1992).

- Virginia A. Walter, *Output Measures and More: Planning and Evaluating Public Library Services for Young Adults* (Chicago: Young Adult Library Services Association, Public Library Association, American Library Association, 1995).

6. The Public Library Association, *Results* series:

- Ethel Himmel and William James Wilson, *Planning for Results: A Public Library Transformation Process* (Chicago: American Library Association, 1998).

- Diane Mayo and Sandra Nelson, *Wired for the Future: Developing Your Library Technology Plan* (Chicago: American Library Association, 1999).

- Sandra Nelson, Ellen Altman, and Diane Mayo, *Managing for Results: Effective Resource Allocation for Public Libraries* (Chicago: American Library Association, 2000).

- Sandra Nelson, *The New Planning for Results: A Streamlined Approach* (Chicago: American Library Association, 2001).

- Diane Mayo and Jeanne Goodrich, *Staffing for Results: A Guide to Working Smarter* (Chicago: American Library Association, 2002).

- Sandra Nelson and June Garcia. *Creating Policies for Results: From Chaos to Clarity* (Chicago: American Library Association, 2003).

References

Access to Public Libraries Study. (Chicago: American Library Association, 1963).

American Library Association. 1948. Post-war Planning Committee. Post-war Planning Committee File, 1941–1948. Available: http://web.library.uiuc.edu/ahx/ala/alacard.asp?RG=93&SG=10&RS=6. (accessed September, 28 2002).

American Library Association. Coordinating Committee on Revision of Public Library Standards. 1956. *Public Library Service: A Guide to Evaluation with Minimum Standards*. Chicago: American Library Association.

American Library Association. Public Library Association, Standards Committee. 1967. *Minimum Standards for Public Library Systems, 1966*. Chicago: American Library Association.

American National Standards Institute. Available: www.ansi.org.

Balcom, Kathleen Mehaffey. 1986. To Concentrate and Strengthen: The Promise of the Public Library Development Program. *Library Journal* 111 (June 15): 36–40.

Bassman, Keri, et al. 1998. *How Does Your Public Library Compare? Service Performance of Peer Groups*. Washington, DC: National Center for Education Statistics. (Release Date: October 27, 1998). Available: http://nces.ed.gov/pubs98/98310.pdf (accessed November 25, 2002).

Bibliostat Connect. Available: www.informata.com.

Blasingame, Ralph, Jr., and Mary Jo Lynch. 1974. Design for Diversity: Alternatives to Standards for Public Libraries. *PLA Newsletter* 13: 4–22.

Brown, Jeffrey L. 2001. Making a Huge Difference in So Many Little Ways. *Public Libraries* 40 (January/February): 24.

Chute, Adrienne. 2003. National Center for Education Statistics Library Statistics Program. In *The Bowker Annual Library and Book Trade Almanac*, 95–102. New York: R. R. Bowker.

Department of Community Affairs. *Georgia Community Indicators*. Available: www.dca.state.ga.us/commind/default.asp.

De Prospo, Ernest R., Ellen Altman, and Kenneth Beasley. 1973. *Performance Measures for Public Libraries*. Chicago: American Library Association.

Durrance, Joan C., and Karen E. Fisher-Pettigrew. 2003. Determining How Libraries and Librarians Help. *Library Trends* 51 (Spring): 541–570.

Fair, E. M. 1934. *Countywide Library Service*. Chicago: American Library Association.

Garceau, Oliver. 1949. *The Public Library in the Political Process: A Report of the Public Library Inquiry*. New York: Columbia University Press.

Goals and Guidelines for Community Library Service. 1975. *PLA Newsletter* 14: 9–13.

Hamilton-Pennell, Christine. Public Library Standards: A Review of Standards and Guidelines from the Fifty States of the U.S. for the Colorado, Mississippi, and Hawaii State Libraries. Mosaic Knowledge Works. Chief Officers of State Library Agencies (COSLA). Available: www.cosla.org (accessed April 2003).

Heckman, James. 2000. Causal Parameters and Policy Analysis in Economics: A Twentieth Century Retrospective. *The Quarterly Journal of Economics* 115 (February): 45–97.

Hennen, Thomas J., Jr. 1999a. Go Ahead, Name Them: America's Best Public Libraries. *American Libraries* 30 (January): 72–76.

Hennen, Thomas J., Jr. 1999b. Great American Public Libraries: HAPLR Ratings: Round Two. *American Libraries* 30 (September): 64–68.

Hennen, Thomas J., Jr. 2000a. Great American Public Libraries: HAPLR Ratings: 2000. *American Libraries* 31 (November): 50–54.

Hennen, Thomas J., Jr. 2000b. Why We Should Establish a National System of Standards. *American Libraries* 31 (March): 43–45.

Hennen, Thomas J., Jr. 2002a. Are Wider Library Units Wiser? *American Libraries* 33.6 (June/July): 65–70. (Also titled, Wider and Wiser Units.) Available: www.haplr-index.com/wider_and_wiser_units.htm.

Hennen, Thomas J., Jr. 2002b. Great American Public Libraries: HAPLR Ratings: 2002. *American Libraries* 33 (October): 64–68.

Hennen, Thomas J., Jr. 2003a. Great American Public Libraries: HAPLR Ratings: 2003. *American Libraries* 34 (October): 44–49.

Hennen, Thomas J., Jr. 2003b. Hennen's American Public Library Ratings. March 2003. Available: www.haplr-index.com/index.html.

Hennen, Thomas J., Jr. 2004. *Hennen's Public Library Planner: A Manual and Interactive CD-ROM*. New York: Neal-Schuman Publishers.

Hennepin County, MN. Office of Planning and Development. 2002. The 50-page 2002 Hennepin County Community Indicators report was published in December 2002 by the Hennepin County Office of Planning and Development. Its 26 indicators relate to several broad areas of community life, including health, self-reliance, transportation, and civic engagement. The report seeks to gauge the effects that county programs and services have on the quality of life experienced by Hennepin County residents. Available: http://www.nextstep .state.mn.us/res_detail.cfm?id=282.

Himmel, Ethel and William James Wilson with the ReVision Committee of the Public Library Association. 1998. *Planning for Results: A Public Library Transformation Process.* Chicago: American Library Association.

Information Use Management and Policy Institute, John C. Bertot, and Charles R. McClure. Public Library Network Statistics: Librarian Education for the Collection, Analysis, and Use of Library Network Services and Resources Statistics. Available: www.ii.fsu.edu/getProjectDetail.cfm?pageID=8&ProjectID=4.

International Institute for Sustainable Development. Compendium of Sustainable Development Indicator Initiatives. Available: www.iisd.org/measure/ compendium.

Jacksonville Community Council. Community Indicators Project. Available: www.jcci.org/indic.htm.

Joeckel, Carleton Bruns. 1935. *The Government of the American Public Library.* Chicago: University of Chicago Press.

Joeckel, Carleton Bruns. 1943. *Post-War Standards for Public Libraries.* Chicago: American Library Association.

Joeckel, Carleton B., and Amy Winslow. 1948. *A National Plan for Public Library Service.* Chicago: American Library Association.

Johnson, Debra Wilcox. 1995. An Evaluation of the Public Library Development Program. Unpublished report for the Public Library Association.

Lance, Keith Curry, and Marti A. Cox. 2000. Lies, Damn Lies and Indexes. *American Libraries* 31 (June-July): 82–87.

Lance, Keith Curry, et al. 2002. *Counting on Results: New Tools for Outcome-Based Evaluation for Public Libraries.* Aurora, CO: Bibliographical Center for Research. Available: www.lrs.org/documents/cor/CoRFin.pdf (accessed November 2, 2003).

Leigh, Robert D. 1950. *The Public Library in the United States: The General Report of the Public Library Inquiry.* New York: Columbia University Press.

Lynch, Mary Jo. 1981. The Public Library Association and Public Library Planning. *Journal of Library Administration* 2 (Summer/Fall/Winter): 29–41.

Martin, Allie Beth. 1972. *A Strategy for Public Library Change: Proposed Public Library Goals—Feasibility Study.* Chicago: American Library Association.

Martin, Lowell. 1972. Standards for Public Libraries. *Library Trends* 21 (October): 164–177.

McClure, Charles R., et al. 1987. *Planning and Role Setting for Public Libraries: A Manual of Options and Procedures.* Chicago: American Library Association.

McCook, Kathleen de la Peña, and Kristin Brand. 2001. Community Indicators, Genuine Progress, and the Golden Billion. *Reference and User Services Quarterly* 40 (Summer): 337–340.

Moorman, John A. 1997. Standards for Public Libraries: A Study in Quantitative Measures of Library Performance as Found in State Public Library Documents. *Public Libraries* 36 (January-February): 32–39.

National Information Standards Association. Available: www.niso.org/index.html.

Nelson, Sandra. 2001. *The New Planning for Results: A Streamlined Approach*. Chicago: American Library Association.

Nelson, Sandra, Ellen Altman, and Diane Mayo. 2000. Managing Your Library's Staff. In *Managing for Results: Effective Resource Allocation for Public Libraries*, 29–110. Chicago: American Library Association.

New York State Library. Bibliostat Connect: Easy Online Access to Public Library Statistics from your State Library. Available: www.nysl.nysed.gov/libdev/libs/biblcnct.htm.

O'Donnell, Peggy. 1988. *Public Library Development Program: Manual for Trainers*. Chicago: American Library Association.

Oregon State Library. *Reporting Public Library Statistics*. Available: www.osl.state.or.us/home/libdev/reportpublibstats.html.

Palmour, Vernon E., et al. 1980. *A Planning Process for Public Libraries*. Chicago: American Library Association.

Public Library Association. 2003. Everything You Want to Know About the *Results Series*. Available: www.pla.org/ala/pla/pla.htm (accessed May 24, 2004).

Public Library Association. Goals, Guidelines and Standards Committee. 1973. Community Library Services: Working Papers on Goals and Guidelines. *Library Journal* 96: 2603–2609.

Public Library Association. Goals, Guidelines and Standards Committee. 1979. *The Public Library Mission Statement and Its Imperatives for Service*. Chicago: American Library Association.

Public Library Association. Public Library Data Service. 1992–present. *Statistical Report* (annual). Chicago: Public Library Association. Continues *Public Library Data Service Statistical Report*. Chicago: Public Library Association, 1988–1991.

Public Library Association. Public Library Principles Task Force. 1982. The Public Library: Democracy's Resource, A Statement of Principles. *Public Libraries* 21: 92.

Pungitore, Verna L. 1992. Dissemination of the Public Library Planning Process Among Smaller Libraries. *Library Quarterly* 62 (October): 375–407.

Pungitore, Verna L. 1993. Planning in Smaller Libraries: A Field Study. *Public Libraries* 32 (November/December): 331–336.

Pungitore, Verna L. 1995. *Innovation and the Library: The Adoption of New Ideas in Public Libraries*. Westport, CT: Greenwood Press.

Schick, Frank L. 1971. Library Statistics: A Century Plus. *American Libraries* 2: 727–741.

Smith, Nancy Milner. 1994. State Library Agency Use of Planning and Role Setting for Public Libraries and Output Measures for Public Libraries. *Public Libraries* 33 (July-August): 211–212.

Standards for Public Libraries. 1933. *ALA Bulletin* 27 (November): 513–514.

Steffen, Nicolle O., and Keith Curry Lance. 2002. Who's Doing What: Outcome-Based Evaluation and Demographics in the "Counting on Results Project." *Public Libraries* 43 (September-October): 271–279.

Steffen, Nicolle O., Keith Curry Lance, and Rochelle Logan. 2002. Time to Tell the Whole Story: Outcome-Based Evaluation and the "Counting on Results Project." *Public Libraries* 43 (July-August): 222–228.

Tucker, Harold W. 1963. The Access to Public Libraries Study. *ALA Bulletin* 57 (September): 742–745.

U.S. National Center for Education Statistics. Public Libraries, Sources of Data. Available: http://nces.ed.gov/pubsearch/getpubList.asp?L1=32&L2=4 (accessed February 18, 2004).

U.S. National Center for Education Statistics. Public Libraries, Survey. Available: http://nces.ed.gov/pubsearch/pubsinfo.asp?pubid=2003398 (accessed February 18, 2004).

U.S. National Center for Education Statistics. Public Library Peer Comparison Tool. Available: http://nces.ed.gov/surveys/libraries/publicpeer (accessed February 18, 2004).

U.S. National Commission on Libraries and Information Science. Library Statistics Cooperative Program. Available: www.nclis.gov/statsurv/surveys/fscs/fscs.html (accessed February 18, 2004).

Van House, Nancy, et al. 1987. *Output Measures for Public Libraries: A Manual of Standardized Procedures*. Chicago: American Library Association.

Walter, Virginia A. 1992. *Output Measures for Public Library Service to Children: A Manual of Standardized Procedures*. Chicago: American Library Association.

Walter, Virginia A. 1995. *Output Measures and More: Planning and Evaluating Public Library Services for Young Adults*. Chicago: American Library Association.

Yan, Quan Liu, and Douglas L. Zweizig. 2000. Public Library Use of Statistics: A Survey Report. *Public Libraries* 39 (March/April): 98–105.

Zweizig, Douglas L., and Eleanor Jo Rodger. 1982. *Output Measures for Public Libraries*. Chicago: American Library Association.

5

Organization, Law, Funding, and Politics

Operating a public library requires an awareness of the social factors that impact the delivery of library services. This chapter treats the political and economic context in which the public library functions, paying particular attention to the organizational, legal, and funding basis. To understand these contexts fully it is critical that librarians scan and understand the national, state, regional, and local political environment, because clearly public policy and legislation at all these levels influences each library's funding and governance. Over fifty years ago, in his work *The Public Library in the Political Process*, Garceau clearly defined this important duty as follows, "Public librarians are inescapably a part of government and involved in 'politics'" (1949: 239). Today public librarians should stay apprised of overarching concerns by reviewing policy issues addressed by organizations such as the National Governors Association, the National Association of Counties, the Alliance for Regional Stewardship, and the U.S. Conference of Mayors. The governance of each public library today takes place within the interlocking contexts of local, regional, state, and national political jurisdictions.

The Organizational Basis of the Public Library

When governing bodies established the first tax-supported public libraries over 150 years ago as a community service, they had no models of governance to follow, and the structure we have today was crafted within the framework of local situations. For the first 50 years of the public library's existence, the city, or in some cases the school district, was the basis of library service. Smaller communities and rural areas generally remained unserved.

The first two periods in the governmental history of the library movement in the United States roughly track the development of municipal government. The first period (1850–1890) was the rise of the "board plan" of administration, as municipalities established boards to oversee new functions and services. As communities established public libraries they commonly adopted this type of structure. During this period state library laws were passed rapidly. Though differing from state to state these laws generally outlined the roles and responsibilities of trustees, authorized taxation for library support, and maintained independence for the library board.

The second period of governmental history (1890–1934) witnessed the development of municipal home rule and a commission form of government. At the state level, the establishment of library agencies served to generate support for the founding of new libraries (Joeckel, 1935). A third period can be identified with the initiation of the American Library Association's active promotion of the extension of library service to unserved rural areas beginning in the 1930s. The national plan of service issued by ALA in 1939 provided a national vision for comprehensive service that would culminate in federal funds for rural library services in the 1950s through the Library Services Act.

The county as a basis for library service emerged as state legislation provided legal means for a broader tax base. In 1898 Ohio (Cincinnati and Hamilton County) and Maryland (Hagerstown and Washington County) authorized taxes by the city and county for library service. Wisconsin and California passed similar legislation in 1901. While each state has a singular experience in the development of library services beyond the municipal level, the story of California serves as the prototype for the county library movement. Ray Held recounts the California story in his comprehensive history, *The Rise of the Public Library in California*, which provides—for those interested—a detailed analysis of steps toward county service.

The inception of larger units of library service as another basis for the organization of libraries was suggested by Joeckel in 1935, to address the needs of regions where municipal or even county organization did not offer economy of scale. These include library districts—an authority authorized by state law to provide library service—and multi-jurisdictional libraries comprised of two or more government entities providing service through an intergovernmental agreement.

While the predominant legal basis of the public library in the United States continues to be municipal government, upon reflection, some conclude that the multicounty and library district units as a basis for library service can provide more resources. Hennen (2002) has developed arguments that demonstrate advantages of wider units of service, including reallocation of administrative costs, equalization of tax rates, and a better basis for long-range planning. Data for conducting research is now available through GEOLIB. A nationwide public library database system, GEOLIB is funded by IMLS and linked to a digital base map, which includes data sets from the U.S. Census and the National Center for Educational Statistics. The database provides consolidated information on public libraries nationwide and is accessible over the Internet.

Figure 5.1 shows that, of the 9,129 public libraries in the United States, the majority is based in municipal government (54.7 percent), followed by nonprofit associations or agencies (14.9 percent), county/parish (10.7 percent), library districts (8.5 percent), multi-jurisdictions (5.4 percent), school districts (3.4 percent), and city/county (1 percent). The remaining libraries are under the aegis of Native American Tribal Government and combined public/school libraries. States vary greatly: Maryland's 24 libraries are wholly county-based, while 98.9 percent of Iowa's 537 libraries are based in municipalities.

The Legal Basis of the Public Library

The legal basis for public libraries resides in state laws that grant a city, town, village, or district the right to establish a library, authorize the power to levy taxes, and determine the structure and powers of the library board that will oversee operation. *Library Law and Legislation in the United States,* is a concise introduction to the three basic areas of law, which relate to libraries—constitutional, statutory, and administrative (Ladenson, 1970; 1982). Constitutional law emanates from the people; statutory law consists of the compilations and codes of law enacted by a legislative body (Congress, state

Figure 5.1: Percentage Distribution of Public Libraries, by Type of Legal Basis and by State: Fiscal Year 2001

State	Number of public libraries	Type of legal basis[1]								Response rate
		Municipal government	County/ parish	City/ county	Multi-jurisdic-tional[2]	Nonprofit association or agency libraries[3]	School district[4]	Library district[5]	Other[6]	
		Percentage distribution								
50 States and DC[7]	9,129	54.7	10.7	1.0	5.4	14.9	3.4	8.5	1.5	100.0
Alabama	207	72.9	7.2	0.5	18.4	0	0	1.0	0	100.0
Alaska	86	48.8	12.8	0	3.5	27.9	0	0	7.0	100.0
Arizona	35	57.1	5.7	0	0	0	0	28.6	8.6	100.0
Arkansas	43	20.9	32.6	2.3	39.5	0	0	0	4.7	100.0
California	179	64.2	25.1	2.2	1.7	0	1.7	5.0	0	100.0
Colorado	116	35.3	16.4	3.4	6.9	0	0.9	37.1	0	100.0
Connecticut	194	50.5	0	0	0	49.5	0	0	0	100.0
Delaware	37	5.4	48.6	2.7	0	0	0	43.2	0	100.0
District of Columbia	1	100.0	0	0	0	0	0	0	0	100.0
Florida	72	31.9	48.6	2.8	15.3	0	0	1.4	0	100.0
Georgia	57	0	42.1	0	57.9	0	0	0	0	100.0
Hawaii	1	0	0	0	0	0	0	0	100.0	100.0
Idaho	106	44.3	0	0	5.7	0	0	50.0	0	100.0
Illinois	629	51.0	0	0	0	0	0	49.0	0	100.0
Indiana	239	14.2	9.6	0	75.3	0	0	0	0.8	100.0
Iowa	537	98.9	0.6	0	0	0	0	0	0.6	100.0

State	Number of public libraries	Municipal govern-ment	County/parish	City/county	Multi-jurisdic-tional[2]	Nonprofit association or agency libraries[3]	School district[4]	Library district[5]	Other[6]	Response rate
					Percentage distribution					
Kansas	321	91.6	4.4	0	0.9	0	0	2.5	0.6	100.0
Kentucky	116	0	7.8	0	0.9	0	0	91.4	0	100.0
Louisiana	65	3.1	90.8	1.5	3.1	0	0	1.5	0	100.0
Maine	273	38.8	0	0	0	61.2	0	0	0	100.0
Maryland	24	0	100.0	0	0	0	0	0	0	100.0
Massachusetts	371	93.5	0	0	0	6.5	0	0	0	100.0
Michigan	381	54.1	5.5	0	0	0	5.2	35.2	0	100.0
Minnesota	140	74.3	8.6	9.3	1.4	0.7	0	0	5.7	100.0
Mississippi	49	4.1	36.7	24.5	34.7	0	0	0	0	100.0
Missouri	150	56.0	28.0	5.3	7.3	0.7	0	0	2.7	100.0
Montana	79	35.4	34.2	16.5	13.9	0	0	0	0	100.0
Nebraska	272	95.6	3.3	0	0.4	0	0	0	0.7	100.0
Nevada	23	8.7	47.8	0	4.3	0	0	39.1	0	100.0
New Hampshire	229	97.4	0	0	0.4	2.2	0	0	0	100.0
New Jersey	309	75.1	4.5	0	1.9	18.1	0	0	0.3	100.0
New Mexico	80	66.3	2.5	0	1.3	12.5	0	1.3	16.3	100.0
New York	750	28.9	1.1	0	0	48.5	17.2	3.6	0.7	100.0
North Carolina	76	14.5	52.6	1.3	19.7	7.9	0	0	3.9	100.0
North Dakota	82	70.7	15.9	1.2	12.2	0	0	0	0	100.0

Type of legal basis[1]

Figure 5.1 continued. Percentage Distribution of Public Libraries

State	Number of public libraries	Municipal government	County/ parish	City/ county	Multi- jurisdic- tional[2]	Nonprofit association or agency libraries[3]	School district[4]	Library district[5]	Other[6]	Response rate
						Percentage distribution				
Ohio	250	9.6	23.2	0	0	7.2	60.0	0	0	100.0
Oklahoma	115	90.4	4.3	0	5.2	0	0	0	0	100.0
Oregon	125	68.8	12.0	0	0	3.2	3.2	12.8	0	100.0
Pennsylvania	459	0	0	0	0	85.8	0	0	14.2	100.0
Rhode Island	48	45.8	0	0	0	54.2	0	0	0	100.0
South Carolina	41	2.4	90.2	0	7.3	0	0	0	0	100.0
South Dakota	126	65.1	7.9	7.1	12.7	0.8	0	0.8	5.6	100.0
Tennessee	184	55.4	40.8	3.8	0	0.8	0	0	0	100.0
Texas	540	56.1	21.9	1.9	1.9	16.7	0	1.5	0.2	100.0
Utah	70	58.6	40.0	1.4	0	0	0	0	0	100.0
Vermont	188	56.9	0	0	6.4	36.2	0	0.5	0	100.0
Virginia	90	25.6	40.0	0	25.6	8.9	0	0	0	100.0
Washington	65	67.7	0	0	0	0	0	32.3	0	100.0
West Virginia	97	49.5	30.9	0	17.5	0	2.1	0	0	100.0
Wisconsin	379	89.4	2.1	0.5	6.1	0	0.3	0	1.6	100.0
Wyoming	23	0	100.0	0	0	0	0	0	0	100.0
Outlying Areas										
Guam	1	0	0	0	0	0	0	0	100.0	100.0
Virgin Islands	1	0	0	0	0	0	0	0	100.0	100.0

Figure 5.1 continued. Percentage Distribution of Public Libraries

1 Type of legal basis refers to the type of local government structure within which the library functions.
2 Multi-jurisdictional—The public library is operated jointly by two or more units of local government under an inter-governmental agreement.
3 Nonprofit association or agency libraries—The public library is privately controlled but meets the statutory definition of a public library in a given state.
4 School district—The public library is under the legal basis of a school district.
5 Library district—A district, authority, board or commission authorized by state law to provide library services.
6 Other—Includes libraries under the legal bases of Native American Tribal Government and combined public/school libraries.
7 50 States and DC totals exclude outlying areas.

NOTE: Detail may not sum to totals because of rounding. Response rate is the percentage of libraries that reported type of legal basis. Data were not reported by the following outlying areas: American Samoa, Northern Marianas, Palau, and Puerto Rico.

SOURCE: U.S. Department of Education, National Center for Education Statistics, Federal-State Cooperative System (FSCS) for Public Library Data, Public Libraries Survey, Fiscal Year 2001.

Figure 5.1 continued. Percentage Distribution of Public Libraries

legislatures, county commissions, city councils); and administrative law governs functions of administrative agencies.

State Law and Legislation

Library laws were compiled by the American Library Association culminating in the series *American Library Laws* that ceased publication in 1983. Current access to the library statutes of most states can be found on the Web site for Chief Officers of State Library Agencies (COSLA), which lists a profile of each state library agency including the current Web site and links to the legislation for libraries currently in force for the state.[1]

Public library directors in each state need to be knowledgeable about their respective laws. Here are examples of a few state declaratory mandates that provide justification and preface these laws:

- Legislative declaration. The general assembly hereby declares that it is the policy of this state, as a part of its provision for public education, to promote the establishment and development of all types of publicly-supported free library service throughout the state to ensure equal access to information without regard to age, physical or mental health, place of residence, or economic status, to aid in the establishment and improvement of library programs, to improve and update the skills of persons employed in libraries through continuing education activities, and to promote and coordinate the sharing of resources among libraries in Colorado and the dissemination of information regarding the availability of library services (Colorado Library Law, 24-90-102).

- It is the purpose of this part to encourage the establishment, adequate financing, and effective administration of free public libraries in this state to give the people of Montana the fullest opportunity to enrich and inform themselves through reading (Montana Code Annotated, 22-1-302).

- The general assembly declares it to be the policy of the state of Vermont that free public libraries are essential to the general enlightenment of citizens in a democracy and that every citizen of the state of Vermont should have access to the educational, cultural, recreational, informational and research benefits of a free public library (Vermont Statutes, 22 VSA 67a).

- The legislature recognizes:
    (a) The importance of free access to knowledge, information and diversity of ideas by all residents of the state;

(b) The critical role played by public, school, special and academic libraries in providing that access;

(c) The major educational, cultural and economic asset is represented in the collective knowledge and information resources of a state's libraries;

(d) The importance of public libraries to the democratic process; and

(e) That the most effective use of a library resources in this state can occur only through interlibrary cooperation among all types of libraries and the effective use of technology (Wisconsin Statutes, 43.001).

These declarations are tangible manifestations of states' commitment to the value of libraries in the lives of their residents. They are the result of the efforts of many people working together over many years to incorporate the library as a public good in law. By way of example, Figure 5.2 is that portion of the Colorado legislation that outlines steps in the method for establishing public libraries.

Local Ordinances

In addition to state law many municipalities and counties have passed local ordinances that enhance or identify local policies relating to library governance. Home rule is the principle or practice of self-government in the internal affairs of a dependent country or other political unit. Powers granted under home rule vary in each state regarding the ability of local governments to raise taxes or impose regulations and vary within states by government functions. To put home rule in context for each state, review *Home Rule in America* (Krane, Rigos, and Hill,2001).

A few examples of local ordinances that provide for public library regulations give an idea of specific instances of local regulation supplementing state legislation.

- Annual report. The board of library trustees shall make a report to the city council immediately after the close of the municipal fiscal year. This report shall contain statements of the condition on the library, the number of books added thereto, the number of books circulated, the amount of fines collected and the amount of money expended in the maintenance of the library during the year, together with such further information as required by the council (Cedar Falls, Iowa, Code, Sec. 2-286).

Figure 5.2: Colorado Revised Statutes

Office of Legislative Legal Services
Colorado General Assembly

ARTICLE 90 - LIBRARIES

24-90-107. Method of Establishment.

(1) A municipal or county library may be established for a governmental unit either by the legislative body of said governmental unit on its own initiative, by adoption of a resolution or ordinance to that effect, or upon petition of one hundred registered electors residing in the proposed library's legal service area. A joint library may be established by the legislative bodies of two or more governmental units, and a library district by the legislative bodies of one or more governmental units, each proceeding to adopt a resolution or an ordinance to that effect. A library district may also be formed by petition of one hundred registered electors residing within the proposed library district addressed to the boards of county commissioners in each county in the proposed library district.

(2) If establishment of a municipal, county, or joint library or a library district is to be by resolution or ordinance, the following procedures shall be followed:

(a) Public hearings following notice shall be held by those governmental units forming the public library. Such notice shall set forth the matters to be included in the resolution or ordinance and shall fix a date for the hearing which shall be not less than thirty nor more than sixty days after the date of first publication of such notice.

(b) Such public hearings shall include discussion of the purposes of the library to be formed and, where more than one governmental unit is involved, the powers, rights, obligations, and responsibilities, financial and otherwise, of each governmental unit.

(c) The resolution or ordinance shall describe the proposed library's legal service area, identifying any excluded areas, shall specify the mill levy and property tax dollars to be imposed or other type and amount of funding, and shall state that the electors of the governmental unit or library district must approve any amount of tax levy not previously established by resolution or ordinance nor previously approved by the electors before the library can be established.

(d) Upon the adoption of the resolution or ordinance, the legislative body or bodies shall establish the public library and provide for its financial support beginning on or before January 1 of the year following the adoption of the resolution or ordinance by all those legislative bodies effecting the establishment or, if any amount of tax levy not previously established by resolution or ordinance nor previously approved by the electors is to provide the financial support, following elector approval of that levy.

(e) Upon establishment of a joint library or library district, and after appointment of the library board of trustees, a written agreement between the legislative body of each participating governmental unit and the library board of trustees shall be effected within ninety days and shall set forth fully the rights, obligations, and responsibilities, financial and otherwise, of all parties to the agreement.

(3) If establishment of a county or municipal library or a library district is by petition of registered electors, the following procedures shall be followed:

(a) The petition shall set forth:

(I) A request for the establishment of the library;

(II) The name or names of the governmental unit or units establishing the library;

(III) The name of the proposed library, and for a library district, the chosen name preceding the words "library district";

(IV) A general description of the legal service area of the proposed public library with such certainty as to enable a property owner to determine whether or not such property owner's property is within the proposed library's legal service area; and

(V) Specification of the mill levy to be imposed or other type and amount of funding and that the electors must approve any amount of tax levy not previously established by resolution or ordinance nor previously approved by the electors before the county or municipal library or library district can be established.

(b) Petitions shall be addressed to the legislative body of the county or municipality, or, in the case of a library district, to the boards of county commissioners of each county having territory within the legal service area of the proposed district.

(c) (I) Except as otherwise provided in subparagraphs (II) and (III) of this paragraph (c), at the time of filing the petition for the establishment of a library district, a bond shall be filed with the county or counties sufficient to pay all expenses connected with the organization of the library district if such organization is not affected.

Figure 5.2 continued. Colorado Revised Statutes

(II) Except as otherwise provided in subparagraph (III) of this paragraph (c), the board of county commissioners of each county having territory within the legal service area of the proposed library district may:

(A) Waive the bonding requirement; and

(B) With the consent of the board of trustees of an existing library, pay for the costs of the election for the proposed library district. If the legal service area of a proposed library district includes two or more counties, the costs of election for such library district to be paid by any county pursuant to this sub-sub-paragraph (B) shall not exceed a percentage of said costs equal to the percentage that the population of the county within the boundaries of the legal service area bears to the total population within the boundaries of such service area.

(III) (A) Subject to the provisions of sub-subparagraphs (B) and (C) of this subparagraph (III), the board of county commissioners of each county having territory within the legal service area of the proposed library district shall pay no less than fifty percent of the costs of the election for such library district if the petition submitted pursuant to subsection (1) of this section contains signatures by registered electors residing in the proposed library district in an amount equal to at least five percent of the total number of votes cast in every precinct in the proposed library district for all candidates for the office of secretary of state at the previous general election.

(B) Payment of election costs for any library district shall not be required of any county under this subparagraph (III) more than once every four years.

(C) In the case where the legal service area of a proposed library district includes two or more counties, the costs of the election for the library district shall be paid on a prorated basis with each county within the boundaries of the proposed library's legal service area paying a percentage of said costs equal to the percentage that the population of the county within the boundaries of the library's legal service area bears to the total population of such service area.

(c.5) Notwithstanding any other provision of this section, the costs of the election of a proposed library district may be assumed by an existing library where the assumption of the costs has been approved by the board of trustees of said library.

(d) Upon receipt of such petition, the legislative body or bodies shall either establish the library by resolution or ordinance, in accordance with subsection (2) of this section, or shall submit the question of the establishment of a public library to a vote of the registered electors residing in the proposed library's legal service area in accordance with the following provisions:

Figure 5.2 continued. Colorado Revised Statutes

(I) In the case of a municipal library, such election shall be held in accordance with article 10 of title 31, C.R.S., and section 20 of article X of the state constitution, and shall be held on the date of the state biennial general election, the first Tuesday in November in odd-numbered years, or the municipal regular election, whichever is earliest; except that such petition shall be filed at least ninety days before such election.

(II) In the case of a library district or county library, such election shall be held in accordance with articles 1 to 13 of title 1, C.R.S., and section 20 of article X of the state constitution, and shall be held on the date of the state biennial general election or the first Tuesday in November in odd-numbered years, whichever is earliest; except that such petition shall be filed at least ninety days before such election.

(III) Public hearings shall be conducted by such legislative body or bodies prior to an election and shall include a discussion of the purposes of the library to be formed and, where more than one governmental unit is involved, the powers, rights, obligations, and responsibilities, financial and otherwise, of each governmental unit.

(e) and (f) (Deleted by amendment, L. 97, p. 411, § 1, effective April 24, 1997.)

(g) If a majority of the electors voting on the question vote in favor of the establishment of a library, the legislative body of each establishing governmental unit shall forthwith establish such library and provide for its financial support beginning on or before January 1 of the year following the election.

(h) Upon establishment of a library district, and after appointment of the library board of trustees, a written agreement between the legislative body of each participating governmental unit and the library board of trustees shall be effected within ninety days and shall set forth fully the rights, obligations, and responsibilities, financial and otherwise, of all parties to the agreement.

(i) If organization of a library district is effected, the district shall reimburse the legislative bodies holding the election for expenses incurred in holding the election.

Source: L. 79: Entire article R&RE, p. 986, § 1, effective July 1. L. 87: (1) and (2) amended, p. 319, § 60, effective July 1. L. 90: Entire section R&RE, p. 1295, § 3, effective July 1. L. 93: (1) amended, p. 1462, § 8, effective June 6. L. 94: (2)(c), (2)(d), and (3)(a)(V) amended, p. 736, § 2, effective July 1. L. 97: (3)(c) to (3)(f) amended, p. 411, § 1, effective April 24. L. 98: (3)(c)(III)(A) amended, p. 831, § 59, effective August 5. L. 2003: (1), (2)(c), (3)(a)(IV), (3)(b), IP(3)(c)(II), (3)(c)(II)(B), (3)(c)(III)(A), (3)(c)(III)(C), and IP(3)(d) amended and (3)(c.5) added, p. 2447, § 8, effective August 15.

Editor's note: (1) This section was contained in an article that was repealed and reenacted in 1979. Provisions of this section, as it existed in 1979, are

Figure 5.2 continued. Colorado Revised Statutes

similar to those contained in 24-90-110 and 24-90-111 as said sections existed in 1978, the year prior to the repeal and reenactment of this article.

(2) Subsections (1), (2)(c), (3)(a)(IV), and (3)(b), the introductory portion to subsection (3)(c)(II), subsections (3)(c)(II)(B), (3)(c)(III)(A), (3)(c)(III)(C), and (3)(c.5), and the introductory portion to subsection (3)(d) were contained in a 2003 act that was passed without a safety clause. The act establishes an effective date of August 15, 2003, for these provisions. For further explanation concerning the effective date, see page vii of this volume.

ANNOTATION

Applied in Ramos v. Lamm, 485 F. Supp. 122 (D. Colo. 1979).

Figure 5.2 continued. Colorado Revised Statutes

- Larceny from libraries. It shall be unlawful for any person, within the township to procure or take in any way from any public library...any book, pamphlet, map, chart, painting, picture, photograph, periodical, newspaper, magazine, manuscript or exhibit or any part thereof with intent to convert the same to his own use or with intent to defraud the owner thereof (Ypsilanti Township, Washtenaw Co., Michigan, Code of Ordinances, Sec. 42-142).

- Sale of books by public library. The New Port Richey Public Library may conduct a sale of books on city owned property upon receiving the prior approval of the city manager. In addition, the Friends of the Library, upon the city manager's prior approval, may conduct a public sale of books on city owned property on behalf of the New Port Richey Public Library. All income, monies, and other proceeds collected from any sale conducted without the assistance of the Friends of the Library shall be deposited in the New Port Richey Public Library Special Revenue Fund. All income, monies, and other proceeds collected from any sale conducted by or with the assistance of the Friends of the Library shall be retained by the Friends of the Library. Notwithstanding the foregoing, all revenue, monies and other proceeds retained by the Friends of the Library shall be used solely for the providing, enhancement of library services offered by the New Port Richey Public Library (New Port Richey, Florida, Code of Ordinances, 2-166).

Multitype laws and legislation are often a collaboration among local governments with state regulation (Fiels, Neumann, and Brown, 1991).

State Library Agencies

The federal government is also important for governance. The federal program that provides funding to libraries is the Library Services and Technology Act (LSTA), a title of the Museum and Library Services Act of 2003. Other federal programs have an impact on various aspects of library service. Federal laws that relate to library issues such as privacy, copyright, and Internet filtering are examples. The LSTA, administered through IMLS, is the piece of federal legislation that impacts local public library funding most directly.

IMLS and State Libraries

The Library Services and Technology Act, the major source of federal funds for public libraries, first became law in 1996, and built upon previous federal library legislation (the Library Services Act and the Library Services and Construction Act). The LSTA takes a state-based approach to strengthening library services.[2] The 2003 reauthorization of Museum and Library Services Act (MLSA, Public Law 108-81) updates the purposes of the Library Services and Technology Act to promote improvements in library services in all types of libraries; to facilitate access to, and sharing of, resources; and to achieve economical and efficient delivery of service for the purpose of cultivating an educated and informed citizenry. It authorizes a doubling of the minimum state allotment under the Grants to States Library Agencies program. This is the Institute of Museum and Library Service's largest program and it helps to coordinate statewide library services and supports a wide array of programs from family literacy to providing broad access to sophisticated databases. It also develops the role of libraries as "information brokers" helping to make resources and services, which are often prohibitively expensive, more readily available (see Institute of Museum and Library Services).

Eligibility for LSTA funds requires that state library agencies submit five-year plans to IMLS. It is through the states' administration of LSTA funds that local plans are developed to conform to LSTA goals. Plans due in 2004 were expected to support LSTA goals in these ways: establish or enhance electronic linkages among or between libraries; link libraries electronically with educational, social, or information services; help libraries access information through electronic networks; encourage libraries in different areas and different types of libraries to establish consortia and share resources; pay costs for libraries to acquire or share computer systems and telecommunications technologies; and target library and information services to persons who have difficulty using a library and to underserved urban and rural communities.

State library agencies coordinate the development of state plans in collaboration with their state's library community to determine use of LSTA funds. For example, the California plan for 2002/3–2006/7 identified six key issues:

1. the economic gap between "haves" and "have nots";

2. increased diversity and growth of the population;

3. quality of education and literacy;

4. technology benefits and challenges;

5. partnership and collaboration; and

6. staying relevant—providing services and programs responsive to the community and having the community aware of them.

Related to these issues, remedies were identified and priority needs defined. An example of a need: "Californians need more access to quality education throughout their lives so that they can achieve their own life goals and be productive members of society," with suggested solutions—deployment of distance learning, functional literacy services, ongoing assessment of the education needs of the library's clientele, intergenerational library programs—provides mechanisms by which the state's libraries can respond with grant applications that provide solutions.

A review of state library plans provides a rich understanding of the variation of mission and goals configured to the needs of each state's people gained through a broad participatory approach. Plans include a description of stakeholder involvement, monitoring, and evaluation. The Chief Officers of State Library Agencies Web site (www.cosla.org) provides links to most current state plans.

Other Federal Legislation

Other Federal legislation (as well as the MLSA) is closely followed by the American Library Association, Washington Office of Government Relations. The Office advocates for the needs of the library community and provides librarians with information on government actions or proposals. Grassroots networks of librarians who will speak with lawmakers about library issues are fostered by events such as National Library Legislative Day, held each May in Washington, DC, to bring librarians, library board members, and library friends to advocate on behalf of libraries. This national event is the culmination of similar events at each state legislature.

Working with direction from the ALA Committee on Legislation the Office of Government Relations monitors issues and develops strategies as outlined each year in the "ALA Federal Legislative Policy." Areas of concern include intellectual freedom, the Freedom of Information Act, postal rates, Internet filtering, privacy, copyright, information technologies, and preservation. The scope of oversight extends to library issues in adult education, American folklife, literacy, and vocational education.

The most publicized recent involvement of libraries at the level of federal law has been the ALA's effort to prevent the linkage of universal service (e-rate) funding to Internet filtering. The Telecommunications Act of 1996 provides discounts in telecommunication costs to schools and libraries. The funding for universal service provides discounted access to the Internet for public libraries and schools. However, passage of the Children's Internet Protection Act (CIPA) and the Neighborhood Children's Internet Protection Act required libraries receiving federal funds to filter Internet access. The American Library Association challenged CIPA in Federal Court as unconstitutional and the case was heard at the Supreme Court (American Library Association, Web site on the Children's Internet Protection Act [CIPA]). The efforts of librarians regarding this Supreme Court case, *American Library Association v. U.S.* (02-361, 2003) demonstrate the library profession's commitment to monitoring all aspects of government policy that impact library service.

Articulation of Legal Considerations

Understanding the expansion of the legal basis of the U.S. public library over the last 150 years requires grounding in the continuum of government from the local to the federal level. Librarians interact most closely with the government of the community served, but state library agencies act as the link between local activity and the federal government through the collaborative development of state library plans. Through state library associations, programs sponsored by the state library agencies, and efforts by the American Library Association, support for public libraries is integrated across all levels of government. The activation involves citizens, who over-see the policies and growth of the library, through their collaborative service on library boards (Minow and Lipinski, 2003).

Library Funding

Local tax dollars primarily fund public libraries. State aid, fed-eral monies, and support from grants, local fundraising, and devel-opment efforts, also contribute to the total budget. In 2001 average public library per capita support was $30.02. Of this $23.20 was local, $3.82 state, $0.17 federal, and $2.82 from other sources (U.S. NCES). The range among states varied from $60.11 per capita (Ohio) to $13.42 (Mississippi).

While some of the difference in level of per capita support for libraries lies in variations of the income of residents, this does not account for all the differences. Texas, for example, has a median income for a family of four of $56,606 and ranks forty-fifth; Florida has a median income for a family of four of $56,824 but ranks thirty-first. Louisiana, with a far lower median income ($51,234), ranks twenty-eighth in library support (U.S. Census Bureau). No correlation exists between a state's income and its level of funding for libraries. These disparate statistics are the result of attitudes over time, zeal of trustees and advocates, and general governmental philosophy.

Local Funding

Local support comes in the form of taxation, which is either appropriated from a general fund, accrues from tax levies, or accrues from special earmarked tax revenues. The level of assess-ment that a property tax can generate is usually set forth in state law. The millage rate is the total number of mills (1 mill = 1/1000 of $1) being levied by each taxing authority. The property tax is, in the main, the primary support for public libraries. Thus, it is the work of the library board in collaboration with the library director and staff that—over time—provides the majority of funds for library operations. Successful strategies for tax campaigns for the support of public libraries are described by Turner (2000) and annual reports in *American Libraries* (Eberhart, 2004) provide an ongoing national progress report.

Library board members and Friends of Libraries also enhance local budgets through a variety of initiatives. These include fund-raising through library endowment development, book sales, and other philanthropic efforts. Friends of Libraries USA (FOLUSA) is a

Figure 5.3: Total Per Capita Operating Income of Public Libraries, by Source of Income and by State: Fiscal Year 2001

| State | Number of public libraries | Total per capita operating income,[1] by source | | | | | | | | | |
| | | Total | | Federal | | State | | Local | | Other | |
		Total	Response rate	Total	Response rate	Total	Response rate	Total	Response rate	Total	Response rate
50 States and DC[2]	9,129	30.02	95.9	0.17	96.4	3.82	96.5	23.20	96.3	2.82	96.2
Alabama	207	15.32	100.0	0.19	100.0	0.95	100.0	12.74	100.0	1.44	100.0
Alaska	86	37.77	100.0	0.92	100.0	1.25	100.0	33.70	100.0	1.90	100.0
Arizona	35	23.10	100.0	0.13	100.0	0.13	100.0	21.96	100.0	0.88	100.0
Arkansas	43	15.10	93.0	0.03	93.0	1.60	93.0	12.32	93.0	1.15	93.0
California	179	25.58	98.9	0.11	98.9	2.23	98.3	21.64	98.9	1.61	98.3
Colorado	116	40.11	100.0	0.05	98.3	0.97	99.1	35.18	100.0	3.90	99.1
Connecticut	194	43.05	92.3	0.08	92.3	0.61	92.3	34.60	92.8	7.76	92.3
Delaware	37	20.49	100.0	0.12	100.0	3.71	100.0	14.19	100.0	2.47	100.0
District of Columbia	1	49.97	100.0	0.96	100.0	0	100.0	47.19	100.0	1.82	100.0
Florida	72	23.49	97.2	0.18	97.2	2.13	97.2	19.78	97.2	1.41	97.2
Georgia	57	19.96	100.0	0.26	100.0	3.62	100.0	14.55	100.0	1.53	100.0
Hawaii3	1	19.71	100.0	0.74	100.0	17.75	100.0	0	100.0	1.22	100.0
Idaho	106	22.70	98.1	0.16	98.1	0.65	98.1	19.23	98.1	2.66	98.1
Illinois	629	45.26	99.4	0.25	99.7	3.31	99.7	36.92	99.4	4.78	99.7
Indiana	239	43.22	100.0	0.14	100.0	3.52	100.0	36.96	100.0	2.60	100.0
Iowa	537	25.08	98.3	0.20	98.5	0.77	98.5	21.90	98.3	2.22	98.5
Kansas	321	34.51	98.1	0.27	98.1	0.84	98.1	29.90	98.1	3.50	98.1
Kentucky	116	19.94	100.0	0.11	100.0	1.26	100.0	16.47	100.0	2.10	100.0

Total per capita operating income,[1] by source

State	Number of public libraries	Total		Federal		State		Local		Other	
		Total	Response rate	Total	Response rate	Total	Response rate	Total	Response rate	Total	Response rate
Louisiana	65	25.08	100.0	0.02	100.0	1.53	100.0	21.55	100.0	1.98	100.0
Maine	273	23.76	98.2	#	98.5	0.15	98.5	17.30	98.2	6.31	98.5
Maryland	24	35.40	100.0	0.36	100.0	4.72	100.0	24.79	100.0	5.53	100.0
Massachusetts	371	34.74	97.8	0.17	97.8	3.26	97.8	28.13	97.8	3.17	97.8
Michigan	381	33.17	100.0	0.06	100.0	1.62	100.0	27.99	100.0	3.51	100.0
Minnesota4	140	30.37	0	0.13	0	2.03	0	26.22	0	1.99	0
Mississippi	49	13.42	100.0	0.27	100.0	2.54	100.0	9.57	100.0	1.04	100.0
Missouri	150	30.09	88.7	0.37	92.0	0.77	94.7	25.68	93.3	3.26	93.3
Montana	79	17.13	100.0	0.05	100.0	0.38	100.0	14.50	100.0	2.20	100.0
Nebraska	272	28.16	82.0	0.22	82.0	0.39	82.0	26.07	82.0	1.49	82.0
Nevada	23	31.47	100.0	0.39	100.0	0.26	100.0	20.86	100.0	9.96	100.0
New Hampshire	229	29.06	94.8	0.04	97.8	0.03	95.6	26.02	95.2	2.97	94.8
New Jersey	309	37.89	93.9	0.18	93.9	1.17	93.9	34.49	93.9	2.05	93.9
New Mexico	80	18.47	93.8	0.14	92.5	0.32	93.8	16.75	93.8	1.26	93.8
New York	750	51.00	100.0	0.22	100.0	2.88	100.0	39.75	100.0	8.15	100.0
North Carolina	76	19.34	100.0	0.16	100.0	2.22	100.0	14.99	100.0	1.97	100.0
North Dakota	82	16.03	100.0	0.14	100.0	1.02	100.0	12.25	100.0	2.62	100.0
Ohio	250	60.11	100.0	0.10	100.0	43.96	100.0	11.14	100.0	4.91	100.0
Oklahoma	115	22.43	90.4	0.11	90.4	0.63	90.4	19.72	90.4	1.97	90.4
Oregon	125	36.16	98.4	0.37	100.0	0.23	99.2	33.16	98.4	2.40	97.6

Figure 5.3 continued. Total Per Capita Operating Income of Public Libraries

Total per capita operating income,[1] by source

State	Number of public libraries	Total		Federal		State		Local		Other	
		Total	Response rate	Total	Response rate	Total	Response rate	Total	Response rate	Total	Response rate
Pennsylvania	459	23.10	100.0	0.22	100.0	6.09	100.0	13.28	100.0	3.51	100.0
Rhode Island	48	34.70	97.9	0.16	97.9	5.75	97.9	21.82	97.9	6.97	97.9
South Carolina	41	18.90	100.0	0.16	100.0	1.74	100.0	16.05	100.0	0.95	100.0
South Dakota	126	25.19	69.0	0.28	73.8	0	84.1	23.23	83.3	1.67	81.0
Tennessee	184	13.82	100.0	0.08	100.0	0.27	100.0	12.22	100.0	1.25	100.0
Texas	540	16.50	100.0	0.16	100.0	0.09	100.0	15.59	100.0	0.66	100.0
Utah	70	25.49	100.0	0.16	100.0	0.41	100.0	23.55	100.0	1.37	100.0
Vermont	188	23.25	92.6	0	100.0	0.07	99.5	16.16	93.6	7.01	92.6
Virginia	90	28.23	100.0	0.20	100.0	2.99	100.0	23.13	100.0	1.90	100.0
Washington	65	39.91	95.4	0.13	100.0	0.25	96.9	37.82	100.0	1.71	92.3
West Virginia	97	14.97	96.9	0.19	100.0	4.63	99.0	8.52	100.0	1.63	97.9
Wisconsin	379	30.90	99.7	0.16	99.7	0.98	100.0	27.71	100.0	2.05	100.0
Wyoming	23	31.88	100.0	0.15	100.0	0.01	100.0	29.22	100.0	2.50	100.0
Outlying Areas											
Guam	1	7.85	100.0	0.35	100.0	0	100.0	7.50	100.0	0	100.0
Virgin Islands	1	24.06	100.0	0.85	100.0	0	100.0	23.21	100.0	0	100.0

Figure 5.3 continued. Total Per Capita Operating Income of Public Libraries

Rounds to zero.
1 Per capita is based on the total unduplicated population of legal service areas. Per capita operating income by source may not sum to total due to rounding. Income is referred to as revenue in other NCES fiscal surveys.
2 50 States and DC totals exclude outlying areas.
3 Hawaii did not receive any operating income from local sources.
4 Nonrespondent (all data are imputed).

NOTE: Detail may not sum to totals because of rounding. Response rate is the percentage of libraries for which the specific item and a nonzero value for population of legal service area were reported. Items with response rates below 100 percent include imputations for nonresponse. Data were not reported by the following outlying areas: American Samoa, Northern Marianas, Palau, and Puerto Rico.

SOURCE: U.S. Department of Education, National Center for Education Statistics, Federal-State Cooperative System (FSCS) for Public Library Data, Public Libraries Survey, Fiscal Year 2001.

Figure 5.3 continued. Total Per Capita Operating Income of Public Libraries

national organization that assists library friends and advocacy groups in developing capacity for fundraising to enhance library development. FOLUSA consists of over 2,000 members united to be effective library advocates.

State Funding

State funding varies greatly. Among the variety of methods are equalization grants, funding incentives, per capita support for direct service, materials grants, or lump sum grants. Others provide funding for competitive grants, interlibrary loan, or construction. Multitype services supporting collaborative or cooperative projects that will extend and support services are also funded. No one has written a straightforward overview of methods used by state library agencies to distribute funds (Himmel, Wilson, and DeCandido, 2000: 13–14). Schaefer made this point clearly in a 2001 study about fund distribution among state libraries. Most state library agencies require that public libraries meet compliance requirements (i.e., hours of service, paid employees, submission of annual reports and statistical data) and then generally distribute state aid funds based on level of compliance. This process establishes minimum levels of public library service within a state.

Federal Funding

Federal funds for local public libraries are primarily administered through state library agencies as LSTA funds. There are two overriding priorities: information access through technology and the provision of information access through empowerment. In 2003, for example, grants of $150 million were made to the states for public libraries according to a population-based formula. States used funds as laid out in respective state plans for a variety of projects including access to technology, early childhood education, family literacy, and workforce readiness. Additional grants under other categories can be sought.

Bertot, McClure, and Ryan (2002) underscore the importance of the state library agencies in coordinating LSTA funds and e-rate procedures.

Foundation Funding

Public and private foundations also provide funding for public libraries. Private foundations generally award grants for special projects or demonstrations. The Gates Program—the largest Foundation award to public libraries since the Carnegie building grants in the early-twentieth century—brought 40,000 computers to libraries in all 50 states increasing computer access to all U.S. residents, with a focus on the most impoverished, between 1997 and 2003.[3] Public libraries can benefit from grants made directly to them from specific foundations or through foundation supported projects of broader scope. One source of information on foundation opportunities is accessible to readers at The Foundation Center (available: http://fdncenter.org), which promotes public understanding of the field and helps grant seekers succeed.

Community foundations are public charities that are nonprofit, tax-exempt, publicly supported, grant-making organizations. They develop broad support from many unrelated donors with a wide range of charitable interests in a specific community. The Community Foundations of America and the Council on Foundations provide resources for working with local community foundations. A Libraries for the Future report noted that 75 percent of community foundations support public library initiatives.

Libraries and the Political Process

Public libraries exist within a nested and overlapping structure of local, regional, state, and national political entities. At each level libraries must work hard to educate policymakers about the fiscal and legal needs of libraries. From the enactment of the first laws for tax-supported libraries in the 1850s to the struggle to de-link universal funds from filtering mandates in 2003, the political process has been central to the progress of libraries. E. J. Josey edited a series of books on the library and the political process that laid out the intricate and interlocking effort that librarians must make to ensure that politicians understand the needs of libraries. ALA Presidents such as Pat Schuman have made advocacy the centerpiece of their presidential year and written compellingly about the librarians' role in the political process (1999).

The American Library Association Public Awareness Advisory Committee has developed online toolkits for advocacy, workshops, and programs in concert with its Washington Office of Governmental Relations. Briefings on key topics are prepared to assist in explaining library issues to policymakers. The national legislative day is held each year in May to bring librarians, library trustees, board members, and other library friends to Washington, DC, to talk with their representatives and senators about issues of concern to the library community. The Public Awareness Committee oversees National Library Week and coordinates the ALA Public Relations Assembly. Each state chapter holds advocacy workshops and a state legislative day.

Public libraries have been effective in gaining funding and support at the local, state, and federal level. The "Campaign for America's Libraries" launched by ALA in 2001 integrates various public relations initiatives ("Advocacy Grows@Your Library"). In 2004 the Public Library Association launched a new initiative during the PLA National Conference demonstrating the ongoing effort to establish the importance of public libraries through national marketing campaigns. John E. Buschman raises some penetrating questions about such programs, which focus on marketing, in his essay on ALA's drift toward the corporate model (2003: 131–147). The challenge for librarians in this century is to develop effective public relations that do not give over to a heedless business model.

Notes

1. Public Library Association, *Library Extension Legislation* (Chicago: American Library Association, 1940); Library Extension Board, *Regional and District Laws* (Chicago: American Library Association, 1942); American Library Association, *American Library Laws* (Chicago: American Library Association) 1930; 1943; 1962 and supplements 1965–1970; 1972 and supplements 1972–1978; 1983. For current legislation, see Chief Officers of State Library Agencies (COSLA), available: www.cosla.org. Some states, such as New York, have compiled statutes and regulations. See Robert Allen Carter, *Public Library Law in New York State* (New York: New York State Library, 1999).

2. The historical development of federal legislation is important to public libraries. For analysis of the LSA and LSCA, see James W. Fry, "LSA and LSCA, 1956–1973: A Legislative History," *Library Trends* 24 (July 1975): 7–28; Jules Mersel, *An Overview of the Library Services and Construction Act, Title 1* (New York: R. R. Bowker, 1969); Edward Gailon Holley, *The Library Services and Construction Act: An Historical Overview from the Viewpoint of Major Participants* (Greenwich, CT: JAI Press, 1983).

3. Several sources provide information on the role and impact of the Gates Foundation on public libraries. See *The Public Access to Computing Project* (available: www.pacp.net/LJ_PAGE_1.html);

Andrew C. Gordon, et al., "The Gates Legacy," *Library Journal* (March 1, 2003): 44–48; and the Bill and Melinda Gates Foundation Web site (available: www.gatesfoundation.org).

References

A National Plan for Libraries. 1935. *ALA Bulletin* 29 (February): 91–98.

A National Plan for Libraries. 1939. *ALA Bulletin* 33 (February): 136–150.

Advocacy Grows@Your Library. 2004. *American Libraries* 35 (February): 32–36.

Alliance for Regional Stewardship. Available: www.regionalstewardship.org.

American Library Association. Washington Office. Available: www.ala.org/washoff. Also available on the Children's Internet Protection Act (CIPA) Web site: www.ala.org/cipa.

Bertot, John Carlo, Charles R. McClure, and Joe Ryan. 2002. Impact of External Technology Funding Programs for Public Libraries: A Study of LSTA, E-Rate, Gates and Others. *Public Libraries* 41 (May-June): 166–171.

Bill and Melinda Gates Foundation. Libraries. Available: www.gatesfoundation.org/libraries (accessed November 2, 2003).

Brawner, Lee. 1993. The People's Choice. *Library Journal* (January): 59–62.

Buschman, John E. 2003. *Dismantling the Public Sphere: Situating and Sustaining Librarianship in the Age of the New Public Philosophy.* Westport, CT: Libraries Unlimited.

California State Library. *California Statewide Plan for Use of Library Services and Technology Funds 2002/03–2006–07.* Available: www.library.ca.gov/assets/acrobat/STATE_PLAN_02-07.pdf (accessed November 6, 2003).

Chief Officers of State Library Agencies (COSLA). Available: www.cosla.org.

Coffman, Steve. 2004. Saving Ourselves: Plural Funding for Public Libraries. *American Libraries* 35 (February): 37–39.

Community Foundations of America. Available: www.cfamerica.org/index.cfm.

Council on Foundations. Community Foundations. Available: www.cof.org.

Eberhart, George M. 2004. Referenda Roundup. *American Libraries* 35 (January): 18–23.

Fiels, Keith Michael, Joan Neumann, and Eva R. Brown. 1991. *Multitype Library Cooperation State Laws, Regulations and Pending Legislation.* Chicago: Association of Specialized and Cooperative Library Agencies.

Foundation Center. Available: http://fdncenter.org.

Friends of Libraries USA (FOLUSA). Available: www.folusa.org.

Garceau, Oliver. 1949. *The Public Library in the Political Process: A Report of the Public Library Inquiry.* New York: Columbia University Press.

GEOLIB. Available: www.geolib.org.

Gordon, Andrew C., et al. 2003. The Gates Legacy. *Library Journal* (March 1): 44–48.

Held, Ray E. 1973. *The Rise of the Public Library in California.* Chicago: American Library Association.

Hennen, Thomas J., Jr. 2002. Are Wider Library Units Wiser? *American Libraries* 33.6 (June/July): 65–70. (Also titled, Wider and Wiser Units.) Available: www.haplr-index.com/wider_and_wiser_units.htm.

Herrera, L. 2003. It's Our Turn. *Public Libraries* 42 (November/December): 343.

Himmel, Ethel E., William J. Wilson, and GraceAnne DeCandido. 2000. *The Functions and Roles of State Library Agencies*. Chicago: American Library Association.

Institute of Museum and Library Services. Available: www.imls.gov/index.htm. See the IMLS Web page on "Grants to State Library Agencies" at: www.imls.gov/grants/library/lib_gsla.asp.

Joeckel, Carleton Bruns. 1935. *The Government of the American Public Library*. Chicago: University of Chicago Press.

Josey, E. J. 1980. *Libraries and the Political Process*. New York: Neal-Schuman Publishers.

Josey, E. J. 1987. *Libraries, Coalitions and the Public Good*. New York: Neal-Schuman Publishers.

Josey, E. J. and Kenneth D. Shearer. 1990. *Politics and the Support of Libraries*. New York: Neal-Schuman Publishers.

Krane, Dale, Platon N. Rigos, and Melvin Hill, Jr. 2001. *Home Rule in America: a Fifty State Handbook*. Washington, DC: CQ Press.

Krois, Jerome W. 2002. An Introduction to Public Library Foundations: A Members Guide. *The Unabashed Librarian* 122: 22–26.

Ladenson, Alex. 1970. Library Legislation: Some General Considerations. *Library Trends* 19 (October): 175–181.

Ladenson, Alex. 1982. *Library Law and Legislation in the United States*. Metuchen, NJ: Scarecrow Press.

Libraries for the Future. Community Foundations and the Public Library. Available: www.lff.org/research/community.html.

Minow, Mary, and Tomas A. Lipinski. 2003. *The Library's Legal Answer Book*. Chicago: American Library Association.

National Association of Counties. Available: www.naco.org/Template.cfm?Section=About_NACo.

National Governors Association. Available: www.nga.org/nga/1,1169,,00.html.

The Public Access to Computing Project: Legacy of Gates U.S. Library Project. Available: www.pacp.net/LJ_PAGE_1.html.

Reed, Sally Gardner. 2004. FOLUSA Turns 25. *American Libraries* 35 (February): 40–41.

Schaefer, Steve W. 2001. Going for the Green: How Public Libraries get State Money. *Public Libraries* 40 (September/October): 298–304.

Schuman, Patricia. 1999. Speaking Up and Speaking Out: Ensuring Equity Through Advocacy. *American Libraries* 30 (October): 50–53.

Turner, Anne M. 2000. *Vote Yes for Libraries: A Guide to Winning Ballot Measure Campaigns for Library Funding*. Jefferson, NC: McFarland and Co.

U.S. Census Bureau. Median Income of Four-Person Families By State. Available: www.census.gov/hhes/income/4person.html.

U.S. Conference of Mayors. Available: www.usmayors.org.

U.S. Department of Education. National Center for Education Statistics. 2003. Public Libraries in the United States. Fiscal Year 2001. E. D. TABS, ed. Adrienne Chute, et al. Available: http://nces.ed.gov/pubsearch/pubsinfo.asp?pubid=2003399 (accessed November 17, 2003).

U.S. National Center for Education Statistics. Public Libraries Data. Available: http://nces.ed.gov/pubsearch/pubsinfo.asp?pubid=2003399 (accessed November 2, 2003).

6

Administration and Staffing

The people employed in the public library are central to the library's fulfillment of its mission. Library workers activate the use of collections, develop community partnerships, and provide the one-on-one service that supports lifelong learning to people of all ages. It takes many people—the library board, library workers, and volunteers—working together to put in place a library that functions as the community's commons.

This chapter presents model organizational charts. It pays attention to the composition and responsibilities of the library board, with consideration of the need to achieve greater diversity. It also provides details about the characteristics of the library director. Based on aggregated national data, this chapter addresses the organization of the library staff. In addition, it describes broad issues such as recruitment, staff development, and the role of unions. Finally, it identifies the role of library volunteers.

Organizational Structures

Librarians must conceive of the administration and staffing of public libraries in the context of overall organizational structure,

135

which exist as a function of municipal, county, or district governance. Public service and civil service structures specify the particular conditions of employment, and due to their local nature, they differ from community to community. The library director most often reports to a library board that is authorized by state statute. There are many variations on the organizational structure of the public library, but two examples—Concord, Massachusetts (population 16,000) and Akron-Summit County, Ohio (population 540,000)—demonstrate the variety of U.S. public library organization.

The Akron-Summit County Public Library (Ohio) provides a very clear example of organization and governance consisting of a central library, seventeen branches and bookmobile/van services. Figure 6.1a depicts the Akron-Summit County Public Library (Ohio) organization chart with the line of authority to the board of trustees. Figure 6.1b shows the Concord Free Public Library (Massachusetts), which reports to a library committee.

Library Boards

Oversight of most public libraries in the United States is by a board of citizens—usually called a board of trustees or directors, but characterized here simply as the "library board." This citizen body has its roots in the structure of the Boston Public Library and parallels the school board in many ways. The enabling legislation for public libraries in each state generally specifies the composition and method of appointment of the library board. Commonly appointed by a governing body, but sometimes elected, the library board has responsibility for a range of functions:

- Analysis of community needs
- Hiring or recommending the director
- Acting in an advocacy role to develop community support for bond issues and taxation
- Budget review and approval
- Policy review and approval
- Commitment to freedom of inquiry and expression
- Formulation of long-range planning

Library board members are supported by national and state level associations in developing intellectual and philosophical aspects of service. The ALA Association for Library Trustees and

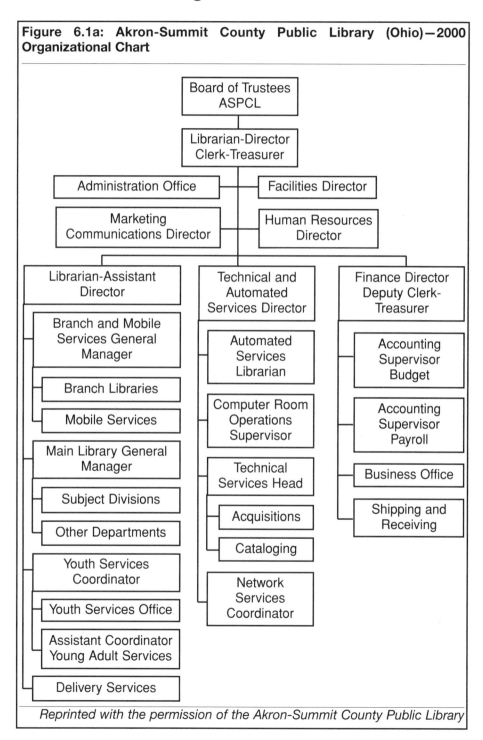

Figure 6.1a: Akron-Summit County Public Library (Ohio)—2000 Organizational Chart

Reprinted with the permission of the Akron-Summit County Public Library

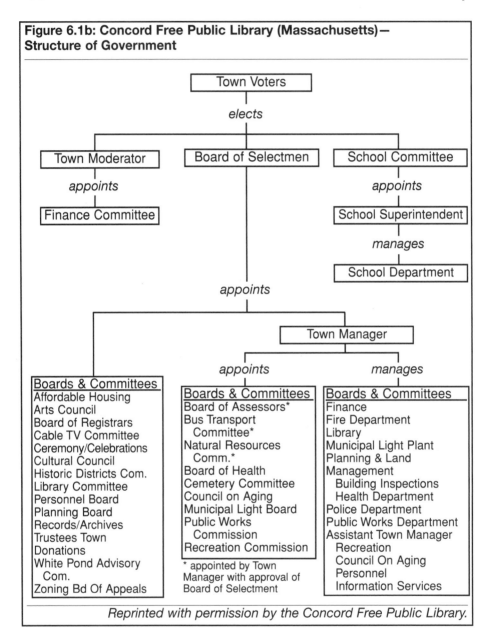

Figure 6.1b: Concord Free Public Library (Massachusetts)—Structure of Government

Town Voters

elects

Town Moderator · Board of Selectmen · School Committee

appoints · *appoints*

Finance Committee · School Superintendent

manages

School Department

appoints

Town Manager

appoints · *manages*

Boards & Committees
Affordable Housing
Arts Council
Board of Registrars
Cable TV Committee
Ceremony/Celebrations
Cultural Council
Historic Districts Com.
Library Committee
Personnel Board
Planning Board
Records/Archives
Trustees Town
Donations
White Pond Advisory
Com.
Zoning Bd Of Appeals

Boards & Committees
Board of Assessors*
Bus Transport
Committee*
Natural Resources
Comm.*
Board of Health
Cemetery Committee
Council on Aging
Municipal Light Board
Public Works
Commission
Recreation Commission

* appointed by Town
Manager with approval of
Board of Selectment

Boards & Committees
Finance
Fire Department
Library
Municipal Light Plant
Planning & Land
Management
Building Inspections
Health Department
Police Department
Public Works Department
Assistant Town Manager
Recreation
Council On Aging
Personnel
Information Services

Reprinted with permission by the Concord Free Public Library.

Advocates (ALTA), founded in 1890, offers educational programs dedicated to excellence in trusteeship. ALTA has approved the "Ethics Statement for Public Library Trustees" (Figure 6.2), which includes support to the fullest of the efforts of librarians in resisting censorship of library materials.

Figure 6.2: Ethics Statement for Public Library Trustees

Voice of
America's
Library
Trustees

Trustees in the capacity of trust upon them, shall observe ethical standards with absolute truth, integrity and honor.

Trustees must avoid situations in which personal interests might be served or financial benefits gained at the expense of library users, colleagues, or the situation.

It is incumbent upon any trustee to disqualify himself/herself immediately whenever the appearance or a conflict of interest exists.

Trustees must distinguish clearly in their actions and statements between their personal philosophies and attitudes and those of the institution, acknowledging the formal position of the board even if they personally disagree.

A trustee must respect the confidential nature of library business while being aware of and in compliance with applicable laws governing freedom of information.

Trustees must be prepared to support to the fullest the efforts of librarians in resisting censorship of library materials by groups or individuals.

Trustees who accept library board responsibilities are expected to perform all of the functions of library trustees.

Adopted by the Board of Directors of the American Library Trustee Association, July, 1985.

Adopted by the Board of Directors of the Public Library Association, July, 1985.

Amended by the Board of Directors of the American Library Trustee Association, July, 1988.

Approval of the amendment by the Board of Directors of the Public Library Association, January, 1989.

American Library Trustee Association (ALTA) a division of the American Library Association. 50 E. Huron St. .Chicago. IL 60611 telephone 312-280-2161 • toll-free 800-545-2433 ext. 2161 • fax 312-280-3257

State library associations and state library agencies also provide programs for library board members, which focus on state issues and organize programs, produce handbooks, and provide other means of support for the work of shared governance. The members of the library board articulate the importance of the library to the general public; therefore, board members' recognition of local and state issues is essential. Each state develops support that reflects its context. For instance, the purposes of the Nebraska Trustee section of the Nebraska Library Association is to bring adequate library service to all Nebraskans through promotion and study of legislation, to encourage adequate funding and to encourage citizen support.

It makes good sense for all public librarians to be aware of their state's efforts to develop strong library boards. The Wisconsin Division for Libraries, Technology, and Community Leaning publishes *Trustee Essentials* (2002), a handbook that includes a job description that succinctly defines the library board member's function: "Participate as a member of a team (the library board) to protect and advance the interests of the broader community by effectively governing the operations and promoting the development of the local public library." The Illinois Trustee Facts (Shaw) identifies key elements that should be provided to new Trustees to enable them to fulfill their roles: board policies; board bylaws; board organization; current library budget; minutes and treasurer reports of at least six months prior to their appointment; state public library standards; library organization chart; a list of library acronyms; and state laws.

The demographic composition of library boards has tended to be fairly homogeneous over time. In his classic 1949 study of boards for the *Public Library Inquiry*, Garceau observed that boards were generally comprised of older, middle-class members of the community. A half-century later Kelley's (1999) study of library trustees in Illinois sent to 4,800 trustees found 70 percent were women, 50 percent were over 55, and occupations were primarily professional (e.g., accounting, banking, education, public service). It is the persistence and advocacy of library boards that provide the community support for building programs, increased taxes or even new operational structures. The Illinois survey found that the state's trustees contributed over 250,000 hours of time in a single year. Although effort has been made to reflect the diversity of communities in library board composition, professional class individuals primarily populate library boards. To recruit library board members that reflect the changing demographics of the United States will require much work; boards greatly need more people from diverse ethnic groups.

We can identify various examples of the dynamic nature of trustee efforts, for instance, in the story of a county rural district formed in Stevens County in Washington state (Hague, 1999), or in a trustee's view of a campaign to pass a library bond issue in New York (Glennon), or in Louisiana trustee Jeanne T. Kreamer's credo on trustee activism (1990). The library board member's contagious enthusiasm and hope is emblematic of the committed dedicated citizen, who has worked side-by-side with librarians to establish, develop, and strengthen library services. Libraries are not mandated by law; they are enabled and voluntary—the roots are nurtured and rise from the people. In addition to the focus on trustee support by the state library agencies and professional state and national library associations, there is a broad literature that helps librarians and trustees develop service.

The Library Director

The library director works closely with the library board to realize the public library mission, develop long-range plans, and implement policies for the library's operations. The director works at the nexus of community and staff. Directors are expected to handle numerous responsibilities, such as the following:

- lead the planning cycles
- organize human resources
- represent the library in the community
- oversee financial operations
- interact with local, state, and national library entities
- develop the library's fiscal base through development and fund-raising
- manage facilities and technology
- plan, design, and evaluate services

Don Sager, president of an executive search and management firm, summarizes the knowledge and skills required by public library directors in his 2001 article. They include these characteristics:

- People skills. Participation in a wide range of community, social, and professional organizations. Experience with collaborative activities and team-centered projects and proficiency in working successfully with diverse groups.

- Vision. Insight into the role the library will play in the future and ability to lead the organization in that direction.

- Marketing Ability. Someone who can sell a new vision of library service to the community.

- Communication. The ability to articulate vision to governance, staff, the public, and funding authorities. Superior writing and public speaking ability and effective use of new technology, as well as creative promotional techniques including representation of the institution in the broadcast media.

- Collaborative Skills. Strength and experience in partnering with a variety of different institutions and groups; skill in forging coalitions with other influential groups in the community; political savvy in gaining the trust of elected officials; team-building talent in marshalling the support of boards, staff, and users; and results-oriented collaborations.

- Technical Skills. Skill in recommending policies for effective use of computers, the Internet, and other, newer resources such as e-books. How to evaluate the impact of new information formats, how to train staff and the public in the latest hardware and software, and how to fund and prepare for the next generation of technology.

- Customer Service Skills. Listening to library users and potential users and seeking feedback.

- Problem-Solving Ability. Faced with challenges to Internet access, diminishing budgets, and an increasingly diverse service base, public library directors with a track record of tackling difficult issues will be sought.

- Risk-Taking. Integrity, courage, and a thick skin are required for the director who must be increasingly innovative.

- Self-Renewal. Astute candidates recognize that the demands of leadership require a personal plan for professional growth. Those who acknowledge this are likely to endure.

Analysis of current position announcements for library director positions demonstrates that library boards value experience with multicultural communities, knowledge of current and developing technologies, understanding of the importance of community involvement, as well as experience working with an advisory board and community groups and elected officials. Figure 6.3, a 2004 announcement

Figure 6.3: Job Description: Executive Librarian

Executive Librarian

Arlington Heights Memorial Library

The Board of Trustees seeks an executive librarian to take charge of this enthusiastically supported public library serving a community of 76,000 in the northwest suburbs of Chicago. The Arlington Heights Memorial Library has a long tradition of strong funding, excellent customer service, and high use. Residents borrow 1.8 million items a year from a collection of 440,000 items. A staff of 200 works in the 132,000-square-foot building. With stable financing and "home rule" taxing authority, the library board sets its own budget, currently $10 million.

The next successful executive will be a collaborative leader and an outstanding communicator capable of inspiring creative patron service in addition to managing finances and technology. Your own vision of excellence and positive handling of challenges will be supported by a strong organization already in place to maintain the high level of service the library's patrons have long enjoyed. You will be working with a library board that consistently supports intellectual freedom and encourages staff participation in the professional library community.

The successful candidate should have an MLS degree from an ALA-accredited program, 10 or more years of public library experience, including a minimum of 5 years as a director or progressively responsible administrative experience in a public library or public library system. The starting salary is negotiable from $100,000, plus excellent benefits.

This ad appeared in the March 2004 issue of *American Libraries* magazine.

for Executive Librarian at Arlington Heights, Illinois, Public Library, is an example. Library directors are expected to be leaders with strong interpersonal, communication, staff development, and customer-service skills.

Organization of the Public Library Staff

Current practice in staffing libraries is more likely to be structured in response to community needs than ever before. Libraries bridge traditional divisions between technical and public services positions by changing technologies, modify divisions through access to external databases, and reconfigure divisions depending on the local situation. The same is true of the composition of staff in terms

Figure 6.4: Examples of Current Position Announcements for Public Library Staff

---

LIBRARIAN, FAMILY AND YOUTH SERVICES. The City of Newport News Public Library System, located in southeastern Virginia, seeks a librarian for family and youth services. The librarian will work with fellow branch staff, families, and children from preschool through young adult and should be knowledgeable of youth literature and collection-development philosophy and methods. This position plans and implements branch-specific preschool, children's, young-adult, and family programs. THIS POSITION REQUIRES knowledge of and a strong interest in working with children and teenagers, and knowledge of computers and information services. Works under the direction of the branch manager and provides assistance with implementing the library system's long-range plan for family and youth services.

BRANCH MANAGER. The West Haven Public Library, West Haven, Connecticut, is seeking a dynamic, full-time (35 hours) branch manager. West Haven is a coastal community, population of 52,000, with miles of beautiful oceanfront and suburban to New York City. The branch manager will be responsible for the daily operations while providing direct service to the neighborhood. DUTIES INCLUDE planning and supervising the work of staff; the ability to provide reference service and readers' advisory; programming and outreach; the ability to select and deselect adult and juvenile collection for the branch; overseeing the physical maintenance of the facility; and budget responsibility for the branch. The branch manager must have computer literacy, good oral and written communication and interpersonal skills, customer service skills, and the ability to identify needs and develop services accordingly.

HEAD OF CATALOGING - LIBRARIAN VI. Duties/Responsibilities: Supervises 25+ staff (including 12 Professionals) in a union environment. Directs cataloging activities for Cleveland Public Library and CLEVNET Consortium. Manages workflow for cataloging 7,000 titles and adding 30,000 copies per month. Serves as primary liaison for OLC and other utilities. Provides leadership for migration to SIRSI Unicorn and recommends solutions to developing migration challenges. Plans and implements technological improvements. Participates in local, regional, national cataloging projects and organizations.

WEB LIBRARIAN. (Charleston County Public Library, South Carolina) is responsible for designing and developing Web pages for the Library's Web presence; creating and delivering continuing education workshops on library technology trends, library applications as available on the local integrated online system, and office automation applications as they apply to the library staff and use by the general public; providing support of library equipment, software, and local area networks; developing and enhancing the technology skills of subordinates and co-workers; preparing statistical reports as requested; answering inquiries regarding equipment and software; carrying out research for Library Administration; and under the direction of the Library Technology Management Administrator, directing up to four subordinate staff supporting internal library e-mail applications, hardware/software repair/replacement, and producing pre-defined reports.

REQUIREMENTS: Master's degree in Library Science from an ALA-accredited library science program or equivalent combination of training and experience. Considerable knowledge of theories and principles of library science; considerable knowledge of library automation concepts and workflow, including circulation, reference, cataloging, and materials purchasing procedures; considerable understanding of computer networking principles, both local and wide-area networks; considerable knowledge of Web page design, and experience in use of Web page development tools; considerable knowledge of building and site preparation related to automation, networking, and telecommunications equipment; considerable skill in using common library machines; considerable skill in using library automated systems; considerable knowledge of modern business management and human resource management principles; considerable knowledge of program planning and execution; considerable skill in creating and delivering technology workshops to the staff and public; considerable skill in communicating effectively with people of varying backgrounds and ages.

Figure 6.4 continued. Position Announcements

of those with the ALA-accredited degree and other staff. The ALA accredits masters-level graduate programs that educate librarians using *Standards for Accreditation* to serve as a mechanism for quality assessment and quality enhancement. The "Library and Information Studies and Human Resource Utilization" policy of the ALA provides guidance as to education and articulation of positions within libraries. Issues relating to interests of support staff are addressed by the ALA within the Library Support Staff Interests Round Table.

While announcements for public library employment still reflect the need for positions that are public service (reference, readers' advisory, youth) or technical service (cataloging, acquisitions, systems) in substance, the on-the-job expectations are more often for a convergence of public and technical skills. New positions such as Web Librarian emerged during the 1990s. See Figure 6.4 for examples of job postings in 2003–2004.

Figure 6.5: Total number of paid full-time equivalent (FTE) staff and paid FTE librarians per 25,000 population of public libraries: Fiscal year 2001

State	Ranking	Total paid FTE staff per 25,000 population [1]	State	Ranking	Paid FTE librarians per 25,000 population
50 States and DC	†	12.18	50 States and DC	†	4.06
Ohio	1	21.66	New Hampshire	1	8.39
Kansas	2	19.42	Nebraska	2	7.72
Indiana	3	19.32	Wyoming	2	7.72
New York	4	18.30	Vermont	4	7.68
Wyoming	5	17.65	Iowa	5	7.11
Connecticut	6	17.07	Massachusetts	6	7.10
Illinois	7	16.12	Connecticut	7	7.07
Massachusetts	8	15.63	Maine	8	6.47
District of Columbia [2]	9	15.30	District of Columbia [2]	9	6.38
New Jersey	10	15.14	Ohio	10	6.07
Rhode Island	11	15.04	New York	11	5.99
Maine	12	14.64	Illinois	12	5.98
New Hampshire	13	14.63	Indiana	13	5.85
Maryland	14	14.62	Kansas	14	5.70
Nebraska	15	14.53	South Dakota	15	5.65
South Dakota	16	14.40	Maryland	16	5.52
Colorado	17	14.33	Wisconsin	17	5.42
Washington	18	13.87	Rhode Island	18	5.19
Oregon	19	13.72	Kentucky	19	4.89
Wisconsin	20	13.67	Alaska	20	4.80
Iowa	21	13.38	North Dakota	21	4.77
Missouri	22	13.21	Colorado	22	4.65
Vermont	23	12.90	Montana	23	4.61
Alaska	23	12.90	Louisiana	24	4.57
Idaho	25	12.70	New Jersey	25	4.48
Minnesota [3]	26	12.14	Michigan	26	4.47
Michigan	27	11.80	West Virginia	27	4.38

Virginia	28	11.68	Oklahoma	28	4.32
Louisiana	29	11.67	Oregon	29	4.12
Utah	30	11.00	Idaho	30	3.93
Mississippi	31	10.78	New Mexico	31	3.92
Hawaii	32	10.73	Minnesota [3]	32	3.91
Pennsylvania	33	10.40	Missouri	33	3.68
New Mexico	34	9.76	Alabama	34	3.65
Florida	35	9.70	Washington	35	3.55
Kentucky	36	9.66	Pennsylvania	36	3.38
Nevada	37	9.62	Mississippi	37	3.37
South Carolina	38	9.61	Hawaii	38	3.30
West Virginia	38	9.61	Virginia	39	3.26
Oklahoma	40	9.57	Utah	40	3.03
Arizona	41	9.47	Florida	41	3.02
North Dakota	42	9.16	South Carolina	41	3.02
North Carolina	43	8.98	Arizona	43	2.80
Montana	44	8.90	Tennessee	44	2.75
Alabama	45	8.69	Delaware	45	2.62
Georgia	46	8.66	Texas	46	2.60
California	47	8.39	Nevada	47	2.50
Tennessee	48	8.28	California	48	2.46
Texas	48	8.28	Georgia	49	2.17
Delaware	50	7.71	Arkansas	49	2.17
Arkansas	51	7.55	North Carolina	51	2.00

[†] Not applicable.

[1] Per 25,000 population is based on the total unduplicated population of legal service areas.

[2] The District of Columbia, while not a state, is included in the state rankings. Special care should be used in comparing its data to state data.

[3] Nonrespondent (all data are imputed).

SOURCE: U.S. Department of Education, National Center for Education Statistics, Federal-State Cooperative System (FSCS) for Public Library Data, Public Libraries Survey, Fiscal Year 2001.

Figure 6.5 continued. Total number of FTE staff and paid FTE librarians

Figure 6.6: Number of paid full-time equivalent (FTE) librarians with ALA-MLS and other paid FTE staff per 25,000 population of public libraries: Fiscal Year 2001

State	Ranking	Paid FTE librarians with ALA-MLS per 25,000 population [1]	State	Ranking	Other paid FTE staff per 25,000 population
50 States and DC	†	2.75	50 States and DC	†	8.13
Connecticut	1	5.25	Ohio	1	15.59
New York	2	5.08	Kansas	2	13.72
District of Columbia[2]	3	4.55	Indiana	3	13.47
Rhode Island	4	4.48	New York	4	12.31
New Jersey	5	4.44	New Jersey	5	10.66
Massachusetts	6	4.35	Washington	6	10.32
Ohio	7	4.23	Illinois	7	10.14
Indiana	8	3.82	Connecticut	8	10.00
Illinois	9	3.70	Wyoming	9	9.93
Hawaii	10	3.30	Rhode Island	10	9.85
Washington	11	3.17	Colorado	11	9.68
Michigan	12	3.11	Oregon	12	9.61
Colorado	13	3.05	Missouri	13	9.52
Maine	14	3.01	Maryland	14	9.10
New Hampshire	15	2.95	District of Columbia[2]	15	8.92
Maryland	16	2.94	Idaho	16	8.77
Alaska	17	2.91	South Dakota	17	8.75
Wisconsin	18	2.89	Massachusetts	18	8.53
Oregon	19	2.87	Virginia	19	8.42
Kansas	20	2.80	Wisconsin	20	8.25
Virginia	21	2.72	Minnesota [3]	21	8.23
Florida	22	2.44	Maine	22	8.17
Pennsylvania	23	2.32	Alaska	23	8.10
Minnesota [3]	23	2.32	Utah	24	7.97
California	25	2.30	Hawaii	25	7.43
South Carolina	26	2.28	Mississippi	26	7.41
Arizona	27	2.25	Michigan	27	7.33
Nebraska	28	2.15	Nevada	28	7.12

Georgia	29	2.03	Louisiana	29	7.10
Iowa	30	1.95	Pennsylvania	30	7.02
Texas	31	1.90	North Carolina	31	6.98
Louisiana	31	1.90	Nebraska	32	6.81
North Carolina	33	1.89	Florida	33	6.68
Missouri	34	1.83	Arizona	34	6.67
Vermont	35	1.82	South Carolina	35	6.59
Nevada	35	1.82	Georgia	36	6.48
Wyoming	37	1.79	Iowa	37	6.27
Oklahoma	38	1.78	New Hampshire	38	6.24
Utah	39	1.64	California	39	5.94
Delaware	40	1.56	New Mexico	40	5.84
New Mexico	41	1.55	Texas	41	5.68
South Dakota	42	1.49	Tennessee	42	5.53
Alabama	43	1.36	Arkansas	43	5.38
Tennessee	44	1.27	Oklahoma	44	5.26
West Virginia	45	1.20	West Virginia	45	5.23
Kentucky	46	1.17	Vermont	46	5.22
Mississippi	47	1.15	Delaware	47	5.09
Idaho	48	1.09	Alabama	48	5.03
Montana	49	1.03	Kentucky	49	4.78
North Dakota	50	0.99	North Dakota	50	4.40
Arkansas	51	0.84	Montana	51	4.29

† Not applicable.

[1] An ALA-MLS is a master's degree from a program of library and information studies accredited by the American Library Association. Per 25,000 population is based on the total unduplicated population of legal service areas.

[2] The District of Columbia, while not a state, is included in the state rankings. Special care should be used in comparing its data to state data.

[3] Nonrespondent (all data are imputed).

SOURCE: U.S. Department of Education, National Center for Education Statistics, Federal-State Cooperative

System (FSCS) for Public Library Data, Public Libraries Survey, Fiscal Year 2001.

Figure 6.6 continued. Number of paid FTE librarians with ALA-MLS and other paid FTE staff

Although no national standards govern the number of staff needed in public libraries, Lynch's (2003) examination of current data offers some guidance. Nationally, in 2001 as shown in Figure 6.5 libraries averaged 12.18 FTE (full-time equivalent staff) per 25,000 population. When the number of staff is reviewed by state, Ohio ranks at the top with 21.66 and Arkansas at the bottom with 7.55.

Some state standards include staffing recommendations. Wisconsin uses population served as a basis for defining staff size. For a population of 25,000 using the Wisconsin algorithm the public library staff would be 12.5 for basic service and 25 for excellent service. Illinois has a similar approach suggesting population as a basis for staff size. For Illinois libraries it is recommended that a library serving 25,000 have a basic staff of 18 adding an additional staff member per 1,000 population.

The percentage of staff with degrees accredited by the American Library Association is 22.5 percent nationwide. Libraries serving populations of 1 million or more report 28.6 percent of staff hold the ALA-accredited degree, but that percent decreases by population size. At population served from 10,000–24,999 the percent of staff with the ALA-accredited degree is 20.1 percent (U.S. NCES, 2003:49). Figure 6.6 displays librarians with the ALA-accredited degree per 25,000 population.

There is also great variation of staffing patterns throughout the United States. Figure 6.7 shows that Connecticut and Hawaii have the highest percentage of staff with the ALA-accredited degree (30.8 percent) and Idaho the lowest (8.5 percent). The national mean for staff with the ALA-accredited degree per 25,000 population is 4.06. Calculating by the number of librarians with the ALA-accredited degree New Hampshire ranks number one with 8.39 librarians per 25,000 of population and North Carolina ranks lowest with 2 librarians per 25,000.

The variation in staffing—both total FTE and percent that hold the ALA-accredited degree—is the result of different states' long-term approach to education and culture. In 2002–2003 the Campaign for America's Librarians initiated by Mitch Freedman, ALA President developed a toolkit to assist libraries in demonstrating the value of library staff to the community (ALA-APA).

Today the "results" model is recognized as the Public Library Association recommended mechanism to develop staffing patterns as outlined in *Managing for Results* (Nelson, Altman, and Mayo, 2000). The model is tied to the integrated approach to planning and resource allocation developed by PLA. Staff is viewed as a resource to be used as efficiently and effectively as possible and engaged in

Figure 6.7: Number of Paid Full-Time Equivalent (FTE) Staff in Public Libraries, by Type of Position; Percentage of Librarians and Total Staff with ALA-MLS; and Number of Public Libraries with ALA-MLS Librarians, by State: Fiscal Year 2001

State	Number of public libraries	Paid FTE staff — Total[1] Total	Total Response rate	Librarians Total	Librarians Response rate	Librarians with ALA-MLS[1] Total	Librarians with ALA-MLS Response rate	Other Total	Other Response rate	Percentage of total FTE librarians with ALA-MLS	Percentage of total FTE staff with ALA-MLS	Number of public libraries with ALA-MLS librarians
50 States and DC[2]	9,129	133,455.6	96.3	44,427.5	96.8	30,093.7	97.5	89,028.2	96.3	67.7	22.5	4,072
Alabama	207	1,544.9	100.0	649.6	100.0	241.6	100.0	895.3	100.0	37.2	15.6	73
Alaska	86	323.4	100.0	120.3	100.0	73.0	100.0	203.0	100.0	60.6	22.6	16
Arizona	35	1,939.9	100.0	573.8	100.0	460.5	100.0	1,366.1	100.0	80.3	23.7	22
Arkansas	43	773.4	97.7	222.2	97.7	85.9	97.7	551.2	97.7	38.7	11.1	35
California	179	11,682.5	98.9	3,416.9	98.9	3,195.8	98.9	8,265.6	98.9	93.5	27.4	169
Colorado	116	2,399.9	100.0	778.8	100.0	510.2	97.4	1,621.0	100.0	65.5	21.3	51
Connecticut	194	2,324.8	94.3	962.9	94.3	715.4	94.3	1,361.9	94.3	74.3	30.8	147
Delaware	37	241.8	100.0	82.2	100.0	48.9	89.2	159.6	100.0	59.6	20.2	23
District of Columbia	1	350.0	100.0	146.0	100.0	104.0	100.0	204.0	100.0	71.2	29.7	1
Florida	72	6,327.2	97.2	1,972.2	97.2	1,593.1	97.2	4,355.0	97.2	80.8	25.2	69
Georgia	57	2,703.9	100.0	678.9	100.0	633.9	100.0	2,025.0	100.0	93.4	23.4	57
Hawaii	1	520.1	100.0	160.0	100.0	160.0	100.0	360.1	100.0	100.0	30.8	1
Idaho	106	577.0	99.1	178.7	99.1	49.3	99.1	398.3	99.1	27.6	8.5	19
Illinois	629	7,297.9	99.5	2,706.3	99.7	1,673.0	99.7	4,591.6	99.5	61.8	22.9	255
Indiana	239	4,386.0	100.0	1,328.4	100.0	867.0	100.0	3,057.7	100.0	65.3	19.8	137
Iowa	537	1,563.7	98.9	831.0	98.7	227.3	100.0	732.7	98.7	27.4	14.5	74
Kansas	321	1,735.2	98.1	509.1	98.1	249.9	98.1	1,226.0	98.1	49.1	14.4	60
Kentucky	116	1,547.9	100.0	782.7	100.0	188.1	100.0	765.2	100.0	24.0	12.2	36

State	Number of public libraries	Paid FTE staff								Percentage of total FTE librarians with ALA-MLS	Percentage of total FTE staff with ALA-MLS	Number of public libraries with ALA-MLS librarians
		Total[1]		Librarians		Librarians with ALA-MLS [1]		Other				
		Total	Response rate	Total	Response rate	Total	Response rate	Total	Response rate			
Louisiana	65	2,086.3	100.0	816.7	100.0	339.5	100.0	1,269.6	100.0	41.6	16.3	51
Maine	273	689.6	98.2	304.7	98.9	141.6	100.0	384.9	98.5	46.5	20.5	82
Maryland	24	3,021.3	100.0	1,141.2	100.0	606.9	100.0	1,880.1	100.0	53.2	20.1	24
Massachusetts	371	3,968.0	98.7	1,803.1	98.7	1,104.9	98.7	2,164.8	98.7	61.3	27.8	248
Michigan	381	4,684.0	100.0	1,773.9	100.0	1,236.0	100.0	2,910.2	100.0	69.7	26.4	198
Minnesota [3]	140	2,389.5	0	769.5	0	456.0	0	1,619.9	0	59.3	19.1	70
Mississippi	49	1,202.0	100.0	376.0	100.0	128.0	100.0	826.0	100.0	34.0	10.6	41
Missouri	150	2,698.9	96.0	752.8	96.0	374.3	96.0	1,946.1	96.0	49.7	13.9	48
Montana	79	320.6	100.0	166.2	100.0	37.0	100.0	154.4	100.0	22.3	11.5	15
Nebraska	272	764.4	73.5	406.0	82.0	113.0	99.6	358.4	73.5	27.8	14.8	28
Nevada	23	768.9	100.0	199.8	100.0	145.3	100.0	569.1	100.0	72.7	18.9	9
New Hampshire	229	716.4	97.8	411.1	99.6	144.4	99.6	305.4	97.8	35.1	20.1	72
New Jersey [4]	309	5,048.7	93.5	1,493.5	95.5	1,480.5	95.5	3,555.2	93.5	99.1	29.3	253
New Mexico	80	610.2	93.8	244.9	92.5	97.2	91.3	365.2	92.5	39.7	15.9	22
New York	750	12,953.3	100.0	4,241.3	100.0	3,596.9	100.0	8,712.0	100.0	84.8	27.8	390
North Carolina	76	2,903.1	100.0	647.1	100.0	612.3	100.0	2,256.0	100.0	94.6	21.1	72
North Dakota	82	202.1	100.0	105.1	100.0	21.9	98.8	97.0	100.0	20.8	10.8	9
Ohio	250	9,834.6	100.0	2,756.8	100.0	1,923.0	100.0	7,077.8	100.0	69.8	19.6	184
Oklahoma	115	1,082.6	90.4	488.1	90.4	200.9	90.4	594.5	90.4	41.2	18.6	31
Oregon	125	1,707.3	100.0	512.4	100.0	356.8	99.2	1,194.9	100.0	69.6	20.9	65

Figure 6.7 continued. Paid FTE Librarians and Staff in Public Libraries with ALA-MLS

State	Number of public libraries	Paid FTE staff								Percentage of total FTE librarians with ALA-MLS	Percentage of total FTE staff with ALA-MLS	Number of public libraries with ALA-MLS librarians
		Total[1]		Librarians		Librarians with ALA-MLS[1]		Other				
		Total	Response rate	Total	Response rate	Total	Response rate	Total	Response rate			
Pennsylvania	459	5,003.4	100.0	1,626.1	100.0	1,116.6	99.6	3,377.3	100.0	68.7	22.3	227
Rhode Island	48	630.6	95.8	217.5	95.8	187.6	97.9	413.1	95.8	86.3	29.8	45
South Carolina	41	1,542.5	100.0	484.2	100.0	366.1	100.0	1,058.3	100.0	75.6	23.7	39
South Dakota	126	342.8	76.2	134.5	85.7	35.3	99.2	208.3	77.8	26.3	10.3	15
Tennessee	184	1,816.3	100.0	603.2	100.0	278.2	100.0	1,213.2	100.0	46.1	15.3	32
Texas	540	6,411.0	99.4	2,014.4	99.6	1,472.7	99.8	4,396.7	99.8	73.1	23.0	179
Utah	70	982.5	100.0	270.4	100.0	146.7	100.0	712.1	100.0	54.3	14.9	18
Vermont	188	297.7	97.9	177.2	97.9	42.0	100.0	120.5	98.9	23.7	14.1	36
Virginia	90	3,304.7	100.0	921.7	100.0	768.9	100.0	2,383.1	100.0	83.4	23.3	82
Washington	65	3,241.7	100.0	830.4	100.0	740.8	98.5	2,411.4	100.0	89.2	22.9	42
West Virginia	97	689.3	100.0	314.2	100.0	86.0	100.0	375.1	100.0	27.4	12.5	36
Wisconsin	379	2,953.6	100.0	1,171.2	100.0	624.3	100.0	1,782.3	100.0	53.3	21.1	152
Wyoming	23	348.6	100.0	152.4	100.0	35.4	100.0	196.2	100.0	23.2	10.2	12
Outlying areas												
Guam	1	24.0	100.0	1.0	100.0	1.0	100.0	23.0	100.0	100.0	4.2	1
Virgin Islands	1	38.0	100.0	7.0	100.0	7.0	100.0	31.0	100.0	100.0	18.4	1

Figure 6.7 continued. Paid FTE Librarians and Staff in Public Libraries with ALA-MLS

1 ALA-MLS: A master's degree from a graduate library education program accredited by the American Library Association (ALA). Librarians with ALA-MLS are also included in total librarians.

2 50 States and DC totals exclude outlying areas.

3 Nonrespondent (all data are imputed).

4 New Jersey collects data on the number of "certified" librarians, not "ALA-MLS" librarians (i.e., the state does not distinguish between master's degrees from programs of library and information studies accredited by the American Library Association (ALA) and all other master's degrees in library science awarded by institutions of higher education). Their "certified" librarians total is included in the ALA-MLS column. Nationally, 4,577 master's degrees were awarded by institutions of higher education in 1999-2000 (U.S. Department of Education, NCES, Digest of Education Statistics, 2001, table 256.) Master's degrees were from ALA-accredited programs totalled 4,201 and accounted for 92 percent of total master's degrees awarded in 1999-2000 (ALA, Office for Human Resource Development and Recruitment, Degrees and Certificates Awarded by U.S. Library and Information Studies Education Programs, 2002.)

NOTE: Detail may not sum to totals because of rounding. Response rate is the percentage of libraries that reported the specific item. Items with response rates below 100 percent include imputations for nonresponse. Data were not reported by the following outlying areas: American Samoa, Northern Marianas, Palau, and Puerto Rico.

SOURCE: U.S. Department of Education, National Center for Education Statistics, Federal-State Cooperative System (FSCS) for Public Library Data, Public Libraries Survey, Fiscal Year 2001.

Figure 6.7 continued. Paid FTE Librarians and Staff in Public Libraries with ALA-MLS

activities that are most important to a library's mission, goals, and objectives. The aspects of staffing considered in the results model are:

1. Identifying activities and when and where they will be performed.

2. Identifying abilities needed to accomplish activities.

3. Determining the number of staff in relation to patron use and staff workload.

4. Understanding how staff currently uses time.

5. Determining how to find staff to accomplish the library's priorities.

To accomplish these actions the book provides work forms, which assist in gathering data to analyze the number and classification of staff required to achieve the library's goals and objectives. The companion volume, *Staffing for Results* (Mayo and Goodrich, 2002), begins at the activity level—a set of tasks that results in a measurable output of things done or services delivered—and supports analysis of work at the task level—the series of sequential actions that converts inputs to outputs. By applying numeric analysis for diagnostic purposes and prescriptive analyses to determine direction reasonable adjustments in assignments can be made.

Broad-Based Issues Relating to Staffing

Recruitment

Recruitment of new librarians continues to be a profession-wide concern that has an impact on staffing. In 2000 the Public Library Association, Executive Committee, issued a report that examined salaries and working conditions as background for the need to develop a recruitment initiative within the profession (PLA, 2000). This work formed the backdrop for the multimillion dollar grants program, "Librarians for the 21st Century," funded by the Institute of Museum and Library Services. The program recognizes the "key role of libraries and librarians in maintaining the flow of information that is critical to support formal education; to guide intellectual, scientific, and commercial enterprise; to strengthen individual decisions; and to create the informed populace that is at the core of democracy." Support to educate the next generation of librarians in the first ten million dollars awarded included a focus on public librarians, especially people of color, and youth services librarians.

Public libraries must make a concerted effort to broaden the diversity of staff at all levels. Although the profession has undertaken many initiatives to create a diverse pool of library workers, the field continues to graduate a predominately white work force (McCook, 2000). In 2000–2001, programs accredited by the ALA ethnicity reported graduates to be 87.7 percent White, 5.6 percent African American, 3.2 percent Hispanic, 2.9 percent Asian-Pacific Islanders, and 0.06 Native Americans (ALISE, 2002).

Scholarships and mentoring for people of color are provided by the ethnic affiliate organizations of the American Library Association: the American Indian Library Association (AILA); Asian/Pacific American Librarians Association (APALA); Black Caucus of the American Library Association (BCALA); Chinese American Librarians Association (CALA); and REFORMA—National Association to Promote Library and Information Services to Latinos and the Spanish-Speaking. The ALA Office for Diversity oversees the SPECTRUM scholarship program for people of color. However, all these efforts have yet to provide a profession-wide profile that reflects the changing U.S. population at large.

Staff Development, Continuing Education, and Certification

> "The employees of the Library represent its most valuable— and most expensive—resource. Investments in staff development and training, particularly in our rapidly changing technologically-driven field, are critical to achieving all other goals."
>
> — Indianapolis-Marion County Public Library, Master Plan for Library Services (available: www.imcpl.lib.in.us/servmp.htm)

Staff development and continuing education for library staff are central to positive performance. Opportunities are made available in a variety of formats, both internal and external to the employing library depending on the library's size and structure. Library-based staff development programs include curricula targeted to new knowledge or skills generally planned by a staff development committee. Ideally a coordinator provides leadership. Other aspects of staff development include funding for travel to conferences; staff institute days; continuing education days; and tuition reimbursement.

The American Library Association has established leadership in continuing education as one of its Action Goals and oversees profession-wide information on continuing education and staff development through its Human Resource Development and Recruitment Office.

In 2000 the ALA sponsored a Congress on Professional Education for Professional Development (COPE 2) to examine the issues and problems related to the continuing professional education of librarians and other professional library staff, with the following goals that illustrate the broad range of concerns that cluster about issues of staff development:

- Improved library service

- Improved professional performance

- Increased credibility and visibility for the library profession

- Increased recognition and compensation for the library profession

- Expanded support from library administrators for continuing professional development activities

- Expanded awareness in the profession of the importance of continuing professional development

- Improved professional development activities in terms of quality, relevance, coverage, availability and currency

- Expanded tools for sharing information about continuing professional development opportunities and best practices

- Recognition of the shared responsibility for continuing professional development between library professionals and their employers

The end result of the COPE 2 conference was to recommend that ALA establish a Web-based clearing house for continuing education, document expenditures by libraries on staff development, and to establish a companion organization to ALA to focus on continuing education and certification. Lynch reported in 2001 that public libraries spent a widely varying amount on staff development, but the mean was 0.98 percent of total payroll in libraries serving over 100,000 (Lynch, 2001). Some libraries spent as much as 8.57 percent.

The American Library Association-Allied Professional Association (ALA-APA) was authorized in 2001 as a companion organization to ALA to promote the mutual professional interests of librarians and other library workers. This new organization focuses on two broad areas:

(1) Certification of individuals in specializations beyond the initial professional degree. The certification program for the Certified Public Library Manager, still in development at this writing, is intended to provide managerial knowledge in budgeting and finance; building planning and maintenance; serving diverse populations; fund-raising and grantsmanship; organization and personnel; politics and networking; marketing; and technology.

(2) Direct support of comparable worth and pay equity initiatives, and other activities designed to improve the salaries and status of librarians and other library workers.

Certification can also take place at the state level. Many states have certification requirements for library directors and other staff. For example, Kentucky has a state board for the certification of librarians that requires directors, assistant directors, department heads, branch librarians, bookmobile librarians, and other full-time staff who provide information service, to be examined. The rationale behind the examination is the board's belief that librarians must increase their skills and knowledge to keep abreast of developments in the information age, and that effort enriches the individual librarian and promotes quality library service. State library agencies have different requirements regarding certification and as one might expect, each state is different.

Unions, Better Salaries and Working Conditions

Union members earn more money, have more benefits, and have more say at work about the best way to get work done. The historical paternalism of the library work place has sometimes allowed libraries to keep salaries below market value, permitted movement of employees from locations at the will of the administration, and sustained a hierarchical workplace. Unions clarify work rules, working conditions and salaries. In a recent *Public Libraries* forum, Johnson observed, "unions can help make libraries better by offering a collaborative model for employee relations that management might want to emulate...union leadership consists of grassroots workplace politics: talking to employees at all levels, building consensus, discussing, persuading, and acting democratically" (Johnson, 2002).

ALA has taken action to advocate for librarians with the formation American Library Association-Allied Professional Association (ALA-APA) in 2001. Salary structure information to enable library workers to make a case for better pay is provided in the online toolkit, *Advocating for Better Salaries and Pay Equity Toolkit*. This instrument was developed as a project of the Campaign for America's Librarians, by the Better Salaries and Pay Equity for Library Workers Task Force, initiated by Mitch Freedman, 2002–2003 ALA President. This new level of advocacy at the national level should provide additional support for the improvement of the status of library workers.

Volunteers

Libraries actively solicit the support of volunteers for library operations. While many come to the library from organized Friends of the Library groups, library Web sites provide online applications for volunteers and report thousands of contributed hours to basic library services. A statewide study in 2000 for Florida reported volunteers contributed time equivalent to 722 full-time staff (nearly 29,000 hours per week) serving in all areas of the state's public libraries—shelving books, checking material in and out, staffing reference and information desks, and providing behind-the-scenes support. In many libraries, coordinators are assigned to organize and make the best use of these community-minded volunteers (Driggers and Dumas, 2002).

Some libraries have developed volunteer programs for teens as a way to provide opportunities for civic responsibility. The Phoenix Public Library recruits and trains teen volunteers to assist library staff and the public during the Summer Reading Program and helps teens develop practical job skills and good customer/public service attitudes. Volunteers also make visits to the homebound, provide homework help, and assist with computer basics. Some state library standards, such as Missouri's, provide for the appraisal of volunteers. The Friends of Libraries USA (FOLUSA) Web site presents a consolidation of volunteer ideas from all over the United States.

References

American Library Association. 1992. *Standards for Accreditation of Master's Programs in Library and Information Studies.* Chicago: American Library Association.

American Library Association. American Indian Library Association (AILA). Available: www.nativeculture.com/lisamitten/aila.html.

American Library Association. Asian/Pacific American Library Association (APALA). Available: www.apalaweb.org.

American Library Association. Black Caucus of the American Library Association (BCALA). Available: www.bcala.org.

American Library Association. Chinese-Americans Library Association (CALA). Available: www.cala-web.org.

American Library Association. Office for Diversity. SPECTRUM Initiative (scholarship program). Available: http://ala.org/diversity.

American Library Association-Allied Professional Association. 2003. *Advocating for Better Salaries and Pay Equity Toolkit.* 3rd ed. Chicago: American Library Association-Allied Professional Association. Available: www.ala-apa.org/tool kit.pdf.

Association for Library and Information Science Education (ALISE). 2002. Students. In *Library and Information Science Education Statistical Report 2002.* Available: http://ils.unc.edu/ALISE/2002/Students/Students01.htm.

Campaign for America's Librarians. American Library Association. 2003. Available: www.ala-apa.org/toolkit.pdf.

Driggers, Preston F., and Eileen Dumas. 2002. *Managing Library Volunteers: A Practical Toolkit.* Chicago: American Library Association.

FLA Friends and Trustees Section. 2000. Floridians Value Their Libraries. *Florida Libraries* 43 (Fall): 18.

Friends of Libraries USA. Available: www.folusa.org. For examples of volunteer effort, see the Web page: www.folusa.org/html/best4.html.

Garceau, Oliver. 1949. The Governing Authority of the Public Library. In *The Public Library in the Political Process: A Report of the Public Library Inquiry,* 53–110. New York: Columbia University Press.

Glennon, Michael. 1997. Developing and Passing a Bond Issue: A Trustee's View. *Public Libraries* 36 (January/February): 24–28.

Hague, Rodger. 1999. A Short History of the Stevens County Rural Library District. *Alki* 15 (July): 22–23.

Illinois Library Association. 1997. Serving Our Public: Standards for Public Libraries. Available: www.sos.state.il.us/library/isl/ref/readyref/pdf/serving/ ILA_Serving.pdf.

Johnson, Cameron. 2002. Professionalism, not Paternalism. *Public Libraries* 41 (May/June): 139–140.

Jordan, Amy. 2002. Can Unions Solve the Low-Pay Dilemma? *American Libraries* 33 (January): 65–69.

Kelley, H. Neil. 1999. Portrait of the Illinois Trustee Community. *Illinois Libraries* 81 (Fall): 222–225.

Kentucky State Board for the Certification of Librarians. Certification Manual, 2001. Available: www.kdla.ky.gov/libsupport/certification/manual.PDF.

Kreamer, Jean T. 1990. The Library Trustee as a Library Activist. *Public Libraries* 29 (July/August): 220–3.

Lynch, Mary Jo. Spending on Staff Development—2001. American Library Association. Available: www.ala.org/ala/hrdr/libraryempresources/spending staff.htm.

Mayo, Diane, and Jeanne Goodrich. 2002. *Staffing for Results*. Chicago: American Library Association.

McCook, Kathleen de la Peña, ed. 2000. Ethnic Diversity in Library and Information Science. *Library Trends* 49 (Summer): 1–214.

Nebraska Library Association, Trustee, User and Friends Section. Nebraska Library Association. Available: www.nol.org/home/NLA/TUFS/index.html.

Nelson, Sandra, Ellen Altman, and Diane Mayo. 2000. Managing Your Library's Staff. In *Managing for Results: Effective Resource Allocation for Public Libraries*, 29–110. Chicago: American Library Association.

Public Library Association. Public Librarian Recruitment. Available: www.pla.org.

Recruitment of Public Librarians. 2000. *Public Libraries* 39 (May/June): 168–172.

REFORMA-National Association to Promote Library and Information Services to Latinos and the Spanish-Speaking. Available: www.reforma.org.

Sager, Donald J. 2001. Evolving Virtues: Public Library Administrative Skills. *Public Libraries* 40 (September/October): 268–272.

Shaw, Jane Belon, et al., eds. Trustee Facts File. Available: www.cyberdrive illinois.com/library/isl/ref/readyref/trustee/index.htm.

U.S. Department of Education. National Center for Education Statistics. 2003. Public Libraries in the United States. Fiscal Year 2001. E.D. TABS, ed. Adrienne Chute, et al. Available: http://nces.ed.gov/pubsearch/pubsinfo.asp?pubid=2003399 (accessed November 17, 2003).

Wisconsin Department of Public Instruction. Trustee Essentials: A Handbook for Wisconsin Public Library Trustees. Available: www.dpi.state.wi.us/dltcl/pld/handbook.html.

Wisconsin Public Library Standards, 2000. 3rd ed. Available: www.dpi.state.wi.us/dltcl/pld/chapter7.html (accessed May 23, 2004).

7

Structure and Infrastructure

This chapter considers the symbolism of the public library building. It summarizes the history of public library buildings in the United States, reviews the role of LSCA in construction during the last third of the twentieth century, and outlines design standards including accessibility. Because the move from federal support of structures through LSCA, to federal support for infrastructure through LSTA, affects all public libraries, we devote attention to this critical topic, as well. This chapter also addresses the challenges that libraries face as they attempt to incorporate new technologies in public library service.

The Symbolism of the Public Library Building

"I have always imagined that Paradise will be a kind of library."

— Jorge Luis Borges, "Poema de los Dones," from *El Hacedor*

The public library building is an emblem of the past, a source of educational and cultural sustenance for the present and a hopeful vision for the future. Public library buildings are at once a symbol of

163

cultural heritage and a testimony to a shared community vision of the commons. The public library can be a factor in community sustainability and redevelopment. It is vital for those working in public libraries to understand the importance of the library to the community's sense of self-identity. Through its structure and infrastructure the library is simultaneously a tangible representation of humanity's ideals and an active system for electronic communication. The library can be a public space that inspires, sustains, and anchors a community's educational and cultural self-perception.

In large library systems with multiple branches, each branch can act as a neighborhood center responding over time to changes in the community. For instance, Chicago Public Library (CPL) with more than 75 branches includes branches that reflect neighborhood diversity in architecture, as well as collections and services. The Rudy Lozano branch, housing CPL's largest Spanish materials collection, features an Olmec pre-Columbian design and art by Latino artists. The involvement of people who will use the facility in the design of public library buildings provides a sense of shared ownership and has come to be an important aspect of community building. In *Better Together*, Putnam and Feldstein (2003) characterize the branches of CPL as "third places," neither work nor home, where people can spend time together. Their case study of CPL's Near North Branch Library, which bridges the wealthy, mainly white Gold Coast and the African American Cabrini-Green community, details the library's role as the heartbeat of the community.

In May, 2004 the new Seattle Public Library designed by Rem Koolhaas opened. The building's angled, soaring architecture captures water views and cityscapes from every floor of its transparent facade. It provides a quantum leap in technology, five main "platforms," or levels, that are pushed and pulled out. Between these platforms are four "floating layers." Koolhaas has said he had observed that existing libraries face a "Sisyphean fight against disorder," so the design aims to incorporate storage for digital information, as well expandable space for books.

The role of the library as an act of civic renewal has been described by Vartan Gregorian in a speech before the Kansas City Club in 2002 wherein he noted, "the new library will grace the city, help stimulate a downtown renaissance and—most importantly—be better able to play its central role in the cultural, intellectual and democratic life of the entire metropolitan community." In Minneapolis the new central library designed by Cesar Pelli is conceived as "a dynamic, resource-rich, downtown destination—an

Figure 7.1: Seattle Public Library—Central Library.

Reprinted with the permission by Seattle Public Library.

essential gathering place that inspires learning, invites interaction, and improves access to information and knowledge for everyone." (Kenney, 2001; see also Minneapolis Public Library).

Public Library Buildings in the Beginning

Early public libraries in the United States were housed in a variety of settings. Individual benefactors provided funds for a building or libraries shared space with other civic agencies, clubs, storefronts, even fire departments. A more focused approach to the development of library facilities came about during the period of Carnegie library philanthropy (1886–1919), which had an impact on library architecture. Initially each community receiving a Carnegie building grant was able to develop its own library architecture and these buildings were emblems of civic pride.

Figure 7.2: New York Public Library—Muhlenberg Branch

Photo courtesy of Miguel A. Figueroa.

Midway (1911) through the program of grants for library buildings, the Carnegie Corporation issued "Notes on Library Buildings" that provided suggested guidelines for libraries built with Carnegie funds. The variety of architectural styles for the 1,689 Carnegie funded libraries included Italian Renaissance, Beaux-Arts, Classical Revival, Spanish Revival, Prairie, Tudor Revival, and Carnegie Classical (Bobinski, 1969). Communities in the United States initially tended to think of public libraries as a civic landmark and a matter of community pride with perhaps less attention to functionality. Carnegie's gifts focused communities on the idea of a public library as a logical community service with some basic standardization of structure. Figure 7.2 depicts a Carnegie branch of New York Public Library.

The American Library Association's *A National Plan for Public Library Service* (Joeckel and Winslow, 1948) assessed the status of the nation's public library buildings in a general fashion noting, "The present [physical plant of the public library] is barely 50 percent adequate for existing public library services. And for the extension of library service to the 35 million people now entirely without public libraries, a great new building program must be undertaken." While specifics were not given as to design, general statements of accessibility, functionality, and the idea of the public library as a "modern educational center" with meeting rooms, film viewing space and listening areas were set forth (Joeckel and Winslow, 1948: 122–129).

Setting National Standards for Facilities and Federal Funds for Construction

The Federal Library Services Act (LSA) and Library Services and Construction Act (LSCA) programs provided support for public library extension, construction and renovation from 1956–1996. The American Library Association responded to this financial support with attention to facilities and buildings in national public library standards. The "Physical Facilities" section of the 1956 *Public Library Service: A Guide to Evaluation with Minimum Standards* noted, "The public library building should serve as a symbol of library service. It should offer to the community a compelling invitation to enter, read, look, listen and learn." This ALA document also provided general specifications for the public library building, such as good signage, a flexible structure that would allow expansion, workrooms, standards for lighting, sound control, and meeting rooms (ALA, 1956: 56). A decade later the *Minimum Standards for Public Library Systems,*

1966 were somewhat more detailed about accommodating additional services such as typewriters for public use, vertical transportation, and study carrels (Public Library Association, 1967: 56–64).

From 1965–1997 LSCA funds provided monies for the construction of new library buildings; the acquisition, expansion, remodeling,

---

Figure 7.3: CFDA No. 84-154—Fiscal Appropriations for Library Construction: 1965–1996

Public Library Construction and Technology Enhancement Grants to State Library Agencies (CFDA No. 84.154)

I. Legislation

Library Services and Construction Act (LSCA), Title II, as amended (20 U.S.C. 351 et seq.) (expires September 30, 1997).

II. Funding History 1/

Fiscal Year	Appropriation	Fiscal Year	Appropriation
1965	$30,000,000	1987	$22,050,000
1970	7,807,250	1988	22,143,100
1975	0	1989	21,877,520
1980	0	1990	18,572,036
1981	0	1991	18,833,395
1982	0	1992	16,383,640
1983	50,000,000	1993	16,252,571
1984	0	1994	17,436,160
1985	24,500,000	1995	17,436,160
1986	21,102,000	1996	16,041,620

1/ There is no time limit for the expenditure of these funds.

Source: U.S. Department of Education. Office of Educational Research and Improvement. Biennial Evaluation Report, 1995-1996. Public Library Construction and Technology Enhancement Grants to State Library Agencies. (CFDA No. 84-154). Accessed November 1, 2003. http://www.ed.gov/pubs/Biennial/95-96/eval/603-97.pdf

and alteration of existing buildings; remodeling to conserve energy; retrofitting to meet standards set by the American with Disabilities Act; purchasing historic buildings for conversion to public libraries; and the acquisition, installation, maintenance or replacement of equipment necessary to provide access to information and communication technologies. This infusion of over $300 million in construction support encouraged state and local governments to match and enhance funding for public library construction. Annual appropriations from 1965–1996 are shown in Figure 7.3.[1]

Illustrative of the passion inspired about library building during this period is the best-documented event in public library building history—the design/build competition for the central Chicago Public Library announced in 1987. The problem of building a civic monument for Chicago was viewed as a clear choice between two distinct alternatives. One option was to build a static tranquil space conducive to the search for knowledge that would project an image of solidity and permanence, a structure that would express civic dignity and monumentality. A second option was to create an image that would reflect the dynamism of the city symbolizing the active collection of information rather than the contemplation of knowledge. The video, *Design Wars,* follows the architects and builders in competition for the Chicago Public Library as they tried to accommodate issues of functionality, safety, public appeal, and expression of a vision of Chicago.

The design selected in 1988, a Beaux-Arts building by Hammond, Beeby and Babka, Inc., has been characterized as fitting aesthetically and architecturally into the city like a glove, with a monumental, decorative, yet profoundly public, innovative, and urban-appropriate form. As hoped, the central library, which opened in 1991 and was named the Harold Washington Library Center (Figure 7.4) after the city's first African American mayor, who died in 1987, sparked a revitalization of Chicago's South Loop District (Six Chicago Architects, 1989; Lane, 1989).

The story of community-wide engagement in the selection of the design for the Chicago Public Library is emblematic of the importance of the library as a great public space (Kent and Myrick, 2003). Public libraries that reach into the heart of a community may be monumental central libraries or small intimate branches. During the LSCA construction grant period, many communities found an opportunity to build public libraries that not only provided educational and recreational needs, but also gave them a great public space during a time of expansive suburbanization and growth in edge cities.

Figure 7.4: Chicago Public Library—Harold Washington Library Center.

Reprinted with permission by Chicago Public Library.

Public Library Buildings for the Twenty-First Century

The Variety of Public Library Buildings

In 1996–1997 the end of the LSCA funds for construction did not halt the period of public library building expansion. Between July 1, 2001 and June 30, 2002 communities throughout the country erected, added to, or renovated, over 200 new public library buildings at a cost of more than $788.4 million. Funding came predominantly from local sources (87 percent). Charitable contributions/gift funds accounted for eight percent and federal and state funds were five percent (Fox, 2002).

To illustrate the variety of building taking place the best sources are the annual features with full-color photographs on new public library buildings that appear in the journals *American Libraries* and *Library Journal.* The 2003 photo spread in *American Libraries* included winners of the American Institute of Architects/ALA

Library Building Awards. The integration of information technology in a service environment was a central feature of these new buildings. While every public library should reflect the needs and spirit of its community, these outstanding examples provide a spectrum of ideas and an annual review of these winners provides ongoing awareness of trends in library architecture and design ("Building for the Future").

- Burbank, California. Buena Vista Branch. Magical forest theme decorates the children's area in a building that triples the 1948 building with 46 computers and a 200-seat community room with view of Abraham Lincoln Park.

- New York Public Library. South Court Branch. A Beaux-Arts branch combining classical, and contemporary themes with skylights in connection to historic architecture.

- Yelm, Washington. Timberland Library System. A linoleum river echoes the community's natural surroundings and defined spaces for study, programs and computers are established through shelving, floor coverings, and glass partitions.

- York Public Library, Maine. Incorporated wetlands in its landscaping. Features community craftsmanship through custom millwork and furniture designed by local craftspersons.

- Little Rock, Arkansas. Central Arkansas Library System. Dee Brown Library. Structural steel and wooden beams; uses clerestory window, overhangs, and a geothermal heating and cooling system.

Public library buildings also provide the opportunity for adaptive reuse of older buildings, while retaining historic features. In 2004 the Kansas City Public Library completed remodeling the First National Bank Building, which had been built in 1906 for $450,000. The remodeling cost over one hundred times that amount, $46,000,000. Tompkins County, New York, renovated a Woolworth store in downtown Ithaca in 2002; Denton, Texas, converted a grocery store into a branch library in 2003. These are projects that involve multiple partners and preserve the character of a community. Rabun (2000) discusses factors to consider in adaptive reuse. It is interesting to note that reuse can go the other way. Older library buildings, especially Carnegie buildings, have been converted to new uses: the Arizona Hall of Fame Museum in Phoenix; professional offices in Fergus Falls, Minnesota; and police facilities in Colusa, California (Jones, 1997).

At the national level, professional support for planning and building library facilities is within the purview of the American Library Association, Library Administration and Management Association, Building and Equipment Section (LAMA BES). LAMA BES exercises responsibility for matters relating to library structure for all types of libraries, including site selection, design, construction, alteration, interior design, furnishings, and equipment. Several publications provide support to those planning buildings: *Planning the Small Library Facility* (Dahlgren, 1996); *Learning Environments for Young Children* (Feinberg, Kuchner, and Feldman, 1998); *Checklist of Building Design Considerations* (Sannwald, 2001); and *Libraries Designed for Users: A 21st Century Guide* (Lushington, 2002). LAMA BES also maintains a list of building consultants.

State library standards provide additional specific information about public library building requirements. The Wisconsin Library Association has provided helpful resources, notably the "Public Library Space Needs: A Planning Outline/1998," developed by Anders C. Dahlgren, which introduces the concept of the "design population." This concept takes into consideration the actual scope of use as contrasted with the defined geographical service area of the library. By using the "Outline" librarians and trustees can estimate space needs based on a library's service goals. The space requirements are organized in six categories with formulas for estimating needs.

- Collection space. Books, periodicals, nonprint resources, and digital materials.

- Reader seating space. Varies depending on type of use (general reading, intensive use by youth doing school work) and size of population should be at least 30 sq. feet per seat.

- Staff work space. Work stations needed to support a library's service program. Between 125 and 150 sq. feet each.

- Meeting space. There are several types of meeting space to be considered: (1) general program room space with theatre or lecture hall seating; (2) conference room space; (3) children's storytime space; (4) computer lab space.

- Special use space. Usually about 10 percent of the library's overall space for index tables, photocopiers, exhibits.

- Non-assignable space. This space—about 25 percent—would be for heating and cooling equipment, storage, corridors, custodial space.

These categories provide a convenient overview of the library spaces that need to be considered in building design.

A new tool, Libris Design software, is a library facility planning information system and downloadable database that was developed for California Public Library planners and funded by the Institute of Museum and Library Services. It permits users to tailor generic library models into building programs and to project estimated costs. It was designed as an expert system to facilitate the creation of generic models that could be tailored to a specific community. The Libris Design software is free on the Web site, which includes technical information and supporting documentation (Campbell, 2003).

Accessibility and Humane Design

In the future, public libraries will need to be bigger, since no services are going away. Beyond traditional functions there needs to be more humane design (accessibility), space for more computers, wireless hotspots for use of laptops, space for the information technology staff to work and repair computers, and a more people-centered orientation with coffee bars and lounge areas. Library redesigns will need to take into account the fact that workstations require space for more than a computer and keyboard, as well as ergonomic support, the need for acoustical barriers to limit computer white noise, and enhanced electrical capacity (Forrest, 2002).

The *Wisconsin Public Library Standards*, 3rd ed., sections on facilities standards emphasize access. The chapter on "Access and Facilities" provides a good overview of current requirements relating to public library buildings. Echoing the enduring aspects of national standards set forth in the 1950s the introduction notes:

> The *physical* library facility also has a direct effect on access. All public library buildings should be easily accessible and offer the community a compelling invitation to enter, read, listen, and learn. Library buildings should be flexible enough to respond to changing use and new technologies. Buildings should be expandable to accommodate growing collections and new services. Buildings should be designed for user efficiency. Building designs also should support staff efficiency,

because staff costs are the major expense in library operation. (2000: 26)

Key criteria in the *Wisconsin Standards'* chapter on "Access and Facilities" that relate to the public library building define the goals of accessibility are:

•   The library provides adequate space to implement the full range of library services that are consistent with the library's long-range plan and the standards in this document.

•   The library has allocated space for child and family use, with all materials readily available, and provides furniture and equipment designed for children and persons with disabilities.

•   At least once every five years, and more frequently if needed, the board directs the preparation of an assessment of the library's long-term space needs. The publication *Public Library Space Needs: A Planning Outline* is helpful.

•   The library building and furnishings meet state and federal requirements for physical accessibility, including the ADA Accessibility Guidelines for Buildings and Facilities (ADAAG). In compliance with the ADAAG, the library provides directional signs and instructions for the use of the collection, the catalog, and other library services, in print, alternate formats, and languages other than English, as appropriate.

•   The library's accessible features (such as entrance doors, restrooms, water fountains, and parking spaces) display the International Symbol of Accessibility.

•   The library building supports the implementation of current and future telecommunications and electronic information technologies.

•   Adequate, safe, well-lighted, and convenient parking is available to the library's patrons and staff on or adjacent to the library's site. The minimum number of required parking spaces may be governed by local ordinance.

•   The exterior of the library is well lighted and identified with signs clearly visible from the street.

•   The entrance is clearly visible and is located on the side of the building that most users approach.

•   Emergency facilities are provided in accordance with appropriate codes; evacuation routes, emergency exits, and the locations of fire extinguishers are clearly marked; emergency first aid supplies are readily available; and the library has a designated tornado shelter.

- Lighting levels comply with standards issued by the Illuminating Engineering Society of North America.

- The library provides facilities for the return of library materials when the library is closed; after-hours material depositories are fireproof.

- The library has public meeting space available for its programming and for use by other community groups, if appropriate. (Wisconsin, chapter 7, 26–27)

The Americans with Disabilities Act Accessibility Guidelines for Buildings and Facilities (ADAAG) are the basis of design requirements of the ADA (U.S. Access Board). The *Wisconsin Standards* are a model response and in accord with the American Library Association policy on "Library Services for People with Disabilities," which states, "libraries must not discriminate against people with disabilities and shall ensure that individuals with disabilities have equal access to library resources."

Planning the Infrastructure: LSCA to LSTA

Certainly the biggest change for those thinking about public library buildings over recent years has been the advent of computer and telecommunications technology. In 1993 the American Library Association held a forum, "Telecommunications and Information Infrastructure Policy Issues," to provide a mechanism for the library community to identify national policy issues, questions and principles in the areas of telecommunications and information infrastructure. Public librarians proved to be highly capable environmental scanners and moved quickly to implement new technologies into their daily work.

Public libraries were among the first to apply for a series of grants for model programs that demonstrated innovative use of network technology in 1994.[2] At Newark Public Library, funds were used to support the Newark Electronic Information Infrastructure Demonstration Project; New York Public Library, working with the Literacy Assistance Center of New York City, tested networked information resources at thirty neighborhood branches for people with limited literacy skills; Danbury Public Library developed a model community Freenet planning process for the state of Connecticut;

three counties in southeast Florida (Broward, Dade, and Palm Beach) developed a Free-Net training infrastructure coordinated by the South East Florida Information Network (SEFLIN); and Salem (Oregon) Public Library developed OPEN (Oregon Public Electronic Network) to enhance the exchange of information between government and citizens (McCook, 2000: 71–72).

Recognizing the complexity of issues relating to information policy, ALA created the Office for Information Technology Policy (OITP) in 1995. This group focuses on enhancing the ability of ALA's Washington Office to follow and influence national issues relating to electronic access to information as a means to ensure the public's right to a free and open information society. The Library Services and Technology Act (LSTA) of 1996 (a title under the Museum and Library Services Act), which replaced the LSCA, emphasizes technology in its grants to libraries. The LSTA has helped libraries to create the technological infrastructure required to obtain and use electronic resources through funding based on required state plans (McCook, 2002; Gregory, 1999).

It may seem hard to believe, but it has been barely a decade since Internet and computer access became widely available in public libraries. The establishment of the LSTA is testimony to the vision of the Clinton-Gore administration's recognition of the need for broad access to the information superhighway and the library community's readiness to work with government to put new projects in place. The rapid adoption of telecommunication technologies and the support to activate them for communities demonstrates the capacity of the nation's public libraries to respond with alacrity to change. Additionally, the Telecommunications Act of 1996 made possible an annual subsidy of $65 million for discounted telecommunication rates to libraries and schools. Through the e-rate (Schools and Libraries Universal Service Support Mechanism) libraries have been able to add telecommunications infrastructure.

The Bill and Melinda Gates Foundation recognized the public library as a partial solution to the "digital divide" between people with and people without computer access. To assist in overcoming this divide the foundation brought computer packages into all fifty states by 2003. The Gates donations—the largest gift to U.S. public libraries since Carnegie—amounted to $250 million for 40,000 computers in 10,000 libraries from 1997–2003. The focus was low-income communities where ten percent of the population earned below the federal poverty line (Gordon, 2003; Bill and Melinda Gates Foundation). Other Gates initiatives included the Native American Access to

Technology Program, which provided computers to tribal libraries in New Mexico, Arizona, Colorado, and Utah (Dorr and Akeroyd, 2001).

The convergence of LSTA, Universal Service, and the Gates Foundation philanthropy, have provided U.S. public libraries with the means to incorporate new technologies and integrate electronic services into the ongoing program of public libraries throughout the nation. Yet each library will still need to develop its own technology strategies from a planning perspective. In *Wired for the Future*, the Public Library Association's manual on technology planning, the following reasons for developing a technology plan are given:

- Libraries of all sizes now recognize that planning for technology is critical if the public is to be provided effective information services.

- Plans are essential to manage the proliferation of technology applications throughout the library.

- Library boards and governing bodies need to be able to comprehend the integration of technology into all library operations.

- A common understanding of technology is required by staff, boards, and funders.

- Universal Service requires technology plans for funding (Mayo and Nelson, 1999: xiv–xvi).

Keeping Up

The public library technology environment requires a high level of engagement to stay aware of new developments. Several online services provide current information. These include ALATechSource, a Web site on library technology, and the *Library Technology Guides* Web site, which provides comprehensive information on library automation, including bibliographies and information on automation companies.

"WebJunction," a public library portal, is an online community of libraries and other agencies sharing knowledge and experience to provide the broadest public access to information technology. The portal is funded by the Bill and Melinda Gates Foundation and is a collaborative project by OCLC (Online Computer Library Center), the Colorado state Library, the Benton Foundation, Isoph, and TechSoup. These groups established WebJunction to share tips, tools, questions, and answers about computing and the Internet—through exchanged conversations, connections, courses and documents. This public library portal intends to provide the best possible public access to information technology for patrons, clients, and customers. *Crossroads*, the newsletter from WebJunction, is delivered free to subscribing libraries and archived on the WebJunction Web site (available: www.webjunction.org/do/Navigation?category=30).

The importance of technology in public libraries as a means to enhance the public's access to information has been made clear by the Institute of Museum and Library Services (IMLS) study, *Public Library Internet Services and the Digital Divide: The Role and Impacts from Selected External Funding Sources* (Bertot, McClure, and Ryan, 2002). This study and findings in the IMLS 2002 report, *Status of Technology and Digitization in the Nation's Museums and Libraries,* assessed the growth of new applications and identified the need for continued funding to extend the impact of technology to small facilities (IMLS, 2002).

Finally, the evolution of laws and legislation regarding technology access must be monitored and each community must work to develop plans in keeping with its own vision. The Children's Internet Protection Act (CIPA) is the most recent example of federal law that has great impact on library infrastructure. Upheld by the Supreme Court in 2003, the law requires that libraries receiving federal funds for Internet access must provide blocking technology. The complexity of application—including the capacity to disable the blocks for adults—requires that librarians assess the current status of such laws through resources such as WebJunction's "Focus on CIPA," and the ALA Office for Intellectual Freedom Web site.

Librarians committed to First Amendment freedoms must monitor ethical and technical issues regarding infrastructure with close attention. As Jaeger and McClure (2004) point out regarding the Supreme Court and CIPA:

> There are, nonetheless, a number of problems with the Court's decision that may offer a basis for challenging the CIPA decision. Equally important is the need for the public library community and government officials to better understand the implications of the decision and how these will affect the application of the decision in local library situations. Yet to be determined is the interest and resolve of the public library community and public library patrons to continue to challenge the CIPA decision and insure that public library users—especially adults—have not had their First

Amendment rights restricted in their access to Internet-based information.

Public librarians must work closely with their boards and local communities to ensure continued access to the Internet. The penalty for not filtering has extended beyond the e-rate to state aid in some parts of the country (National Conference of State Legislatures, 2004). The convergence of infrastructure challenges with the freedom to read requires ongoing effort to safeguard a robust commons for those who use public libraries in the United States.

Notes

1. For background on overall public library construction funded by the LSCA from 1965–1997, examine the archived report of the U.S. Department of Education. Office of Educational Research and Improvement. *Biennial Evaluation Report, 1995–1996. Public Library Construction and Technology Enhancement Grants to State Library Agencies* (CFDA No. 84-154). Available: www.ed.gov/pubs/Biennial/95-96/eval/603-97.pdf (accessed November 1, 2003). Other sources of information include ERIC reports and state library agency reports. For example, Rhode Island has provided a well-done state funding history of public library construction beginning in 1965 that documents the distribution of local, state, and federal funds. Available: www.lori.ri.gov/construction/intro/funding.php (accessed November 1, 2003). State library association journals are another source for summaries of the impact of LSCA construction funds. For example, Bridget L. Lamont, "The Legacy of the Library Services and Construction Act in Illinois," *Illinois Libraries* 80, no. 3 (Summer 1998): 93–184.

2. Telecommunications and Information Infrastructure Assistance Program, TIIAP, today called the Technology Opportunities Program, funded by the U.S. Department of Commerce, National Telecommunications and Information Administration. Available: www.ntia.doc.gov/otiahome/top/index.html.

References

ALATechSource. Available: www.techsource.ala.org.

American Library Association. 2003. Library Services for People with Disabilities. In *ALA Handbook of Organization, 2003–2004,* 54.3.2. Chicago: American Library Association.

American Library Association. Coordinating Committee on Revision of Public Library Standards. 1956. *Public Library Service: A Guide to Evaluation with Minimum Standards*. Chicago: American Library Association.

Bertot, John Carlo, Charles R. McClure, and Joe Ryan. 2002. Impact of External Technology Funding Programs for Public Libraries: A Study of LSTA, E-Rate, Gates and Others. *Public Libraries* 41 (May–June): 166–171.

Bill and Melinda Gates Foundation. Libraries. Available: www.gatesfoundation.org/libraries (accessed November 2, 2003). See especially the Library Program Fact Sheet at: www.gatesfoundation.org/MediaCenter/Publications/Library Factsheet-021201.htm.

Bobinski, George S. 1969. Carnegie Library Architecture. In *Carnegie Libraries: Their History and Impact on American Library Development*, 57–75. Chicago: American Library Association.

Building for the Future. 2003. *American Libraries* 34 (April): 41–62.

Campbell, Anne L. 2003. Magical Models. *Library Journal* (February 15): 38–40.

Crossroads. Available: www.webjunction.org/do/Navigation?category=30.

Dahlgren, Anders C. 1996. *Planning the Small Library Facility*. 2nd ed. Chicago: American Library Association.

Dahlgren, Anders C. Public Library Space Needs: A Planning Outline/1998. Wisconsin Department of Public Instruction: Public Library Development. Available: www.dpi.state.wi.us/dltcl/pld/plspace.html#Introduction (accessed November 1, 2003).

Dorr, Jessica, and Richard Akeroyd. 2001. New Mexico Tribal Libraries: Bridging the Digital Divide. *Computers in Libraries* 21, no. 8 (October): 36–43. Available: www.infotoday.com/cilmag/oct01/dorr&akeroyd.htm.

Feinberg, Sandra, Joan F. Kuchner, and Sari Feldman. 1998. *Learning Environments for Young Children: Rethinking Library Spaces and Services*. Chicago: American Library Association.

Forrest, Charles. 2002. Building Libraries and Library Building Awards—Twenty Years of Change: An Interview with Anders C. Dahlgren. *Library Administration and Management Journal* 16 (Summer): 120–125.

Fox, Bette-Lee. 2002. The Building Buck Doesn't Stop Here: Library Buildings 2002. *Library Journal* 127.20 (December): 42–55.

Goldberger, Paul. 2004. High-Tech Bibliophilia. *The New Yorker* (May 24): 90–92.

Gordon, Andrew C., et al. 2003. The Gates Legacy. *Library Journal* (March 1): 44–48.

Gregorian, Vartan. Libraries as Acts of Civic Renewal. Kansas City Public Library. Available: www.kclibrary.org/support/central/index.cfm.

Gregory, Gwen. 1999. The Library Services and Technology Act: How Changes from LSCA are Affecting Libraries. *Public Libraries* 38 (November-December): 378–382.

Institute of Museum and Library Services. Status of Technology and Digitization in the Nation's Museums and Libraries, 2002 Report. Available: www.imls.gov/reports/techreports/intro02.htm.

Jaeger, Paul T., and Charles R. McClure. 2004. Potential Legal Challenges to the Application of the Children's Internet Protection Act (CIPA) in Public

Libraries: Strategies and Issues. *First Monday* 9 (February). Available: http://firstmonday.org/issues/issue9_2/jaeger/index.html.

Joeckel, Carleton B., and Amy Winslow. 1948. *A National Plan for Public Library Service*. Chicago: American Library Association.

Jones. Theodore. 1997. *Carnegie Libraries Across America: A Public Legacy*. New York: John Wiley.

Kenney, Brian. 2001. Minneapolis PL to Revitalize Its Downtown. *Library Journal* 126 (June 15): 12.

Kent, Fred, and Phil Myrick. 2003. How To Become a Great Public Space. *American Libraries* 34 (April): 72–76.

LAMA Building Consultants List. Available: https://cs.ala.org/lbcl/search (accessed May 23, 2004).

Lane, Christian K. 1989. Chicago Public Library Competition. *Chicago Architectural Journal* 7: 6–27.

Library Technology Guides: Key Resources and Content Related to Library Automation. Available: www.librarytechnology.org/index.pl?SID=20030413217346191&UID=&auth.

Libris Design. Available: www.librisdesign.org/index.html (accessed November 1, 2003).

Lushington, Nolan. 2002. *Libraries Designed for Users: A 21st Century Guide*. New York: Neal-Schuman Publishers.

MARZ Associates, in association with WGBH, Boston. 1989. Nova: Design Wars. VHS. Boston: WGBH Educational Foundation.

Mayo, Diane, and Sandra Nelson. 1999. *Wired for the Future: Developing Your Library Technology Plan*. Chicago: American Library Association.

McCook, Kathleen de la Peña. 2000. *A Place at the Table: Participating in Community Building*. Chicago: American Library Association.

McCook, Kathleen de la Peña. 2002. *Rocks in the Whirlpool: The American Library Association and Equity of Access*. ERIC ED462981. Chicago: American Library Association. Available: www.ala.org/ala/ourassociation/governingdocs/key actionareas/equityaction/rockswhirlpool.htm.

Minneapolis Public Library. New Central Library. Available: www.mplib.org/ncl_ projectsummary102803.asp.

National Conference of State Legislatures. *Children and the Internet: Laws Relating to Filtering, Blocking and Usage Policies in Schools and Libraries*. Available: www.ncsl.org/programs/lis/CIP/filterlaws.htm

Oklahoma Territorial Museum and Carnegie Library. Available: www.okhistory.mus .ok.us/mus-sites/masnum21.htm.

Public Library Association, Standards Committee. 1967. *Minimum Standards for Public Library Systems*, 1966. Chicago: American Library Association.

Putnam, Robert D., and Lewis M. Feldstein. 2003. Branch Libraries: The Heartbeat of the Community. In *Better Together: Restoring the American Community*, 34–54. New York: Simon and Schuster.

Rabun, J. Stanley. 2000. *Structural Analysis of Historic Buildings: Restoration, Preservation and Adaptive Reuse Applications for Architects and Engineers*. New York: Wiley.

Sannwald, William W. 2001. *Checklist of Building Design Considerations*. 4th ed. Chicago: American Library Association.

Seattle Public Library. Capital Projects. Available: www.spl.org/lfa/central/building anewcentral.html.

Six Chicago Architects: Impressions of the Chicago Public Library Competition. 1989. *Chicago Architectural Journal* 7: 28–37.

Supreme Court Upholds CIPA. 2003. *Newsletter on Intellectual Freedom* 52 (September): 173; 187–191.

Tompkins County Public Library. Available: www.tcpl.org/index.html.

U.S. Access Board. Accessibility Guidelines and Standards. Available: www.access board.gov/indexes/accessindex.htm.

U.S. National Telecommunications and Information Administration. Technology Opportunities Program. Available: www.ntia.doc.gov/otiahome/top/index.html.

The Universal Service Administrative Company. Available: www.sl.universalservice.org (accessed November 2, 2003).

Wisconsin Public Library Standards, 2000. 3rd ed. Available: www.dpi.state.wi .us/dltcl/pld/chapter7.html (accessed May 23, 2004).

8

Adult Services

Since the establishment of public libraries in the 1850s the scope of services for adults has expanded from the initial development and oversight of collections organized mainly for serious adult reading, to a broader collection focus that includes recreational reading. Gradually, over the twentieth century more active services were added such as reference and information, adult education, readers' advisory, community programming, career support, genealogy, and local history. Librarians worked thoughtfully as a profession during the twentieth century to define and measure the ideal configuration of public library adult services.

Each public library determines the structure of its adult services. The difficulty in characterizing adult services derives from their diversity and from the profession's organization within the American Library Association that does not place coordinated emphasis on adult services as an area of practice. The professional focus for development of adult service standards resides primarily within two associations of the ALA—the Reference and User Services Association (RUSA) and the Public Library Association (PLA), but adult services are not addressed as a whole in the same way as library services to children or young adults. Services for adults are addressed as individual services, which makes it a challenge to convey adult services as a unified focus for public librarians. This chapter provides a brief history of the development of adult services in public libraries and then an overview of the current status of the most common adult services.

Definitions and Milestones

"Adult services" is an inclusive term designating all services provided to adults in the public library. Adult services include:

- selection of resources for the library's collection;
- providing access to the collection, including instruction, readers' advisory, and guidance;
- reference and information services;
- activation of use of the library's resources for individuals and community groups.

From the time of their founding, public libraries provided support to adults seeking self-education. This included reading guidance, service to community organizations, and adaptation of service for people with special needs. The conflict between librarians who felt libraries should only develop collections as their central purpose—evident in the ALA presidential address of Hiller C. Wellman (1915)—and those who felt that educational services were important—evident in the president address of Walter L. Brown two years later (1917)—continued for decades.

Formalization of the public library's commitment to adult services became clearer in the 1920s with the publication of several major studies relating to adult education. *The American Public Library and the Diffusion of Knowledge*, by William S. Learned (1924), resonated among librarians already involved in a variety of adult services. Adult services scholar Monroe characterized Learned's book as "a perceptive synthesis and orderly summation of significant services already envisioned and initiated in public libraries" (1963: 29). It also provided the intellectual justification for ALA to take action with the appointment of a Commission on the Library and Adult Education. The Commission report, *Libraries and Adult Education* (1926), studied the role of adult education and became the foundation of the subsequent expansion of adult services in public libraries. ALA then established a Board on Library and Adult Education, which reported activities in the journal, *Adult Education and the Library*

(1924–1930), and later the ALA *Bulletin.* These included reading studies, the "Reading with a Purpose Project" and ongoing work with the American Association for Adult Education.

In 1934 John Chancellor was appointed to the ALA Headquarters staff to initiate a ten-year assessment of adult education development in public libraries. Libraries were viewed as deeply conscious that they were an adult education agency; readers' advisory services gained acceptance; and librarians interacted with other adult education agencies. Alvin Johnson developed the argument that the public library can be a vibrant provider of knowledge, in his 1938 study, *The Public Library—A People's University*, which continues to be the source of a frequent characterization of the public library.

By the late 1930s, librarians began to use the term "adult services" more broadly than to mean "adult education," but projects within the ALA under the rubric, "adult education" continued. These included the establishment of the Adult Education Section within the Public Library Division in 1946; the American Heritage Project (funded by the Ford Foundation Fund for Adult Education—FAE) from 1951–1954; and creation of the Office of Adult Education at ALA, which awarded subgrants of $1.5 million to libraries to stimulate adult education activities (1951–1961). Funds were provided for Great Books and political education emphasizing discussion groups. A national survey of 1,692 public libraries conducted by Helen Lyman, *Adult Education Activities in Public Libraries,* was published in 1954—the first effort to describe the scope of adult services across the United States.

In 1957 after these landmark efforts, the organization of services to adults within ALA had outgrown its place within the Public Library Division and was granted division status as the Adult Services Division (ASD). At its founding ASD identified five aspects to adult services:

1. Indirect guidance (displays, reading lists)

2. Advisory services (informed and planned reading)

3. Services to organizations and groups (exhibits, readings lists, booktalks, program-planning support)

4. Library sponsored programs (films, discussion groups, radio, television)

5. Community advisory services

The Notable Books Council and other bibliographic projects relating to adult materials also fell under ASD. The Division published the *ASD Newsletter*, which incorporated the *Library Services to Labor Newsletter* in 1964. Projects carried out included the Library-Community project, the "Reading for an Age of Change" series, and work with adult new readers (McCook, 1990; Phinney, 1967).

In 1970 the ASD jointly adopted the policy, "Library Rights of Adults: A Call for Action," with the Reference Services Division (RSD), which stated that each adult should have the right to a library that seeks to understand both his needs and his wants and that uses every means to satisfy them. Given the common goals of the two divisions, a merger took place in 1972 to form the Reference and Adult Services Division (RASD). Adult services within RASD were the focus of several committees, including the "Service to Adults Committee."

During the late 1960s and 1970s U.S. libraries generally made a stronger commitment to equal service to all and adult services expanded in focus. Libraries in the south desegregated and libraries throughout the nation focused on outreach (Josey, 1994; Weibel, 1982). In 1970 ALA established the Office for Library Service to the Disadvantaged, now the Office for Literacy and Outreach Services. The purposes of the Office were (1) to promote the provision of library service to the urban and rural poor, of all ages, and to those people who are discriminated against because they belong to minority groups; (2) to encourage the development of user-oriented informational and educational library services to meet the needs of the urban and rural poor, ethnic minorities, the underemployed, school dropouts, the semiliterate and illiterate, and those isolated by cultural differences; and (3) to insure that librarians and others have information and access to technical assistance and continuing education opportunities to assist them in developing effective outreach programs (McCook, 2001b).

In *The Service Imperative for Libraries* (1982) the adult services paradigm for public libraries was presented in a series of essays in honor of Margaret E. Monroe. The four basic adult services functions identified were information, guidance, instruction, and stimulation. Monroe viewed stimulation as a library's response to community needs along a continuum from highly innovative to extensions of existing services (Schlachter, 1982).

In 1983 the Services to Adults Committee of RASD won an ALA Goal Award to conduct a national survey of adult services among 1,758 libraries serving populations of 25,000 or more. This survey extended the work done by Helen Lyman 30 years earlier was titled the "Adult Services in the Eighties"(ASE) Project. Results appeared in the 1990 monograph, *Adult Services: An Enduring Focus for Public Libraries*, with essays focusing on key services: lifelong learning; services to minorities, job seekers, labor, parents, older adults, people with disabilities, and genealogists; support for economic development; and public access microcomputers. Analysis conducted by Wallace included comparison of regional differences in service provision and demographic differences (Heim and Wallace, 1990).

RASD became the Reference and User Services Association (RUSA) in 1996, at which time the designation "adult services" disappeared from the organizational structure of the American Library Association. Rather than being the specific focus of a particular ALA unit, adult services development today is located in both RUSA and the Public Library Association. Thus, there is no single access point within the ALA for the public librarian desiring information about "adult services" that parallels the youth services associations.[1] A new service launched in 2004 by the ALA Office for Literacy and Outreach Services is a searchable database on library outreach: bookmobiles; activities for seniors; and national heritage celebrations that demonstrates the scope of adult services.

After the widespread adoption of the planning process for public libraries in the 1980s adult services in public libraries were characterized as aspects of public library roles: community activities center, community information center, formal education support center, independent learning center, popular materials library, reference library, and research center (McClure, et al., 1987). When the planning process changed terminology from "library roles" to "service responses" in the 1990s, the various adult services reached another stage in development as particular service responses (Nelson, 2001).

Types of Adult Services Today

It is one of the aims of this book to tie together the various resources that support public librarianship within the context of current practice. Instead of presenting adult services as the 13 discrete "service responses" delineated in *The New Planning for Results,* the variety of adult services in relationship to the service responses is organized here to reflect a larger vision of the public library's importance to its communities. Thus, the services are discussed in four categories, and youth services are similarly characterized in the next chapter, as follows:

- Public Sphere
- Cultural Heritage
- Education
- Information

Public Sphere

The public library in its most expansive role is as a central component of a community's "public sphere." In this capacity librarians can support the community's links to the daily reality and discourse of those it serves. It is through enhancement of the public sphere that the library builds community and encourages authentic dialogue. The service responses that serve enhancement of the public sphere are "Commons," "Community Referral," and "Current Topics and Titles."[2]

Commons

The public library is an important part of the public sphere and functions as a commons where community voices come together. Libraries provide the means to foster authentic dialogue, and librarians can work to ground the discussion of the public library's service in justice (McCook, 2001a). The importance of the public library in providing a commons was the topic of several books at the beginning of the new century that explored the larger role of the public library in connection to civil society: *Libraries and Democracy: The Cornerstones of Liberty* (Kranich, 2001); *Civic Librarianship* (McCabe, 2001); *A Place at the Table: Participating in Community Building* (McCook, 2000a); and *Civic Space/Cyberspace* (Molz and Dain, 1999). Community building and the role of the commons in the democratic process were the focus of ALA's millennium presidents, Sarah Ann Long (1999–2000) and Nancy Kranich (2000–2001). Extensive testimony to this public library response appears in the *Encyclopedia of Community* (Christensen and Levinson, 2003), which characterizes the public library as the starting point for a wide range of community projects.

The American Library Association, Public Programs Office (PPO) fosters programming that supports the role of the public library as a commons. It acts as a catalyst and promotes good practices in programming and exhibitions and develops high-quality national programs designed to encourage dialogue among community members and expose the community to new ideas and viewpoints. While there is considerable overlap in PPO's contributions to the development of the public library's response as a commons with the lifelong learning response, it is the big questions asked through programs developed by the PPO that contribute to the intellectual foundation of the library as providing stimulus for civic engagement.

In the tradition of the American Heritage Project of the 1950s the PPO has promoted reading and viewing discussion programs in the new century. Hundreds of public libraries have played the important role as a commons with programs such as "One Community, One Book"; "End of the World or World Without End;" "Long Gone: The Literature and Culture of African American Migration"; and "One Vision, Many Voices: Latino Literature in the U.S."

Community Information and Referral

Public libraries have a long history providing community information. This includes information about community agencies and organizations. The 1970s were the defining period for "information and referral" (I & R) with the Detroit Public Library's "The Information Place [TIP]" a model of a library organized to provide community information, as conceptualized by director, Clara S. Jones. The classic work covering practical case studies and the actual delivery of library-based I & R, *Information and Referral in Public Libraries*, provided an intellectual and philosophical analysis of the profession's work to develop I & R in the seventies (Childers, 1984). The appropriate role of libraries in I & R and community information was defined at the national level in the 1983 National Commission on Libraries and Information Science report, which recommended that community information and I & R are best accomplished with an interdisciplinary coordination of social service agencies and libraries.

Putting I & R and community information services into action was formalized within the American Library Association by the Community Information Section (CIS) of the Public Library Association beginning in 1979. The CIS has been committed to developing standards for information and referral for over 25 years, producing four editions of *Guidelines for Establishing Community Information and Referral Services in Public Libraries* (Maas and Manikowski, 1997).

With the advent of the Internet, community networking emerged as a complement to I & R systems (whether library-based or not). Librarians were well represented among early rounds of grantees from the Telecommunications and Information Infrastructure Assistance Program (McCook, 2000c). Committed community information librarians utilized new technologies as they developed to serve community information needs. In 1999 the possibilities of yoking I & R and electronic Web-based information as the Internet exploded were addressed in *The Community Networking Handbook* (Bajjaly, 1999).

Durrance and Pettigrew (2002) identify the contributions libraries make as providers of community information. They view the library and its staff as uniquely qualified to coordinate the provision of community information (CI) in local communities, especially as CI becomes widely available in digital formats and distributed by multiple agencies. This research has affected the development of approaches that permit librarians to determine, from the perspective of citizens, the outcomes of such community focused services as: community databases of social service information, community-technology programs for teens that seek to bridge the digital divide, and services designed to help immigrants gain the skills they need to become citizens.

The Public Library Association, Community Information Services committee promotes, publicizes, and emphasizes the role of the public library in actively providing community information to identified target groups. The committee connects with the national 2–1–1 initiative for social services information and works to integrate social service referral with library community referral (McCook, 2000c).

Current Topics and Titles

Reading and readers' services for the general reader—what most people think of as the central purpose of the public library—are addressed in *New Planning for Results* under the service response of "Current Topics and Titles." A central focus for most public libraries continues to be acquiring, organizing, and making available current collections for adults.

Decades of debate over the role of fiction in the public library collection provide an interesting history of this primary public library activity. A substantive summary of the discussions appears in two volumes by Esther Carrier, *Fiction in Public Libraries, 1876–1900* and *Fiction in Public Libraries, 1900–1950*, which provide a comprehensive analysis of the debate between adherents of "quality" fiction and those who feel that fiction of all types should be included in collections (Carrier, 1965; 1985).

Librarians responsible for collection development and readers' advisory services are most effective by being aware of the history and sociology of reading and its role in the lives of library users. Karetzky's summary of the history of reading research (1982) provides an intellectual guide to the work of early reading theorists. Knowledge of the investigations of reading provides an intellectual basis for public library collection development. Key works like *The Reading Interests and Habits of Adults* (Gray and Munroe, 1929); *What People Want to Read About* (Waples and Tyler, 1931); *Living With Books* (Haines, 1935); and *The Geography of Reading* (Wilson, 1938) are classic studies that help provide an appreciation of the role of librarians in the promotion and support of reading.

Understanding reading in the life of adults is beneficial to librarians whose role is to select and promote books. Several analyses provide excellent context:

- Korda. *Making the List* (2001)
- Salwak. *A Passion for Books* (1999)
- Radway. *A Feeling for Books* (1997)
- Manguel. *A History of Reading* (1996)
- Appleyard. *Becoming a Reader* (1990)
- Howell. *Beyond Literacy: The Second Gutenberg Revolution* (1989)
- Nell. *Lost in a Book* (1988)

These works examine reading and try to distill the meaning of the act of reading—what McCook has characterized as "the first virtual reality," or as Manguel has observed, trying to describe the variety of moods in reading:

We read in slow, long motions, as if drifting in space, weightless. We read full of prejudice, malignantly. We read generously, making excuses for the text, filling gaps, mending faults. And sometimes, when the stars are kind, we read with an intake of breath, with a shudder, as if someone or something had "walked over our grave," as if a memory had suddenly been rescued from a place deep within us—the recognition of something we never knew was there, or of something we vaguely felt as a flicker or a shadow, whose ghostly form rises and passes back into us before we can see what it is, leaving us older and wiser. (1996: 303)

The shaping of collections that will cause this intake of breath, this rescued memory is a trust that the public grants librarians. In the early 1990s the profession moved so far from the idea of shaping the collection that librarians such as Charles Robinson advocated, "Give 'Em What They Want"—and selection began to be viewed by some as primarily a reaction to demand. This abdication of responsibility has been tempered by leaders, such as Sarah Ann Long, who has noted, "We were fitting in with a tide of stylish opinion that was sweeping the country that was both anti-intellectual and anti-authority" (2001: viii). The public has also shown an appreciation for some clarity in book selection as expressed by Vivian Gornick in a February 20, 1998, piece in the *New York Times* about books that matter: "I cannot help thinking, 50 years ago in the Bronx, if the library had responded to my needs instead of shaping my needs, what sort of reader would I have become?"

Public librarians serving adults should know the history of reading and reading culture to be able to strike a balance between popular books and the classic and meaningful books that lead to introspection and understanding. The Notable Books Council of the American Library Association produces an annual list of recommended books that demonstrates this balance (Wyatt, 2002).

In addition to philosophical and sociological grounding in book culture, the public sphere is enhanced by librarians' stimulation of reading current topics and titles. A local example with national impact is the Adult Reading Round Table (ARRT) founded in 1984 based in concern over the profession's lack of attention to readers' advisory services for adults. A renaissance of interest in readers' advisory services took place during the 1990s—the same years that so much of the profession's focus was on technology, the Internet and digitization (Balcolm, 2002). The popularity of all kinds of fiction is underscored by the publication of five editions of *Genreflecting* since 1982 (Herald).

Examples of specific activities librarians can undertake to generate interest in current topics and titles include:

- "one community-one book" programs (*One Book, One Community Planning Guide*)
- booktalks (Booktalking: Quick and Simple)
- book discussion groups (Balcolm, 1992)

- author programs (Sager 1998)
- readers' advisory[3]
- displays (Hawthorne and Gibson)
- promotion of award books[4]

The Center for the Book at the Library of Congress and State Centers for the Book develop activities that promote each state's book culture and literary heritage. Book festivals at the national, state, and local level emerged during the 1990s as a new focus for people who care about reading.[5] The National Endowment for the Humanities and state Humanities Councils support research, education, preservation, and public programs. By working closely with these entities public librarians can extend community dialogue based on reading to topics of current importance.

Library historians seeking to capture the library experience from the users' angle of vision, and that of others involved with libraries, can make clearer the role of libraries in the life of the individual and in the intellectual, cultural, and social life of those who live in the United States. For instance, examining the library experience will further increase understanding of the extent to which librarians have attempted to mediate between the reader and the book to lead the reader to "high" culture (Carpenter, 1996). Herein may be the heart of the librarian's role in the transcendence of the public sphere. The meaning of carefully developed library collections, expert readers' advisory service, and the importance of books in our society is reinforced by musing upon the power of the humanities. In *Riches for the Poor*, Earl Shorris tells the story of the poor in the United States; he shows how the poor are much like everyone else; he shows that the difference between a comfortable life and a life of poverty is often the failure of the poor to enter the political life—a life that requires reflection. The power of reading to change lives through cultivation of the public sphere in libraries is mighty.

Cultural Heritage

Public libraries have long played an important role in preserving and activating cultural heritage and often included museum-like collections (Dilevko, 2003). Reading discussion groups, lectures, film series, exhibits, and celebrations of different cultures, are central adult services that are the basis for partnerships that have expanded the library's involvement in local communities. Additionally, attention to cultural heritage connects the library to state and national organizations that have cognate missions. Three especially come to mind: the National Endowment for the Humanities, the Center for the Book, and the Institute of Museum and Library Services.

Since 1979 the National Endowment for the Humanities (NEH) has supported opportunities for the public to explore the humanities and culture through activities such as exhibitions, reading and film discussion series, catalogs, lectures, symposia, and Web sites. State humanities councils affiliated with NEH have strengthened cultural heritage presence with a regional focus. The American Library Association, most often through its Public Programs Office, has collaborated with NEH to develop library-based humanities programming and its mission "Linking Libraries, Communities, and Culture," underscores the integral role libraries play in providing a forum for cultural exploration.[6] The Public Programs Office fosters cultural programming as an integral part of library service in all types of libraries.

The cultural heritage mission is further enhanced through public libraries' connection to the Center for the Book at the Library of Congress, established in 1977 under the aegis of then Librarian of Congress, Daniel J. Boorstin, who saw great value in the Library of Congress actively promoting books and reading. The National Book Committee (1954–1974) and the U.S. Governmental Advisory Committee on International Books and Library Programs (1962–1977) supported by the State Department merged to became the first Advisory Committee for the Center for the Book. The Center for the Book and its state affiliates work closely with libraries to promote national reading campaigns.

In 1996 the Institute of Museum and Library Services (IMLS) was established as an independent federal grant-making agency that fosters innovation, leadership, and a lifetime of learning by supporting the nation's museums and libraries. Grants and programs supported by IMLS have strengthened the ties between libraries and other cultural heritage institutions—especially museums. The IMLS focus on the learner in a changing world through collaborative partnerships strengthens public library ties to cultural heritage values.

The service responses in *New Planning for Results* that correspond to the cultural heritage category are "Lifelong Learning," "Cultural Awareness," and "Local History and Genealogy."[7]

Lifelong Learning

Lifelong learners have been defined as adults involved in learning activities other than compulsory (K–12) education. They include those involved in voluntary learning activities, as well as in activities that are required for legal, professional, or other reasons (U.S. DOE, 2000). Public librarians can call upon a long tradition of commitment to the development of human capabilities to provide continuing emphasis on the humanistic aspects of adult learning (Lee, 1966; Monroe, 1963; Van Fleet, 1990; Van Fleet and Raber, 1990).

The Public Library Association, Adult Continuing and Independent Learning Services Committee supports librarians serving lifelong learners by identifying, assembling, and making widely available, information about existing continuing and independent learning and resources in public libraries. Recent guides to adult programming provide libraries with methods to integrate programming and lifelong learning (Lear, 2002; Mates, 2003; Rubin, 1997).

Cultural Awareness

Helping users to understand and appreciate the culture of others is an important aspect of adult services. However, identifying resources and evaluating them can be difficult without specific expertise. The Ethnic and Multicultural Information Exchange Round Table (EMIERT) of the ALA serves as a source of information on ethnic collections, services, and programs and the PLA Services to Multicultural Populations Committee develops strategies for providing public library service to diverse populations.

Librarians of color have formed separate organizations to focus more clearly on service to people from different cultures. These include the American Indian Library Association (AILA); Asian/Pacific American Librarians Association (APALA); Black Caucus of the American Library Association (BCALA); Chinese American Librarians Association (CALA); and REFORMA—National Association to Promote Library and Information Services to Latinos and the Spanish-Speaking. The American Library Association works closely with these affiliates through its Offices of Diversity and the Office for Literacy and Outreach Services, which sponsors the annual Jean E. Coleman lecture on outreach.[8] By working in collaboration with organizations of librarians of color, public librarians will find the resources and support to develop services that honor and respect the cultural heritage of the many people who comprise the diverse population of the United States (McCook, 2000b).

The Gay, Lesbian, Bisexual, and Transgendered Round Table (GLBTRT) works to develop service models. Carmichael, in *Daring to Find Our Names: The Search for Lesbigay Library History* (1998), describes how the energies of the GLBTRT have been devoted to service concerns for lesbigay patrons through subject headings that are not pejorative and promotion of gay literature. Joyce has reviewed the literature for public librarians and described the challenges to fully inclusive service for the gay, lesbian, and transgendered community.

Local History and Genealogy

For many communities the public library provides access to community memory through the development of local history collections and genealogy services. The RUSA Genealogical Committee, which has issued its booklet, "Guidelines for Establishing Local History Collections" that state at the outset that libraries should connect with other community agencies. A key partnership is the American Association for State and Local History, which provides leadership and support to preserve and interpret state and local history in order to make the past more meaningful to all Americans. Preserving and safeguarding local history is a central contribution that librarians can make to build local communities (Archibald, 1999).

The responsibility of public libraries to serve the needs of patrons interested in genealogical research is addressed by the RUSA Genealogical Committee, which has issued its booklet, "Guidelines for Developing Beginning Genealogical Collections and Services." Services to genealogists are an important aspect of cultural heritage service that connects cultural awareness and local history concerns.

Education

Public libraries provide adult support for education primarily through the library responses from *New Planning for Results* for "Basic Literacy Services," "Information Literacy," and "Formal Learning Support."[9]

Basic Literacy

The 2002 NCES report, *Programs for Adults in Public Library Outlets* (U.S. DOE, 2002), reported that 17 percent of public library outlets offered adult literacy programs including adult basic literacy, pre-GED, GED, English as a Second Language, and family literacy. Larger libraries were most likely to offer programs. Today U.S. public librarians are allied with the national movement on literacy through the National Institute for Literacy (NIFL), which serves as a focal point for public and private activities that support

the development of high-quality regional, state, and national literacy services. The goal of NIFL is to ensure that all Americans with
literacy needs have access to services that can help them gain the
basic skills necessary for success in the workplace, family, and community in the twenty-first century.

The ALA Committee on Literacy works with the ALA Office for
Literacy and Outreach Services (OLOS) as liaison to NIFL and to
provide policy input at the national level. BuildLiteracy, an OLOS
project, is an interactive how-to Web site for building and sustaining
literacy coalitions, collaborations, and partnerships. Examples of
public library literacy services are included in *Literacy and Libraries:
Learning From Case Studies* published in 2001 (DeCandido, 2001).

Two Public Library Association committees help support literacy services. The "Basic Education and Literacy Services" committee
identifies resources useful in developing, implementing, and maintaining literacy activities, and works to make librarians aware of the
value of cooperation with other agencies in the formation and execution of literacy programs. The "Resources for the Adult New Reader"
committee informs publishers that librarians have a growing interest in professional and learning materials in areas of adult education: literacy, GED, career information, and various other areas and
encourages publishers to produce and market more titles on these
subjects. The committee also compiles the "Best Books for the Adult
New Reader 2003" list.[10]

Fundamental questions about the focus of public libraries and
the provision of adult literacy services are analyzed in McCook
and Barber (2002b). They contend that if librarians do not incorporate adult lifelong learning theory with literacy and make a broader
commitment to "learning for life," librarians may not achieve the goal
of a learning society for residents of the United States. Recognition of
the facets of public policy in the G. W. Bush administration that provide literacy support only for purposes of earning must be confronted
so that public libraries serve the larger humanistic needs for culture
and education.

Information Literacy

Providing resources for users to find, evaluate and use information effectively involves individual and group support. The
Information Literacy Toolkit (ACRL) provides this definition:

> Information literacy is related to information technology
> skills, but has broader implications for the individual, the

educational system, and for society. Information technology skills enable an individual to use computers, software applications, databases, and other technologies to achieve a wide variety of academic, work-related, and personal goals. Information literate individuals necessarily develop some technology skills.[11]

The American Library Association's reports of the Presidential Committee on Information Literacy and the study by Spitzer, Eisenberg, and Lowe (1998) connect public libraries to this adult service. While most research and writing has focused on academic settings, the findings are applicable to public library development of information literacy services.

The 2002 NCES report, *Programs for Adults in Public Library Outlets*, reported that 92 percent of all public libraries provide Internet access. To support librarians providing service to these users of electronic information RUSA has issued "Guidelines for the Introduction of Electronic Information Resources to Users" and "Electronic Information Sources Guidelines for Training Sessions."

Formal Learning Support

Services provided as part of the "Information Literacy" response flow into those for "Formal Learning Support." This response includes services for homeschooling families, families with children enrolled in charter schools, distance learners, and enrolled students for whom the public library may be more easily accessible than the academic library. As education becomes less campus based, the role of the public library in support of formal learning is likely to expand.

Many families that homeschool their children rely on the public library to provide them with resources they use in their educational endeavors and with services, such as library tours, story programs, and computer instruction (Kleist-Tesch, 1998). Guidelines for academic distance learners also provide structure for public libraries supporting formal education (ACRL).

Information

Four public library responses from *New Planning for Results* are organized around the broad category of information. These include "General Information," "Business and Career Information," "Consumer Information," and "Government Information."[12] The 2003 *Professional Competencies for Reference and User Services*

Librarians (RUSA) outline the characteristics of information services librarians, who are responsive to user needs, carefully analyze sources and services, keep current with developments in the field, utilize new knowledge to enhance service, and communicate the nature of the services provided to users. Information services should be effectively designed and organized to meet the needs of the primary community, promoted to users, and evaluated and assessed on an ongoing basis. RUSA's *Guidelines for Behavioral Performance of Reference and Information Service Providers* have been revised to provide guidance in serving remote as well as in person users.

General Information

Information services take a variety of forms—direct individual assistance, signs, directories, Web site links, and telephone and e-mail reference. "Guidelines for Information Services" developed by the Reference and User Services Association (RUSA, 2000), addresses six categories:

- Services—stressing accuracy, accessibility, instruction, publicity, community information, adding value to information, and referral.

- Resources—the information collection should be current and reflect the spectrum of the population served; when necessary, external reference sources should be consulted.

- Access—information services should be well configured with attention to the needs of people with disabilities; state-of-the-art communications methods; and services available to meet the community's needs.

- Personnel—staff should have knowledge and preparation to meet information needs of the library's clientele; effective interpersonal communication skills; competency in using information technology.

- Evaluation—services should be evaluated for response time; accessibility; effectiveness for various groups among the population served; effectiveness in meeting the community's needs; and statistical data for comparison with national norms.

- Ethics—the ALA Code of Ethics governs conduct of those providing information services.

General information services are undergoing much change as information services evolve to accommodate an increasingly digital world. *Professional Competencies for Reference and User Services Librarians* outline the information services librarian's responsibilities to maintain currency and engagement with these changes, and *Guidelines for Behavioral Performance of Reference and Information Service Providers* provide strategies regardless of format (RUSA).

Government Information

Government information is highly complex and can require special expertise especially in the case of laws and regulations. Although the Internet has made resources more widely available, there are still many aspects of access to government information that require interpretation and mediation by librarians. The Government Documents Roundtable of the ALA provides oversight about access to documents and appoints task forces to ensure the continuation of availability. It is also important to recognize that provision of government information includes all levels and jurisdictions—local and state, as well as the documents of foreign governments and international bodies, such as the United Nations. If the provision of government information is selected as a key response the library will need to determine the categories of documents.

Business and Career Information; Consumer Information

Libraries are an important source of information for economic development for the community. Business Information includes services for community economic development and services for the individual. The Business Reference and Services Section (BRASS) of RUSA provides extensive resources for addressing the needs of the business community and includes committees that focus on service to public libraries. BRASS publishes the "Public Libraries Briefcase," "Guidelines for Medical, Legal, and Business Responses," and "'Best of the Best' Business Web Sites."

The PLA Career and Business Services Committee supports public library service to business and studies the validation of public library services to the business community, as well as the impact of business services and the return on this investment. Services to job seekers, especially in times of economic downturn, may also be a focus of service. The cost of books, periodicals, a functional computer, and online access to the Internet required to carry out basic job searches, study for the GED, or develop work skills are beyond the means of this large portion of the population. Underemployment has grown as the 1996 Personal Responsibility and Work Opportunity Reconciliation Act has placed strict limits on public assistance. These factors combined make public libraries a critical component in the effort of poor people to participate in workforce development.

Service for All

Adult services configured to respond to community needs must take into consideration the needs of individual adults and the challenges to provide access for everyone in the community. Implementation of the goal to provide service for all has many aspects, including usability for people with disabilities; linguistic diversity by providing materials and services for people with different languages; as well as helping communities overcome economic barriers, such as the digital divide.

The American Library Association has established key action areas to promote access for all, notably, Equity of Access (Osborne, 2004; McCook, 2002). The implementation takes place through various association initiatives such as the "Library Services for People with Disabilities Policy," advocated by Rhea Rubin, which states:

> Libraries play a catalytic role in the lives of people with disabilities by facilitating their full participation in society. Libraries should use strategies based upon the principles of universal design to ensure that library policy, resources and services meet the needs of all people.

Guidelines for Library Services to Older Adults (RUSA) demonstrate the multifaceted approach that must be taken to develop equitable service for any special category of users. The *Guidelines* consider accessibility, respect, communication, programming, materials, and community partnerships. They provide an overall structural approach that parallels specific services responses.

For the 47 million U.S. residents (18.2 percent) who speak a language other than English at home, public libraries must provide resources to assist in learning English as a second language and provide access to materials in native languages (EMIERT). Consider that there are 28 million U.S. residents who speak Spanish. The challenges in serving this population are great: many come from countries where public library services do not exist, they may not be literate in their spoken language, library signage and forms may be only in English, and few librarians are of Latino heritage (Güereña, 2000).

There are 34.6 million people in the United States whose earnings are below the official poverty rate ($18,392 for a family of four) and poverty disproportionately affects people of color (24.1 percent African American; 21.8 percent Hispanic origin). The ALA policy, "Library Services for the Poor," advocated by Sanford Berman, a founder of the SRRT Task Force on Hunger, Homelessness and Poverty, states, "it is crucial that libraries recognize their role in enabling poor people to participate fully in a democratic society" (American Library Association, 2003: 54). Librarians need to study communities to determine the best configuration of services. Ours is a nation of extremes. At the Pine Ridge Indian reservation in Shannon County, South Dakota, which is 94.2 percent Native American, the per capita income is $6,286. Anne Arundel County in Maryland is 81 percent white with a per capita income of $27,578. They both need equitable library service.

Serving communities that are at once poor and represent a different culture requires a commitment by librarians for social justice and equity. In the essays for the book *Poor People and Library Services*, we note there are no "problem" patrons—just people who might need help (Venturella, 1998). Librarians configuring adult services must consider all aspects of the human condition.

Notes

1. For additional background, see articles by Kathleen de la Peña McCook, "Adult Services as Reflective of the Changing Role of the Public Library," *RQ* 26 (Winter 1986): 180–187; "The Developing Role of Public Libraries in Adult Education: 1966 to 1991," in *Partners for Lifelong Learning: Public Libraries and Adult Education*, 21–53 (Washington, DC: U.S. Department of Education, 1991); and "Where Would We Be Without Them? Libraries and Adult Education Activities: 1966–1991," *RQ* 32 (Winter 1992): 245–253.

2. Sandra Nelson. *The New Planning for Results: A Streamlined Approach* (Chicago: American Library Association, 2001), "Commons," 161–165; "Community Referral," 166–171; "Current Topics and Titles," 183–187.

3. Joyce G. Saricks and Nancy Brown, *Readers' Advisory Services in the Public Library*, 2nd ed. (Chicago: American Library Association, 1997). See also Kenneth D. Shearer and Robert Burgin, *Readers' Advisor's Companion* (Littleton, CO: Libraries Unlimited,

2002); Ricki Nordmeyer, "Readers' Advisory Websites," *Reference and User Services Quarterly* 41 (Winter 2001): 139–143; Duncan Smith, "Talking with Readers: A Competency Based Approach to Readers' Advisory Services," *Reference and User Services Quarterly* 40 (Winter 2000): 135–142; Mary K. Chelton, "What We Know and Don't Know about Reading, Readers, and Readers' Advisory Services," *Public Libraries* 38 (Jan/Feb 1999): 42–47; Kenneth D. Shearer, *Guiding the Reader to the Next Book* (New York: Neal-Schuman, 1996); Kathleen de la Peña McCook and Gary O. Rolstad, *Developing Readers' Advisory Services: Concepts and Commitments* (New York: Neal-Schuman Publishers, 1993). Librarians can find many guides and resources for specific types of readers' advisory, for example, Diana Tixier Herald, *Genreflecting: A Guide to Reading Interests in Genre Fiction,* 5th edition (Libraries Unlimited, 2000); Joyce G. Saricks, *The Readers' Advisory Guide to Genre Fiction* (Chicago: American Library Association, 2001).

4. Award books provide a focal point for exhibits, displays and discussion. Major sites include the Notable Books Council (American Library Association, Reference and User Services Association). Available: www.ala.org/rusa/notable.html. Bookwire provides links to major award sites. Available: www.bookwire.com/bookwire/other books/Book-Awards.html.

5. The 2003 National Book Festival featured more than eighty award-winning and nationally known authors, illustrators, poets, and storytellers, as well as storybook characters from children's classics. Library of Congress, National Book Festival. Available: www.loc.gov/bookfest/relatedsites/index.html. Many states and local communities also hold book festivals. See for instance:

- Arizona Book Festival. Available: www.azbookfestival.org.

- Border Book Festival. Available: www.zianet.com/bbf/history.htm.

- Louisiana Book Festival. Available: www.louisianabook festival.org.

- Texas Book Festival. Available: www.texasbookfestival.org.

- Virginia Festival of the Book. Available: www.vabook.org.

- Wisconsin Book Festival. Available: www.wisconsinbook festival.org/overview.

Many more are listed at the Web site of the Institute of Museum and Library Services. Available: www.imls.gov/pubs/bookfest.htm.

6. In 1965 the National Foundation on the Arts and Humanities Act was passed creating the National Endowment for the Humanities (NEH). In 1979 a program to support humanities programs in public libraries was established. National Endowment for the Humanities, *NEH and America's Libraries* (Washington, DC: NEH, 1998). National Endowment for the Humanities, "Who We Are—Timeline." Available: www.neh.gov/whoweare/timeline.html (accessed April 17, 2002).

7. Nelson, *The New Planning*, "Life Long Learning," 211–215; "Cultural Awareness," 178–182; "Local History and Genealogy," 216–220.

8. These various organizations are accessible online:

- American Library Association. Office for Diversity. Available: www.ala.org/diversity.

- American Library Association. Office for Literacy and Outreach Services. Jean E. Coleman Lecture. Available: www.ala.org/ala/olos/olosprograms/jeanecoleman/firstjeanecoleman.htm.

- American Indian Library Association (AILA). Est. 1979. Available: www.nativeculture.com/lisamitten/aila.html.

- Asian/Pacific American Librarians Association (APALA). Est. 1980. Available: www.uic.edu/depts/lib/projects/resources/apala.

- Black Caucus of the American Library Association (BCALA). Est. 1970. Available: www.bcala.org.

- Chinese American Librarians Association (CALA). Est. 1983. Available: www.cala-web.org.

- REFORMA: The National Association to Promote Library and Information Service to Latinos and the Spanish Speaking. Est. 1971. Available: www.reforma.org.

9. Nelson, *The New Planning*, "Basic Literacy," 151–155; "Information Literacy," 205–210; "Formal Learning Support," 188–194.

10. Public Library Association, Basic Education and Literacy Services Committee and Resources for the New Adult Reader Committee. These continue earlier ALA projects on materials for the new reader: Helen H. Lyman, *Library Materials in Service to the*

Adult New Reader (Chicago: ALA, 1973); *Reading and the Adult New Reader* (Chicago: ALA, 1976); *Literacy and the Nation's Libraries* (Chicago: ALA, 1977).

11. Association of College and Research Libraries. *Information Literacy Toolkit*. Available: www.ala.org/ACRLTemplate.cfm. The ACRL Information Literacy Institute includes partnerships with public libraries, as well as best practices.

12. Nelson, *The New Planning*, "General Information," 195–199; "Business and Career Information," 156–160; "Consumer Information," 172–177; "Government Information," 200–204.

References

American Library Association. 2003. *Library Services for the Poor*. ALA Handbook of Organization, 2003–2004. Chicago: American Library Association. Available: www.ala.org/ala/ourassociation/handbook20032004/2003handbookPDF.pdf

American Library Association. Office on Literacy and Outreach Services. Outreach at your Library. Available: http://cs.ala.org/olos/outreach/participating.cfm.

Appleyard, J. A. 1990. *Becoming a Reader: The Experience of Fiction from Childhood to Adulthood*. Cambridge, MA: Cambridge University Press.

Archibald, Robert R. 1999. *A Place to Remember: Using History to Build Community*. Walnut Creek, CA: Rowman and Littlefield.

Association for College and Research Libraries (ACRL). Information Literacy Toolkit. Available: www.ala.org/acrl. See especially the ACRL paper, Guidelines for Distance Learning Library Services.

Bajjaly, Stephen T. 1999. *The Community Networking Handbook*. Chicago: ALA Editions.

Balcom, Ted. 1992. *Book Discussion for Adults: A Leader's Guide*. Chicago: American Library Association.

Balcom, Ted. 2002. The Adult Reading Round Table. *Reference and User Services Quarterly* 41 (Spring): 238–243.

Birge, Lynn E. 1981. *Serving Adult Learners: A Public Library Tradition*. Chicago: American Library Association.

Bleiweiss, Maxine. 1997. *Helping Business: The Library's Role in Community Economic Development*. New York: Neal-Schuman Publishers.

Booktalking: Quick and Simple. Available: http://nancykeane.com/booktalks.

Breivik, Patricia Senn, Vicki Hancock, and J. A. Senn. 1998. A Progress Report on Information Literacy: An Update on the American Library Association Presidential Committee on Information Literacy: Final Report. Chicago: Association of College and Research Libraries. Available: www.ala.org/ala/acrl/acrlpubs/whitepapers/progressreport.htm.

Brown, Walter L. 1917. The Changing Public. *ALA Bulletin* 11 (July): 91–95.

BuildLiteracy. American Library Association. Available: www.buildliteracy.org/index.htm.

Carmichael, James V., Jr. 1998. *Daring to Find Our Names: The Search Lesbigay Library History*. Westport, CN: Greenwood.

Carpenter, Kenneth E. 1996. *Toward a History of Libraries and Culture in America*. Washington, DC: Library of Congress.

Carr, David W. 2000. In the Context of the Possible. *RBM* 1: 117–135.

Carrier, Esther Jane. 1965. *Fiction in Public Libraries, 1876–1900*. New York: Scarecrow Press.

Carrier, Esther Jane. 1985. *Fiction in Public Libraries, 1900–1950*. Littleton, CO: Libraries Unlimited.

Childers, Thomas. 1984. *Information and Referral: Public Libraries*. Norwood, NJ: Ablex.

Christensen, Karen, and David Levinson, eds. 2003. *Encyclopedia of Community*. Thousand Oaks, CA: Sage Publications. See especially the articles, Information Communities, 657–660; Public Libraries, 1114–1117; and Libraries Build Community, Appendix 2, 1533–1551.

Croneberger, Robert, and Carolyn Luck. 1975. Defining Information and Referral Service. *Library Journal* 100 (November 1): 1984–1987.

Dane, William J. 1990. John Cotton Dana: A Contemporary Appraisal of His Contributions and Lasting Influence on the Library and Museum Worlds 60 Years After His Death. *Art Libraries Journal* 15: 5–9.

DeCandido, GraceAnne, ed. 2001. *Literacy and Libraries: Learning From Case Studies*. Chicago: American Library Association.

Dilevko, Juris, and Lisa Gottlieb. 2003. Resurrecting a Neglected Idea: The Re-Introduction of Library-Museum Hybrids. *Library Quarterly* 73 (April): 160–198.

Durrance, Joan C., and Karen E. Pettigrew. 2002. *Online Community Information: Creating a Nexus at Your Library*. Chicago: American Library Association.

Gray, William S., and Ruth Munroe. 1929. *The Reading Interests and Habits of Adults*. New York: Macmillan.

Güereña, Salvador. 2000. *Library Services to Latinos*. Jefferson, NC: McFarland and Co.

Haines, Helen E. 1935. *Living with Books: The Art of Book Selection*. New York: Columbia University Press.

Heim (de la Peña McCook), Kathleen M., and Danny P. Wallace. 1990. *Adult Services: An Enduring Focus for Public Libraries*. Chicago: American Library Association.

Herald, Diana Tixier. 2000. *Genreflecting: A Guide to Reading Interests in Genre Fiction*. 5th ed. Englewood, CO: Libraries Unlimited.

Howell, R. Patton. 1989. *Beyond Literacy: The Second Gutenberg Revolution*. San Francisco: Saybrook.

Johnson, Alvin. 1938. *The Public Library—A People's University*. New York: American Association for Adult Education.

Jones, Clara S. 1978. *Public Library Information and Referral Service*. Syracuse, NY: Gaylord Professional Publications.

Josey, E. J. 1994. Race Issues in Library History. In *Encyclopedia of Library History*, ed. W. A. Wiegand and D. G. Davis, 533–537. New York: Garland Publishing.

Joyce, Steven. 2000. Lesbian, Gay and Bisexual Library Service: A Review of the Literature. *Public Libraries* 39 (September/October): 270–279.

Karetzky, Stephen. 1982. *Reading Research and Librarianship: A History and Analysis*. Westport, CT: Greenwood Press.

Kleist-Tesch, Jane M. 1998. Homeschoolers and the Public Library. *Journal of Youth Services* 11 (Spring): 231–241.

Korda, Michael. 2001. *Making the List: A Cultural History of the American Best Seller, 1900–1999*. New York: Barnes and Noble.

Kranich, Nancy, ed. 2001. *Libraries and Democracy: The Cornerstones of Liberty*. Chicago: American Library Association.

Lear, Brett W. 2002. *Adult Programs in the Library*. Chicago: American Library Association.

Learned, William S. 1924. *The American Public Library and the Diffusion of Knowledge*. New York: Harcourt.

Lee, Robert Ellis. 1966. *Continuing Education for Adults through the American Public Library 1833–1966*. Chicago: American Library Association.

Library of Congress. Center for the Book: State Center Affiliates. Available: www.loc.gov/loc/cfbook/stacen.html.

Library of Congress. National Book Festival. Available: www.loc.gov/bookfest/relatedsites/index.html.

Library Rights of Adults. 1970. *ASD Newsletter* 8 (Winter): 2–3.

Local Book Festivals and Reading Programs. Institute of Museum and Library Services. Available: www.imls.gov/pubs/bookfest.htm.

Long, Sarah Ann. 2001. Foreword. In *Civic Librarianship: Renewing the Social Mission of the Public Library*, ed. Ronald B. McCabe, vii-ix. Lanham, MD: Scarecrow Press.

Lyman, Helen. 1954. *Adult Education Activities in Public Libraries*. Chicago: American Library Association.

Maas, Norman L., and Dick Manikowski. 1997. *Guidelines for Establishing Community Information and Referral Services in Public Libraries*. 4th ed. Chicago: American Library Association.

Manguel, Alberto. 1996. *A History of Reading*. New York: Penguin.

Mates, Barbara T. 2003. *5-Star Programming and Services for your 55+ Customers*. Chicago: American Library Association.

McCabe, Ronald B. 2001. *Civic Librarianship: Renewing the Social Mission of the Public Library*. Lanham, MD: Scarecrow Press.

McClure, Charles R., et al. 1987. *Planning and Role Setting for Public Libraries: A Manual of Options and Procedures*. Chicago: American Library Association.

McCook, Kathleen de la Peña. 1990. Adult Services: An Enduring Focus. In *Adult Services: An Enduring Focus for Public Libraries*. eds. Kathleen M. Heim (de la Peña McCook) and Danny P. Wallace, 11–26. Chicago: American Library Association.

McCook, Kathleen de la Peña. 1993. The First Virtual Reality. *American Libraries* 24 (July/August): 626–628.

McCook, Kathleen de la Peña. 2000a. *A Place at the Table: Participating in Community Building.* Chicago: American Library Association.

McCook, Kathleen de la Peña, ed. 2000b. Ethnic Diversity in Library and Information Science. *Library Trends* 49 (Summer): 1–214.

McCook, Kathleen de la Peña. 2000c. Service Integration and Libraries. *Reference and User Services Quarterly* 40 (Winter): 22–25.

McCook, Kathleen de la Peña. 2001a. Authentic Discourse as a Means of Connection Between Public Library Service Responses and Community Building Initiatives. *Reference and User Services Quarterly* 40 (Winter): 127–133.

McCook, Kathleen de la Peña. 2001b. Poverty, Democracy, and Public Libraries. In *Libraries and Democracy: The Cornerstones of Liberty.* ed. Nancy Kranich, 28–46. Chicago: American Library Association.

McCook, Kathleen de la Peña. 2002. *Rocks in the Whirlpool: The American Library Association and Equity of Access.* ERIC ED462981. Chicago: American Library Association. Available: www.ala.org/ala/ourassociation/governingdocs/key actionareas/equityaction/rockswhirlpool.htm.

McCook, Kathleen de la Peña, and Peggy Barber. 2002a. *Chronology of Milestones for Libraries and Adult Lifelong Learning and Literacy.* ERIC. Washington, DC.

McCook, Kathleen de la Peña, and Peggy Barber. 2002b. Public Policy as a Factor Influencing Adult Lifelong Learning, Adult Literacy and Public Libraries. *Reference and User Services Quarterly* 42.1 (Fall): 66–75.

Molz, Redmond Kathleen, and Phyllis Dain. 1999. *Civic Space/Cyberspace: The American Public Library in the Information Age.* Cambridge, MA: MIT Press.

Monroe, Margaret E. 1963. *Library Adult Education: The Biography of an Idea.* New York: Scarecrow Press.

Monroe, Margaret E. 1981. The Cultural Role of the Public Library. *Advances in Librarianship* 11: 1–49.

National Endowment for the Humanities. State Humanities Councils. Available: www.neh.gov/whoweare/statecouncils.html.

National Institute for Literacy. Available: www.nifl.gov.

Nell, Victor. 1988. *Lost in a Book: The Psychology of Reading for Pleasure.* New Haven, CT: Yale University Press.

Nelson, Sandra. 2001. *The New Planning for Results: A Streamlined Approach.* Chicago: American Library Association.

One Book, One Community Planning Guide. 2003. Chicago: American Library Association.

Osborne, Robin. 2004. *From Outreach to Equity: Innovative Models of Library Policy and Practice.* Chicago: American Library Association.

Phinney, Eleanor. 1967. Ten Years from the Vantage Point of the Executive Secretary. *AD Newsletter* 4 (Summer): 11–14.

Radway, Janice A. 1997. *A Feeling for Books: The Book-of-the-Month Club, Literary Taste, and Middle Class Desire.* Chapel Hill, NC: University of North Carolina Press.

Reference and User Services Association (RUSA). 1993. Guidelines for Establishing Local History Collections. Available: www.ala.org/ala/rusa/rusaprotools/ referenceguide/guidelinesestablishing.htm.

Reference and User Services Association (RUSA). 1995. Electronic Information Sources Guidelines for Training Sessions. Available: www.ala.org/ala/ rusa/rusaprotools/referenceguide/electronicinformation.htm.

Reference and User Services Association (RUSA). 1996. Guidelines for Behavioral Performance of Reference and Information Service Providers. Available: www.ala.org/ala/rusa/rusaprotools/referenceguide/guidelinesbehavioral.htm.

Reference and User Services Association (RUSA). 1997. Guidelines for the Introduction of Electronic Information Resources to Users. Available: www.ala.org/ala/rusa/rusaprotools/referenceguide/guidelinesintroduction.htm.

Reference and User Services Association (RUSA). 1999a. Guidelines for Developing Beginning Genealogical Collections and Services. Available: www.ala.org/ ala/rusa/rusaprotools/referenceguide/guidelinesdeveloping.htm.

Reference and User Services Association (RUSA). 1999b. Guidelines for Library Services to Older Adults. Available: www.ala.org/ala/rusa/rusaprotools/ referenceguide/libraryservices.htm.

Reference and User Services Association (RUSA). 2000. Guidelines for Information Services. Available: www.ala.org/ala/rusa/rusaprotools/referenceguide/guide linesinformation.htm.

Reference and User Services Association (RUSA). 2003. Professional Competencies for Reference and User Services Librarians. Available: www.ala.org/ala/rusa/ rusaprotools/referenceguide/professional.htm.

Rubin, Rhea Joyce. 1997. *Humanities Programming: A How-To-Do-It Manual*. New York: Neal-Schuman Publishers.

Sager, Donald J., ed. 1998. Authors in Public Libraries. *Public Libraries* 37 (July/August): 237–241.

Salwak, Dale. 1999. *A Passion for Books*. New York: St. Martin's Press.

Schlachter, Gail A. 1982. *The Service Imperative for Libraries: Essays in Honor of Margaret E. Monroe*. Littleton, CO: Libraries Unlimited.

Shorris, Earl. 2000. *Riches for the Poor*. New York: W. W. Norton and Company.

Spitzer, Kathleen L., Michael B. Eisenberg, and Carrie A. Lowe. 1998. *Information Literacy: Essential Skills for the Information Age*. ERIC ED427780. Syracuse, NY: *ERIC Clearinghouse on Information and Technology*.

Stevenson, Grace T. 1954. The ALA Adult Education Board. *ALA Bulletin* 48b (April): 226–231.

U.S. Department of Education. 2000. *Lifelong Learning NCES Task Force: Final Report, Volume II, Working Paper No. 2000-16b*. Washington, DC: U.S. Department of Education.

U.S. Department of Education. National Center for Education Statistics. 2002. *Programs for Adults in Public Library Outlets*. Washington, DC: National Center for Education Statistics.

U.S. National Commission on Libraries and Information Science. 1983. *Final Report to the National Commission on Libraries and Information Science from the*

Community Information and Referral Task Force. ERIC ED241014. Washington, DC: National Commission on Libraries and Information Science.

Van Fleet, Connie. 1990. Lifelong Learning Theory and the Provision of Adult Services. In *Adult Services: An Enduring Focus for Public Libraries,* ed. Kathleen M. Heim (de la Peña McCook) and Danny P. Wallace, 166–211. Chicago: American Library Association.

Van Fleet, Connie, and Douglas Raber. 1990. The Public Library as a Social/Cultural Institution: Alternative Perspectives and Changing Contexts. In *Adult Services: An Enduring Focus for Public Libraries,* ed. Kathleen M. Heim (de la Peña McCook) and Danny P. Wallace, 456–500. Chicago: American Library Association.

Venturella, Karen M. 1998. *Poor People and Library Services.* Jefferson, NC: McFarland and Co.

Wallace, Danny P. 1990. The Character of Adult Services in the Eighties. In *Adult Services: An Enduring Focus for Public Libraries,* eds. Kathleen M. Heim (de la Peña McCook) and Danny P. Wallace, 27–165. Chicago: American Library Association.

Waples, Douglas, and Ralph W. Tyler. 1931. *What People Want to Read About: A Study of Group Interests and a Survey of Problems in Adult Reading.* Chicago: University of Chicago Press.

Weibel, Kathleen. 1982. The Evolution of Library Outreach 1960–75 and Its Effect on Reader Services: Some Considerations. Occasional Paper Number 16. Urbana, IL: Graduate School of Library and Information Science. Also available as ERIC ED231376.

Wellman, Hiller C. 1915. The Library's Primary Duty. *ALA Bulletin* 9 (July): 89–93.

Wilson, Louis R. 1938. *The Geography of Reading: A Study of the Distribution and Status of Libraries in the United States.* Chicago: University of Chicago Press.

Wyatt, Neal. 2002. A Year Inside Notable Books. *Reference and User Services Quarterly* 41 (Summer): 340–343.

9

Youth Services

by

Linda Alexander and Barbara Immroth

Youth Services in Public Libraries

Youth services in public libraries have grown and adapted for more than a century, as youth librarians have worked with commitment and focus to define and develop services appropriate for young people. These services began in the 1800s in public libraries with collections of books for the educational and cultural development of children and broadened to include designated rooms for youth. Library story hours, programs, and outreach were added to the scope of services during the twentieth century. This chapter reviews the history of public library services for youth, details national initiatives such as competency statements, and characterizes youth services in the context of the Public Library Association's *New Planning for Results* model (Nelson, 2001).

History

Beginnings to 1951

During the nineteenth century the societal view of children and their needs slowly changed. The growth of cities and industrialization brought the realization that children could be an economic asset, especially for the poor, but at the same time the need for children to achieve literacy was addressed by the formation of Sunday School libraries for children whose parents could not afford to pay for private school. These libraries were primarily religious books, but included a broader range of subjects and were a source of free books for many children in the 1820s and 1830s. They probably influenced the inclusion of district libraries in common schools (F. K. Walter, 1941).

Wealthy individuals such as Caleb Bingham, the Salisbury, Connecticut, bookseller, donated books for nine- to sixteen-year olds for a small library in 1803. In 1810 the town appropriated funds to buy additional books, making it "probably the first example of an American municipal government allocating support for a public library" (Fenwick, 1976: 332). Although several states passed school district laws incorporating the concept of school libraries in the 1830s to the 1850s, no appropriations for collections and staff were made. Although these early libraries were not direct forerunners of later public children's and school libraries, their existence demonstrates a growing awareness of the need to provide reading material for children.

The idea of providing library access to children came to national attention with the establishment of public libraries in the mid-1850s, the growth of literature for children, and changing attitudes toward the improvement of child welfare. Fletcher addressed age restrictions on library use and the quality of books being published for children in the 1876 report, *Public Libraries in the United States of America; Their History, Condition, and Management.* The need for staff trained to select books and guide reading of youth was slowly recognized by the library profession.

For an extensive analysis of the development of children's services in public libraries from 1876–1906, see Thomas (1982), who identifies five conditions that allowed for the emergence of youth services: (1) specialized collections; (2) specialized space; (3) specialized personnel; (4) specialized programs; and (5) the existence of organizations and agencies devoted to youth. Jenkins (2000) used Thomas's model to discuss the research literature of youth services librarianship, and her review provides a broad context for those serving youth today.

Key librarians in the nineteenth and early-twentieth century who developed the foundation of library services to youth include:

- Caroline Hewins, librarian at Hartford, CT, Public Library, who published a list of the best children's books available in 1882 and wrote yearly reports on "Reading for the Young."

- Mary Wright Plummer, librarian at Pratt Institute, who advocated for libraries to take an active role in children's reading; designed the first public library children's room, 1895 (Lundin, 1996: 840–850).

- Lutie Stearns, Milwaukee Public Library, who wrote "Report on Reading for the Young" and held a general meeting about children's issues at the 1894 American Library Association, signifying acceptance of children's services by the library profession (Fenwick, 1976: 337).

- Anne Carroll Moore, Superintendent for Work with Children at Pratt Institute, in 1896 began giving lectures on children's services. She wrote "Special Training for Children's Librarians" (1898) and included a children's room in every branch of the New York Public Library, where she worked as a Children's Librarian from 1906–1941.

In the 1890s some public libraries abolished age restrictions and established separate children's rooms that included collections and staff. In the public schools the progressive movement championed a change from textbook teaching to use of a broader range of resources, and public libraries in some cities began to provide schools with special collections and services. In 1899 the National Education Association published the "Report of the Committee on the Relations of Public Libraries to Public Schools" that recommended cooperation between schools and public libraries and a small library in every elementary school.

Professional education for children's librarianship began in the first decade of the twentieth century. In addition to Hewins's classes at Pratt, Frances Jenkins Olcott started classes for children's librarians at the Carnegie Library in Pittsburgh, which became the Training School for Children's Librarians in 1901 and continued to train children's librarians exclusively until 1917 (Fenwick, 1976: 341). In the public schools activity-centered learning required use of numerous resources as students made new demands on library collections. Public libraries responded in several ways. Some provided classroom collections on loan to schools, or opened a branch library in the school, some shared responsibility for library collections with the schools, and in some places the schools began their own libraries.

High schools had collections of books earlier than elementary schools.

Other high points in the early development of youth services as a public library specialization included establishment of the American Library Association's Section for Children's Librarians, organized in 1900; Louise Seaman Bechtel's appointment as the first head of a juvenile department at a publisher, Macmillan (1919); and Children's Book Week organized in 1919 by Frederick Melcher, chair of the American Booksellers Association. Recognizing the success of publishers, booksellers, and librarians working together, and the dedication and professionalism of children's librarians, Melcher was the driving force in establishing the John Newbery Medal in 1922 for the most distinguished children's book published in the United States each year, which is administered by the Association for Library Services to Children of the ALA.

The years 1920–1950 were a time of consolidation, standardization, and broadening horizons for library service to children. During the Depression public library circulation soared, and circulation to children was 40–45 percent of the total. Children's librarians continued to provide services that had been established earlier: individual reader guidance, book selection, and provision of reading promotion materials. Storytelling programs provided a literacy experience for older children and libraries instituted youth and preschool story hours.

The need to bridge the gap between children's and adults' reading was recognized by the opening of special rooms for teens, the first in 1925 at the Cleveland Public Library. In 1930 the Young People's Reading Round Table was established in the American Library Association. In 1941 three groups within the American Library Association, children's librarians, young peoples' librarians, and school librarians, formed the Division of Libraries for Children and Young People with Mildred Batchelder as the Executive Secretary. In 1951 when the American Association of School Librarians (AASL) became a separate ALA division, Batchelder remained as Executive Secretary of the Children's Service Division and the Young People's Services Division. However, as Jenkins notes, youth services were largely neglected in the landmark Public Library Inquiry of the late 1940s.

Serving Youth of Color

The story of public library service to youth of color is not told in the mainstream histories. Native American children were often sent to boarding schools—detribalized in institutions like the Carlisle

Indian Industrial School. African American children were not provided with equal access to libraries during the first part of the twentieth century due to segregation (Gleason, 1941). Yet there have been bright spots. Early children's librarians reached out to immigrant children and provided small neighborhood book collections with missionary zeal.

While it is difficult to characterize fully the lack of resources and support devoted to serving African American youth in the first half of the twentieth century (Mussman, 1998), it is important to take note of leaders who did lay the foundation for better days to come. Charlemae Hill Rollins, children's librarian and scholar of African American literature for children worked at Chicago Public Library from 1927–1963. In 1957 Mrs. Rollins was the first African American to head the ALA Children's Services Division. Augusta Braxton Baker, storyteller, author, and consultant based at the New York Public Library from 1937–1974, initiated the series *The Black Experience in Children's Books* and wrote the classic, *Storytelling: Art and Technique*. Fannette H. Thomas edited a collective biography on African American youth services librarians who protected African American children from racism and discrimination and challenged these social problems in the adult society.

1951 to the Present

The 1954 court decision Brown v. Board of Education declared separate but equal educational facilities inherently unequal and urged desegregation of public schools with all deliberate speed. Public libraries followed at varying rates. Birmingham, Alabama, which had duplicate facilities and collections for African Americans and Whites, integrated by 1963. The story of the desegregation of public libraries can be found in disparate regional analyses, but youth services librarians today can be proud that some librarians were active in the desegregation struggle (Cresswell, 1996).

An increasing use of media and resources beyond the book for teaching in schools impacted library services for children and youth during the period 1950–1975. The 1956 Library Services and Construction Act (LSCA) provided federal funding for public libraries to experiment with new outreach programs for the unserved (Walter, 2001: 7). Public libraries also experienced a shift in patrons, with poorer, less educated patrons in the central cities and more affluent families moving to the suburbs. Desegregation presented new challenges. Supporting the teaching of basic reading literacy skills and providing collections that appealed to minorities became more important for central city libraries. Preschool story-times became more popular, as did storytellers in languages other than English.

Young adults became a more visible focus of librarians with the establishment of the ALA Young Adult Services Division in 1957. High school students were more than half of the users of public libraries, placing new demands on collections and staff (Fenwick, 1976: 358). In 1963 the Library of Congress named Virginia Haviland the head of the Children's Book Section, later the Children's Literature Center. She was a leader in national and international children's literature activities.

Federal education funding during the 1960s and early 1970s provided money to purchase school library books and to hire school librarians. This brought about discussion and research on school-public library cooperation, shared collection building, and other joint ventures which extend to present day (Woolls, 2001). An influential book by Margaret A. Edwards of the Enoch Pratt Library in Baltimore, *The Fair Garden and the Swarm of Beasts: The Library and the Young Adult,* was published in 1969. This book for library professionals provided a "well-defined philosophy for services for teens and discussions for best practice" (Walter and Meyers, 2003: 10).

Proposition 13 in California in 1978 and similar initiatives in other states led to large local tax cuts, and public library expenditures all over the country declined. During the 1980s funding became a major issue for library services (Walter and Meyers, 2003: 26). Society placed an increased emphasis on social, cultural, and educational growth of youth, urging the passage of state and federal laws requiring public library professionals to provide books and materials to day-care centers and parents of preschool children. ALA task forces specified and defined goals, policies, and recommendations to implement these services (ALA, 1984; Rollock, 1988). Circulation statistics, quantitative evaluation methods, and accountability were required to validate effectiveness and justify the use of tax money to administer services and programs. Public libraries wrote mission statements, and strategic planning was a point of convergence for connecting information to libraries. About half of all public library users were under the age of eighteen, with one-fourth being between the ages of twelve and eighteen (U.S. NCES, 1988).

As a response to the needs of teens, YASD published books about young adult services such as *Young Adults Deserve the Best: Competencies for Libraries Serving Youth* (YALSA, 1981); *You are Not Alone* (1986); and *Teen Pregnancy Crisis* (1989). Lists of "Quick Picks" for reluctant readers and "Best Books for Young Adults" became popular with young library patrons. A 1986 conference in New York, *Libraries Serving Youth: Directions for Service in the 1990s* was indicative of the reawakening of librarians to the needs of youth (Rovenger and Wigg, 1986; Rollock, 1988: 187–198). YASD became the Young Adult Library Services Association (YALSA) in 1992.

In 1982 the Public Library Association issued *Output Measures for Public Libraries* (Zweizig and Rodger, 1982). A decade later ALSC commissioned Virginia Walter to write a companion volume to assist children's librarians in evaluating their services in a similar fashion but tailored to the realities of children's services, *Output Measures for Public Library Service to Children: A Manual of Standardized Procedures* (1992). YALSA followed ALSC's lead and Walter produced *Output Measures and More: Planning and Evaluating Public Library Services for Young Adults* (1995).

A group of experienced children's librarians created the "Prototype of Public Library Services for Young Children and Their Families" at a U.S. Department of Education supported conference in Austin, Texas in 1994. The Prototype is based on research in child development and emergent literacy and advocates significant improvements in preschool services in public libraries (Immroth and Ash-Geisler, 1995). The ALA President Mary Somerville's theme, "Kids Can't Wait...Library Advocacy Now!" in 1996-97 emphasized a focus on youth services and youth services librarians.

Professional Associations

Each public library determines the scope of youth services that it provides. Some libraries have children's services staff; some have children 's and young adult services staff; and some have youth services staff, who provide services to young people from birth to 18 years. Several American Library Association units focus on youth. Organizational units within ALA addressing the needs of children and young adults were created in 1957 when the Association of Young People's Librarians split into the Children's Services Division (now the Association for Library Service to Children) and the Young Adult Services Division (now the Young Adult Library Services Association). ALSC and YALSA develop partnerships on the national level with the "Liaison with National Organizations Serving Children and Youth" (ALSC) and "Partnerships Advocating for Teens" (YALSA). They work in collaboration with the American Association of School Librarians on public library-school partnerships and with the Public Library Association on issues of common interest.

The Association for Library Service to Children

The Association for Library Service to Children (ALSC) "is interested in the improvement and extensions of library services to children (preschool through eighth grade) in all types of libraries." Priority areas include child advocacy; evaluation of media; awards and scholarships; partnerships; and professional development. ALSC committees determine the Caldecott Award, the Newbery Award, and five other annual awards for outstanding children's materials. Other committees compile annual lists of notable books, recordings, videos, and computer software for children.

ALSC committee members advocate for children on the local, state, and national levels on issues including intellectual freedom and legislation. The ALSC journal is *Children and Libraries: The Journal of the Association for Library Service to Children.*

Young Adult Library Services Association

The mission statement of the Young Adult Library Services Association (YALSA) "is to advocate, promote, and strengthen service to young adults as part of the continuum of total library service, and to support those who provide service to this population." Reaching this goal involves seven areas: advocacy for free and equal access to materials and services; evaluating and promoting materials and services; identifying research needs; formal and continuing education; promoting the expansion of young adult service in professional associations and agencies; representing the interests of librarians and staff working with young adults; and creating and maintaining communication links with other units within ALA. *Young Adult Library Services* is the official journal of YALSA.

Public Library Association

Various units of the Public Library Association (PLA) provide some activities for those serving the youth population. The Preschool Literacy Initiatives is an interdivisional task force of PLA/ALSC with the charge "to serve as a liaison between the two divisions to develop preschool literacy initiatives...and to promote effective implementation of these initiatives." Three committees under the PLA Library Services Cluster aim to address the needs of children and youth and promote service to a particular population: Services to Elementary School Age Children and their Caregivers; Services to Preschool Children and their Caregivers; and Services to Teenagers and their Caregivers.

Competencies

Competencies For Librarians Serving Children in Public Libraries (ALSC, 1999) are broadly categorized in seven areas: knowledge of the client group; administrative and managerial skills; communications skills; materials and collection development; programming skills; advocacy, public relations and networking; and professionalism and professional development (see Walter and Meyers, 2003). School library media specialists have a separate set of competencies for information literacy standards created jointly by the American Association of School Librarians (AASL) and the Association for Educational Communications and Technology (AECT) called *Information Power: Building Partnerships for Learning* (1998). YALSA competencies for librarians serving young adults, *Young Adults Deserve the Best: Competencies for Librarians Serving Young Adults,* were developed in 1981 and revised in 1998 and 2003.

Censorship

Banning books goes back to the time of Plato, who "argued that banishing various poets and dramatists was essential for the moral good of the young" (Nilsen and Donelson, 2001: 395). During the late-nineteenth and early-twentieth centuries, Anthony Comstock imprisoned "evil" authors, destroyed what he conceived of as bad literature, and published *Traps for the Young* on temptations for youth (Bremmer, 1967). The 1896 American Library Association conference attendees questioned whether Crane's *Red Badge of Courage* should be on the list of recommended books (Nilsen and Donelson, 2001: 396).

During the twentieth century, librarians discussed what was appropriate for young people to read or view. Court cases document the multitude of challenges to books and other materials and free speech issues throughout the United States. It is imperative that all library professionals be informed on these issues and that they develop policies and procedures to address potential challenges to the accessibility of materials. We cannot emphasize enough that being ready when the censor arrives is part of the responsibility of all personnel working in libraries. *Intellectual Freedom for Children: The Censor is Coming* (ALSC, 2000) provides guidance; the YALSA and ALSC Web sites also provide information about dealing with banned and challenged materials. Since material for children and youth are among the most frequently challenged in library collections, it is especially important for librarians serving these populations to understand the issues and know how to react if items in their collections are challenged.

Internet connections available to children, the fear of danger to children, and the societal upheaval in the wake of 9/11 resulted in sweeping new federal legislation and brought intellectual freedom issues into national prominence during the end of the twentieth century and the beginning of the twenty-first century. The Children's Internet Protection Act (CIPA) requires "the installation and use by schools and libraries of technology for filtering or blocking material on the Internet on computers with Internet access to be eligible to receive or retain universal service assistance." In their insightful article, Jaeger and McClure (2004) summarize potential legal challenges to CIPA.

Types of Children and Youth Services Today

It is one of the aims of this book to tie together the various resources that support public librarianship within the context of current practice. Instead of presenting youth services as the 13 discrete "service responses" delineated in *The New Planning for Results* (Nelson, 2001), we organize the variety of youth services in relationship to four categories of service responses, to reflect a larger vision of the public library's importance to our communities using the service responses. (The treatment of adult services in Chapter 8 follows this same scheme.)

- Public Sphere
- Cultural Heritage
- Education
- Information

Public Sphere

The public library in its most expansive role is a central component of a community's "public sphere." In this capacity, librarians can support the community's links to the daily reality and discourse of those it serves. It is through enhancement of the public sphere that the library builds community and encourages authentic dialogue. The service responses that enhance the public sphere are "Commons," "Community Referral," and "Current Topics and Titles."[1]

Commons

People, especially youth, have a need to meet and interact with others in the community and to participate in public discourse about community issues. The commons allows libraries to provide program opportunities that draw the diverse community of youth together. The public library provides meeting spaces, events bulletin boards, e-mail accounts, and a common environment as a public place (McCook, 2001).

The introduction of technology has changed how American library buildings are designed. New building design includes places for teens to use the new technologies, to read magazines, listen to music, and just hang out. In a study on attracting youth to public libraries, Bishop and Bauer identified strategies and programs that could help libraries and librarians become community partners serving young adults. Findings from surveys and interviews with librarians and young adults suggested that teens wanted spaces for snack machines (or coffee shops), publicity in the library, encouragement to bring friends, research sources, Internet access, and volunteer opportunities (2002: 41–42). The C. Burr Artz Library branch of the Frederick County Public Libraries, in Maryland, has developed a "Teen Zone"—a place just for teens. Equipped with bright décor, upholstered chairs, and tables for doing homework, Teen Zone (Carty, 2003) has an updated collection of fiction, nonfiction, magazines, videos, and audio books.

The New Port Richey Public Library (Florida) offers poetry slams, karaoke, teen lock-ins, debate club, coffee house, teen advisory club, arts and crafts, Mommy and Me, and numerous other programs on educational and social issues. The library provides meeting rooms, computer labs, as well as a children's library and young adult section (Dillinger and Sewell, 2003).

Community Referral

Community Referral service in public libraries refers to the provision of information related to services offered by community agencies and organizations. Libraries develop databases of available services with phone numbers and addresses of helping agencies and additionally provide information about qualifications required for receiving specific services. Services may be in the form of responding to walk-ins or providing toll-free phone numbers or easy access to information via the Internet (Nelson, 2001). One community referral example is Austin Public Library (Texas). The program provides for children and youth community technology programs, which seek to bridge the digital divide. Dell's Wired for Youth Center involves the use of computer workstations at 10 branches throughout the city of Austin to assist at risk youth aged 8–18 with homework, community and electronic resources, as well as to provide computer games and surfing opportunities on the Net. A youth librarian serves each branch for this purpose (Wired for Youth).

Current Topics and Titles

Making collections available for children and young adults is one of the main focuses for collection development in public libraries. Anne Carol Moore, who was one of the first children's librarians in the early 1900s, noted that there were few books published specifically for children. She was challenged to search the adult shelves for materials that might be suitable for youth in order to stock shelves in children's rooms (Walter, 2001: 20). When publishers saw a potential market for juveniles, they began to publish special lines of children's books along with their trade books. Schools and public libraries were the main markets until cuts in library funding and the increase in the number of bookstores made the retail market more significant. New electronic retail distribution outlets like Amazon.com have some effect on the children's book trade industry (Walter, 2001: 21).

In *My Roads to Childhood: Views and Reviews of Children's Books,* Moore offers principles for book selection and evaluation standards that came to be accepted by the profession (Walter, 2001: 20). Evaluation of multicultural materials for youth adds another criterion for book selection, in addition to cultural accuracy and authenticity. Selected professional literature relating to this response is included under cultural awareness in the section on Cultural Heritage.

Youth in our communities want information about popular culture, social trends, and recreational experiences. The library provides a current collection and readers' advisory to meet the individualized needs for reader guidance. Readers' Advisory and Reference Services are the mainstays of library services to children and youth. Children ask more questions at the reference desk than do grownups. To serve them well, the craft of answering reference questions often involves connecting the child with the book. Highly skilled youth librarians, who know how to "gently probe" for clues about reading preferences, demonstrate that there is an art to readers' advisory services (Walter, 2001: 29).

A broad collection includes best sellers, classic titles, and materials in multiple formats, supported by children's and young adult booktalks, bibliographies by subject or author, displays, author signings, and previews for nonbook media such as videos, CD and audio formats, puppets, and computer resources and games. Collections for youth should reflect popular demand in terms of paperback and hardback books and magazines published specifically for children and young adults. Anyone can access Readers' Advisory via a computer connected to the Internet, for a multitude of award lists, book reviews, and lists of recommended books and related materials (Nelson, 2001).

Awards for Books and Materials

A long-standing activity of youth librarians is the evaluation and selection of appropriate books and materials. ALSC and YALSA give a number of awards for outstanding materials each year and prepare lists of recommended titles in numerous formats, all of which would be outstanding additions to collections for children and youth. Beginning with the Newbery Award in 1922 and the Caldecott Award in 1938, children's librarians have a distinct visible record of highlighting excellent books and materials. *Children's Book Awards International, 1990 through 2000* (L. Smith, 2003) lists 141 children's book awards in the United States. Best known awards include:

- The John Newbery Award, established in 1922, given annually to the author who has made the most distinguished contribution to American literature for children in the preceding year.

- The Randolph Caldecott Award, established in 1938, given to the artist of the most distinguished picture book for children.

- The Mildred Batchelder Award, established in 1968, given to an American publisher for "the most outstanding [children's] book originally published in a foreign language in a foreign country and subsequently published in English in the United States" (ALA, 2003: 78).

- The Laura Ingalls Wilder Award, established in 1954, given to an author or illustrator whose books have made a substantial and lasting contribution to literature for children for a period of years.

- The Coretta Scott King Award, established in 1969, given to African American authors and illustrators who have published distinguished books that promote an understanding and appreciation of the culture and contribution of all people for the American dream. This award was initially given under the auspices of ALA SRRT, now EMIERT (H. M. Smith, 1994; 1999; 2004).

- The Pura Belpré Award, established in 1996, given to a Latino/Latina writer and illustrator whose work best portrays, affirms, and celebrates the Latino cultural experience in an outstanding work of literature for children and youth. This award is given by ALSC and REFORMA National Association to Promote Library Services to Latinos and the Spanish Speaking.

- The Virginia Hamilton Literary Award, created in 1998 to give recognition to authors and illustrators whose work was a lasting contribution to multicultural literature for children and young adults (see the award's Web site: http://dept.kent.edu/virginiahamiltonconf/litawd1.htm).

The three YALSA Awards that stand out are the following:

- Alex Award, which selects from the previous year's publications ten books written for adults that have special appeal for young adults.

- Margaret A. Edwards Award, established in 1988, given for an author's lifetime achievement for writing books that have been popular with teenagers, published in the United States within the past five years.

- Michael L. Printz Award, established in 2000, given for a book that exemplifies literary excellence in young adult literature published in the United States in the preceding year.

Promotion of books and reading takes many forms: summer reading programs, booktalks, story hours, puppet shows, author programs, displays, and celebrating Children's Book Week, Teen Read Week, International Children's Book Day, and El Dia de los Niños/El Dia de los Libros. Increased emphasis on literature and programs that celebrate diversity have emerged in response to changing demographics in the United States and a new awareness and response to the ensuing needs (Campbell, 1994). The publishing industry is more open to having members of ethnic groups write these books instead of others telling their stories for them. Epstein explains that "editors with both mainstream publishers and alternative presses are continuing to look for multicultural stories..." but they are "on guard against inadvertent cultural domination or outright mistakes" (Epstein, 2001: 34).

Cultural Heritage

Public libraries have long played an important role in preserving and activating cultural heritage. Reading discussion groups, lectures, film series, exhibits, and celebrations of different cultures are central adult services that are the basis for partnerships that have expanded the library's involvement in local communities. Richard Jensen has noted, "culture is composed of the things that define us, the physical manifestations of what we as a collective people bring to a place." He also said that planning library spaces for the teen culture must "challenge traditions to be authentic" (Walter and Meyers, 2003: 65; Jensen, 2000: 10). The service responses in *New Planning for Results* that correspond to the cultural heritage category are "Lifelong Learning," "Cultural Awareness," and "Local History and Genealogy."[2]

Lifelong Learning

The public library provides a number of services to assist youth in opportunities for self-directed personal growth and development, such as easy access to the circulating collection through the online catalog, with emphasis on nonfiction titles. A library responding to this need will provide such services as Born to Read, Mommy and Me, bibliographic instruction, family literacy, homework assistance, tours for schools and homeschoolers, and GED services. The target population includes all ages. A Born to Read program typically teaches parents the importance of reading to their small children and uses videos, lectures, and demonstrations to model for parents the best techniques for reading and sharing books. This collaboration of ALSC and the Department of Health and Human Services/Head Start is open to all parents, but is designed to reach at-risk children of teen and low-income parents.

Multnomah County Libraries (Oregon) encourage early childhood programming using youth librarians in all 18 branches. Services include storytimes, puppet shows, music programs, storytellers, and art programs. Librarians visit child-care facilities for storytimes and provide library tours for students in child care. The books for babies and toddlers are the most circulated books in the collection. Outreach services include delivering books to child-care centers, Head Start locations, homeless shelters, and preschools. Summer reading programs provide incentives for school children to keep reading during summer vacation (Arnold, 2002).

Cultural Awareness

Examples of programs that provide cultural awareness to youth are author programs, music and drama groups, and workshops on creative writing (Programs for School-Age Youth). Such public library services can help youth gain understanding of their own cultural heritage and that of others. Services can involve providing in-depth collections, multilingual and ethnic resource centers, forums on cultural sensitivity and library materials in several languages. These service responses can target children in Head Start projects, sponsor Holocaust memorials, or spotlight any culture in the community using collections in many languages, programming, outreach, fairs, and performing arts and exhibits.

The ALA Ethnic and Multicultural Information Exchange Round Table (EMIERT) focuses on materials that enhance cultural awareness. Various subcommittees of EMIERT include the Jewish Information Committee, the Children's Services committee, and the Multicultural Awards Committee. EMIERT has published *Venture into Cultures: A Resource Book of Multicultural Materials and Programs* (Kuharets, 2001), *Directory of Ethnic and Multicultural Publishers, Distributors and Resource Organizations* (Wertsman, 2003), and *The EMIE Bulletin.*

Broward County Library system in Florida has a large population of immigrants from Haiti, Jamaica, Cuba, and Trinidad. Broward youth librarians have responded to their communities' cultural needs by hosting an Asian New Year Program and a teen-generated Caribbean Festival (Wexler, 2001). Putnam County Library in Cookeville, Tennessee, offers a Facing History and Ourselves Program with the Chance Residential Center for girls aged thirteen to seventeen. The program explores community and identity, ethnicity, human rights, religious group membership, tolerance, and the power of propaganda around the central theme of the historical Holocaust. The program also involves a book review program, in which teens evaluate new young adult books (Schmitzer, 2003). Mongan branch of the Kenton County Public Library, in Covington, Kentucky, features "De Colores." With the assistance of community partners, it was originally designed as a literacy outreach project for Hispanics. This service provides a bilingual storytime program using invited speakers (Howrey, 2003).

REFORMA promotes an annual national day of observance called El Dia de los Niños/El Dia de los Libros (Children's Day/Book Day). This Mexican style festival "celebrates children, literacy, language, and books for children of all linguistic and cultural backgrounds." The El Dia de los Niños/El Dia de los Libros Web sites list many ideas and activities from years of festivals all over the nation. Pat Mora, an outstanding children's writer, supports this celebration of children and books.

Local History and Genealogy

Libraries that offer services in local history and genealogy do so in response to citizens in the community, who want to know and better understand personal or community heritage. The services may include instruction in research methods, archives, oral histories, and photographs. Although most of these services may be geared to the adult population, family tree assignments in elementary school and lessons about the community from preschool to college are opportunities for young patrons to learn about personal, family, or community history. An example is the Kentucky Library and Museum in Bowling Green, which offers a vast assortment of Civil War relics and diaries, displays from the Victorian times, opportunities for family tree searches using a card catalog for the historical collection, the Robert Penn Warren collection, artifacts, and archives, all of which are open for touring by school and other groups. On the property sits a fully furnished cabin from the early 1900s, which is accessible during visits by school children; teachers can arrange to visit the cabin through the educational programs librarian. Visits of the buildings are generally open to the public. These types of services and programs help children find genealogical roots.

Education

It is in the interest of society to educate parents about the developmental needs of children. To accomplish this, children's and youth librarians can make a difference by being actively available for assistance with community customers. Dan White, a children's services librarian in Oregon, supports the concept that the relationships librarians develop with children and families is the most important aspect of encouraging use of the community library. Building relationships requires an ongoing commitment involving brief transactions over a long period of time. There is a tremendous opportunity to serve reading needs in the community, which will in turn have a positive impact on the community at large (White, 2002: 15). Public library responses under this category are in terms of "Basic Literacy Services," "Information Literacy," and "Formal Learning Support."[3]

Basic Literacy Services

Target audiences for basic literacy services for youth might include a group of teens, parents of preschoolers, or members of families who are recent immigrants (Nelson, 2001: 152). PLA and ALSC collaborated on an early literacy project in 2001 to create materials to conduct parent/caregiver workshops on early literacy. This project began as part of the effort to implement the "Preschool Literacy Initiative." Some of the components of basic literacy services for youth involve family literacy, such as English as a second language (ESL) programs, tutoring involving multiple generations—teaching parents to read to their kids, and developing language appreciation and skills through spoken and written language activities.

Literacy services include high/low literacy collections; active outreach programs for preschoolers; tutoring students in reading; teen services that focus on study skills, life skills, and positive values; GED preparation programs; family literacy programs that address the needs of parents and caregivers; and English as a second language (ESL) classes, tutoring, and computer skills instruction.

We cannot discuss information literacy services without mentioning the multitude of links on the ALSC Web site. Under the ALSC "Resources" link users can find various links to basic literacy services, information literacy services, learning support for children and teens. One particularly worthy link is the Online Children's Library link to the Internet Public Library (IPL) for Youth, with further links to Kidspace and TeenSpace, both of which have some of the best educational links to be found. Subjects covered on the pages for teens include career, books and writing, arts and entertainment, homework help, money matters, health, sports, dating, and style. You can also find numerous links to technology and computers, even some teaching children and teens how to create Web pages and learn HTML. Links to Filamentality and Learning HTML are examples of information to help youth learn to use computer technology for learning and creative purposes. There are links to Web sites that are safe for kids such as ALFY and the Amazing Picture Machine. Blue Web'n alone has over 1,000 searchable databases that are outstanding Internet learning sites. Along with links to Ready Reference, Reading Room, story hour, and POTUS (Presidents of the United States), these sites include a Culture Quest World Tour for information about countries all over the world and searching tools for pathfinders for developing research skills. An exploration of the YALSA site uncovers similar links for teens.

Information Literacy

Much of the discussion in this section can be tied to the preceding section on Basic Literacy services. Information Literacy services address the need to help patrons develop skills for finding, evaluating, and using information effectively. AASL puts emphasis on information literacy as an important skill, especially for school age students. Youth must develop skills to assist them with academic projects, such as research papers, as well as life challenges. Pathfinders are often used to teach these skills.

Various efforts focus on digital literacy, which target youth with special links on the local library Web site or teen pages for homework and recreational resources. Sites with names like Cyber-Kids and Cyber-Teens offer Internet and electronic resources training, most often requiring a large number of staff and a well-equipped computer lab for training.

Reference information can be integrated to offer full-text databases, word processing, and spreadsheet software. Children learn computer skills, how to use reference sources, and listen to stories to gather information and to express information in their own words. Some public libraries partner with the public schools with shared digital/electronic technologies. Information literacy skills refers to how to understand and use information in any format. It is important to stress that the development of computer skills/use is too narrow; the use of a computer serves as a *means* for accomplishing goals for research and creativity rather than an *end*.

Formal Learning Support

Formal learning support helps students enrolled in a formal program of education, or who are pursuing their education through a program of homeschooling to attain their educational goals. Examples of this service are parent education, emergent literacy, school visits and class visits to the library, retaining reading skill levels through summer reading, computer access and instruction in Web page design, easily accessible Web pages devoted to sources for children and young adults, GED instruction, and bibliographic instruction.

Research indicates that formal learning support services are inadequate to meet the needs of youth. Findings from one study of public library services revealed that only 33 percent of public libraries provided computer, Internet, and Web design workshops. The same study showed that a mere 23.4 percent of public libraries support homework assistance by providing space, "hotlines," and staff to help in tutoring (Programs for School-Age Youth, 1999).

Youth services librarians view themselves as educators. Danley describes the role of the children's librarian as being first and foremost that of an educator. The librarian is one who "guides the children to become independent information gatherers" (Danley, 2003: 98). She refers to the use of constructivist principles from psychology by successful children's librarians, who know how to relate to and guide young patrons in meeting their information needs. Using principles of child development and cognition, librarians can be dynamic in helping children become self-directed learners for meeting educational and information needs. Youth library responses to these needs can include intergenerational services to youth and their care givers. Family literacy activities can be based on story hour stories, nursery rhymes, kits for science fair projects, and other areas of the curriculum, such as social studies, math, and reading, for middle school students to encourage parents to become more involved with their child's learning.

After-school programs with reading enrichment or neighborhood-based homework help programs can use peer and adult tutors, who can be available at special centers to help students understand and complete their homework. The library can make available collections that support curriculum and computer stations with online access to electronic resources. Based on an active partnership with school district personnel, school visits by public library staff and cooperation of school counselors can be used to locate peer tutors.

In 1998, 23.4 percent of libraries offered homework help by providing library spaces for youth to work in private, reference sources, telephone hotlines, and tutoring programs using adults and older youth volunteers (Programs for School-Age Youth, 1999: 71). Public libraries have sometimes found outside funding to offer homework assistance to students during after-school hours. The County of Los Angeles Public Library (COLAPL) has had homework centers in at least 30 branches for over 10 years. With staff, computers, and materials, they help children and young adults with tough questions and assignments using a subscribed service called Tutor.com. Although the service is not free to the library, funding is continually sought to keep their homework programs going (Minkel, 2002: 39).

Information

Public libraries have played an important role in providing youth with general information, government information, business, consumer, and career services. Information should be provided and organized to meet the needs of children and youth. Four public library responses from *New Planning for Results* are organized around the broad category of information. These include "General Information," "Business and Career Information," "Consumer Information," and "Government Information."[4]

General Information

Youth need information on a broad array of topics related to work, school, and personal life. Library services for youth include services that teach or help children to answer their many questions. Librarians have long debated whether to find the resources for students seeking information or to teach them to use current print and electronic reference resources to locate materials on their own. In public library settings, just-in-time individual research instruction on a flexible and individual basis can provide a level of competence for future information needs. Additionally, youth librarians can make available bibliographic instruction classes or programs to teach young customers to learn efficient ways to find important sources of information. Many of the services already discussed encompass reference services for children and youth and for their teachers and caregivers. Instruction in use of electronic databases and print library resources is discussed under some of the services listed above. Training for staff and volunteers who work with children is necessary for assisting with information-seeking behavior of different age groups.

Government Information

School assignments or other queries often call for information about elected officials and governmental agencies that enable people to learn how to participate in the democratic process. For many reasons, including the need for an educated citizenry, youth need an awareness of the existence of government publications, and the ability to access education laws, rules, practices, and information about health, jobs, and their communities. In the United States, government agencies publish reliable and authentic information on almost every field of inquiry on the local, state and federal levels. The topics in government publications range from gardening and fertilizers to information about railroads, engineering, education, NASA, and the

Internet. The various government agencies even publish coloring books and cookbooks for children. Normally, only large public libraries that are designated as "Depository Library" receive the many series of printed documents due to space or other issues. Print collections of documents are not generally housed in such a way as to be good browsing collections and can be difficult to locate by even the most savvy researcher. There are over 1,400 designated government depository libraries in the United States, many of which are part of university or large public library collections.

Since the mid-1990s, each agency of the government has begun to provide free public access to much government information via the World Wide Web. In a public library, local government-published information can include grassroots campaigns, or locally published brochures on topics of health, education, community meetings, and profiles on neighborhoods in that city. Government information can be useful resources for adults who work with children, as well as students in middle and high school. Web sites for state and federal documents can also be accessed through Internet-connected computer terminals.

The U.S. government is the most prolific publisher in the world with publishing demands that exceed what the Government Printing Office (GPO) can meet. Due to the large number of documents, many government documents are subcontracted to commercial publishers to fulfill publishing requirements. For example, Rand McNally publishes many government and commercial maps and atlases. One such example of government Web sites of interest to youth, teachers, and parents is Ben's Guide to U.S. Government for Kids. This site includes tools for K–12, teaches how the government works and includes locators to government sites developed for youth. Ben's Guide is an educational component of GPO Access provided by the Superintendent of Documents. Librarians serving youth can provide assistance to youth in finding many electronic sources, whereas various print sources may come in the formats of pamphlets, W2 forms, and other documents provided by the public library as a service to local citizens. Specialized training is a must for any librarian working with services regarding government information.

Business and Career Information: Consumer Information

These services address the need for information related to business, careers, personal finance, and obtaining employment. In a 1999 report of a survey of more than 1,200 libraries serving youth, only 19.2 percent of libraries reported that they provided career development programs. Examples included sponsoring career fairs, where invited professionals demonstrated or discussed information related to current fields in which they worked (Programs for School-Age Youth, 1999: 71).

Children and youth learn about business in their educational and recreational endeavors. Career guidance for youth can be especially important to groups such as teen mothers and dropouts who need to work. Materials for resume writing can be provided and extensive job listings are available in books, newspapers, and online resources. Libraries can provide consumer information on a wide variety of topics. College resources and many other career topics are available in print, CD-ROM, and online formats; for example, the *Dictionary of Occupational Titles* (DOT) can be in CD-ROM format with older versions appearing in print.

Consumer information lists can include educational information from public domain and government sources. Health and child care information can be provided to high-risk teen mothers, or to Hispanic Mothers in Spanish, using e-mail lists on the Internet terminals housed in the library computer labs. Using images to supply information to people with low literacy skills, the library can develop databases with local content about health, education, and jobs.

Looking at the Future of Youth Services

The Public Library Data Service (PLDS) *Statistical Report 2003* includes the fifth in a series of Children's Services Surveys. In addition to information about holdings, materials budget, population, annual circulation, and annual program attendance, PLDS added questions about early literacy, borrowing policies, and contracts with other agencies for Internet resources. The data are reported by the size of the population served in nine categories from 1,000,000 and over to under 5,000. The *Statistical Report* provides longitudinal comparative data.

"Emergent Literacy" is what children learn about reading and writing before they can do either (White, 2002: 16). Since research suggests that over a third of children lack basic reading readiness skills upon school entrance, targeting services toward parents for preparing their children works well. Relationships with parents and caregivers, built over time on a voluntary basis, can affect the child's entire school career.

Barriers to access must be lowered. Using outreach services can be an educational and economic equalizer (White, 2002: 19). Youth librarians need to promote outreach services to families and the community and emphasize that they can help provide guidance for book selection and other services. Outreach to day-care centers and schools, family resource centers, teen parent programs, and girls and boys clubs is vital in expanding contacts with youth in the community. By our encounters with young and not-so-young customers, over time we can build relationships that remind them to call on the public library to serve their educational, cultural, and information needs.

Notes

1. Nelson, *The New Planning*, "Commons," 161–165; "Community Referral," 166–171; "Current Topics and Titles," 183–187.

2. Nelson, *The New Planning*, "Life Long Learning," 211–215; "Cultural Awareness," 178–182; "Local History and Genealogy," 216–220.

3. Nelson, *The New Planning*, "Basic Literacy," 151–155; "Information Literacy," 205–210; "Formal Learning Support," 188–194.

4. Nelson, *The New Planning*, "General Information," 195–199; "Business and Career Information," 156–160; "Consumer Information," 172–177; "Government Information," 200–204.

References

Agosto, Denise E. 2001. Bridging the Cultural Gap: Ten Steps Toward a More Multicultural Youth Library. *Journal of Library Services in Libraries* 4 (Spring); 38–41.

American Association of School Librarians and Association for Educational Communications and Technology. 1998. *Information Power: Building Partnerships for Learning.* Chicago: American Library Association.

American Library Association. 1984. *Realities: Educational Reform in a Learning Society.* Chicago: American Library Association.

American Library Association. 2003. *ALA Handbook of Organization: 2003–2004.* Chicago: American Library Association.

American Library Association. Ethnic and Multicultural Information Exchange Round Table. Available: http://lonestar.utsa.edu/jbarnett/emie.html.

Arnold, Renae. 2002. Coming Together for Children: A Guide to Early Learning Childhood Programming. *Journal of Youth Services in Libraries* 15 (Winter): 24–30.

Association for Library Services to Children (ALSC). 1999. *Competencies for Librarians Serving Children in Public Libraries.* Available:www.ala.org/alsc.

Association for Library Service to Children (ALSC). 2000. *Intellectual Freedom for Children: The Censor is Coming.* Chicago: American Library Association.

Baker, Augusta, and Ellin Greene. 1987. *Storytelling Art and Technique.* New York: Bowker.

Bingham, Anne. 2002. Goin' Someplace Special: Trends in Children's Literature. *Alki* 18 (July): 14–15.

Bishop, Kay, and Pat Bauer. 2002. Attracting Young Adults to Public Libraries: Frances Henne/YALSA/VOYA Research Grant Results. *Journal of Youth Services in Libraries* 15 (Winter): 36–44.

Booktalking: Quick and Simple. Available: http://nancykeane.com/booktalks.

Bremmer, Robert. 1967. *Traps for the Young.* Cambridge, MA: Harvard University Press.

Campbell, Patty. 1994. The Sand in the Oyster: White Children's Book Authors' Books on Multicultural Topics. *The Horn Book Magazine* 70 (July/August): 491.

Carty, Natasha S. 2003. Teen Zone: C. Burr Artz Library, Frederick County Public Libraries, Frederick, Maryland. *Voice of Youth Advocates* 26 (August): 204–205.

Chelton, Mary Kay. 1997. Three in Five Public Library Users Are Youth. *Public Libraries* (March/April): 104–108.

Cresswell, Stephen. 1996. The Last Days of Jim Crow in Southern Libraries. *Libraries and Culture* 31 (Summer/Fall): 557–573.

Council on Interracial Books for Children. 1980. *Guidelines for Selecting Bias-free Textbooks and Storybooks.* New York: Council on Interracial Books for Children.

Danley, Elizabeth. 2003. The Public Children's Librarian as Educator. *Public Libraries* 42 (March/April): 98–101.

Day, Frances Ann. 1999. *Multicultural Voices in Contemporary Literature: A Resource for Teachers.* Rev. ed. Portsmouth, NH: Heinemann.

Dia de los Niños, Dia de los Libros. Available: http://reforma.org/resources/ninos/dia.html.

Dictionary of Occupational Titles. CD-ROM. U.S. Department of Employment and Training. U.S. Employment Service, 1998.

Dillinger, Susan, and Tracey Sewell. 2003. *Interviewees.* New Port Richey Library, New Port Richey, FL. Monday, November 24.

Epstein, Connie C. 2001. Create a World for Young Readers. *The Writer* 114 (June): 34.

Fenwick, Sara Innis. 1976. Library Services to Children and Young People. *Library Trends* 25 (Summer): 329–360.

Fitzgibbons, Shirley. 2001. Libraries and Literacy: A Preliminary Survey of the Literature. *IFLA Journal* 27: 91–106.

Fletcher, William I. 1876. *Public Libraries and the Young. In Public Libraries in the United States: Their History, Condition and Management,* 412–418. Washington, DC: Department of the Interior, Bureau of Education.

Gleason, Eliza Atkins. 1941. *The Southern Negro and the Public Library: A Study of Government and Administration of Public Library Service to Negroes in the South.* Chicago: University of Chicago Press.

Gregory, Vicki L., Marilyn Stauffer, and Thomas Keene, Jr. 1999. *Multicultural Resources on the Internet: The United States and Canada.* New York: Neal-Schuman Publishers.

Hewins, Caroline. 1892. Yearly Report on Boys' and Girls' Reading. *Library Journal* 7 (July/August): 182–190.

Howrey, Sara P. 2003. De Colores: The Universal Language of Bilingual Storytime. *American Libraries* 34 (October): 38–40, 42–43.

Immroth, Barbara Froling and Vicki Ash-Geisler. 1995. *Achieving School Readiness: Public Libraries and National Education Goal 1. With A Prototype of Public Library Services for Young Children and Their Families.* Chicago: American Library Association.

Institute of Museum and Library Services (IMLS). Available: www.imls.gov (accessed December 3, 2003).

Jaeger, Paul T., and Charles R. McClure. 2004. Potential Legal Challenges to the Application of the Children's Internet Protection Act (CIPA) in Public Libraries: Strategies and Issues. *First Monday* 9 (February). Available: http://firstmonday.org/issues/issue9_2/jaeger/index.html.

Jenkins, Christine A. 1996. Women of ALA Youth Services and Professional Jurisdiction: Of Nightingales, Newberies, Realism, and the Right Books, 1937–1945. *Library Trends* 44 (Spring): 813–839.

Jenkins, Christine A. 2000. The History of Youth Services Librarianship: A Review of the Research Literature. *Libraries and Culture* 35 (Winter): 103–139.

Jensen, Richard. 2000. *Clark and Menefee.* New York: Princeton Architectural Press. 10.

Jones, Patrick. 1998. *Connecting Young Adults and Libraries: A How-To-Do-It Manual.* 3rd ed. New York: Neal-Schuman Publishers.

Jones, Patrick. 2001. Why We Are Kids Best Assets. *School Library Journal* 47 (November): 44–47.

Kuharets, Olga. R., ed. 2001. *Venture Into Cultures.* 2nd ed. Chicago: American Library Association.

Kuipers, Barbara. 1995. *American Indian Reference and Resource Books for Children and Young Adults.* 2nd ed. Englewood, CO: Libraries Unlimited.

Kruse, Ginny Moore, and Kathleen Horning. 1991. *Multicultural Literature for Children and Young Adults.* Madison, WI: Wisconsin Department of Public Instruction.

Lundin, Anne. 1996. The Pedagogical Context of Women in Children's Services and Literature Scholarship. *Library Trends* 44 (Winter): 840–850.

Malone, Cheryl Knott. 2000. Toward a Multicultural American Public Library History. *Libraries and Culture* 35 (Winter): 77–87.

McCook, Kathleen de la Peña. 2001. Authentic Discourse as a Means of Connection between Public Library Service Responses and Community-Building Initiatives. *Reference and User Services Quarterly* 41 (Winter): 127–133.

Minkel, Walter. 2002. When Homework is Good Politics. *School Library Journal* 48 (April): 39.

Moore, Anne Carroll. 1898. Special Training for Children's Librarians. *Library Journal* 12 (August): 81.

Moore, Anne Carroll. 1939. *My Roads to Childhood: Views and Reviews of Children's Books*. New York: Doubleday, Doran.

Muse, Daphne. ed. 1997. *The New Press Guide to Multicultural Resources for Young Readers*. New York: New Press.

Mussman, Klaus. 1998. The Ugly Side of Librarianship; Segregation in Library Services from 1900–1950. In *Untold Stories: Civil Rights, Libraries and Black Librarianship,* 78–92. Champaign, IL: University of Illinois, Graduate School of Library and Information Science.

National Education Association. 1899. *Report of the Committee on the Relations of Public Libraries to Public Schools*. Washington, DC: National Education Association.

Nelson, Sandra. 2001. *The New Planning for Results: A Streamlined Approach*. Chicago: American Library Association.

New York Library Association. Task Force on Standards for Youth Services. 1984. *Standards for Youth Services in Public Libraries of New York State*. New York: Youth Services Section of NYLA.

Nilsen, Alleen, and Kenneth L. Donelson. 2001. *Literature for Today's Young Adults*. 6th ed. New York: Longman.

Programs for School-Aged Youth in Public Libraries: Report of a survey conducted for the DeWitt Wallace-Reader's Digest Fund. 1999. *Teacher Librarian* 27 (October): 71–72.

Public Library Association. 2003. *Public Library Data Service Statistical Report, 2003*. (Special Section Children's Services Survey): Chicago: American Library Association.

Rollock, Barbara T. 1988. *Public Library Services for Children*. Hamden, CT: Shoe String Press.

Rovenger, Judith, and Ristiina Wigg. 1986. *Libraries Serving Youth; Directions for Service in the 1990s*. New Paltz, NY: New York Library Association.

Schmitzer, Jeanne C. 2003. YOYA's Most Valuable Program for 2003: Making Personal Connections with History. *Voice of Youth Advocates* 26 (October): 276–28.

Sims, Rudine. 1982. *Shadow and Substance: Afro-American Experience in Contemporary Children's Fiction*. Urbana, IL: National Council of Teachers of English.

Slapin, Beverly, and Doris Seala, ed. 1992. *Through Indian Eyes: The Native Experience in Books for Children*. 3rd ed. Philadelphia, PA: New Society Publishers.

Smith, Henrietta M. 1994. *The Coretta Scott King Awards Book: From Visions to Reality*. Chicago: American Library Association.

Smith, Henrietta M. 1999. *The Coretta Scott King Awards Book, 1970–1999*. Chicago: American Library Association.

Smith, Henrietta M. 2004. *The Coretta Scott King Awards Book, 1970–2004.* Chicago: American Library Association.

Smith, Laura. 2003. *Children's Book Awards International, 1990 through 2000.* Jefferson, NC: McFarland and Co.

Steiner, Stanley F. 2001. *Promoting a Global Community through Multicultural Children's Literature.* Englewood, CO: Libraries Unlimited.

Thomas, Fannette H. 1982. The Genesis of Children's Library Services in the American Public Library, 1876–1906. PhD diss., University of Wisconsin-Madison.

Thomas, Fannette H. 1993. The Black Mother Goose: Collective Biography of African-American Children's Librarians. In *Culture Keepers: Enlightening and Empowering Our Communities: Proceedings of the First National Conference of African American Librarians,* ed. Stanton F. Biddle, 196–200. Newark, NJ: Black Caucus of the American Library Association.

U.S. Department of the Interior. Bureau of Education. 1876. *Public Libraries in the United States of America: Their History, Condition, and Management. Special Report.* Washington, DC: U.S. Government Printing Office. Repr., as Monograph Series, no. 4, Champaign, IL: University of Illinois, Graduate School of Library Science.

U.S. National Center for Education Statistics. 1988. *Services and Resources for Young Adults in Public Libraries.* Washington, DC: U.S. Government Printing Office.

Virginia Hamilton Literary Award. Available: http://dept.kent.edu/virginiahamilton conf/litawd1.htm.

Walter, Fran K. 1941. A Poor But Respectable Relation—the Sunday School Library. *Library Quarterly* 12 (July): 734.

Walter, Virginia A. 1992. *Output Measures for Public Library Service to Children: A Manual of Standardized Procedures.* Chicago: American Library Association.

Walter, Virginia A. 1995. *Output Measures and More: Planning and Evaluating Public Library Services for Young Adults.* Chicago: American Library Association.

Walter, Virginia A. 2001. *Children and Libraries: Getting It Right.* Chicago: American Library Association.

Walter, Virginia A., and Elaine Meyers. 2003. *Teens and Libraries: Getting It Right.* Chicago: American Library Association.

Watson, Dana. 1998. Multicultural Children's Literature Selection and Evaluation: Incorporating the World Wide Web. *The Acquisitions Librarian* 20: 171–83.

Wertsman, Vladimir, F. 2003. *Directory of Ethnic & Multicultural Publishers, Distributors and Resource Organizations.* 5th ed. Niles. IL: Ethnic and Multicultural Information Exchange Round Table.

Wexler, Synda R. 2001. Fantastic Fiestas in the Library: Florida Teens Connect with their Caribbean and Hispanic Roots. *Voice of Youth Advocates* 24 (October): 247–249.

White, Dan R. 2002. Working Together to Build a Better World: The Importance of Youth Services in the Development and Education of Children and Their Parents. *OLA Quarterly* 8 (Fall): 15–19.

Wired for Youth. Available: www.wiredforyouth.com (accessed December 8, 2003).

Woolls, Blanche. 2001. Public Libraries-School Library Cooperation: A View from the Past with a Predictor for the Future. *Journal of Youth Services in Libraries* 14 (Spring): 8–10.

Wright, Lisa A. 1996. Public Library Circulation Rises along with Spending. *American Libraries* 27 (October): 57–58.

Young Adult Library Services Association. 2003. *Young Adults Deserve the Best. Professional Development Center.* Available: www.ala.org/ala/yalsa/ professionaldev/yacompetencies/competencies.htm.

Zweizig, Douglas L., and Eleanor Jo Rodger. 1982. *Output Measures for Public Libraries.* Chicago: American Library Association.

10

Connections

No Public Library Is an Island

Public librarians have demonstrated prescient leadership in collaboration beyond their own local boundaries to extend and expand library service. Initially this collaboration was through professional affiliation that laid the groundwork for more formal cooperation. Public libraries are connected through local cooperative agreements, multitype library consortia (MLCs), state library agencies, multistate regional networks, and national/international cooperatives such as OCLC. These entities comprise a complex series of overlapping networks in which public libraries function.

Librarians have long worked at the state and national level to develop policies on all aspects of service from interlibrary loan to cataloging standards. Through state library agencies librarians have worked on statewide plans, professional development, collaborative grants, and cooperative licensing. Through multitype library consortia librarians have focused on common regional concerns, such as reciprocal borrowing and shared cataloging. These collaborations have continuously shifted with different groups taking on different projects at different times in different places. Oftentimes the same

241

leaders have shaped a plan at different levels. Interlocking work to extend library service is one of the greatest achievements of public librarianship in the United States.

In addition to understanding the local political processes that govern the daily operations of the public library, it is important that librarians recognize the relationships the public library has to larger systems that provide support and connections to additional resources. These various components in the overall network of librarians and libraries provide opportunities to carry on professional connections that enrich careers and strengthen ties to others. The spirit and energy of individual librarians have built the foundation of this network. We turn attention in this chapter to the growth of public library cooperative initiatives in the United States, noting three factors: the role of professional associations, the work of state library agencies, and the growth of multitype library consortia.

Professional Associations

American Library Association

Librarians were one of the first occupational groups in the United States to organize as a professional association. The American Library Association, established in 1876, provided an ongoing mechanism for discussing, planning, and developing cooperative initiatives. One of the first committees established by librarians in the United States was a committee on cooperation that sought to provide shared cataloging. The 1876 publication of the report, *Public Libraries in the United States of America: Their History, Condition, and Management: Special Report* (U.S. Bureau of Education), which included histories and statistics of libraries, greatly enhanced the collaborative work of librarians. The *Special Report* provided a context of growth and development by which libraries could establish goals and future development. The establishment of *Library Journal*, which was the official publication of the ALA until 1908 when the *ALA Bulletin* began, also contributed to the capacity of librarians to work together and share ideas. Thus, in 1876 librarians realized two key elements—baseline data and a mechanism for ongoing communication—that paved the way for collaborative progress.

In the years since U.S. librarians formally organized themselves as the American Library Association, they have focused on the concerns of public libraries, broadly speaking. But under the umbrella of this larger association, special associations, divisions, sections, or committees have paid special attention to public libraries. Sixty years ago (1944) the Division of Public Libraries was formed within ALA and merged with the Library Extension Division in 1950 to become the Public Library Division. In 1958 this Division was reorganized as the Public Library Association, which today is the national overarching professional association for most public librarians. (See Figure 10.1.)

The Public Library Association consisted of over 10,000 members in 2003 and its current strategic plan determines its core purpose: *To strengthen public libraries and their contribution to the communities they serve* (Tekker and PLA, 2002). PLA is guided by the following essential and enduring principles:

- Provides visionary leadership ever open to new ideas

- Dedicated to lifelong learning

- Focused on and responsive to member needs

- Committed to a free and open exchange of information and active collaboration

- Respects diversity of opinion and community needs

- Committed to excellence and innovation

Public librarians also participate in other units of the American Library Association, based upon their primary interests: Association for Library Collections and Technical Services, Association for Library Services to Children (ALSC), Association for Library Trustees and Advocates, Library Administration and Management Association (LAMA), Library and Information Technology Association, Reference and User Services Association (RUSA), and Young Adult Library Services Association (YALSA). Each of these units of the American Library Association has, over the years, developed cooperative projects, formulated standards and guidelines, recommended best practices, and provided opportunity for librarians to collaborate to improve and expand the quality of public library services. Twice yearly (at the ALA Annual Conference and Midwinter Meetings) 15,000–20,000 librarians from all over the United States meet to plan, exchange ideas, and learn about new developments in the field. In addition to these two major conferences, the Public Library Association holds its own biennial national conference and spring symposia to provide continuing education for the nation's public librarians. Much communication among public librarians also takes place electronically to conduct the work of the association.

A snapshot of programs and projects that took place at the national level in 2003 gives an idea of the scope of work of the professional association activity of public librarians:

- Writing Effective Public Library Policies
- Emerging Immigrant Communities: The Public Library Responds
- Evaluation of Public Library Service to Preschool Children
- The Information Commons Challenge
- Print and Electronic Approval Plans in the Twenty-First Century
- Workload Measures and Staffing Patterns
- Cataloging Needs of Public Libraries

The leadership of public libraries at the national level as represented by the presidents of the Public Library Association of the ALA has been compiled as Figure 10.1. These individuals have represented large and small public libraries from every region of the United States. The contributions of these presidents to the development of public libraries through their focus on advocacy, the political process, strategic planning, and program provision, are part of the rich heritage of connections that have laid the groundwork for an enduring institution.

State and Regional Library Associations

For many public librarians state or regional associations—chapters of the American Library Association—provide a parallel, but more local, opportunity to meet and collaborate. There are fifty-seven state and regional library association chapters affiliated with the American Library Association, each including at least a committee or section that addresses public library issues. Generally, these associations hold an annual conference, as well as ongoing workshops and programs. The five largest chapters and their respective membership totals are: Texas (7,310), Ohio (3,691), New York (3,000), Illinois (2,925), and Indiana (2,706). A few highlights taken from the Web sites of state chapters in 2003 demonstrate the types of cooperative activities of chapter associations and the scope of public library networking.

Figure 10.1: Public Library Association Presidents—1945–2005

1. Amy Winslow, 1945-1946, Cuyahoga County Library, OH
2. Carl Vitz, 1946-47, Head, Public Library of Cincinnati & Hamilton County
3. Forrest Spaulding, 1947-48, Librarian, Des Moines, IA
4. Louis Nourse, 1948-49, Asst. Librarian, St. Louis, MO
5. John S. Richards, 1949-50, Librarian, Seattle Public Library
6. Helen M. Harris, 1950-51, Librarian McGhee Library Knoxville TN
7. Harold Brigham, 1951-52, Director, Indiana State Library
8. Ruth Rutzen, 1952-53, Director Home Reading Service, Detroit Public Library
9. Jack B. Spear, 1953-54, Head, Traveling Libraries, New York State Library
10. Ruth W. Gregory, 1954-55, Head Librarian, Waukegan Public Library, Waukegan, IL
11. Mildred W. Sandoe, 1955-56, Personnel Director, Cincinnati
12. John T. Eastlick, 1956-57, City Librarian, Denver
13. Arthur H. Parsons, Jr., 1957-58, Director, Omaha Public Library, NE
14. Laura Currier, 1958-59, Director, Mississippi Library Commission
15. James E. Bryan, 1959-60, Director, Newark Public Library
16. Elinor Walker, 1960-61, Coordinator of work with young people, Carnegie Library of Pittsburgh
17. Harold Hamill, 1961-62, City Librarian, Los Angeles Public Library
18. Clara Breed, 1962-63, City Librarian/Director, San Diego Public Library
19. Ransom L. Richardson, 1963-64, Director, Flint Public Library, MI
20. William Chait, 1964-65, Director, Dayton and Montgomery County Public Library
21. Alta Parks, 1965-66, Asst. Director, Gary Public Library, IN
22. David M. Stewart, 1966-67, Chief Librarian, Nashville Public Library
23. Helen E. Fry, 1967-68, Staff Librarian, U.S. Army DCSPER SPEC SERV HQ 4th Army, Ft. Sam Houston, TX
24. Willard O. Youngs, 1968-69, City Librarian, Seattle Public
25. June E. Bayless, 1969-70, City Librarian, Beverly Hills Public
26. Andrew Geddes, 1970-71, Director, Nassau Library System, New York
27. Effie Lee Morris, 1971-1972, San Francisco Public Library Children's Services coordinator
28. David Henington, 1972-1973, Director, Houston Pub. Library
29. Lewis C. Naylor, 1973-1974, Director, Toledo-Lucas County Library
30. Dorothy M. Sinclair, 1974-1976, Prof. of Lib. Sci., Case Western Reserve University
31. Genevieve M. Casey, 1976-1978, Wayne State University, Detroit, professor of library science
32. Ronald A. Dubberly, 1978-1980, Director, Seattle Public Library

33. Robert Rohlf, 1980-1981, Director, Hennepin County Libr., Minnesota
34. Agnes M. Griffen, 1981-1982, Director, Montgomery County Dept. Pub. Libraries, MD
35. Donald J. Sager, 1982-1983, Director, Elmhurst Pub. Libr., IL.
36. Nancy M. Bolt, 1983-1984, President, JNR Associates
37. Charles W. Robinson, 1984-1985, Director, Baltimore County Public Library
38. Patrick O'Brien, 1985-1986, Director, Dallas Public Library
39. Kathleen M. Balcom, 1986-1987, Director, Downers Grove Public Library
40. Susan S. Kent, 1987-1988, Deputy lib. dir., Tucson Public Library
41. Melissa Buckingham, 1988-1989, Free Library of Philadelphia
42. Sarah Ann Long, 1989-1990, Sys. Dir., North Suburban Libr. Sys., Wheeling, IL.
43. Charles M. Brown, 1990-1991, Director of Libraries, Arlington, VA
44. June Garcia, 1991-1992, Extension Svcs. Adminstr., Phoenix Public Library
45. Elliot Shelkrot, 1992-1993, Director, Free Library of Philadelphia
46. Pat A. Woodrum, 1993-1994, Executive Director, Tulsa City-County Library System
47. Judy Drescher, 1994-1995, Director, Memphis/Shelby Co. Public Library, TN
48. LaDonna Kienitz, 1995-1996, City Librarian, Newport Beach
49. Linda Mielke, 1996-1997, Director, Carroll County Public Library, MD
50. Ginnie Cooper, 1997-1998, Director, Multnomah County Library, OR
51. Christine L. Hage, 1998-1999, Director, Rochester Hills Public Library, MI
52. Harriet Henderson, 1999-2000, Director, Louisville Public Library, KY
53. Kay Runge, 2000-2001, Director, Scott County Library System, IA
54. Toni Garvey, 2001-2002, Phoenix Public Library
55. Jo Ann Pinder, 2002-2003, Director, Gwinnett County Public Library, GA
56. Luis Herrera, 2003-2004. Director, Pasadena Public Library, CA
57. Clara Nalli Bohrer, 2004-2005. Director, West Bloomfield Township Public Library, MI

Figure 10.1 continued. PLA Presidents—1945–2005

- Arizona Library Association—Service to Diverse Populations Interest group
- California Library Association—Fair Compensation for Library Workers
- Idaho Library Association—Standards for Idaho Public Library Services
- Illinois Library Association—New Trustee Manual

- New Hampshire Library Association—Statement on the Use of Internet filters
- North Carolina Library Association—Branch managers Network
- Texas Library Association—TALL Texans Leadership Development Institute

The web of relationships created by public librarians working at national and state levels to set policies, develop standards, and provide continuing education opportunities is a great strength of U.S. public librarianship. For well over a century librarians in the United States have gotten to know each other in a sustained and engaged manner, which has provided the foundation for more formalized cooperative relationships.

State Library Agencies

State library agencies have been mentioned in previous chapters, for their role in supporting the establishment of public libraries, but they also stand out as a catalyst for a great deal of the motivation for public library cooperation. Founded beginning in the 1890s to encourage public library development, state library agencies have come to play an increasingly larger role in enhancing library cooperation, extension, and collaboration. Public library leaders in the early-twentieth century recognized that the creation of independent public libraries affiliated with municipal government could not meet the library needs of the nation. Some communities were too small or distances too great to provide adequate library services based on local taxing districts. Over the years, state library agencies played a major role in encouraging larger units of service to provide library resources. The Library Services Act and the Library Services and Construction Act were keystones in the goal of providing library service throughout the nation.

In the early 1960s the Association of State Libraries initiated a survey to review the status of state library agencies to make recommendations for their future. The 1966 report, *The Library Functions of the States,* identified "coordination and cooperation" among each state's libraries as a key function of state library agencies (Monypenny, 1966), a point that was made the following year with strong emphasis in the National Advisory Commission on Libraries (U.S. NACL) report, *Libraries at Large: Traditions, Innovations and the National Interest* (Nelson, 1967). This report included the recommendation that the LSCA be amended to strengthen state library agencies and specifically that this is done so that state library agencies could "coordinate planning for total library service." This was a major watershed for library cooperation, because it set policy for the future of library cooperation, as a means by which public libraries could serve the broadest possible range of people.

LSCA and Planning

The ALA worked diligently through its Washington Office to see that the NACL recommendation that state library agencies be strengthened was implemented through amendments to the LSCA in 1970. State plans were required, but states were given latitude in the way that they expended funds to coordinate and strengthen library services. Each state developed a different pattern of service throughout the LSCA period. The plans provide a history of the innovation and cooperative efforts made by each state to strengthen the nation's library services.

To provide an overview of the substance of the cooperative activities of the libraries of the United States as coordinated by the state library agencies during the LSCA period, we provide a few illustrative abstracts of model plans. It should be noted that library development in each state was configured to its own needs. Many state library agency plans and annual reports are available through the U.S. Department of Education, Education Resources Information Center (ERIC) and taken together provide a detailed history of the manner in which state library agencies encouraged innovation during the LSCA period. The following four examples, selected from a 25-year period of plans submitted to the federal government, show a variety of the manifestations that each state exhibited. Every state has its own variation on the development of services through the state library agencies. The complete documents are available through the ERIC system.

Those wishing to compile a historical record of any state's library development will find that the plans submitted to state library agencies are a vital primary source, as demonstrated by these brief selections.

Illinois State Library—Annual Program LSCA, 1974

Brief summaries are provided of 17 library projects being conducted in Illinois during 1974. These deal with the following matters:

1. The development of the Illinois State Library

2. Library manpower training

3. Library research

4. The Illinois State Library Materials Processing Center

5. The professional development of library personnel

6. The demonstration of library services to groups without libraries

7. The provision of services to groups lacking adequate libraries

8. Library resources, research, and references

9. Bibliographic control and access to resources

10. Public library system development

11. A children's book review and examination center

12. Multimedia services

13. Library services to the institutionalized

14. Library services to the blind and the physically handicapped

15. Local public library services

16. Multitype library activities. Each summary provides a brief description of the project, including details about its goals and major activities, the agencies that support it, and the legislation that enables it (ERIC ED089712, 1974).

Wyoming State Library—Five Year Plan, 1974–1978

An overview is presented of the Wyoming State Library Five-Year Plan. The first major component deals with demographic characteristics, giving data on the state's geographic area, population, racial characteristics, and the location of minority groups. The second main component provides a brief review of the Wyoming State Library Advisory Council and the means by which it facilitates broader participation in planning library services, while the third component summarizes the methods used to evaluate present services and to develop new programs. These include formal liaison with the Advisory Council, personal contact with library personnel, systems studies of programs, and analyses of demographic and other statistical data. State Library publications and financial statements will be used for dissemination purposes. The final component lists the goal of library service as being to provide informational, cultural, and recreational services and materials to all citizens in the state.

Specific objectives related to this goal are enumerated, including the provision of: (1) consultant, financial, and reference services to libraries; (2) services to the handicapped, the institutionalized, and the disadvantaged; (3) library services to rural areas; (4) research and library development services; and (5) aid with library construction (ERIC ED089714, 1974).

New York State Library—Long-Range Plan, 1987-1992

The State of New York submitted its long-range plan under the title, "Library Service to the People of New York State. A Long-Range Program, October 1, 1987–September 30, 1992, for the Improvement of Library Services Utilizing Local, State and Federal Resources." This annual report on the comprehensive five-year program for the enhancement of libraries in New York State achieves the following: (1) provides a benchmark for the continuing planning, development, and evaluation of state library services; (2) summarizes the objectives, policies, and programs undertaken for the improvement of those services; (3) serves as a guide to library networks, regional planning groups, and other agencies that wish to participate in the Federal Library Services and Construction Act (LSCA) program; and (4) meets the LSCA requirements. An overview of the state library environment is offered; library systems and networks are profiled; statewide resource sharing and technological change are summarized; constraints on services are outlined; and the program's goals and objectives are discussed. Tables provide summary statistics on public, academic, school, institution, and medical libraries; the New York State Library; public library systems; systems and libraries by region; and state appropriations for higher education. A 23-item bibliography of major documents for the New York State library service program and lists of New York members of the LSCA Advisory Council and the Regents Advisory Council on Libraries are also provided. "LSCA Program Purposes—Needs and Intended Actions" and "Policy Guidelines on the Administration of LSCA Funds 1987–88" are included as supplements (ERIC ED286536, 1987).

The South Carolina Program for Library Development, 1991–1994

This report outlines the long-range program of the Library Services and Construction Act (LSCA) in South Carolina. The first of five chapters presents excerpts of the LSCA that describe its Titles I–III programs; explains the evolution of South Carolina's long-range

Program for Library Development; discusses the dissemination of publications related to the LSCA programs in South Carolina; and touches on how LSCA programs are coordinated. Focusing on the library public, the second chapter discusses the probable impact of population increases on information needs and library services, and inventories the special needs of the economically disadvantaged, the illiterate, the blind and physically handicapped, persons with limited English-speaking ability, the elderly, and the institutionalized. The third chapter focuses on South Carolina libraries and their needs, including the South Carolina State Library, public libraries, institutional libraries, academic libraries, technical college learning resource centers, school library media centers, and special libraries. Library education programs in South Carolina institutions of higher education are also described, and maps and statistics are provided for public, institutional, and college and university libraries, and the South Carolina Library Network. A copy of the state aid agreement form between the South Carolina State Library and the state's public library systems is included. The adequacy, priorities, and evaluation procedures of Title I, II, and III projects are the focus of the fourth chapter, and the fifth presents the four goals of the state library together with objectives designed to meet those goals (ERIC ED345688, 1992).

As can be seen from these abstracts of reports from Illinois, Wyoming, New York, and South Carolina from different years covering the period of LSCA funding, the cooperative and collaborative activities of the states relied heavily upon individual libraries participating in the planning process. Libraries worked to forge innovative services to extend library resources to the underserved, enhance personnel development, and build the capacity of libraries to respond to the needs of each state's residents in the manner most suitable for them. In each and every state the habit of cooperative planning grew among librarians and fostered a climate for working together toward common goals at a state level, while focusing on local service.

LSTA and the Future for State Library Agencies

The passage of the Library Services and Technology Act (LSTA) in 1996 shifted the manner in which the federal government funded state activities, but the work of state library agencies continues to revolve around the enhancement of library services. In 2000 the Association of Specialized and Cooperative Library Services (ASCLA) and the Chief Officers of State Library Agencies (COSLA) issued *The Functions and Roles of State Library Agencies* (Himmel,

Wilson, and DeCandido, 2000), which replaced the earlier series of *Standards for Library Functions at the State Level.* The ASCLA-COSLA study described state library agency services in three broad categories:

1. Services to the public. Reference and interlibrary loan to the public; statewide reference services; virtual and digital libraries; library for the blind and physically handicapped; state centers for the book; and state history museums.

2. Services to government. Law collections; reference and interlibrary loan services to state government; state documents collections and state documents depository systems; state archives; state computer center and data operations; preservation for state agencies.

3. Services to libraries. Administration of federal ad state aid; certification of librarians; gathering of statistics; consulting services; continuing education programs; database development; Internet access; library legislation preparation and review; library evaluation and research; literacy; statutory responsibility for public libraries and multitype library systems; summer reading programs.

Each year the National Center for Education Statistics (U.S. NCES) issues a report on the range of roles played by state library agencies and the various combinations of fiscal, human, and informational resources invested in such work (Holton, 2004). The 2002 survey of state library agencies provides data on governance, services to libraries in the respective state, service transactions, staff, income, expenditures for assistance to libraries, and LSTA expenditures. Figure 10.2 shows the variety of library development activities carried out by the agencies in 2002. This annual report lays out the scope of statewide projects that are the result of statewide collaboration through development of statewide plans.

You can see the intensity of effort made to gain grassroots input, when federal funding switched from the LSCA to the LSTA, in the work done in California. A statewide convocation was held at the outset of the implementation of the LSTA in 1997, *Providing Public Library Service to California's 21st Century Population.* This was convened by the California State Library with the goal of creating a vision of public library service for the state. Over 100 library leaders and supporters gathered for two days of meetings and work sessions on California's twenty-first century population: a demographic profile,

Figure 10.2: Library Development Activities of State Library Agencies by Type of Activity and State: Fiscal Year 2002

State	Number of public libraries	Total per capita[1] operating expenditures, by type							
		Total		Staff		Collection		Other[2]	
		Total	Response rate	Total	Response rate	Total	Response rate	Total	Response rate
50 States and DC[3]	9,129	27.64	96.0	17.70	96.1	4.19	96.2	5.75	96.2
Alabama	207	15.03	99.0	9.61	99.0	2.22	100.0	3.21	100.0
Alaska	86	36.60	98.8	23.43	98.8	4.18	98.8	9.00	98.8
Arizona	35	21.83	100.0	13.51	100.0	3.53	100.0	4.79	100.0
Arkansas	43	13.24	93.0	8.02	93.0	2.29	93.0	2.92	93.0
California	179	23.21	98.9	15.21	97.8	2.98	98.9	5.02	98.9
Colorado	116	36.42	100.0	22.52	100.0	6.20	100.0	7.70	99.1
Connecticut	194	39.51	92.3	26.94	91.8	5.38	91.8	7.19	91.8
Delaware	37	18.83	100.0	11.63	100.0	2.94	100.0	4.27	100.0
District of Columbia	1	47.61	100.0	34.48	100.0	4.56	100.0	8.56	100.0
Florida	72	21.48	95.8	12.65	95.8	3.66	95.8	5.17	95.8
Georgia	57	18.57	100.0	12.52	100.0	2.47	100.0	3.58	100.0
Hawaii	1	19.97	100.0	13.18	100.0	2.81	100.0	3.98	100.0
Idaho	106	21.68	98.1	13.83	97.2	2.88	97.2	4.97	96.2
Illinois	629	37.80	99.0	24.11	99.7	5.73	99.7	7.95	99.0
Indiana	239	40.83	100.0	23.53	100.0	6.75	100.0	10.55	100.0
Iowa	537	24.23	98.1	15.30	98.0	4.02	97.8	4.91	98.1
Kansas	321	33.16	98.1	19.65	98.1	5.52	98.1	7.99	98.1

| State | Number of public libraries | Total per capita[1] operating expenditures, by type | | | | | | | |
| | | Total | | Staff | | Collection | | Other[2] | |
		Total	Response rate	Total	Response rate	Total	Response rate	Total	Response rate
Kentucky	116	17.58	100.0	9.92	100.0	2.88	100.0	4.78	100.0
Louisiana	65	21.95	100.0	12.66	100.0	2.88	100.0	6.41	100.0
Maine	273	22.62	96.3	14.54	97.4	3.38	98.2	4.70	97.8
Maryland	24	34.33	100.0	23.20	100.0	5.86	100.0	5.26	100.0
Massachusetts	371	33.08	97.8	22.40	97.8	5.66	97.8	5.03	97.8
Michigan	381	28.76	100.0	16.59	100.0	3.64	100.0	8.53	100.0
Minnesota4	140	29.52	0	20.43	0	4.02	0	5.07	0
Mississippi	49	12.28	100.0	8.08	98.0	1.71	100.0	2.48	100.0
Missouri	150	26.10	94.0	15.74	94.7	5.07	95.3	5.29	96.7
Montana	79	14.20	100.0	9.56	100.0	1.93	100.0	2.71	100.0
Nebraska	272	26.65	82.0	17.01	82.0	5.05	82.0	4.59	82.0
Nevada	23	26.50	100.0	16.84	100.0	4.50	100.0	5.17	100.0
New Hampshire	229	28.22	94.8	18.97	95.2	4.20	95.2	5.05	94.8
New Jersey	309	$36.60	93.5	$24.93	93.5	$4.85	93.5	$6.81	93.5
New Mexico	80	17.84	93.8	11.91	93.8	2.84	93.8	3.10	93.8
New York	750	46.78	100.0	31.01	100.0	6.35	100.0	9.42	100.0
North Carolina	76	17.99	100.0	11.65	100.0	2.80	100.0	3.54	100.0
North Dakota	82	14.85	100.0	8.98	100.0	2.91	100.0	2.95	100.0
Ohio	250	51.58	100.0	31.64	100.0	9.58	100.0	10.36	100.0
Oklahoma	115	19.95	90.4	12.25	90.4	3.24	90.4	4.46	90.4

Figure 10.2 continued. Library Development Activities of State Library Agencies

| State | Number of public libraries | Total per capita[1] operating expenditures, by type | | | | | | | |
| | | Total | | Staff | | Collection | | Other[2] | |
		Total	Response rate	Total	Response rate	Total	Response rate	Total	Response rate
Oregon	125	37.08	98.4	23.41	99.2	4.92	98.4	8.75	98.4
Pennsylvania	459	22.71	99.8	13.88	99.8	3.57	100.0	5.26	100.0
Rhode Island	48	33.58	97.9	22.33	97.9	4.16	97.9	7.09	97.9
South Carolina	41	18.71	100.0	11.76	100.0	3.45	100.0	3.50	100.0
South Dakota	126	23.12	79.4	15.56	78.6	3.77	85.7	3.80	85.7
Tennessee	184	13.39	99.5	8.54	100.0	2.20	99.5	2.65	99.5
Texas	540	16.02	99.8	10.73	99.4	2.46	100.0	2.83	99.8
Utah	70	25.54	100.0	16.35	100.0	5.08	100.0	4.12	100.0
Vermont	188	24.13	89.4	15.64	92.6	3.37	91.5	5.13	89.4
Virginia	90	27.38	100.0	16.98	100.0	4.54	100.0	5.86	100.0
Washington	65	37.12	98.5	25.74	100.0	5.27	98.5	6.11	100.0
West Virginia	97	13.83	100.0	8.62	100.0	2.35	100.0	2.85	100.0
Wisconsin	379	29.86	100.0	20.25	100.0	4.19	100.0	5.42	100.0
Wyoming	23	30.08	100.0	21.17	100.0	3.20	100.0	5.71	100.0
Outlying Areas									
Guam	1	7.15	100.0	5.83	100.0	0	100.0	1.32	100.0
Virgin Islands	1	23.21	100.0	18.76	100.0	1.68	100.0	2.77	100.0

Figure 10.2 continued. Library Development Activities of State Library Agencies

1 Per capita is based on the total unduplicated population of legal service areas. Per capita expenditures by type may not sum to total due to rounding.

2 This includes all expenditures other than those for staff and collection, such as binding, supplies, repair or replacement of existing furnishings and equipment, and costs incurred in the operation and maintenance of physical facilities.

3 50 States and DC totals exclude outlying areas.

4 Nonrespondent (all data are imputed).

NOTE: Detail may not sum to totals because of rounding. Response rate is the percentage of libraries for which the specific item and a nonzero value for population of legal service area were reported. Items with response rates below 100 percent include imputations for nonresponse. Data were not reported by the following outlying areas: American Samoa, Northern Marianas, Palau, and Puerto Rico.

SOURCE: U.S. Department of Education, National Center for Education Statistics, Federal-State Cooperative System (FSCS) for Public Library Data, Public Libraries Survey, Fiscal Year 2001.

Figure 10.2 continued. Library Development Activities of State Library Agencies

perspective papers on access, collection development, community collaboration and outreach, lifelong learning, promoting the value of libraries, staffing to serve California's twenty-first century population, and technology in libraries. Input was sought from the California Library Association, public libraries, library schools, and library supporters.

The evolution of state library agencies in each state has been a journey shared by the public librarians and the people of the state. On the Web site of COSLA—Chief Officers of State Library Agencies—there are links to the plans of each state. These plans were developed in collaboration with public librarians to achieve statewide service. State library agency staff also exchange information and ideas by participation in the ALA unit devoted to their concerns. These agencies have worked for over a century to establish library service, act as an intermediary between the states and the federal government, provide resources for long-range planning and development, and foster library cooperation.[1]

Systems, Networks, Consortia

Becker formulated an early general definition of libraries working together, "When two or more libraries engage formally in a common pattern of information exchange, through communications, for some functionally interdependent purpose, we have a library network" (1979). The world's biggest library network is the Online Computer Library Center (OCLC), founded in 1967 by university presidents in Ohio to share library resources and reduce costs by using computers and technology. Online shared cataloging for libraries was introduced in 1971; interlibrary loan service in 1979; and First-Search introduced as a reference tool in 1991. OCLC is a cooperative venture that gives a library access to WorldCat, the global union catalog, and offers fee-access to a wide range of services and databases. OCLC's membership comprises the world's largest library consortium. It exists to further access to the world's information and reduce library costs by offering services for libraries and their users.

The growth of networks in the late-twentieth century is viewed by Woodsworth (1991) as a response to the OCLC policy that shared cataloging would take place through networks, rather than individual libraries. Seventeen regional service providers, such as Amigos, PALINET, and SOLINET, contract with OCLC to provide support and training for OCLC services.[2] Each of these networks has an interesting history and exploring these histories provides a look at the overlapping efforts among professional associations, government funding, and individual institutional commitment that leads to cooperation.

For instance, PALINET—"a premier network guiding information-service organizations in shaping tomorrow for themselves and their clients in a highly competitive environment through innovation, service, entrepreneurship, cooperation, and collaboration"—serves libraries in Pennsylvania, Delaware, New Jersey, Maryland, and West Virginia. The network traces its roots back nearly 70 years to the Union Library Catalogue of the Philadelphia Metropolitan Area. When PALINET merged with the Pittsburgh Regional Library Center in 1995, over 600 libraries—public, academic, and special—joined together in pursuit of better library service (PALINET).

The vision of networks as described in strategic plans is also important for public librarians scanning the environment for future direction. AMIGOS, serving the southwestern United States, began in 1974 to bring OCLC access to libraries in the region. The "AMIGOS Strategic Plan for 2000–2003" goes much further in goals to include training, access, and electronic technology advances (AMIGOS). Exploring the history and vision of any of the OCLC regional service providers demonstrates the passion librarians have shown to develop better access for library users. Every public librarian should take the time to learn the history, development, and future plans of the regional service provider to which they belong.

Multitype Library Cooperatives

Libraries working regionally in collaborative arrangements are variously called multitype library cooperatives, systems, networks, or consortia. Today the term that has gained the broadest use is multitype library cooperative or MLC. The MLC has increased in importance to the daily life of public librarians since the 1970s. It is difficult to generalize about MLCs, because even more than state library agencies MLCs have developed directly in response to local needs. They have evolved from the combined efforts of librarians working through professional associations in collaboration with state library agencies. It is most likely, however, that an MLC will be more operational in the daily work of a library than a professional association, state library agency, or regional service provider. Long's definition of library cooperation marks a recent evolution in the concept, "an independent library-related entity with an autonomous governing board whose responsibilities include library cooperation and improvement of member libraries" (1995).

The MLC is the latest evolution of the long push for larger units of library service, first described in the 1920s and legitimized in the LSA, which called for state plans to promote service to rural areas. The 1967 addition of Title III to the LSTA specifically promoted multitype library development, and the public library standards issued by the Public Library Association were titled, *Minimum Standards for Public Library Systems, 1966.* The library system as discussed in the *Standards* was intended to provide accessibility through branches, cooperating libraries, and bookmobile stops, plus a pool of resources and services used in common by all the outlets. Nelson Associates' 1969 study provided an overview of the growth of these systems, structures, and institutions, during the height of public library-based system implementation.

The increase in scope of the MLCs in the 1970s and 1980s strongly contributed to public library development and acted as a mechanism to help equalize services for all people. Consulting services and continuing education provided by the MLCs rendered support to small libraries without professional staff. Some MLCs purchased core collections to share among member libraries, established review centers, or coordinated cooperative collection development. By 1990 standards had been established for MLCs and state laws consolidated to support further development (ASCLA, 1990; Fiels, Neumann, and Brown, 1991).

Support for librarians working in MLCs or system environments comes from two units of the American Library Association. The InterLibrary Cooperation and Networking (ICAN) Section of the Association of Specialized and Cooperative Library Agencies (ASCLA) provides discussions, programs, and planning activities for the effective delivery of quality library services through multitype library networks. The "Public Library Systems" cluster of the Public Library Association encourages improved library service through the involvement of public libraries in multi-jurisdictional library systems and the participation of public libraries in multitype library systems.

The ALA has produced key publications guiding the current development of MLCs, including *Library Networks in the New Millennium*, which identifies ten trends that will guide MLC activities in this century (Laughlin, 2000):

- Complex rapidly changing electronic information environment

- Restructuring of work

- Rethinking education/distance education

- Cooperative purchasing

- High demand for skilled workers

- Diversifying funding

- Collaboration, partnering and community building

- One-stop shopping

- Accountability

- Demand for extraordinary service

The most recent analysis (2003) of the future of MLCs was initiated by the Light Bulb Group (LBG); five multitype library directors interested in the current status and activities of multitype library systems commissioned a study to develop a "snapshot" of exemplary library systems in the United States. Of special interest to the LBG were the challenges that systems were addressing, their use of innovation, and successful leadership skills. As one could expect, cooperative planning and developing consensus was viewed (next to funding) as the main challenge. The scope of multitype library consortia, systems, and networks can best be assessed by perusing the 30 pages of listings in the *American Library Directory* (Information Today).

Librarians Ignoring Boundaries That All May Read

Public librarians serve their local communities with a strong community focus. They are also motivated by an overarching commitment to preserve the human record and make it accessible to all. These parallel goals have been central to U.S. public librarianship since the first interlibrary loan. Perhaps the most long-standing example of cooperating across boundaries is the National Library Service for the Blind and Physically Handicapped, which began with the Pratt-Smoot Act in 1931 and is now a national network of cooperating libraries for Braille and audio books, that "all may read." Each public library in the United States acts as a contact in a national network to provide materials.

Another example of public librarians spanning boundaries is the joint-use library, which services different user constituencies in one facility. Joint-use libraries established over the decade include:

- Harmony Library in Fort Collins, Colorado (Front Range Community College and City of Fort Collins);

- Seminole Community Library, Florida (town of Seminole and St. Petersburg College);

- Dr. Martin Luther King, Jr. Library (San Jose, California Public Library and San Jose State University);

- Alvin Sherman Library, Research and Information Technology Center (Nova Southeastern University and Broward County Libraries Florida).

Characterized as the ultimate form of cooperation, joint-use libraries require intergovernmental agreements, collaborative policies, and a spirit of mutual goal development. Dornseif (academic librarian) and Draves (public librarian) have addressed the benefits of a more varied collection; expanded hours of operation; and efficiency (Dornseif and Draves, 2003). Bundy (2003) has addressed the challenges to design of facilities.

The Colorado Digitization Program, initially funded by an LSTA grant in 1999, is an example of collaboration among various agencies (public libraries, museums, historical societies). The mission of the Colorado Digitization Program (available: www.cdpheritage.org/about/mission.html) underscores this commitment to working across institutional boundaries:

> Through digitization, the Collaborative Digitization Program, a collaboration of archives, historical societies, libraries and museums of the West, enables access to cultural, historical and scientific heritage collections, thereby increasing understanding of the past and informing future generations.

The realization of such a mission is possible by the value public librarians have long placed on providing access to the cultural and historical record.

Public librarians have internalized resource sharing as part of their professional ethos, so new technological advances that transcend geographical perimeters, such as Internet portals, metadata standards, collaborative digitization projects, or 24/7 information services, are simply extensions of the public librarians' ideal of service without boundaries. Because of their emphasis on boundary spanning and resource sharing, public librarians have natural connections with national organizations, such as the metropolitan focused Alliance for Regional Stewardship or the rural focused Cooperative State Research, Education, and Extension Service (CSREES). The Alliance fosters collaboration among government units to advance economic, social, and environmental progress, while maintaining a sense of place in metropolitan regions. The CSREES assists rural areas in sustainability and building quality communities. Librarian's associations, state library agencies, and MLCs provide public librarians with the means to develop policies, seek grant support and activate new plans in congruence with larger societal visions for the enhancement of quality of life.

Notes

1. Within ALA, the ASCLA State Library Agency Section purpose is to develop and strengthen the role and functions of state library agencies in providing leadership and services that foster and improve the delivery of library services and to stimulate the continued professional development of state library agency personnel in discharging their unique functions in such areas as statewide planning and evaluation, services to state governments and legislatures, services to local libraries, services to users with special needs, and so forth. Discussion groups within the Section are Consultants for Service to Children and Young People, General Consultants, Information Needs of State Government, Internet, LSTA Coordinators, and State Agency Consultants to Institutional Libraries.

2. Each of these systems has a different history. They are connected in their shared cataloging connection to OCLC. See:

- OCLC. "Regional Service Providers." Available: http://oclc.org/contacts/regional/default.htm.

- AMIGOS. Available: www.amigos.org.

- BCR. Bibliographical Center for Research. Available: www.bcr .org.

- ILLINET. Available: www.cyberdriveillinois.com/departments/library/who_we_are/OCLC/home.html.

- INCOLSA. Indiana Cooperative Library Services Authority. Available: www.incolsa.net.

- MLC. Michigan Library Consortium. www.mlnc.org.

- MLNC. Missouri Library Network Corporation. Available: www.mlnc.org.

- MINITEX. Available: www.minitex.umn.edu.

- NEBASE. Nebraska's OCLC Connection. Available: www.nlc .state.ne.us/netserv/nebase/nebserv.html.
- NELINET. Available: www.nelinet.net.
- NYLINK. Available: http://nylink.suny.edu.
- OHIONET. Available: www.ohionet.org.
- PALINET. Available: www.palinet.org.
- SOLINET. Southeastern Library Network. Available: www .solinet.net.
- WiLS. Wisconsin Library Services. Available: www.wils.wisc.edu.

References

Alliance for Regional Stewardship. 2003. *Inclusive Stewardship: Emerging Collaborations Between Neighborhoods and Regions.* Denver, CO: The Alliance.

American Library Association. Chapter Relations Office. Chapter Profile Survey, 2003, ALA Chapters Fact Sheet. Available: www.ala.org.

AMIGOS. Available: www.amigos.org.

Association of Specialized and Cooperative Library Agencies. 1990. *Standards for Cooperative Multitype Library Organizations.* Chicago: American Library Association.

Becker, Joseph. 1979. Network Functions. In *The Structure and Governance of Library Networks,* ed. Alan Kent and Thomas J. Galvin, 89. New York: Marcel Dekker.

Bundy, Alan. 2003. Joint-Use Libraries: The Ultimate Form of Cooperation. In *Planning the Modern Library Building,* ed. Gerald B. McCabe and James R. Kennedy, 129–148. Westport, CT: Libraries Unlimited.

Colorado Digitization Program. Available: www.cdpheritage.org.

Cooperative State Research, Education, and Extension Service. Research, Education and Economics. Available: www.reeusda.gov/ecs/rrdc.htm.

Dornseif, Karen, and Ken Draves. 2003. The Joint-Use Library: The Ultimate Collaboration. *Colorado Libraries* 29 (Spring): 5–7.

Fiels, Keith Michael, Joan Neumann, and Eva R. Brown. 1991. *Multitype Library Cooperation State Laws, Regulations and Pending Legislation.* Chicago: Association of Specialized and Cooperative Library Agencies.

Himmel, Ethel E., and William J. Wilson. Library Systems and Cooperatives. Himmel and Wilson Library Consultants. Available: www.libraryconsultant .com/LibrarySystems.htm (accessed July 7, 2004).

Himmel, Ethel E., William J. Wilson, and GraceAnne DeCandido. 2000. *The Functions and Roles of State Library Agencies.* Chicago: American Library Association.

Information Today. Networks, Consortia, and Other Cooperative Library Organizations. In *American Library Directory 56th Edition, 2003–2004*, 2411–2440. Medford, NJ: Information Today.

Keller, Shelly G., ed. 1997. *Proceedings of the Convocation on Providing Public Library Service to California's 21st Century Population*. ERIC ED422000. Sacramento, California, May 22–23.

Laughlin, Sara. 2000. *Library Networks in the New Millennium: Top Ten Trends*. Chicago: American Library Association.

Library of Congress. National Library Service for the Blind and Physically Handicapped. Available: www.loc.gov/nls.

Long, Sarah Ann. 1995. Systems, Quo Vadis? An Examination of the History, Current Status, and Future Role of Regional Library Systems. *Advances in Librarianship* 19: 118.

Monypenny, Phillip. 1966. *The Library Functions of the States*. Chicago: American Library Association.

National Library Service for the Blind and Physically Handicapped. Library of Congress. Available: www.loc.gov/nls/index.html.

Nelson Associates, Inc. 1969. *Public Library Systems in the United States: A Survey of Multijurisdictional Systems*. Chicago: American Library Association.

Nelson Associates, Inc., in association with National Advisory Commission on Libraries. 1967. *American State Libraries and State Library Agencies: An Overview with Recommendations*. ERIC ED022486. New York: National Advisory Commission on Libraries. Repr., in *Libraries at Large: Traditions, Innovations and the National Interest*, ed. Douglas M. Knight and E. Shepley Nourse, 400–411. New York: R. R. Bowker, 1969.

PALINET. Available: www.palinet.org.

Public Library Association. 1967. *Minimum Standards for Public Library Systems, 1966*. Chicago: American Library Association.

Tekker Consultants, L.L.C., in association with Public Library Association, 2002. Strategic Plan, June 2002. Available: www.ala.org/ala/pla/plaorg/plastrategic plan/stratplan.pdf.

U.S. Department of the Interior. Bureau of Education. 1876. *Public Libraries in the United States of America: Their History, Condition, and Management. Special Report*. Washington, DC: U.S. Government Printing Office. Repr., as Monograph Series, no. 4, Champaign, IL: University of Illinois, Graduate School of Library Science.

U.S. National Advisory Commission on Libraries. 1969. *Libraries at Large: Traditions, Innovations, and the National Interest*, ed. Douglas M. Knight and E. Shepley Nourse. New York: R. R. Bowker.

U.S. National Center for Education Statistics. 2004. *State Library Agencies, Fiscal Year 2002*. Washington, DC: U.S. Department of Education. Available: http://nces.ed.gov/pubs2004/2004304.pdf.

Woodsworth, Anne. 1991. Governance of Library Networks: Structures and Issues. *Advances in Librarianship* 15: 155–174.

11

Global Perspectives on Public Libraries

by

Barbara J. Ford

"The public library, the local gateway to knowledge, provides a basic condition for lifelong learning, independent decision-making and cultural development of the individual and social groups."

— IFLA/UNESCO Public Library Manifesto, 1994

The United Nations (UN) Millennium Declaration of 2000 committed countries to do all they can to eradicate poverty, promote human dignity and equality, and achieve peace, democracy, and environmental sustainability. The goals that emanated from this declaration include the achievement of universal primary education and an increase in literacy. In *Millennium Development Goals: A Compact Among Nations to End Human Poverty* the connection between meaningful political engagement and social reform is described (UNDP, 2003: 141–142). The global perspective provided by the annual reports on human development issued by the UN provides the context for presenting this chapter's introduction to public libraries from an international viewpoint.

History and Purpose of Public Libraries: A World View

The United Nations Educational, Scientific and Cultural Organization (UNESCO) first issued the "Public Library Manifesto" in 1949, then revised it in 1972, and again in 1994 and 1998. The Manifesto was prepared in cooperation with the International Federation of Library Associations and Institutions (IFLA) and can be seen in over twenty languages on the IFLA Web site. The latest available UNESCO "Public Library Manifesto" (1994) has several sections, including mission, funding, legislation, networks, operation, management, and implementing the Manifesto. The Manifesto proclaims "UNESCO's belief in the public library as a living force for education, culture and information, and as an essential agent for the fostering of peace and spiritual welfare through the minds of men and women." To supplement the UNESCO Manifesto, many countries in all parts of the world have their own declarations, adopted by their library profession or government agencies, about the mission and purpose of public libraries.

The history of public libraries is virtually unique to each country. Each country's public libraries have developed along different lines, with varying degrees of government interest, citizen involvement, mechanisms for financial support, and structure. Changes in public libraries can occur very rapidly as the national situation changes or evolve slowly when resources are limited or there is no impetus for change. The exact number of public libraries in the world today is difficult to assess, and it is impossible to prepare a single list of their goals and objectives. With wide differences in distribution, financial support, and population characteristics, few general statements can possibly apply universally. Since the middle of the nineteenth century the tax-supported, open-to-all, public library has become a part of the cultural life of many nations.

Public libraries have often been created in communities around the world as part of a societal change process, to become the source of knowledge and basis for lifelong learning. Periods of turbulence and rapid change often result in renewed focus on what the public library has to offer. The public library can become an informal classroom to ensure that groups are included in governmental processes and have equal access to knowledge and information. Today in some countries, public libraries are seen as a potential line of defense against threats against democracy and social disintegration partly caused by the digital revolution.

Adaptation to changes in technology and digital information has led to discussions of the role of the public library. Public libraries range from those that make use of the latest technology, such as those found in Singapore, to camel delivery services in Africa, and from multimedia- and Internet-based institutions to libraries building on oral traditions in countries with low literacy rates. In recent years many countries have been reviewing public libraries in light of the Internet and digitization. Equal access to information, the need to promote information literacy, and lifelong learning are key concepts for the future of public libraries. Substantial investment in infrastructure has been necessary and is essential to foster the growth of technical skills among the populations served.

Great Britain

The growth of public libraries in Great Britain demonstrates one example of how development has taken place in a pattern most like the United States. The Public Libraries Act of Great Britain passed in 1850 provided for spending for the establishment and maintenance of a public library open to all and supported by taxes. The Act was motivated by the instabilities of the time, including the industrial revolution, and public libraries were conceived as help for the working class, contributors to economic growth, and cultivators of democracy. New libraries did not reach significant numbers until donations from the Carnegie Corporation began in the 1880s. By the 1960s and 1970s library service became more a matter of national government concern and funds were provided to put up new buildings, expand holdings, and hire more staff. By the 1970s public libraries in the United Kingdom had moved toward larger units of service and the national government was providing some funding. In 1997 the British Arts Minister announced a fund to bring local public libraries to the forefront of the information technology revolution. The complexity of the role of the public library has been explored by Black, who exhorts librarians "to resurrect the true, radical essence of its philosophy: the enhancement and emancipation of the self within the context of progress and social justice" (2000: 171).

Worldwide Snapshot

The *International Dictionary of Library Histories* (Stam, 2001) provides a worldwide survey of public libraries and some important landmarks, giving a global snapshot of public library development. In Africa the planned development of libraries was rare until after the 1920s. Subscription libraries existed in South Africa as early as 1838 and were later developed into the public library system. Libraries in Lagos, Nigeria, were founded and supported by the British Colonial Office and funded by the Carnegie Corporation. The first national public library service established by statute in sub-Saharan Africa was the Ghana Library Service in 1948. Public library development in Africa escalated in the 1960s and 1970s with local librarians trained abroad.

Public libraries in the areas encompassed by the former British Empire generally followed a similar pattern of development. Originating as institutions such as subscription libraries for the wealthy elite, libraries slowly broadened their scope to include service to all. After independence the trend toward service to all continued. In the English-speaking Caribbean region, organized public library services were created in the nineteenth century after financial assistance from the Carnegie Corporation and British Council helped set up library services. Provision for public library development in India has been included in its five year plans since independence from colonial rule, but public library services are available by and large only to urban residents. The Delhi Public Library in India was established as a pilot project in 1951 in cooperation with UNESCO and has become a model public library for South Asian countries. Very slow progress has been made in the development of rural libraries in India, and there is a fundamental challenge in convincing communities that information can be a vital resource for development (Vashishth, 1995).

While private libraries developed quite early in Islamic history, public libraries are a recent development in Islamic countries. New public library buildings and expanded services in countries like the United Arab Emirates are notable in recent years. In nearby Bhutan and the Maldives public libraries are virtually nonexistent. Public library services in southeast Asia range from initial development in Thailand, to a broad-based joint effort in Malaysia, where public library development is the responsibility of state, federal, and local government authorities, to the remarkable development in Singapore, where the National Library operates the public library system. In 1966 public libraries were opened in Nepal with the assistance of the Danish International Development Agency, UNESCO, and the Nepal National Library. Development of public libraries in the Pacific islands dates primarily from after World War II.

In China public libraries did not exist before their introduction through missionaries in the early 1900s. After the Communist takeover, however, the government decreed in 1957 that public libraries were to be part of a system to inculcate citizens with patriotism and socialism and make them good party members. China's Cultural Revolution in 1966 led to the closure or destruction of many public libraries. Since that time certain cities and provinces have slowly reestablished public libraries (Yitai and Gorman, 2000). The pattern was similar in the Balkan countries, where public libraries emerged in the mid-nineteenth century as part of a national emancipation movement. During the post World War II period, the communist states supported large-scale programs to change their library systems and libraries to political propaganda tools for mass indoctrination with Marxist-Leninist ideology. Poor infrastructures and the absence of national standards and trained personnel have slowed recent attempts to automate library services in the Balkans. In Central and Eastern Europe following the Communist era, various organizations (e.g., the Mellon Foundation, Soros Foundation, and the Council of Europe) poured significant funding into automation and infrastructure upgrades.

In Finland nationalism and the quest for education established public libraries in the 1860s, followed in the 1920s by written standards enforced by library inspectors. Sweden's combination of education and religious movements facilitated the creation of public libraries, originally aimed at the lower classes. In the mid-nineteenth century reading societies in Iceland evolved into public libraries in rural parts of the country. Spain's public library movement as defined by a 1901 ruling has led to a service orientation toward the public. The proliferation and growth of Iberian libraries after the 1970s has been remarkable. Both Spain and Portugal have modernized their libraries with the advent of the Internet and Web-based digital technology. Spain held its first national conference on public libraries in 2002, with papers and discussions illustrating the innovative programs existing in Spain's public libraries.

IFLA and UNESCO

The International Federation of Library Associations and Institutions (IFLA) is the leading international body representing the interests of library and information services and their users. It is the global voice of the library and information profession with 1,700 members from more than 150 countries. The roots of IFLA are at the International Congress of Librarians and Booklovers held at Prague in 1926. It was there that Gabriel Henriot, then president of the *Association des bibliothécaires francais* and professor at the

American Library School in Paris, recommended the creation of a standing international library committee, to be elected by individual national organizations. The impetus was part of the international movement to promote cooperation across national frontiers that followed World War I.

One year later, in 1927, the International Federation of Library Associations (IFLA) was founded in Edinburgh during the celebration of the fiftieth anniversary of the Library Association of the United Kingdom. IFLA's first constitution was approved in 1929 at the First World Congress of Librarianship and Bibliography in Rome. Wieder and Campbell (2002) tell the story of IFLA's first 50 years, primarily summarizing early development and pointing out the importance of IFLA's formal agreement with the United National Educational, Scientific and Cultural Organization (UNESCO). Founded in 1946, UNESCO assumed the goal of assisting libraries and promoting the development of documentation, library, and archival services as part of the national information infrastructures. IFLA was officially recognized as the principal nongovernmental organ for UNESCO's cooperation with professional library associations in Oslo in 1947. At the same time UNESCO promised financial support for the execution of IFLA's program.

In recent years the advent of computer and telecommunications technology that permit the international exchange of information in digital format and the governmental reform movement have brought a renewed interest in public libraries. Eradicating the digital divide has become a major topic of concern for national governments, private foundations, nongovernmental organizations, and the computer industry. A core value of IFLA is the belief that people, communities, and organizations need universal and equitable access to information, ideas, and works of imagination for their social, educational, cultural, democratic, and economic well-being.

Documents developed by IFLA including the *IFLA Internet Manifesto* and the *Glasgow Declaration on Libraries, Information Services and Intellectual Freedom* (Figure 11.1) illustrate the importance of these issues. IFLA was active in the support of the World Summit on the Information Society in Geneva in December 2003 and will be active in the second phase in Tunis in December 2005.

Since the mid-1960s the objectives of public libraries in many parts of the world have been the subject of regular review to examine whether they respond adequately to the needs of communities. With social changes there have been increased demands for citizens for improved access to information and education while advances in the

Figure 11.1: Glasgow Declaration on Libraries, Information Services, and Intellectual Freedom

Years of IFLA

Meeting in Glasgow on the occasion of the 75th anniversary of its formation, the International Federation of Library Associations and Institutions (IFLA) declares that:

IFLA proclaims the fundamental right of human beings both to access and to express information without restriction.

IFLA and its worldwide membership support, defend and promote intellectual freedom as expressed in the United Nations Universal Declaration of Human Rights. This intellectual freedom encompasses the wealth of human knowledge, opinion, creative thought and intellectual activity.

IFLA asserts that a commitment to intellectual freedom is a core responsibility of the library and information profession worldwide, expressed through codes of ethics and demonstrated through practice.

IFLA affirms that:

- Libraries and information services provide access to information, ideas and works of imagination in any medium and regardless of frontiers. They serve as gateways to knowledge, thought and culture, offering essential support for independent decision-making, cultural development, research and lifelong learning by both individuals and groups.

- Libraries and information services contribute to the development and maintenance of intellectual freedom and help to safeguard democratic values and universal civil rights. Consequently, they are committed to offering their clients access to relevant resources and services without restriction and to opposing any form of censorship.

- Libraries and information services shall acquire, preserve and make available the widest variety of materials, reflecting the plurality and diversity of society. The selection and availability of library materials and services shall be governed by professional considerations and not by political, moral and religious views.

- Libraries and information services shall make materials, facilities and services equally accessible to all users. There shall be no discrimination for any reason including race, national or ethnic origin, gender or sexual preference, age, disability, religion, or political beliefs.

- Libraries and information services shall protect each user's right to privacy and confidentiality with respect to information sought or received and resources consulted, borrowed, acquired or transmitted.

IFLA therefore calls upon libraries and information services and their staff to uphold and promote the principles of intellectual freedom and to provide uninhibited access to information.

This Declaration was prepared by IFLA/FAIFE.

Approved by the Governing Board of IFLA 27 March 2002, The Hague, Netherlands.

Proclaimed by the Council of IFLA 19 August 2002, Glasgow, Scotland.

Figure 11.1 continued. IFLA's Glasgow Declaration

production and distribution of information have increased expectations. The public library has traditionally responded to such demands and become a focal point for the aspirations of citizens and vital to many governments. The role of public libraries in communities cannot be overlooked, as they are often the most successful focal point of democratic local life and support continuous lifelong learning.

Public Libraries Section of IFLA; IFLA Standards and Guidelines

Public libraries have important responsibilities in providing the public access to information. UNESCO'S *World Culture Report* (1998) shows the distribution of public libraries in the world can lead to inequity and imbalance. In Finland the proportion of the population who were registered public library users from 1989–1994 was 47 percent, compared with 28 percent in Jamaica, 7 percent in Malaysia, and 1 percent in Zimbabwe. The number of books in public libraries per 100 people was 712 for Finland, 47 for Jamaica, 41 for Malaysia, and 10 for Zimbabwe. It appears from the statistics and literature about public libraries that there is a strong relationship between the level of development and the use of public libraries and that development often increases public library use.

The IFLA Public Libraries Section provides an international forum and network for the development and promotion of public libraries. The goals, objectives, and strategies of the section are developed within the context of the principles enshrined in the "Public Library Manifesto" and the IFLA Professional Priorities. The Section of Public Libraries has over 300 members and many others look to the Section for professional direction and guidance. Section program goals include: promote equal access to all; raise the quality of services in public libraries by defining standards, developing guidelines, and documenting and disseminating best practices; promote the importance of training and professional development for librarians; defend the role of the public library in democratizing access to and the use of information technology; promote literacy, reading development, and lifelong learning projects; promote networking and cooperation between libraries and other agencies to balance the needs of users with the intellectual property rights of authors; promote the role of libraries in society.

In 1973 IFLA published "Standards for Public Libraries," which was reissued with slight revisions in 1977. In 1986 this document was replaced by "Guidelines for Public Libraries." As their titles suggest, they represent two different approaches to providing practical guidance to librarians. The introduction to the 1973 Standards stated that separate standards were not considered desirable, since the general objectives in all countries were the same, the modifying factor being the pace at which development could take place. The 1973 version therefore provided a range of quantitative standards, including the size of collections, size of administrative units, opening hours, staffing levels, and building standards. The 1986 Guidelines took a different view recognizing that when needs and resources vary so widely there can be no common standards for services. The Guidelines offered not rules but advice, based on experience drawn from many different countries and useful for general application. The Guidelines recognized that recommendations on desirable levels of library service, based on past experience in quite different circumstances, are bound to be unreliable and misleading.

The next approach to standards took the form of consultative meetings in Amsterdam (1998), Bangkok (1999), and Jerusalem (2000), to develop a set of guidelines for the twenty-first century framed to provide assistance to librarians in any situation to develop an effective public library service related to the requirements of their local community. *The Public Library Service: IFLA / UNESCO Guidelines for Development* were published in 2001 and consisted of six major standards pertaining to the following areas:

- Role and purpose of the public library
- Legal and financial framework
- Meetings the needs of the users
- Collection development
- Human resources
- Management and marketing of public libraries

Users can access this document in a number of languages directly from the IFLA Web site. These guidelines and standards can be relevant to any public library at some point in its development. Where public libraries cannot meet all the standards and recommendations immediately, it is hoped that they provide a target for the future.

Around the world, people are becoming aware of the key role of public libraries in providing access to information to help everyone participate in the democratic process and develop their country. Countries are slowly learning the role that information can play in solving problems and advancing national development goals. Some parts of the world still face challenges to gain access to technology that allows public libraries to be linked with networks internationally. Some countries do not have national information policies or a national information infrastructure. Public librarians are collaborating and working beyond traditional boundaries with public information networks for citizens and providing opportunities for lifelong learning. Digitization is providing sets of images to be stored and indexed and made accessible to the public. A good balance between print collections and electronic materials is needed. Networking can and is transforming and revitalizing public libraries. In many countries public libraries are working to provide access to new technologies and to make use of the IFLA/UNESCO *Guidelines for Development.*

User Services, Collection Development, and Intellectual Freedom

The range of possible services offered by public libraries varies considerably, since the public library has a very broad charge and serves everyone. Most public libraries offer separate services for children and adults. Students are often the greatest users of public libraries in much of the world, sometimes as a quiet place to study and at other times as an important source of information for homework or family and personal needs.

Collections are the concrete expressions of the public library's mission; and issues relating to the preservation of intellectual freedom and guaranteeing the right to read are central to collection development. In developing countries, there may be less opportunity to develop balanced collections, since space is valuable and there are many donated books with limited resources for acquiring materials. Libraries often import expensive materials from abroad and in addition to purchase costs and shipping costs, issues related to customs and import duties may present difficulties. In some cases, collections may be largely or wholly dependent on international donations.

The Committee on Multicultural Library Services of the Swedish Library Association produced *Library at the Centre of the World: Multicultural Library Services* (1999) to illustrate what is being done in public libraries today and to demonstrate the importance of the public library in multicultural integration. The topics covered illustrate the wide range of service to users that many public libraries must address. They include services to users whose first language is different from the majority, to elderly immigrants, and to minorities. Programs such as purchasing books at international book fairs and using databases and the Internet to serve multicultural populations are some of the responses suggested by the committee.

Africa has its own unique challenges, since libraries were often founded to serve urban educated populations and not those with primarily oral traditions. Some claim that the public library has not been a notable success in Africa, because it is an imported institution that African governments have never financed at levels that allow it to be effective (Sturges and Neill, 1998). Public libraries often survive on donations and minimal financial support. Students seeking a quiet place to study their own textbooks are often the largest group of users. The demand currently is from children and the services appropriately are directed at children. Large numbers of schoolchildren and college students doing homework and making limited use of collections and services may lead to more use by the next generation. While services built on highly literate and sophisticated users often are not offered or requested currently, they may be needed in the future. The trend of population growth gives reason to believe that a reading society, which will need library services, is in the process of emerging in Africa. Currently libraries must be stocked to meet the needs of the children and students who are the primary clientele.

Elsewhere in Africa some rural information and cultural centers have been developed to find new ways to reach the general public with library service. Rural audio libraries have been founded to address the preservation and transmission of oral cultures in Mali, Swaziland, Zimbabwe, and Tanzania. A lending service provided out of a van or truck or by bicycle or camel may serve towns that cannot support a library building or librarian. Box book schemes to remote rural areas are a typical way of responding to needs for materials to read where a room is available and people cannot be served in any other way. Many countries including, Kenya, Ghana, Tanzania, and Sierra Leone, instituted mobile library services to rural areas in the 1960s and 1970s. Financial, staffing, and management problems must be addressed since these issues often have led to failure of innovative library services.

In some parts of the world, community action spontaneously created new public libraries. Senegal's tiny libraries, which can be found as part of community centers in suburbs of Dakar, funded by local societies and donor organizations, are a case in point. Working with the Soros Foundation, Haitian communities have developed community libraries around the country. In Mexico, new presidential leadership has led to the creation of a substantial number of new public libraries in the early part of the twenty-first century.

Article 19 of the UNESCO Universal Declaration of Human Rights provides the basis for discussion of intellectual freedom and access to information. In 1997 IFLA created a Committee focusing on the Freedom of Access to Information and Freedom of Expression (FAIFE) to speak for all libraries on their role regarding intellectual freedom. IFLA's executive board strongly endorsed FAIFE as an essential activity for the Federation to support as a priority for libraries and a crucial activity for IFLA. The main task for FAIFE is to promote freedom of speech and emphasize the vital role of the library as the doorway to information and knowledge. In 2001 the first IFLA/FAIFE "World Report on Libraries and Intellectual Freedom" was published. The report and others that followed includes a short, factual summary of the situation in a number of countries, including the general situation concerning libraries, librarianship, and intellectual freedom; specific cases of challenges of censorship or other violations of intellectual freedom; the legislation of libraries and intellectual freedom; and library association positions related to intellectual freedom including professional codes of conduct or ethics.

Because of the important role of information in contemporary society, a new class of people, who are information poor, has emerged, resulting in what is often referred to as the digital divide. Many cannot buy a computer and many who own them cannot use them effectively. Public libraries that have the technology and skills have a responsibility to aid and guide those who do not. By providing access, training, and the chance to experiment, public libraries can help users meet their educational needs. The importance of strong, well-funded public libraries for economic and social development in contemporary society cannot be underestimated.

Governance and Funding

The public library is generally the responsibility of local and national authorities, supported by specific legislation and financed by national and local governments. Private funds provide important supplements in many locations. International financial support can be of benefit, but strong local government support is necessary for development of new programs and maintenance of existing services. The constraints on libraries often relate to the lack of funds and therefore lack of facilities, materials, and staff salaries. Disruptions, including political and economic conflicts, poverty, war, and disease, can erode the hard work and achievements of libraries.

In many countries, public libraries are faced with diminishing financial resources. At the same time, ways of delivering information are expanding and librarians are convinced that public libraries should provide information in print and nonprint formats. The use of electronic information often causes extra financial pressures. Funding is one of the major challenges for public libraries around the world, and public libraries are reacting in a number of ways to these changes. Recruiting volunteers to reduce personnel costs, raising costs for patrons by initiating annual charges, charging for lending a particular item, and different rates for different services have been among the strategies used. Promoting the public library in an effective way has become essential and one strategy to achieve this is through cooperation with social and cultural organizations. Sponsorship of projects for public libraries by the private sector is also becoming more common.

While the UNESCO "Public Library Manifesto" (Figure 11.2) states that the public library shall in principle be free of charge, in libraries there is an ongoing discussion about payment for services. Some argue for equal and easy access to free services, and others insists that fiscal concerns and market mechanisms point to the need

Figure 11.2: UNESCO Public Library Manifesto

November 1994

Freedom, prosperity and the development of society and of individuals are fundamental human values. They will only be attained through the ability of well-informed citizens to exercise their democratic rights and to play an active role in society. Constructive participation and the development of democracy depend on satisfactory education as well as on free and unlimited access to knowledge, thought, culture and information.

The public library, the local gateway to knowledge, provides a basic condition for lifelong learning, independent decision- making and cultural development of the individual and social groups.

This Manifesto proclaims UNESCO's belief in the public library as a living force for education, culture and information, and as an essential agent for the fostering of peace and spiritual welfare through the minds of men and women.

UNESCO therefore encourages national and local governments to support and actively engage in the development of public libraries.

The Public Library

The public library is the local centre of information, making all kinds of knowledge and information readily available to its users.

The services of the public library are provided on the basis of equality of access for all, regardless of age, race, sex, religion, nationality, language or social status. Specific services and materials must be provided for those users who cannot, for whatever reason, use the regular services and materials, for example linguistic minorities, people with disabilities or people in hospital or prison.

All age groups must find material relevant to their needs. Collections and services have to include all types of appropriate media and modern technologies as well as traditional materials. High quality and relevance to local needs and conditions are fundamental. Material must reflect current trends and the evolution of society, as well as the memory of human endeavour and imagination.

Collections and services should not be subject to any form of ideological, political or religious censorship, nor commercial pressures.

Missions of the Public Library

The following key missions which relate to information, literacy, education and culture should be at the core of public library services:

1. creating and strengthening reading habits in children from an early age;

2. supporting both individual and self conducted education as well as formal education at all levels;

3. providing opportunities for personal creative development;

4. stimulating the imagination and creativity of children and young people;

5. promoting awareness of cultural heritage, appreciation of the arts, scientific achievements and innovations;

6. providing access to cultural expressions of all performing arts;

7. fostering inter-cultural dialogue and favouring cultural diversity;

8. supporting the oral tradition;

9. ensuring access for citizens to all sorts of community information;

10. providing adequate information services to local enterprises, associations and interest groups;

11. facilitating the development of information and computer literacy skills;

12. supporting and participating in literacy activities and programmes for all age groups, and initiating such activities if necessary.

Funding, legislation and networks

- The public library shall in principle be free of charge.

The public library shall in principle be free of charge. The public library is the responsibility of local and national authorities. It must be supported by specific legislation and financed by national and local governments. It has to be an essential component of any long-term strategy for culture, information provision, literacy and education.

- To ensure nationwide library coordination and cooperation, legislation and strategic plans must also define and promote a national library network based on agreed standards of service.

- The public library network must be designed in relation to national, regional, research and special libraries as well as libraries in schools, colleges and universities.

Operation and management

- A clear policy must be formulated, defining objectives, priorities and services in relation to the local community needs. The public library has to be organized effectively and professional standards of operation must be maintained.

Figure 11.2 continued. UNESCO Public Library Manifesto

- Cooperation with relevant partners - for example, user groups and other professionals at local, regional, national as well as international level- has to be ensured.

- Services have to be physically accessible to all members of the community. This requires well situated library buildings, good reading and study facilities, as well as relevant technologies and sufficient opening hours convenient to the users. It equally implies outreach services for those unable to visit the library.

- The library services must be adapted to the different needs of communities in rural and urban areas.

- The librarian is an active intermediary between users and resources. Professional and continuing education of the librarian is indispensable to ensure adequate services.

- Outreach and user education programmes have to be provided to help users benefit from all the resources.

Implementing the Manifesto

Decision makers at national and local levels and the library community at large, around the world, are hereby urged to implement the principles expressed in this Manifesto.

The Manifesto is prepared in cooperation with the International Federation of Library Associations and Institutions (IFLA).

Figure 11.2 continued. UNESCO Public Library Manifesto

for charges and payment. Some libraries are introducing registration or subscription charges for public library membership. These strategies become more common with political and economic changes and reductions in funds.

A trend in local government in some parts of the world is to merge libraries into larger units of leisure or culture or education. The head of the library service may be a librarian who also manages programs outside the library sector, or a nonlibrarian who is responsible for a range of services including libraries. Certain countries in some parts of the world, faced with diminishing governmental resources, have considered radical changes. One option is to contract out the public library service, so that it is provided by an outside company on behalf of a local or central government body. Not many jurisdictions have adopted this course, since most people think it is important that the public library is an independent and impartial institution that provides education, culture, recreation, and information to all.

Networking and resources are particularly essential today. No single library can buy everything its users need. Public libraries are more often being used for education and personal development and as information resource centers. Economic necessity and the need to increase the effectiveness of individual libraries have spurred cooperative efforts among groups of libraries to achieve equity of access. Many new library networks are multitype and broker remote access to information. With electronic sources of information becoming key to the provision of reference and information services, networks are becoming more common and more essential.

Information about the current state of public libraries in Europe has been facilitated by the creation of the European Union and the European Commission. A green paper on the role of libraries in the information society was issued in 1997 (Thorhauge, et al., 1997). Nations in northern Europe were shown to have relatively higher percentages of the national population registered as borrowers from public libraries.

In countries such as Malaysia and Singapore public libraries are being built up on a planned basis with strong direction by the national library. The role of the public library as a cultural center is key in some countries. In Bulgaria public libraries are housed in cultural centers, and in the United Kingdom most metropolitan public libraries are administered as part of a leisure or cultural directorate. With social, technological, and telecommunications advances, one of the responses of public libraries has been to create large units of administration and to fund coordinating mechanisms. In 2001 Mexico held their first international conference on public libraries, with speakers from Germany, Canada, Spain, the USA, France, Italy, and Mexico. As libraries are expanded, Mexico has benefited from a substantial donation from the Bill and Melinda Gates Foundation to bring technology to public libraries and librarians working with government officials to enhance the technological infrastructure.

Librarians have in recent years begun to address the issue of the value of the public library, in terms of the ways in which libraries contribute to the economic development of the local community. An Australian management consultant asserts that politicians and librarians underestimate the current and potential economic value of public libraries and suggests that the benefit created is twice as much as the funds spent (Haratsis, 1995). Consultants in New Zealand developed a cost-benefit methodology for assessing the value of library output. The role of the library in economic development can involve a wide range of activities, from encouragement of literacy to the provision of specialized business services. With financial constraints and the perceived need to provide new services while maintaining book and multimedia collections and delivering specialized services to minority groups, there are discussions about which services are basic—and therefore should be free of charge—and which might be fee based. Many libraries face stable or diminishing budgets and the need to provide new services and meet increased demands.

International Library Development Initiatives

Public libraries around the world have received targeted support from philanthropic organizations, such as the Carnegie Corporation, Bertelsmann Foundation, British Council, Book Aid International, and more recently the Bill and Melinda Gates Foundation, among others. When countries have fewer resources, public libraries may be viewed as a new concept imported from the West. At the beginning of the last century, Andrew Carnegie was instrumental in spreading the influence of libraries through countries that were part of the former British Commonwealth. Carnegie provided funds for over 2,800 public library buildings, most of them in the English-speaking world. Carnegie required that the community donate space for the building and provide for the operating expenses. Since the 1990s the Carnegie Corporation has again focused on libraries in Africa.[1]

Bill and Melinda Gates Foundation

The Bill and Melinda Gates Foundation International Library Initiative supports libraries throughout the world to help individuals improve their lives through information and technology. The foundation has supported the "Abre Tu Mundo" (Open Your World) project in Chile, which has given Chilean residents no-cost access to computers and the Internet in Chile's 368 public libraries, as well as training on the use of new information technologies and the generation of local content for the Internet (Bibliloredes).

The Access to Learning Award funded by the Bill and Melinda Gates Foundation is given annually to a public library or similar organization outside the United States that has shown a commitment to offering the public free access to information technology through an existing innovative program (Council on Library and Information Resources). Recent awards have included:

- Biblioteca del Congreso, Argentina—one of the few libraries in the country that provides services to the public free of charge, including a computer center that is open around the clock.

- Biblored, Colombia—a network of 19 public libraries in Bogotá that offers no-cost access to digital information in some of the city's poorest neighborhoods.

- Helsinki City Library, Finland—among the first public libraries in the world to offer Internet access to the public. It established the Information Gas Station, a portable unit providing immediate information by phone, fax, or text messages.

- Proyecto Bibliotecas (Probigua), Guatemala—has libraries and technology centers in rural communities. These centers include computer training labs that teach new skills to underserved populations.

The most recent award, for 2003, was the Smart Cape Access Project of Cape Town South Africa, for its innovative efforts to connect residents, particularly in low-income neighborhoods, with no-cost public access to computers and the Internet. The Access to Learning Award made it possible to install computers in all Cape Town Libraries.

Open Society Institute, Soros Foundation

The Open Society Institute (OSI) is a private operating and grant-making foundation based in New York City that serves as the hub of the Soros Foundation's network, a group of autonomous foundations and organizations in more than 50 countries. OSI and the network implement a range of initiatives that aim to promote open societies by shaping government policy and supporting education, media, public health, and human and women's rights, as well as social, legal, and economic reform. To diminish and prevent the negative consequences of globalization, OSI seeks to foster global open society by increasing collaboration with other nongovernmental organizations, governments, and international institutions.

The Library Program of the OSI of the Soros Foundation helped libraries transform themselves into public and service-oriented centers for their communities. The Network Library Program developed model libraries that function as civic information centers. In 1999 and 2000, 15 such model libraries were supported in eight countries of Central and Eastern Europe and Russia with support from local government. In 2000 the program was merged into an integrated Information Program. The Electronic Information for Libraries consortium launched in late 1999 provides a structural solution to the digital divide in content access. The consortium, which includes 2000 libraries and public information institutions in 39 countries, enables low-cost access to several thousand social science and business journals. A second component in partnership with the World Health Organization provides medical journals and databases.

The OSI Information Program promotes the equitable deployment of knowledge and communications resources and is based on three premises. First, human beings are not passive subjects or only economic agents seeking personal gain, but civic beings who share a world, which they have the power to shape. Second, the ability to exchange ideas, knowledge, and information is the lifeblood of citizenship and participation in a shared public sphere. Third, while traditional media remain essential to citizenship, new digital technologies hold potential for enhancing civic life that is still largely untapped.

Bertelsmann Foundation

Since its inception in 1977 the Bertelsmann Foundation has conducted projects in the sphere of public libraries where they emphasize the construction and promotion of model libraries, as well as the development of future-oriented methods of library management. The Bertelsmann Foundation International Network of Public Libraries works to pool international know-how, to strengthen the exchange of experience among public library experts, to develop concepts for modern library management and above all, to promote the transfer of such model solutions into practice (International Network of Public Libraries). With 16 experts from 10 counties, the network strives to create a forum in which people can share information and expertise to increase the effectiveness and efficiency of libraries. The two modules are international research and preparation of model solutions on issues of modern library management and implementation of these solutions at the practical level to test their suitability for everyday use. Volume one of a series of case studies sponsored by the Bertelsmann Foundation International Network of Public Libraries outlines successful solutions. The report of the Canterbury Public Library, serving the city of Christchurch, New Zealand, and the methodology used to evaluate its ability to meet the challenges of the twenty-first century provides guidelines and recommendations on how to implement change in a meaningful way (Windau, 1999).

British Council

Since 1934 librarians in the British Council have created an international library network and helped lay the foundations of public library systems in the developing world (Coombs, 1988). The Council maintained its own libraries, administered book aid schemes, encouraged professional interchange and education, and ran courses in librarianship. In 1959 the public library development scheme emerged to sponsor public library systems more or less from scratch. The areas of most intense activity were West and East Africa. By the 1970s the Council felt the need to provide integrated and more sophisticated information service. More recently, people have questioned the relevance of the British model, based partly on the fact that materials that were appropriate were difficult to acquire from indigenous publishers. The focus of the British Council has changed, and support for this work is less today.

Mortenson Center for International Library Programs

The Mortenson Center for International Library Programs, at the University of Illinois at Urbana-Champaign, designs programs for working professionals to exchange ideas and upgrade their knowledge and skills, through experiences and internships. This is achieved through a structured program of skills development, formal coursework, consultation with library and library school faculty, and literature reviews, as well as library tours and conferences. Since 1991 librarians from 76 countries have participated in the program.

World Library Partnership

The World Library Partnership (WLP) takes a different approach and among other activities sends librarians to developing countries to assist in library programs primarily in rural areas. WLP forms partnerships between libraries in developing countries and the United States, which focus on cultural exchange and raising funds to support small libraries. In corporation with UNESCO they also developed *Libraries for All: How to Start and Run a Basic Library* (Wendell, 1998).

Book Donation Programs

Several hundred book donation programs operate throughout the world, which function with varying degrees of success. The key is to be certain that books that are not needed, or dated materials, are not sent at a great financial cost. Book Aid International is a major donor of new and used books. They have teamed with African Books Collective to promote African titles abroad and to ease their distribution internationally within Africa.

The Canadian Organization for Development through Education, the Norwegian Agency for Development Cooperation, the Danish International Development Agency, and other agencies have provided funding for libraries. A number of useful workshop meetings devoted to the organization of library services have occurred, heavily facilitated by IFLA's advancement of Librarianship in the Third World Programme (ALP). In French-speaking Africa, a network of centers was set up to provide access to information media. The cultural center as focus for information activity is a well-established concept in francophone West Africa. Senegal is an example, wherein the Ministry of Culture provides each administrative region of the country with a major cultural center. Cultural promotion and association with a complex of other cultural activities had led to library activity.

In the end, each country and community must decide what kind of public library is needed and develop the local support to ensure its success. International programs can help, but local support and leadership is essential.

Community Outreach and Services

An international comparison of public library services and statistics reveals that of the wide range of services provided, including books, interlibrary lending, and children's services are nearly universal (Hanratty and Sumsion, 1996). The library is for many people the reason for coming to the central city and is considered by people of many cultures to be a safe and nonthreatening environment. In Australia the relationship of libraries and shopping centers has created some of the most successful library service points. Chile has recently expanded the number of public libraries and the technology available using the leverage of a grant from the Gates Foundation to receive additional resources from the government.

Public Libraries and the Information Society, prepared for the European Commission, proposes a vision for public libraries for the twenty-first century. This report outlines the necessity of developing national policies and strategies for public libraries and the importance of continuing education for librarians (Thorhauge, et al., 1997). The report discusses how the public library fulfills a variety of functions, including local cultural center, local learning center, general information center, and social center. Libraries can help all people prosper in an information society and be a key part of the educational system. Public libraries are a key component for a civil society and lifelong learning, education, and democratic process in an open society.

Similar evaluations took place in other parts of the world, including discussions of the barefoot librarian in Africa (Onwubiko, 1996). Access to knowledge and lifelong learning is vital in democracies. Unequal access to information and technology, as well as information illiteracy, may create additional social divisions, but public libraries can help, and changes in government can lead to opportunities to renew public libraries. Administrative reform can lead to changes, but most countries remain committed to financing them by public budgets.

Outreach services such as bookmobiles, providing electronic information, and cooperation with other libraries to improve services are important. Bookmobiles can expand service by reaching out to people who cannot get to a library. Those managing public libraries must find a balance between varied goals, such as using marketing techniques and providing a collection that is not based on commercial interests. The introduction of the Camel Library Service by the Kenya National Library Service is an innovative approach to delivering services to those with a nomadic lifestyle (Atuti, 1999). Rahman (2000) reports on the status of rural and small libraries in Bangladesh, describing the reality of isolation, poor telecommunications infrastructure, and neglect faced by many rural libraries around the world that sometimes serve illiterate populations.

Libraries respond to community needs in ways that are most appropriate to their setting and resources. Camel book boxes, bicycle book carts, donkey drawn book carts, and other programs illustrate ingenious ways librarians respond to community needs and deliver services. Mali has a library in a railway car that serves ten communities along the railway line. In Zimbabwe a donkey cart is used as a means of conveyance. Pack mules have been used in South America to transport collections of books to remote communities. Bicycles can move information workers and small quantities of materials at low cost over difficult terrain.

Telecommunication infrastructures vary widely among nations. Donations of computer information systems are increasingly common, but internal funds may not be available for ongoing maintenance and upgrades. Digital and Internet-based projects provide new opportunities for public libraries. In countries without a strong public library tradition, it is difficult to show relevance and need for the Internet and technology. The Internet democratizes information and empowers users and public libraries can be gateways to information and assist people in learning how to use these resources.

Library cooperation is a major means for providing services today, and libraries throughout the world have become more connected to each other through systems and networks, making it easier to share resources. Systems, networks, and databases make it possible to search for information in other libraries. As the local gateway to information, the public library has to meet the information needs of a community by using not only their collection, but also those of others. The changing financial situation for public libraries and rapidly changing technology mean that skilled leadership and staff are essential.

Crossroads

Public librarianship follows a variety of models in different parts of the world, including technology centers, cultural centers, and study centers, among others. The UNESCO Libraries portal provides access to over 200 library sites around the world for comparative analysis. As society continues to undergo ideological, political, cultural, social, economic, and technological changes, public libraries must develop policies and strategies that demonstrate their relevance. Libraries are perceived to be at a crossroads in their history. People wonder whether they will have a central place in the electronic society or remain on the margins, and whether they will be able to attract the funds to provide the varied resources and programs needed by the public. Issues of censorship and the wide range of materials available on the Internet, copyright and intellectual property rights, and providing services free at the point of delivery are key for future public library services. Public libraries play an essential role in providing and organizing electronic materials for use and in helping and training users to use digital resources. Users demand that libraries provide not only the software and hardware needed, but also the professional support to help independent learners use resources. Through participation in the American Library Association International Relations Round Table, programs like

Sister Cities (Sager, 2000), or attendance at the International Federation of Library Associations and Institutions, U.S. librarians can work to be part of World Librarianship. The global library community has many challenges and opportunities ahead. The crucial issue is how to facilitate the development of public libraries, which provide equal and open access to information for all citizens and thus lead to free and economically developed societies.

Notes

1. *Public Libraries in Africa: A Report and Annotated Bibliography*, comp. Aissa Issak (Oxford: International Network for the Availability of Scientific Publications, 2000), and *The Book Chain in Anglophone Africa: A Survey and Directory,* ed. Roger Stringer (Oxford: International Network for the Availability of Scientific Publications, 2002), were published with the financial support of the Carnegie Corporation. To learn more, visit: www.carnegie.org and www.inasp.info.

References

Atuti, Richard M. 1999. Camel Library Service to Nomadic Pastoralists: the Kenyan Scenario. *IFLA Journal* 25: 152–158.

Biblioredes (Chile). Available: www.biblioredes.cl.

Bill and Melinda Gates Foundation. International Library Initiatives. Available: www.gatesfoundation.org.

Black, Alistair. 2000. *The Public Library in Britain, 1914–2000.* London: The British Library.

Caballero, Maria Cristina. 2003. *Biblored: Colombia's Innovative Library Network.* Washington, DC: Council on Library and Information Resources.

Coombs, Douglas. 1988. *Spreading the Word: The Library Work of the British Council.* London: Mansell Publishing Limited.

Council on Library and Information Resources. Access to Learning Award. Available: www.clir.org/fellowships/gates/gates.html.

Greenhalgh, Liz, Ken Worpole, and Charles Landry. 1995. *Libraries in a World of Cultural Change.* London: UCL Press.

Hanratty, Catherine, and John Sumsion. 1996. *International Comparison of Public Library Statistics.* Loughborough, UK: Loughborough University, Library and Information Statistics Unit.

Haratsis, Brian. 1995. Justifying the Economic Value of Public Libraries in a Turbulent Local Government Environment. *Australasian Public Libraries and Information Services* 8: 164–172.

Hassner, Karen. 2004. Promoting the Public Library Guidelines. *IFLA Section of Public Libraries Newsletter* 29 (February): 22.

International Federation of Library Associations and Institutions. Core Values. Available: www.ifla.org.

International Federation of Library Associations and Institutions. Glasgow Declaration. Available: www.ifla.org/faife/policy/iflastat/gldeclar-e.html.

International Federation of Library Associations and Institutions and Freedom of Access to Information and Freedom of Expression. 2001. *Libraries and Intellectual Freedom: IFLA/FAIFE World Report: Denmark.* Denmark: IFLA/FAIFE Office.

International Federation of Library Associations and Institutions. 2001. *The Public Library Service: IFLA/UNESCO Guidelines for Development.* München: K. G. Saur.

International Network of Public Libraries Available: www.public-libraries.net and www.bertelsmann-stifung.de.

McCook, Kathleen de la Peña, Barbara J. Ford, and Kate Lippincott. 1998. *Libraries: Global Reach—Local Touch.* Chicago: American Library Association.

New Zealand Library and Information Association. 1996. *Valuing the Economic Costs and Benefits of Libraries: a Study Prepared for the N Strategy.* Wellington, New Zealand: New Zealand Library and Information Association.

Onwubiko, Chidi P. C. 1996. The Practice of Amadi's Barefoot Librarianship in African Public Libraries. *Library Review* 45: 39–47.

Open Society Institute, Soros Foundation. Available: www.soros.org. Examples of the Soros Foundation's support of international public libraries include the following:

Electronic Information for Libraries. Available: www.osi.hu/nlp.

Information Program. Available: www.soros.org/initiatives/information.

Rahman, Faizur. 2000. Status of Rural and Small Libraries in Bangladesh: Directions for the Future. *Rural Libraries* 20: 52–64.

Rudolf, Málek. 1970. On the Origin of the International Organization of Librarians (IFLA): the Congress of Librarians in Prague, 1926. *Libri* 20: 222–224.

Sager, Donald. J. 2000. The Sister Libraries Program. *Public Libraries* 39 (July/August): 195–199.

Soros Foundation. Open Society Institute. Available: www.soros.org.

Stam, David H., ed. 2001. *International Dictionary of Library Histories.* Chicago: Fitzroy Dearborn Publishers.

Sturges, Paul, and Richard Neill. 1998. *The Quiet Struggle: Information and Libraries for the People of Africa.* 2nd. ed. London: Mansell.

Swedish Library Association. 1999. *Library at the Centre of the World: Multicultural Library Services.* Lund, Sweden: Committee on Multicultural Library Services of the Swedish Library Association.

Thorhauge, J., et al. 1997. *Public Libraries and the Information Society.* Luxembourg: European Commission.

UNESCO. The IFLA/UNESCO Public Library Manifesto. Available: www.ifla.org/documents/libraries/policies/unesco.htm.

UNESCO. 1998. *World Culture Report 1998: Culture, Creativity and Markets.* France: UNESCO.

United Nations. Millennium Declaration. Available: www.un.org/millennium/declaration/ares552e.htm.

United Nations Development Programme. 2003. *Human Development Report 2003: Millennium Development Goals: A Compact Among Nations to End Human Poverty.* New York: United Nations.

University of Illinois Library at Urbana-Champaign. Mortenson Center for International Library Programs. Available: www.library.uiuc.edu/mortenson.

Vashishth, C. P., ed. 1995. *Libraries as Rural Community Resource Centres: Papers and Proceedings of the Workshop on Rural Community Resource Centres.* Delhi: B. R. Publishing.

Wedgeworth, Robert. 1998. Global Perspective. In *Libraries: Global Reach-Local Touch,* ed. Kathleen de la Peña McCook, Barbara J. Ford, and Kate Lippincott, 6–11. Chicago: American Library Association.

Wendell, Laura. 1998. *Libraries for All: How to Start and Run a Basic Library.* Paris: UNESCO.

Wieder, Joachim, and Harry Campbell. 2002. IFLA's First Fifty years. *IFLA Journal* 28: 107–117.

Windau, Bettina, ed. 1999. *International Network of Public Libraries.* 6 vols. Lanham, MD: Scarecrow Press.

World Library Partnership. Available: http://worldlibraries.org.

World Summit on the Information Society. Available: www.itu.int/wsis.

Yitai, Gong, and G. E. Gorman. 2000. *Libraries and Information Services in China.* Lanham, MD: Scarecrow Press.

12
Twenty-First Century Trends in Public Librarianship

Humans have a long history of looking into the sky and forming stories from the constellations of stars—stories that correspond to their own history and culture. The Seven Sisters or Pleiades of the Greeks are the Flint Boys to the Navajo, and to the Hindus they are the Krttika, divorced wives of the Rishi sages. The public library is like a constellation, whose history and purpose differ depending upon the teller of the tale and the culture that it serves. Summarizing the future trends that will affect public libraries is a challenge, requiring interpolation from an array of points.

Each public library faces rapidly shifting demographics. The foreign-born population in the United States grew 57.4 percent in the 1990s. By 2000 more new immigrants lived in the suburbs than in inner cities (Singer, 2004). A library in Roxbury, Massachusetts, may need to plan for the arrival of new residents from Somalia, while Miami-Dade Public Library in Florida greets people transplanted from Honduras. One public library builds a new central library as part of a downtown revitalization project, while another develops neighborhood libraries. One public library collaborates with a history museum to digitize photographs from the city's past; another works with a botanical society to create neighborhood gardens. Close

293

up these public libraries are different in the activation of programs and services, from a distance they form a celestial brilliance, a starry sky, a connection of lights.

Public libraries in the United States continuously face the need to cope with fiscal challenges. During the first years of the twenty-first century, economic recession was exacerbated by the states' inability to meet unfunded federal mandates, which in turn meant less monies were available for state support of other programs. Additionally, the losses of high-paying jobs and underemployment throughout the economy further restricted tax revenues available to public libraries. To overcome these challenges, library boards and staff need to work closely with government officials as repositioning takes place to make the best use of the "community capital" that will provides the means for growth in a knowledge economy (Johnson, 2002).

Public libraries are well suited to be part of economic repositioning and can develop services that will assist communities and individuals. The "return on investment" study carried out by Holt in 2001 provides a model for communicating the estimated return and value derived from taxpayer investment to constituents. Additionally, through skillful use of the planning process public libraries can anticipate broad social movements and consolidate past efforts to ensure that services articulate with larger community planning initiatives (McCook, 2001: 28–43).

Four sweeping trends will affect public libraries in the next decade:

1. Sense of Place (SoP) in the Context of Regionalism

2. Convergence of Cultural Heritage Institutions

3. Inclusive Service Mandates and Social Justice Commitment

4. Sustaining the Public Sphere

Sense of Place (SoP) in the Context of Regionalism

A sense of place (SoP) is the sum total of all perceptions—aesthetic, emotional, historical, supernal—that a physical location, and the activities and emotional responses associated with that location, invoke in people. The public library provides a sense of place that can transcend new development, big-box stores, and malls, to help a community retain its distinct character. The current emphasis on sustainable and livable communities encourages creation of public spaces that are true community places. Yet the question that faces the public librarian is how to accommodate a community's desire for its public library to provide an SoP with the library's additional mandate to provide service beyond its defined community borders?

This question can be addressed by comparing the regional vision of modern planners with community emphasis on a new urbanism; that is, the ideal of resolving community issues together with environmental challenges. The need for regional vision is described by the Alliance for Regional Stewardship, which takes a "smart growth" approach and focuses on links and connections among multiple governments in regions that surround cities like Pittsburgh, Miami, Chicago, or Los Angeles. As Frug (2002) pointed out in his analyses of the need to transcend local governments for regional goals, the new direction of regions must be to work across boundaries of the sectors for common projects. Public librarians, through long experience, have spanned the boundaries of local communities to provide reciprocal borrowing, collaborative information services, and group licensing of electronic resources. At the same time, through work with planners, public libraries can provide an SoP for the local community.

Yet, concurrent with recognition of regional issues by the Alliance for Regional Stewardship and similar groups such as Citistates, the future of life in the United States is likely to be grounded more and more in the ideal of the livable local community. The mission of the Alliance is "to foster collaborative multi-sector regional stewardship as a means for advancing economic, social and environmental progress, while maintaining a sense of place, in America's metropolitan regions." Perhaps the success of public librarians in achieving regional services while maintaining an SoP can be their ability to serve as a fulcrum for leveraging the library's role in larger planning issues.

The public library stands as a true "third place"—as Oldenburg (2001) characterizes the place—not home and not work—where people gather. While some libraries enhance this role more than others, the urban planning design focus on livable communities with emphasis on walkable environments and accommodating civic spaces capitalizes on those aspects of public libraries that provide an SoP (Congress for the New Urbanism). When the town of Hays, Kansas, chose to restore a 1911 Carnegie Public Library as a vital downtown anchor in 2004, we witnessed how compelling the SoP can be to a community (Miller, 2004). The public library's ability to be part of the revitalization of downtowns and neighborhoods makes it an important polestar for the community, in the face of an increase in gated developments, urban sprawl, and unplanned growth.

Convergence of Cultural Heritage Institutions

The Sphinx, both real and virtual, is the central image in Stille's book, *The Future of the Past,* which explores *the* past, as it exists today and the prospects for its future. The scholars from many disciplines and their various solutions to preserving the past for future generations crowd Stille's book and bring to clarity the impact that digitization is making on the cultural heritage of the world. In any public library with an Internet connection, school children and adults can access museums, listen to music from all over the globe, watch videos of dancers, or gain access to the riches of special archival collections.

The new convergence of cultural heritage institutions is not only a manifestation of technological possibilities, but also the result of a different way of looking at lifelong learning. At the 2001 conference, "21st Century Learner: Exploring Community Partnerships for Life Long Learning," sponsored by the U.S. Institute of Museum and Library Services (IMLS) the free-choice learning model was identified as the direction of future. Free-choice learning accounts for half of all learning (formal school and work account for the rest) and a holistic system will integrate the resources of libraries, museums, and the broadcast media. Achieving this goal and expanding the benefit of lifelong learning is a goal of IMLS. This same theme is manifested in the library-public broadcasting partnership, Storylines, sponsored by the ALA and the National Endowment for the Humanities. The Urban Libraries Council study that examined the role of libraries, museums, and public broadcasting (Walker and Manjarrez, 2003) explored this concept in depth.

Through grant awards that foster collaboration IMLS is now making a financial investment to encourage partnerships among cultural heritage institutions. The "Library-Museum Collaboration" program supports innovative projects that model how museums and libraries can work together to expand their service to the public—with emphasis on serving the community, using technology, or enhancing education. Examples of grants between libraries and museums in 2003 include the following:

• Burpee Museum of Natural History—Rockford, IL

Grant in collaboration with 61 small libraries in northern Illinois and southern Wisconsin to attract the public through shared exhibitions and learning activities. Centers on a recently excavated dinosaur named Jane.

- Child's Museum of Texas and Houston Public Library—Houston, TX

  Para los Niños, a joint project, will provide monolingual Spanish-speaking parents of children up to age seven with Spanish-language parenting materials, toolkits, and hands-on workshops for parents and children.

- Public Library of Charlotte and Mecklenburg County—Charlotte, NC

  Cultural Connections, a collaboration with the Mint Museum of Art, will extend the benefits of a library card to include discounts for admission and special programs at the Mint Museum.

- Olympic Peninsula Tribal Association and the University of Washington Libraries—Seattle, WA

  A digitization project that will document artifacts, stories and events of tribal heritage in the Pacific Northwest through photographs, videotapes, and oral histories.

Capacity building among librarians, archivists, and museum professionals, through programs such as the Web-Wise Conferences on "Libraries and Museums in the Digital World" or the "Digitization for Cultural Heritage Professionals" programs, provides the skills to improve public access to cultural heritage information. These learning opportunities also encourage interaction among those working in different institutions. Discussion of these developments takes place at WebJunction, the online portal where public librarians share knowledge and experience to provide the broadest public access to information technology.

Public library programs that bring communities together to explore one book or discuss history, literature, or science, are increasingly collaborating with other cultural heritage institutions to deepen understanding. The provision of books, music, videos, DVDs, access to the Internet, and electronic resources sustains and deepens each learner's journey. Carr muses on the responsibilities of libraries in *The Promise of Cultural Heritage Institutions:*

It is our common trust to serve and assist the American journey, fearless, in this transformed century. We are perhaps at
the edge of understanding that our institutions, like all of our
culture, are about the energies of dream, and courage, solace
and renewal. And at that edge, perhaps we can assist others
(and ourselves) to understand that what we want most deeply
to know as true, we must craft for ourselves (2003: 172).

Librarians who ponder the development of the cultural heritage
role, find themselves as caretakers of the future of the past. Yet, as
libraries undertake these new ventures, some time should be spent
to assay the effect of commercial support of enterprises, as well as
the blurred distinction between visitors and users that convergence
can create (Dilevko and Gottlieb, 2003).

Inclusive Service Mandates and Social Justice Commitment

Public libraries have a long history of moving toward inclusive
service to all community residents. The goal of equity of access, long
advocated by the American Library Association, is simple in concept,
yet complex in implementation (McCook, 2002). Today the U.S. population presents many challenges to the goal of equity of access:
there are over 50 million people in the United States with some sort
of disability that must be accommodated; 20 percent of the United
States speaks a language other than English in the home; 12.1 percent of the population lives below the poverty level; 19.8 percent of
the U.S. population is foreign born. Each of these groups presents a
set of special service responses requirements if the public library is
to provide equity of access.

As government services and social services contract, people will
find the public library to be the most well situated agency to assist
them in making use of a variety of needed services, such as literacy,
career development, and health information. While specialized programs in the community may provide more developed support for
any given service, the public library has the capacity to develop a
service integration approach in helping people begin and locate services they require.

Libraries can achieve this goal in many ways. The vanguard of
service-integration in the twenty-first century is the 2–1–1 initiative,
which provides callers with information and referral in times of crisis and for every-day needs. The 2–1–1 initiatives that now serve 82
million people in 25 states provide callers with information about

and referrals to human services for every day needs and in times of crisis (2–1–1. Get Connected). Public libraries can align themselves to be a vital component of the growing movement for comprehensive community initiatives. The New York State Library has developed guidelines for library involvement that serve as a national model for 2–1–1 collaboration. The library's director alone cannot do this. Staff at all levels of the organization must develop the leadership capacity to help full integration of services through setting direction, setting boundaries, and creating alignment with other community agencies (Polend, 2002).

The public library has a strong intellectual and philosophical commitment to equity of access as manifested in national policy statements approved by the ALA, such as the "Library Services for People with Disabilities Policy," the policy on "Library Services for the Poor," and the work of associations that focus on the special reading and information needs of people from diverse cultures. It becomes part of the task of librarians in different communities to identify demographic composition of the population and develop responsive services. In 2004 the Bill and Melinda Gates Foundation issued the report, *Toward Equality of Access*, which emphasized the need for continued support of librarians, policy makers and community advocates to continue to overcome the digital divide to ensure equity.

Social justice is activated as librarians work to provide all community members with inclusive services regardless of age, ethnicity, language, physical or mental challenges, or economic class. As demonstrated by Carla Hayden's 2004 presidency on Equity of Access in From Outreach to Equity (Osborne, 2004), new models are developing all the time to improve access to information for all. Whether ensuring that there is online access in rural public libraries or bringing bookmobiles to urban centers, public librarians contribute to human development and enrichment. In a world of inequality, as Sennett (2003) describes the United States today, the respect that librarians provide for all members of their public is a rare yet precious mode of daily work.

Sustaining the Public Sphere

The importance of the public library as a commons, listed as one of the service responses in *New Planning for Results,* will grow in the years to come. The commons role is part of the larger metaphor of the "public sphere" in democratic societies. The idea of the public sphere has been developed using the work of philosopher Jürgen Habermas, who has described the significance of people connecting ideas through broad discussion: "Reaching mutual understanding through discourse indeed guarantees that issues, reasons, and information are handled reasonably, but such understanding still depends on contexts characterized by a capacity for learning, both at the cultural and the personal level" (1996: 324–325). A vibrant public sphere provides an opportunity for the discourse that will enliven democracy. Public libraries that recognize the importance of sustaining the public sphere will respond to their community's desire for a place to address critical issues in their lives.

The national library leadership has focused on the importance of the commons function in libraries. Kranich (2003) notes that, "information, too, is a common asset that is essential to advancing teaching, learning, and civic participation, and also encourages the development of civil society. When people are better informed, they are more likely to deliberate about policies that affect their lives and commons concerns. Most importantly, citizens need a commons where they can speak freely, discern different perspectives, share similar interests and concerns." The role of public library collection development so that librarians ensure that materials are available to meet the needs and interests of all segments of their communities continues to be an important way that the public sphere can be enhanced (Budd and Wyatt, 2002).

However, real threats to the availability of information for public discourse exist. In *Dismantling the Public Sphere,* Buschman (2003) provides a critique of librarianship in light of increasing commercialization of information and the broad reach of authoritarian populism. To assure continued availability of the materials for meaningful discussion and deliberation about important issues also requires a free press and free access to media. As McChesney and Nichols (2002) argue, this requires awareness of the limitations of the mass media resulting from corporate voices. Librarians must be aware of the complex factors that delimit what is available and work to extend collection development beyond the usual sources.

Public librarians also seek to protect readers from intrusions allowed by the USA PATRIOT Act and have drawn criticism from the government for doing so. The USA PATRIOT Act was passed after the terrorist acts on September 11, 2001 with almost no debate. The ACLU states, "Many parts of this sweeping legislation take away checks on law enforcement and threaten the very rights and freedoms that we are struggling to protect. For example, without a warrant and without probable cause, the FBI now has the power to access your most private medical records, your library records, and your student records...and can prevent anyone from telling you it was done."

The American Library Association resolution on the USA PATRIOT Act notes, "The American Library Association (ALA) opposes any use of governmental power to suppress the free and open exchange of knowledge and information or to intimidate individuals exercising free inquiry...ALA considers that sections of the USA PATRIOT ACT are a present danger to the constitutional rights and privacy rights of library users." (Lichtblau, 2003; American Library Association). Most state library associations have also passed resolutions regarding the threat of the USA PATRIOT Act to the democratic process.

The Children's Internet Protection Act (CIPA) is another case in which librarians have worked to protect public access to information—specifically unfiltered Internet access in public libraries. CIPA requires that libraries receiving e-rate funds must filter out material that is obscene or harmful to minors. The Supreme Court declared CIPA constitutional on June 23, 2003. However, the constitutionality was based on libraries' ability to disable filtering software. This case continues to be one that will engage public librarians through the decade (Sobel, 2003). The dilemma is noted by Jaeger and McClure (2004):

> CIPA represents the intersection of the constitutional right to freedom of speech and the desire of the government to protect children from harm. The potential legal challenges created by the application of CIPA result from the fact that these two abstract notions, when combined in a community space, are not always mutually compatible or feasible.

Librarians stand together across the United States as defenders of the people's right to know. The legal context must be monitored closely by all who work in and oversee policy implementation for public libraries.

Public librarians also stimulate community discussion on issues through support of events like the National Issues Forum, reading discussion programs, such as, "A Response to September 11," and reading viewing programs, such as, "The Sixties: Decade of Crisis and Change" (American Library Association, Public Programs Office, National Endowment for the Humanities, National Video Resources). Public libraries activate the public sphere through support of lifelong learning and discussion programs and strengthen the public's desire for opportunities to address issues that are salient to the community.

Taken together, the provision of a commons, materials in all formats to support exploration of important issues, and offering opportunity for communities to come together are important public library contributions to a rich public sphere. If discourse becomes more democratic through consensus building, it is partly because authentic discourse enables people to move from personal opinions to informed ideas (McCook, 2001).

Final Words

Public libraries and the library workers who are committed to the continuation of this most democratic of all institutions face the future with the charge of maintaining a sense of place in the context of regionalism; being mindful of the convergence of cultural institutions; being sensitive to the effort that is required to extend inclusion in the spirit of social justice; and being committed to the sustainability of an open public sphere. The public library at one and the same time preserves the multiple heritages of the societies it serves, acts on the edge of change, and gives support to dreamers who would play *The Glass Bead Game* (Hesse, 1969). More prosaically, we find the need to make sense of the information landscape explored in the 2003 OCLC study, *Pattern Recognition*.

Public libraries as a place of welcome to all learners will contribute to the development of social capital (Healy, et al., 2001; Balatti and Falk, 2002) and thereby help bring to fruition a world in which people can follow their individual interests with attention to socioeconomic progress. By supporting the development of human capabilities in the United States and throughout the world, humanity may yet come to a place free from deprivation and insecurity (Sen, 2003). The convergence of cultural institutions and the consilience of science and the humanities predicted by Gould portend a future in which public libraries will play an important part. The public library is endowed with a history of grassroots support for its development, the ongoing commitment of thousands of friends and users, and staffs comprised of thoughtful and engaged individuals who tend to its future.

References

2-1-1. Get Connected. Get Answers. United Way. Alliance for Information and Referral Services. Available: www.211.org.

Alliance for Regional Stewardship. Available: www.regionalstewardship.org.

American Civil Liberties Union. Keep America Safe and Free. Available: www.aclu.org/SafeandFree/SafeandFree.cfm?ID=12126&c=207.

American Library Association. Office for Intellectual Freedom. For resolutions and resources regarding the USAPATRIOT Act see the ALA Web site: www.ala.org/oif/ifissues/isapatriotact.

American Library Association. Office for Intellectual Freedom. 2002. *Intellectual Freedom Manual*. 6th ed. Chicago: American Library Association.

American Library Association. Public Programs Office. Available: www.ala.org/publicprograms.

Balatti, Jo, and Ian Falk. 2002. Socioeconomic Contributions of Adult Learning to Community: A Social Capital Perspective. *Adult Education Quarterly* 52 (August): 281–298.

Bill and Melinda Gates Foundation. 2004. Toward Equality of Access: The Role of Public Libraries in Addressing the Digital Divide. Available: www.gatesfoundation.org/nr/Downloads/libraries/uslibraries/reports/TowardEqualityofAccess.pdf.

Budd, John M., and Cynthia Wyatt. 2002. "Do You Have Any Books On—": An Examination of Public Library Holdings. *Public Libraries* 41 (March/April): 107–112.

Buschman, John E. 2003. *Dismantling the Public Sphere: Situating and Sustaining Librarianship in the Age of the New Public Philosophy*. Westport, CT: Libraries Unlimited.

Carr, David. 2003. *The Promise of Cultural Institutions*. Walnut Creek, CA.: AltaMira Press.

Center for Rural Librarianship. Rural Librarianship and Bookmobile and Outreach Services. Available: http://eagle.clarion.edu/~grads/csrl/csrlhom.htm.

Congress for the New Urbanism. Available: www.cnu.org/index.cfm.

Dilevko, Juris, and Lisa Gottlieb. 2003. Resurrecting a Neglected Idea: The Reintroduction of Library-Museum Hybrids. *Library Quarterly* 73 (April): 160–198.

First Amendment Center. Available: www.firstamendmentcenter.org/default.aspx.

Frug, Gerald. E. 2002. Beyond Regional Government. *Harvard Law Review* 115 (May): 1763–1836.

Global Insight. 2003. U.S. Metro Economies: Types of Jobs Lost and Gained 2001–2005. U.S. Conference of Mayors. Available: www.usmayors.org/USCM/home.asp.

Gould, Stephen Jay. 2003. *The Hedgehog, the Fox and the Magister's Pox: Mending the Gap Between Science and the Humanities*. New York: Harmony Books.

Habermas, Jürgen. 1996. *Between Facts and Norms: Contributions to a Discourse Theory of Law and Democracy*. Translated by William Rehg. Cambridge, MA: The MIT Press.

Healy, Tom, et al. 2001. *The Well-Being of Nations: The Role of Human and Social Capital*. Paris: Organisation for Economic Co-operation and Development.

Hesse, Hermann. 1969. *The Glass Bead Game (Magister Ludi)*. Translated by Richard and Clara Winston. New York: Holt, Reinhart and Winston.

Holt, Glen E. 2001. *Public Library Benefits Valuation Study.* St. Louis Public Library. Available: www.slpl.lib.mo.us/using/valuation.htm.

Holt, Glen E., and Donald Elliott. 2003. Measuring Outcomes: Applying Cost-Benefit Analysis to Middle-Sized and Smaller Public Libraries. *Library Trends* 51 (Winter): 424–440.

Institute of Museum and Library Services (IMLS). Available: www.imls.gov (accessed December 3, 2003).

Jaeger, Paul T., and Charles R. McClure. 2004. Potential Legal Challenges to the Application of the Children's Internet Protection Act (CIPA) in Public Libraries: Strategies and Issues. *First Monday* 9 (February). Available: http://firstmonday.org/issues/issue9_2/jaeger/index.html.

Johnson, James H. Jr. 2002. A Conceptual Model for Enhancing Community Competitiveness in the New Economy. *Urban Affairs Review* 37 (July): 763–780.

Lichtblau, Eric. 2003. Ashcroft Mocks Librarians and Others Who Oppose Parts of Counterterrorism Law. *New York Times* (September 16, Section A, p. 23.)

McChesney, Robert, and John Nichols. 2002. *Our Media, Not Theirs: The Democratic Struggle Against Corporate Media.* New York: Seven Stories Press.

McCook, Kathleen de la Peña. 2000. *A Place at the Table: Participating in Community Building.* Chicago: American Library Association.

McCook, Kathleen de la Peña. 2001. Authentic Discourse as a Means of Connection Between Public Library Service Responses and Community Building Initiatives. *Reference and User Services Quarterly* 40 (Winter): 127–133.

McCook, Kathleen de la Peña. 2002. *Rocks in the Whirlpool: The American Library Association and Equity of Access.* ERIC ED462981. Chicago: American Library Association. Available: www.ala.org/ala/ourassociation/governingdocs/key actionareas/equityaction/rockswhirlpool.htm.

Miller, Malanie. 2004. The Castle is Back. *American Libraries* 35 (April): 70–72.

National Conference of State Legislatures. NCSL Calls Upon the Federal Government to Meet Its Responsibilities To The States-July 2003. Available: www.ncsl.org.

National Issues Forum. Available: www.nifi.org.

National Video Resources. Available: www.nvr.org.

Nelson, Sandra. 2001. *The New Planning for Results: A Streamlined Approach.* Chicago: American Library Association.

New York State Library. 2–1–1 in New York State: Information for Libraries. Available: www.nysl.nysed.gov/libdev/outreach/211nys.htm.

OCLC. 2003 Environmental Scan: Pattern Recognition. Available: www.oclc.org/ membership/escan/default.htm.

Oldenburg, Ray. 2001. *Celebrating the Third Place.* New York : Marlowe & Co.

Osborne, Robin, ed. 2004. *From Outreach to Equity: Innovative Models of Library Policy and Practice.* Chicago: American Library Association.

Pokorny, Renee E. 2000. Library Services to Immigrants and Non-Native Speakers of English. *Bookmobiles and Outreach Services 6*: 21–34.

Polend, Nancy L. 2002. Making Service Integration a Reality. *Policy and Practice of Public Human Services* 60 (September): 24–27.

Sen, Amartya. 2003. The Social Demands of Human Rights. *New Perspective Quarterly* 20 (Fall): 83–84.

Sennett, Richard. 2003. *Respect in a World of Inequality*. New York: W. W. Norton.

Singer, Audrey. The Rise of Immigrant Gateways. The Brookings Institution. Available: www.brookings.edu/urban/pubs/20040301_gateways.pdf (accessed February 2004).

Sobel, David. L. Net Filters and Libraries. First Amendment Center. Available: www.firstamendmentcenter.org/default.aspx (accessed November 2003).

Talen, Emily. 1999. Sense of Community and Neighborhood Form: An Assessment of the Social Doctrine of New Urbanism. *Urban Studies* 36: 1361–1379.

U.S. Census Bureau. 2002. Coming to America: A Profile of the Nation's Foreign-Born (2000 update). Washington, DC: U.S. Census Bureau. Available: www.census.gov/prod/2002pubs/cenbr01-1.pdf (accessed November 13, 2003).

Urban Library Council. Available: www.urbanlibraries.org.

Walker, Chris, and Carlos A. Manjarrez. 2003. *Partnerships for Free Choice Learning: Public Libraries, Museums and Public Broadcasters Working Together*. Washington, DC: Urban Institute. Evanston, IL: Urban Libraries Council.

Appendix A
Selected Readings

1. The Landscape of Public Libraries at the Beginning of the Twenty-First Century

General

Florida Resources and Environmental Analysis Center. Public Library Geographic Database. Available: www.geolib.org/PLGDB.cfm.

Garceau, Oliver. 1949. *The Public Library in the Political Process: A Report of the Public Library Inquiry.* New York: Columbia University Press.

Joeckel, Carleton Bruns. 1935. *The Government of the American Public Library.* Chicago: University of Chicago Press.

Shera, Jesse H. 1949. *Foundations of the Public Library: The Origins of the Public Library Movement in New England, 1629–1855.* Chicago: University of Chicago Press. Repr., Hamden, CT: Shoestring Press, 1965.

U.S. Department of Education. National Center for Education Statistics. 2003. Public Libraries in the United States. Fiscal Year 2001. E.D. TABS, ed. Adrienne Chute, et al. Available: http://nces.ed.gov/pubsearch/pubsinfo.asp?pubid =2003399.

U.S. Department of the Interior, Bureau of Education. 1876. *Public Libraries in the United States of America: Their History, Condition, and Management. Special Report.* Washington, DC: U.S. Government Printing Office. Repr., as

Monograph Series, no. 4, Champaign, IL: University of Illinois, Graduate School of Library Science.

Tribal Community Libraries

American Indian Library Association. 1976. *American Indian Libraries Newsletter.* Fall issue.

American Library Association. American Indian Library Association (AILA). Available: www.nativeculture.com/lisamitten/aila.html.

Bill and Melinda Gates Foundation. Native American Access to Technology. Available: http://gatesfoundation.org/Libraries/NativeAmericanAccessTechnology.

Grounds, Richard A., et al. 2003. *Native Voices: American Indian Identity and Resistance.* Lawrence, KS: University Press of Kansas.

Hills, Gordon H. 1997. *Native Libraries: Cross-Cultural Conditions in the Circumpolar Countries.* Lanham, MD: Scarecrow Press.

Patterson, Lotsee. 2000. History and Status of Native Americans in Librarianship. *Library Trends* 49, no. 1 (Summer): 182–193.

Patterson, Lotsee. 2001. History and Development of Libraries on American Indian Reservations. In *International Indigenous Librarians' Forum Proceedings*, ed. Robert Sullivan, 38–44. Auckland, New Zealand: Te Ropu Whakahau.

Roy, Loriene. 2000. To Support and Model Native American Library Services. *Texas Library Journal* 76 (Spring): 32–35.

Roy, Loriene, and A. Arro Smith. 2002. Supporting, Documenting and Preserving Tribal Cultural Lifeways: Library Services for Tribal Communities in the United States. *World Libraries* 12 (Spring): 28–31.

Roy, Loriene. 2003. Interviewed by Kathleen de la Peña McCook. December 2, 2003.

Roy, Loriene, et al. 2004. *Tribal Libraries, Archives and Museums: Preserving our Language, Memory and Lifeways.* Lanham, MD: Scarecrow Press.

Roy, Loriene. School of Information, University of Texas at Austin. If I Can Read, I Can Do Anything. Available: www.ischool.utexas.edu/~ifican.

U.S. Institute of Museum and Library Services. Native American Library Services. Available: www.imls.gov/grants/library/lib_nat.asp#po. See also on this Web page the link to Advisory Meeting on Native American Library Services (accessed January 13, 2000).

U.S. National Commission on Libraries and Information Science. 1992. Pathways to Excellence: A Report on Improving Library and Information Services for Native American Peoples. Available: www.nclis.gov/libraries/nata.html.

2. Brahmins, Bequests, and Determined Women: The Beginnings to 1918

Books and Chapters in Books

American Library Association. 1963. *Access to Public Libraries.* Chicago: American Library Association.

Amory, Hugh, and David D. Hall, eds. 2000. *A History of the Book in America.* Vol. 1 of *The Colonial Book in the Atlantic World.* Cambridge, MA: Cambridge University Press.

Basbanes, Nicholas A. 1995. *A Fine Madness: Bibliophiles, Bibliomanes, and the Eternal Passion for Books.* New York: Henry Holt and Company.

Bixby, A. F., and A. Howell. 1876. *Historical Sketches of the Ladies' Library Associations of the State of Michigan, 1876.* Adrian, MI: Times and Expositor Steam Print. Reprinted in Kathleen Weibel, Kathleen Heim (de la Peña McCook), and Dianne J. Ellsworth. *The Status of Women in Librarianship, 1876–1976*, pp. 3–4. Phoenix, AZ: Oryx Press, a Neal-Schuman Professional Book, 1979.

Boston Public Library. 1852. *Report of the Trustees of the Public Library to the City of Boston.* Reproduced in Jesse H. Shera, *Foundations of the Public Library: The Origins of the Public Library Movement in New England, 1629–1855.* Chicago: University of Chicago Press, 1949. Repr., Hamden, CT: Shoestring Press, 1965). 267–290.

Boylan, Anne M. 1988. *Sunday School: the Formation of an American Institution, 1790–1880.* New Haven, CN: Yale University Press.

Brown, Richard D. 1989. *Knowledge Is Power: The Diffusion of Information in Early America, 1700–1865.* New York: Oxford University Press.

Casper, Scott E., Joanne D. Chaison, and Jeffrey D. Groves, eds. 2002. *Perspectives on American Book History: Artifacts and Commentary.* Amherst: University of Massachusetts Press.

Cazden, Robert E. 1978. Libraries in the German-American Community and the Rise of the Public Library Movement. In *Milestones to the Present: Papers from Library History Seminar V*, 93–211. Syracuse, NY: Gaylord Professional Publications.

Cornelius, Janet Duitsman. 1991. *When I Can Read My Title Clear: Literacy, Slavery and Religion in the Antebellum South.* Columbia, SC: University of South Carolina Press.

Dain, Phyllis P. 1972. *The New York Public Library: A History of Its Founding and Early Years.* New York: New York Public Library.

Davis, Donald G., Jr. 2002. *Winsor, Dewey, and Putnam: the Boston Experience.* Champaign, IL: University of Illinois, Graduate School of Library and Information Science.

Davis, Donald G., Jr., and John Mark Tucker. 1989. *American Library History: A Comprehensive Guide to the Literature.* Santa Barbara, CA: ABC-CLIO.

Ditzion, Sidney H. 1947. *Arsenals of a Democratic Culture: A Social History of the American Public Library Movement in New England and the Middle States from 1850–1900.* Chicago: American Library Association.

Du Mont, Rosemary Ruhig. 1977. *Reform and Reaction: The Big City Public Library in American Life.* Westport, CT: Greenwood Press.

Edwards, Edward. 1859. *Memoirs of Libraries, Including a Handbook of Library Economy.* London: Trubner.

Edwards, Edward. 1869. *Free Town Libraries, Their Function, Management, and History in Britain, France, Germany, and America.* London: Trubner.

Freeman, Robert S. 2003. Harper & Brothers' Family and School District Libraries, 1830–1846. In *Libraries to the People: Histories of Outreach*, ed. Robert S. Freeman and David M. Hovde. Jefferson, NC: McFarland and Co.

Freeman, Robert S., and David M. Hovde, eds. 2003. *Libraries to the People: Histories of Outreach*. Jefferson, NC: McFarland and Co.

Garrison, Dee. 1979. *Apostles of Culture: The Public Librarian and American Society, 1876–1920*. New York: The Free Press.

Gilmore, William J. 1989. *Reading Becomes a Necessity: Material and Cultural Life in Rural New England, 1780–1835*. Knoxville, TN: University of Tennessee Press.

Gleason, Eliza Atkins. 1941. *The Southern Negro and the Public Library: A Study of Government and Administration of Public Library Service to Negroes in the South*. Chicago: University of Chicago Press.

Goetsch, Lori A., and Sarah B. Watstein. 1993. *On Account of Sex: An Annotated Bibliography on the History of Women in Librarianship, 1987–1992*. Metuchen, NJ: Scarecrow Press.

Graham, Patterson Toby. 2002. *A Right to Read: Segregation and Civil Rights in Alabama's Public Libraries, 1900–1965*. Tuscaloosa, AL: University of Alabama Press.

Grotzinger, Laurel Ann, James Vinson Carmichael and Mary Niles Maack. 1994. *Women's Work: Vision and Change in Librarianship*. Champaign, IL: University of Illinois.

Hall, David D. 1989. *Worlds of Wonder, Days of Judgment: Popular Religious Belief in Early New England*. New York: Alfred A. Knopf.

Harris, Michael H. 1975. *Role of the Public Library in American Life: A Speculative Essay*. Occasional Paper No. 117. Champaign, IL: University of Illinois, Graduate School of Library and Information Science.

Harris, Michael H. 1995. *History of Libraries in the Western World*. 4th ed. Lanham, MD: Scarecrow Press.

Hayes, Kevin J. 1996. *A Colonial Woman's Bookshelf*. Knoxville, TN: University of Tennessee Press.

Hildenbrand, Suzanne, ed. 1996. *Reclaiming the American Library Past: Writing the Women In*. Norwood, NJ: Ablex.

Hoyt, Dolores J. 1999. *A Strong Mind in a Strong Body: Libraries in the German-American Turner Movement*. New York: Peter Lang.

Jewett, Charles Coffin. 1851. Report on the Public Libraries of the United States of America, January 1, 1850. In *Report of the Board of Regents of the Smithsonian Institution*. Washington, DC: Smithsonian Institution.

Joeckel, Carleton Bruns. 1935. *The Government of the American Public Library*. Chicago: University of Chicago Press.

Jones, Plummer Alston, Jr. 1999. *Libraries, Immigrants, and the American Experience*. Westport, CT: Greenwood Press.

Josey, E. J. 1970. *The Black Librarian in America*. Metuchen, NJ: Scarecrow Press.

Kaser, David. 1978. Coffee House to Stock Exchange: A Natural History of the Reading Room. In *Milestones to the Present: Papers from Library History Seminar V*, ed. Harold Goldstein, 238–254. Syracuse NY: Gaylord Professional Publications.

Kaser, David. 1980. *A Book for a Six Pence: The Circulating Library in America*. Pittsburgh, PA: Beta Phi Mu.

Kelly, Thomas. 1957. *George Birbeck: Pioneer of Adult Education*. Liverpool University Press.

Knight, Frances R. 2000. A Palace for the People: the Relationships that Built the Boston Public Library. Diss. University of Oxford.

Knowles, Malcolm S. 1977. *A History of the Adult Education Movement in the United States: includes Adult Education Institutions through 1976*. Huntington, NY: Robert E. Krieger Publishing Company.

Kruger, Betsy, and Catherine A. Larson. 2000. *On Account of Sex: An Annotated Bibliography on the History of Women in Librarianship, 1993–1997*. Lanham, MD: Scarecrow Press.

Ladenson, Alex. 1982. *Library Law and Legislation in the United States*. Metuchen, NJ: Scarecrow Press.

Laugher, C. T. 1973. *Thomas Bray's Grand Design*. Chicago: American Library Association.

Lehmann-Haut, Hellmutt, et al. 1952. *The Book in America: A History of the Making and Selling of Books in the United States*. New York: Bowker.

Lehuu, Isabel. 2000. *Carnival on the Page: Popular Print Media in Antebellum America*. Chapel Hill, NC: University of North Carolina Press.

Marshall, A. P. 1976. Service to African-Americans. In *Century of Service: Librarianship in the United States and Canada,* ed. H. Jackson and E. J. Josey, 62–78. Chicago: American Library Association.

McCauley, Elfrieda B. 1971. The New England Mill Girls: Feminine Influence in the Development of Public libraries in New England, 1820–1860. Doctoral Thesis, Columbia University.

McCook, Kathleen de la Peña, and Katharine Phenix. 1984. *On Account of Sex: An Annotated Bibliography on the History of Women in Librarianship, 1977–1981*. Chicago: American Library Association.

McMullen, Haynes. 2000. *American Libraries Before 1876*. Beta Phi Mu Monograph Series, no. 6. Westport, CT: Greenwood Press.

Miksa, Francis. 1982. The Interpretation of American Public Library History. In *Public Librarianship: A Reader,* ed. Jane Robbins-Carter, 73–90. Littleton, CO: Libraries Unlimited.

Musmann, V. K. 1982. Women and the Founding of Social Libraries in California, 1859–1910. PhD diss., University of Southern California.

Mussman, Klaus. 1998. The Ugly Side of Librarianship; Segregation in Library Services from 1900–1950. In *Untold Stories: Civil rights, Libraries and Black Librarianship*, 78–92. Champaign, IL: University of Illinois, Graduate School of Library and Information Science.

Phenix, Katharine, and Kathleen de la Peña McCook. 1989. *On Account of Sex: An Annotated Bibliography on the History of Women in Librarianship, 1982–1986*. Chicago: American Library Association.

Shera, Jesse H. 1949. *Foundations of the Public Library: The Origins of the Public Library Movement in New England, 1629–1855.* Chicago: University of Chicago Press. Repr., Hamden, CT: Shoestring Press, 1965.

Stielow, Frederick J., and James Corsaro. 1993. The Carnegie Question and the Public Library Movement in Progressive Era New York. In *Carnegie Denied: Communities Rejecting Carnegie Library Construction Grants, 1898–1925,* ed. Robert Sidney Martin, 35–51. Westport, CT: Greenwood Press.

Tucker, John M. 1998. *Untold Stories: Civil Rights, Libraries and Black Librarianship.* Champaign, IL: University of Illinois, Graduate School of Library and Information Science.

Tyack, David. B. 1967. *George Ticknor and the Boston Brahmins.* Cambridge, MA: Harvard University Press.

U.S. Department of the Interior, Bureau of Education. 1876. *Public Libraries in the United States of America: Their History, Condition, and Management. Special Report.* Washington, DC: U.S. Government Printing Office. Repr., as Monograph Series, no. 4, Champaign, IL: University of Illinois, Graduate School of Library Science.

Wadlin, Horace Greeley. 1911. *The Public Library of the City of Boston: A History.* Boston: The Trustees.

Watson, Paula D. 2003. Valleys Without Sunsets: Women's Clubs and Traveling Libraries. In *Libraries to the People: Histories of Outreach,* ed. Robert S. Freeman and David M. Hovde, 73–95. Jefferson, NC: McFarland and Co.

Weibel, Kathleen, Kathleen Heim (de la Peña McCook), and Dianne J. Ellsworth. 1979. *The Status of Women in Librarianship, 1876–1976.* Phoenix, AZ: Neal-Schuman Publishers.

Wellman, Hiller C., and Elizabeth Putnam Sohier. 1953. In *Pioneering Leaders in Librarianship,* ed. Emily Miller Danton. Boston: Greg Press.

Whitehill, Walter Muir. 1956. *Boston Public Library; A Centennial History.* Cambridge, MA: Harvard University Press.

Wiegand, Wayne A. 1986a. The Historical Development of State Library Agencies. In *State Library Services and Issues: Facing Future Challenges,* ed. Charles R. McClure, 1–16. Norwood, NJ: Ablex.

Wiegand, Wayne A. 1986b. *The Politics of an Emerging Profession: The American Library Association, 1876–1917.* New York: Greenwood Press.

Wiegand, Wayne A. 1989. *An Active Instrument for Propaganda: The American Public Library During World War I.* Westport, CT: Greenwood Press.

Williams, Julie Hedgepeth. 1999. *The Significance of the Printed Word in Early America.* Westport, CT: Greenwood Press.

Wittmann, Reinhard. 1999. Was There a Reading Revolution at the End of the Eighteenth Century? In *A History of Reading in the West,* ed. Guglielmo Cavallo and Roger Chartier, 284–312. Amherst, MA: University of Massachusetts Press, 1999.

Wolf, Edwin. 1988. *The Book Culture of a Colonial American City: Philadelphia Books, Bookmen, and Booksellers.* New York: Oxford University Press.

Wyss, Hilary E. 2000. *Writing Indians: Literacy, Christianity and Native Community in Early America.* Amherst, MA: University of Massachusetts Press.

Young, Arthur P. 1981. *Books for Sammies: The American Library Association and World War I.* Pittsburgh, PA: Beta Phi Mu.

Zboray, Ronald J. 1993. *A Fictive People: Antebellum Economic Development and the Reading Public.* New York: Oxford University Press.

Zboray, Ronald, and Mary Saracino Zboray. 2000. *A Handbook for the Study of Book History in the United States.* Washington, D. C.: Center for the Book, Library of Congress.

Articles

Augst, Thomas. 2001. American Libraries and Agencies of Culture. *American Studies* 42 (Fall): 12.

Blazek, R. 1979. The Development of Library Service in the Nation's Oldest City: The St. Augustine Library Association, 1874–1880. *Journal of Library History* 14: 160–182.

Cresswell, Stephen. 1996. The Last Days of Jim Crow in Southern Libraries. *Libraries and Culture* 31 (Summer/Fall): 557–573.

Dawson, Alma. 2000. Celebrating African-American Librarians and Librarianship. *Library Trends* 49 (Summer): 49–87.

Ditzion, Sidney H. 1940. The District School Library, 1835–1855. *Library Quarterly* 10: 545–547.

Du Mont, Rosemary Ruhig. 1986. Race in American Librarianship: Attitudes of the Library Profession. *Journal of Library History* 21 (Summer): 488–509.

Fain, Elaine. 1978. The Library and American Education: Education Through Secondary School. *Library Trends* (Winter): 327–352.

Hall, David D. 1994. Readers and Reading in America: Historical and Critical Perspectives. In *Proceedings of the American Antiquarian Society* 104: 337–357.

Harris, Michael H. 1973. The Purpose of the American Public Library: A Revisionist Interpretation of History. *Library Journal* 98 (September 15): 2509–2514.

Harris, Michael H. 1974. Everett, Ticknor and the Common Man: Fear of Societal Instability as the Motivation for the Founding of the Boston Public Library. *Libri* 24: 249–275.

Harris, Michael H. 1976. Public Libraries and the Decline of Democratic Dogma. *Library Journal* 101 (November 1): 2225–2230.

Harris, Steven R. 2003. Civil Rights and the Louisiana Library Association. *Libraries and Culture* 38 (Fall): 322–350.

Held, Ray E. 1959. The Early School District Library in California. *Library Quarterly* 29: 79.

Houlette, W. D. 1934. Parish Libraries and the Work of Rev. Thomas Bray. *Library Quarterly* 4: 588–609.

McMullen, Haynes. 1985. The Very Slow Decline of the American Social Library. *Library Quarterly* 55: 207–225.

Malone, Cheryl Knott. 2000a. Books for Black Children: Public Library Collections in Louisville and Nashville, 1915–1925. *Library Quarterly* 70 (April): 179–200.

Malone, Cheryl Knott. 2000b. Toward a Multicultural American Public Library History. *Libraries and Culture* 35 (Winter): 77–87.

Mattson, Kevin. 2000. The Librarian as Secular Minister to Democracy: The Life and Ideas of John Cotton Dana. *Libraries and Culture* 35 (Fall): 514–534.

Richards, E. M. 1940. Alexandre Vattemare and His System of International Exchanges. *Bulletin of the Medical Library Association* 32: 413–448.

Steiner, Bernard C. Rev. 1896. Thomas Bray and his American Libraries. *American Historical Review* 2 (October): 59–75.

Story, R. 1975. Class and Culture in Boston: The Athenaeum, 1807–1860. *American Quarterly* 27: 178–199.

Todd, Emily B. 2001. Antebellum Libraries in Richmond and New Orleans and the Search for the Practices and Preferences of Real Readers. *American Studies* 42 (Fall): 195–209.

Tucker, Harold W. 1963. The Access to Public Libraries Study. *ALA Bulletin* 57 (September): 742–745.

Watson, Paula D. 1994. Founding Mothers: The Contribution of Women's Organizations to Public Library Development in the United States. *Library Quarterly* 64 (July): 237.

Watson, Paula D. 1996. Carnegie Ladies, Lady Carnegies: Women and the Building of Libraries. *Libraries and Culture* 31 (Winter): 159–196.

Young, Arthur P. 2002. Books, Libraries and War. *Illinois Library Association Reporter* 20 (April): 10–11.

Law

Massachusetts, State of. *1848 Acts and Resolves, Chapter 52.* Boston: State of Massachusetts.

Web Sites

General Federation of Women's Clubs. Available: www.gfwc.org.

A Separate Flame Western Branch: The First African-American Public Library. Available: http://lfpl.org/western/htms/welcome.htm.

3. Public Library Growth and Values: 1918–2004

Books and Chapters in Books

American Library Association. 1936. *The Equal Chance: Books Help to Make It.* Chicago: American Library Association.

American Library Association. Commission on the Library and Adult Education. 1926. *Libraries and Adult Education.* Chicago: American Library Association.

American Library Association. Library Extension Board. 1926. *Library Extension: A Study of Public Library Conditions and Needs.* Chicago: American Library Association.

American Library Association. Library Extension Board. 1927a. *Equalizing Library Opportunities.* Chicago: American Library Association.

American Library Association. Library Extension Board. 1927b. *How to Organize a County Library Campaign*. Chicago: American Library Association.

American Library Association. Office for Intellectual Freedom. 2002. *Intellectual Freedom Manual*. 6th ed. Chicago: American Library Association.

Asheim, Lester. 1950. *A Forum on the Public Library Inquiry*. New York: Columbia University Press. Repr. Westport, CT: Greenwood Press, 1970.

Berelson, Bernard. 1949. *The Library's Public: A Report of the Public Library Inquiry*. New York: Columbia University Press.

Bowerman, George F. 1931. *Censorship and the Public Library*. New York: H. W. Wilson.

Bryan, Alice I. 1952. *The Public Librarian: A Report of the Public Library Inquiry*. New York: Columbia University Press.

Carmichael, James V., Jr. 1988. *Tommie Dora Barker and Southern Librarianship*. Chapel Hill, NC: The University of North Carolina.

Carnovsky, Leon, and Lowell A. Martin. 1944. *The Library and the Community*. Chicago: University of Chicago Press.

Casey, Genevieve M., ed. 1975. Federal Aid to Libraries: Its History, Impact, Future. Special issue, *Library Trends* 24 (July).

Conable, Gordon. 2002. Public Libraries and Intellectual Freedom. *Intellectual Freedom Manual*. 6th ed. Chicago: American Library Association.

Ditzion, Sidney H. 1947. *Arsenals of a Democratic Culture: A Social History of the American Public Library Movement in New England and the Middle States from 1850–1900*. Chicago: American Library Association.

Dix, William S., and Paul Bixler. 1954. *Freedom of Communications: Proceedings of the First Conference on Intellectual Freedom, New York City, June 28–29, 1952*. Chicago: American Library Association.

Garceau, Oliver. 1949. *The Public Library in the Political Process: A Report of the Public Library Inquiry*. New York: Columbia University Press.

Geller, Evelyn. 1984. *Forbidden Books in American Public Libraries, 1876–1939: A Study in Cultural Change*. Westport, CT: Greenwood Press.

Holley, Edward G., and Robert Schremser. 1983. *The Library Services and Construction Act: An Historical Overview from the Viewpoint of Major Participants*. Greenwich, CN: JAI Press.

Joeckel, Carleton Bruns. 1935. *The Government of the American Public Library*. Chicago: University of Chicago Press.

Joeckel, Carleton Bruns. 1943. *Post-War Standards for Public Libraries*. Chicago: American Library Association.

Joeckel, Carleton B., and Amy Winslow. 1948. *A National Plan for Public Library Service*. Chicago: American Library Association.

Johnson, Alvin. 1938. *The Public Library—A People's University*. New York: American Association for Adult Education.

Knight, Douglas M., and E. Shepley Nourse, eds. 1969. *Libraries at Large: Traditions, Innovations and the National Interest; The Resource Book Based on the Materials of the National Advisory Commission on Libraries*. New York: R. R. Bowker.

Knowles, Malcolm S. 1977. *A History of the Adult Education Movement in the United States: includes Adult Education Institutions through 1976.* Huntington, NY: Robert E. Krieger Publishing Company.

Kranich, Nancy, ed. 2001. *Libraries and Democracy: The Cornerstones of Liberty.* Chicago: American Library Association.

Kunitz, Stanley. 2000. The Layers. In *The Collected Poems*, 217–218. New York: W. W. Norton.

Learned, William S. 1924. *The American Public Library and the Diffusion of Knowledge.* New York: Harcourt.

Leigh, Robert D. 1950. *The Public Library in the United States: The General Report of the Public Library Inquiry.* New York: Columbia University Press.

Martin, Lowell A. 1962. LSA and Library Standards. In *The Impact of the Library Services Act,* ed. Donald E. Strout, 1–16. Champaign, IL: University of Illinois.

Martin, Lowell A. 1967. *Baltimore Reaches Out: Library Services to the Disadvantaged.* Baltimore, MD: Enoch Pratt Free Library.

Martin, Lowell A. 1969. *Library Response to Urban Change: A Study of the Chicago Public Library.* Chicago: American Library Association.

Mason, Marilyn Gell. 1983. *The Federal Role in Library and Information Services.* White Plains, NY: Knowledge Industry Publications.

McCook, Kathleen de la Peña. 1994. *Toward a Just and Productive Society: An Analysis of the Recommendations of the White House Conference on Library and Information Services.* Washington, DC: National Commission on Libraries and Information Science.

Milam, Carl H. 1922. *What Libraries Learned from the War.* Washington, DC: U.S. Office of Education.

Molz, Redmond Kathleen. 1984. *National Planning for Library Service: 1935–1975.* Chicago: American Library Association.

Monroe, Margaret E. 1963. *Library Adult Education: The Biography of an Idea.* New York: Scarecrow Press.

Monypenny, Phillip. 1966. *The Library Functions of the States.* Chicago: American Library Association.

Public Library Association. Goals, Guidelines and Standards Committee. 1979. *The Public Library Mission Statement and Its Imperatives for Service.* Chicago: American Library Association.

Pungitore, Verna L. 1995. *Innovation and the Library: The Adoption of New Ideas in Public Libraries.* Westport, CT: Greenwood Press.

Raber, Douglas. 1997. *Librarianship and Legitimacy: The Ideology of the Public Library Inquiry.* Westport, CT: Greenwood Press.

Reagan, Patrick D. 2000. *Designing a New America: The Origins of New Deal Planning, 1890–1943.* Amherst MA: University of Massachusetts Press.

Robbins, Louise S. 1996. *Censorship and the American Library: The American Library Association's Response to Threats to Intellectual Freedom: 1939–1969.* Westport, CT: Greenwood Press.

Shera, Jesse H. 1949. *Foundations of the Public Library: The Origins of the Public Library Movement in New England, 1629–1855.* Chicago: University of Chicago Press. Repr., Hamden, CT: Shoestring Press, 1965.

Sullivan, Peggy. 1976. *Carl H. Milam and the American Library Association.* New York: H. W. Wilson Company.

Thomison, Dennis. 1978. *A History of the American Library Association, 1876–1972.* Chicago: American Library Association.

U.S. National Commission on Libraries and Information Science. 1975. *Toward a National Program for Library and Information Services: Goals for Action.* Washington, DC: U.S. Government Printing Office.

U.S. National Commission on Libraries and Information Science. 1992. Pathways to Excellence: A Report on Improving Library and Information Services for Native American Peoples. Available: www.nclis.gov/libraries/nata.html.

Van Fleet, Connie. 1990. Lifelong Learning Theory and the Provision of Adult Services. In *Adult Services: An Enduring Focus for Public Libraries*, ed. Kathleen M. Heim (de la Peña McCook) and Danny P. Wallace, 166–211. Chicago: American Library Association.

White House Conference on Library and Information Services. 1980. *Information for the 1980's: Final Report of the White House Conference on Library and Information Services, 1979.* Washington, DC: National Commission on Libraries and Information Science.

White House Conference on Library and Information Services. 1991. *Information 2000: Library and Information Services for the 21st Century.* Washington, DC: The Conference.

White House Conference on Library and Information Services Task Force. 1997. *Summary of Actions to Implement the 96 Recommendations and Petitions of the 1991 White House Conference on Library and Information Services: March 1994 through December 1996.* Washington, DC: National Commission on Libraries and Information Science. (Release Date: Jan. 1997). Available: http:// purl.access.gpo.gov/GPO/LPS4122 (accessed 28 Sept. 2002).

Wiegand, Wayne A. 1989. *An Active Instrument for Propaganda: The American Public Library During World War I.* Westport, CT: Greenwood Press.

Wilson, Louis R. and Edward A. Wight. 1935. *County Library Service in the South: A Study of the Rosenwald County Library Demonstration.* Chicago: University of Chicago Press.

Articles

12 Ways Libraries are Good for the Country. 1995. *American Libraries* 26 (December): 1113–1119.

ALA Responds to CIPA Decision. 2003. *Newsletter on Intellectual Freedom* (September): 175.

Berelson, Bernard. 1938. The Myth of Library Impartiality. *Wilson Library Bulletin* 13 (October): 87–90.

Berninghausen, David K. 1948. Library Bill of Rights. *ALA Bulletin* 42 (July-August): 285.

Fenwick, Sara Innis. 1976. Library Services to Children and Young People. *Library Trends* 25 (Summer): 329–360.

Fuller, Peter F. 1994. The Politics of LSCA During the Reagan and Bush Administrations: An Analysis. *Library Quarterly* 64 (July): 294–318.

Fry, James W. 1975. LSA and LSCA, 1956–1973: A Legislative History. *Library Trends* 24 (July): 7–28.

Graham, Frank P. 1932. Citizen's Library Movements. *Library Extension News* 14 (May): 2.

Haines, Helen E. 1924. Modern Fiction and the Public Library. *Library Journal* 49 (May 15): 458–460.

Jenkins, Christine A. 2000. The History of Youth Services Librarianship: A Review of the Research Literature. *Libraries and Culture* 35 (Winter): 103–140.

Kelly, Melody S. 2003. Revisiting C. H. Milam's "What Libraries Learned from the War" and Rediscovering the Library Faith. *Libraries and Culture* 38 (Fall): 378–388.

Lee, Dan R. 1991. Faith Cabin Libraries: A Study of an Alternative Library Service in the Segregated South, 1932–1960. *Libraries and Culture* 26 (Winter): 169–182.

Library Projects Under Public Works, Civil Works and Relief Administrations. 1933. *ALA Bulletin* 27 (December): 539.

Lincove, David A. 1994. Propaganda and the American Public Library from the 1930s to the Eve of World War II. *RQ* 33 (Summer): 510–523.

Lingo, Marci. 2003. Forbidden Fruit: The Banning of The Grapes of Wrath in the Kern County Free Library. *Libraries and Culture* 38 (Fall): 351–377.

Looking Toward National Planning. 1934. *ALA Bulletin* 28 (August): 453–460.

Maack, Mary Niles. 1994. Public Libraries in Transition: Ideals, Strategies and Research. *Libraries and Culture* 29 (Winter): 79.

McCook, Kathleen de la Peña, and Peggy Barber. 2002. Public Policy as a Factor Influencing Adult Lifelong Learning, Adult Literacy and Public Libraries. *Reference and User Services Quarterly* 42.1 (Fall): 66–75.

McCook, Kathleen de la Peña, and Maria A. Jones. 2002. Cultural Heritage Institutions and Community Building. *Reference and User Services Quarterly* 41 (Summer): 326–329.

McReynolds, Rosalee. 1990/1991. The Progressive Librarians Council and Its Founders. *Progressive Librarian* 2 (Winter): 23–29.

Milam, Carl H. 1934. National Planning for Libraries. *ALA Bulletin* 28 (February): 60–62.

A National Plan for Libraries. 1935. *ALA Bulletin* 29 (February): 91–98.

A National Plan for Libraries. 1939. *ALA Bulletin* 33 (February): 136–150.

Public Library Association, Public Library Principles Task Force. 1982. The Public Library: Democracy's Resource, A Statement of Principles. *Public Libraries* 21: 92.

Raber, Douglas. 1995. Ideological Opposition to Federal Library Legislation: the Case of the Library Services Act of 1956. *Public Libraries* 34 (May/June): 162–169.

Resolution on the USAPATRIOT Act and Related Measures that Infringe on the Rights of Library Users. 2003. *Newsletter on Intellectual Freedom* (May): 93.

Robbins, Louise S. 2001. The Overseas Library Controversy and the Freedom To Read: U.S. Librarians and Publishers Confront Joseph McCarthy. *Libraries and Culture* 36 (Winter): 27–39.

Stielow, Frederick J. 1983. Censorship in the Early Professionalization of American Libraries. *Journal of Library History* 18 (Winter): 42–47.

Stielow, Frederick J. 1990. Librarian Warriors and Rapprochement: Carl Milam, Archibald MacLeish, and World War II. *Libraries and Culture* 25 (Fall): 516.

Web Sites

American Library Association. Washington Office. Available: www.ala.org/washoff.

Institute of Museum and Library Services. 1996. Museum and Library Services Act of 1996. Available: www.imls.gov/about/abt_1996.htm.

Institute of Museum and Library Services. 2003. Highlights of the New Law (2003). Available: www.imls.gov/whatsnew/current/092503a.htm.

Martin, Robert S. 2003. Cultural Policies in Knowledge Societies: the United State of America. Speech presented at UNESCO Ministerial Roundtable: Toward Knowledge Societies, UNESCO Headquarters, Paris, France, October 10, 2003. Available: www.imls.gov/whatsnew/current/sp101003.htm.

U.S. National Commission on Libraries and Information Science (USNCLIS). 1995. NCLIS at 25. Available: www.nclis.gov/about/25yrrpt.html.

U.S. National Commission on Libraries and Information Science (USNCLIS). 1999. NCLIS Adopts "Principles for Public Service." Available: www.nclis.gov/news/pressrelease/pr99/ppls99.html.

4. Statistics, Standards, Planning, and Results

Books and Chapters in Books

American Library Association. Committee on Economic Opportunity Programs. 1969. *Library Service to the Disadvantaged: A Study Based on Responses to Questionnaires from Public Libraries Serving Populations Over 15,000.* Chicago: American Library Association.

American Library Association. Coordinating Committee on Revision of Public Library Standards. 1956a. *Public Library Service: A Guide to Evaluation with Minimum Standards.* Chicago: American Library Association.

American Library Association. Coordinating Committee on Revision of Public Library Standards. 1956b. *Public Library Services; Supplement: Costs of Public Library Services in 1956.* Chicago: American Library Association.

American Library Association. Public Library Association, Standards Committee. 1967. *Minimum Standards for Public Library Systems, 1966.* Chicago: American Library Association.

Bassman, Keri, et al. 1998. *How Does Your Public Library Compare? Service Performance of Peer Groups.* Washington, DC: National Center for Education Statistics. (Release Date: October 27, 1998). Available: http://nces.ed.gov/pubs98/98310.pdf (accessed November 25, 2002).

Bertot, John Carlo, Charles R. McClure, and Joe Ryan. 2001. *Statistics and Performance Measures for Public Library Networked Services.* Chicago: American Library Association.

Childers, Thomas. 1975. Statistics That Describe Libraries and Library Service. *Advances in Librarianship* 5: 107–20.

Chute, Adrienne. 2003. National Center for Education Statistics Library Statistics Program. In *The Bowker Annual Library and Book Trade Almanac,* 95–102. New York: R. R. Bowker.

De Prospo, Ernest R., Ellen Altman, and Kenneth Beasley. 1973. *Performance Measures for Public Libraries.* Chicago: American Library Association.

Fair, E. M. 1934. *Countywide Library Service.* Chicago: American Library Association.

Garceau, Oliver. 1949. *The Public Library in the Political Process: A Report of the Public Library Inquiry.* New York: Columbia University Press.

Hamilton-Pennell, Christine. Public Library Standards: A Review of Standards and Guidelines from the Fifty States of the U.S. for the Colorado, Mississippi, and Hawaii State Libraries. Mosaic Knowledge Works. Chief Officers of State Library Agencies (COSLA). Available: www.cosla.org (accessed April 2003).

Harrington, Michael. 1962. *The Other America: Poverty in the United States.* New York: Macmillan.

Hennen, Thomas J., Jr. 2004. *Hennen's Public Library Planner: A Manual and Interactive CD-ROM.* New York: Neal-Schuman Publishers.

Himmel, Ethel, and William James Wilson with the ReVision Committee of the Public Library Association. 1998. *Planning for Results: A Public Library Transformation Process.* Chicago: American Library Association.

Joeckel, Carleton Bruns. 1935. *The Government of the American Public Library.* Chicago: University of Chicago Press.

Joeckel, Carleton Bruns. 1943. *Post-War Standards for Public Libraries.* Chicago: American Library Association.

Joeckel, Carleton B., and Amy Winslow. 1948. *A National Plan for Public Library Service.* Chicago: American Library Association.

Johnson, Debra Wilcox. 1995. An Evaluation of the Public Library Development Program. Chicago: Public Library Association.

Leigh, Robert D. 1950. *The Public Library in the United States: The General Report of the Public Library Inquiry.* New York: Columbia University Press.

Lynch, Mary Jo. 1987. *Libraries in an Information Society: A Statistical Summary.* Chicago: American Library Association.

Lynch, Mary Jo. 1983. *Sources of Library Statistics: 1972–1982.* Chicago: American Library Association.

Martin, Allie Beth. 1972. *A Strategy for Public Library Change: Proposed Public Library Goals—Feasibility Study.* Chicago: American Library Association.

McClure, Charles R., et al. 1987. *Planning and Role Setting for Public Libraries: A Manual of Options and Procedures.* Chicago: American Library Association.

McCook, Kathleen de la Peña. 1982. Stimulation. In *The Service Imperative for Libraries: Essays in Honor of Margaret E. Monroe,* 120–154. Littleton, CO: Libraries Unlimited.

Nelson, Sandra. 2001. *The New Planning for Results: A Streamlined Approach.* Chicago: American Library Association.

Nelson, Sandra, Ellen Altman, and Diane Mayo. 2000. Managing Your Library's Staff. In *Managing for Results: Effective Resource Allocation for Public Libraries,* 29–110. Chicago: American Library Association.

Palmour, Vernon E., et al. 1980. *A Planning Process for Public Libraries.* Chicago: American Library Association.

Public Library Association. Everything You Want to Know About the *Results* Series. Available: www.ala.org/ala/pla/plapubs/resultsseriesrfq/resultsseries.htm (accessed May 24, 2004).

Public Library Association. Goals, Guidelines and Standards Committee. 1979. *The Public Library Mission Statement and Its Imperatives for Service.* Chicago: American Library Association.

Public Library Association. Public Library Data Service. 1992–present. *Statistical Report* (annual). Chicago: Public Library Association. Continues *Public Library Data Service Statistical Report.* Chicago: Public Library Association, 1988–1991.

Public Library Association. Request for Submission of Qualifications (RSQ) From People Interested in Writing a Book in the PLA *Results* Series. Available: www.pla.org (accessed November 2, 2003).

Pungitore, Verna L. 1995. *Innovation and the Library: The Adoption of New Ideas in Public Libraries.* Westport, CT: Greenwood Press.

Samek, Toni. 2001. *Intellectual Freedom and Social Responsibility in American Librarianship, 1967–1974.* Chicago: American Library Association.

Steffen, Nicolle O., and Keith Curry Lance. 2002. Who's Doing What: Outcome-Based Evaluation and Demographics in the 'Counting on Results Project.' *Public Libraries* 43 (September-October): 271–279.

Van House, Nancy, et al. 1987. *Output Measures for Public Libraries: A Manual of Standardized Procedures.* Chicago: American Library Association.

Wallace, Danny P., and Connie Jean Van Fleet. 2001. *Library Evaluation: A Casebook and Can-Do Guide.* Englewood, CO: Libraries Unlimited.

Walter, Virginia A. 1992. *Output Measures for Public Library Service to Children: A Manual of Standardized Procedures.* Chicago: American Library Association.

Walter, Virginia A. 1995. *Output Measures and More: Planning and Evaluating Public Library Services for Young Adults.* Chicago: American Library Association.

Zweizig, Douglas L. 1996. *The Tell It! Manual; The Complete Program for Evaluating Library Performance.* Chicago: American Library Association.

Zweizig, Douglas L., and Eleanor Jo Rodger. 1982. *Output Measures for Public Libraries.* Chicago: American Library Association.

Articles

Balcom, Kathleen Mehaffey. 1986. To Concentrate and Strengthen: The Promise of the Public Library Development Program. *Library Journal* 111 (June 15): 36–40.

Blasingame, Ralph, Jr., and Mary Jo Lynch. 1974. Design for Diversity: Alternatives to Standards for Public Libraries. *PLA Newsletter* 13: 4–22.

Bloss, Meredith. 1976. Standards for Public Library Service—Quo Vadis? *Library Journal* 101 (June): 1259–1262.

Brown, Jeffrey L. 2001. Making a Huge Difference in So Many Little Ways. *Public Libraries* 40 (January/February): 24.

Durrance, Joan C., and Karen E. Fisher-Pettigrew. 2003. Determining How Libraries and Librarians Help. *Library Trends* 51 (Spring): 541–570.

Goals and Guidelines for Community Service. 1975. *PLA Newsletter* 14: 9–13.

Heckman, James. 2000. Causal Parameters and Policy Analysis in Economics: A Twentieth Century Retrospective. *The Quarterly Journal of Economics* 115 (February): 45–97.

Hennen, Thomas J., Jr. 1999a. Go Ahead, Name Them: America's Best Public Libraries. *American Libraries* 30 (January): 72–76.

Hennen, Thomas J., Jr. 1999b. Great American Public Libraries: HAPLR Ratings: Round Two. *American Libraries* 30 (September): 64–68.

Hennen, Thomas J., Jr. 2000a. Great American Public Libraries: HAPLR Ratings: 2000. *American Libraries* 31 (November): 50–54.

Hennen, Thomas J., Jr. 2000b. Why We Should Establish a National System of Standards. *American Libraries* 31 (March): 43–45.

Hennen, Thomas J., Jr. 2002a. Are Wider Library Units Wiser? *American Libraries* 33.6 (June/July): 65–70. (Also titled, Wider and Wiser Units.) Available: www.haplr-index.com/wider_and_wiser_units.htm.

Hennen, Thomas J., Jr. 2002b. Great American Public Libraries: HAPLR Ratings: 2002. *American Libraries* 33 (October): 64–68.

Hennen, Thomas J., Jr. 2003. Great American Public Libraries: HAPLR Ratings: 2003. *American Libraries* 34 (October): 44–49.

Johnson, Debra Wilcox. 1993. Reflecting on the Public Library Data Service Project: Public Libraries Over Five Years, 1987–1991. *Public Libraries* 32 (Sept./Oct.): 259–61.

Lance, Keith Curry, and Marti A. Cox. 2000. Lies, Damn Lies and Indexes. *American Libraries* 31 (June-July): 82–87.

Lynch, Mary Jo. 1981. The Public Library Association and Public Library Planning. *Journal of Library Administration* 2 (Summer/Fall/Winter): 29–41.

Lynch, Mary Jo. 1985. Public Library Statistics, the National Center for Education Statistics, and the Public Library Community. *Public Libraries* 24 (Summer): 62–64.

Lynch, Mary Jo. 1988. An Impossible Dream Come True? *Public Libraries* 27 (Winter): 170–171.

Lynch, Mary Jo. 1991. New, National and Ready to Fly: the Federal State Cooperative System (FSCS) for Public Library Data. *Public Libraries* 30 (November/December): 358–361.

Martin, Lowell. 1972. Standards for Public Libraries. *Library Trends* 21 (October): 164–177.

McCook, Kathleen de la Peña, and Kristin Brand. 2001. Community Indicators, Genuine Progress, and the Golden Billion. *Reference and User Services Quarterly* 40 (Summer): 337–340.

Moorman, John A. 1997. Standards for Public Libraries: A Study in Quantitative Measures of Library Performance as Found in State Public Library Documents. *Public Libraries* 36 (January-February): 32–39.

Public Library Association. Goals, Guidelines and Standards Committee. 1973. Community Library Services: Working Papers on Goals and Guidelines. *Library Journal* 96: 2603–2609.

Public Library Association. Public Library Principles Task Force. 1982. The Public Library: Democracy's Resource, A Statement of Principles. *Public Libraries* 21: 92.

Pungitore, Verna L. 1993. Planning in Smaller Libraries: A Field Study. *Public Libraries* 32 (November/December): 331–336.

Robinson, Charles W. 1983. Libraries and the Community. *Public Libraries* 22 (Spring): 7–13.

Schick, Frank L. 1971. Library Statistics: A Century Plus. *American Libraries* 2: 727–741.

Smith, Nancy Milner. 1994. State Library Agency Use of Planning and Role Setting for Public Libraries and Output Measures for Public Libraries. *Public Libraries* 33 (July-August): 211–212.

Standards for Public Libraries. 1933. *ALA Bulletin* 27 (November): 513–514.

Steffen, Nicolle O., and Keith Curry Lance. 2002. Who's Doing What: Outcome-Based Evaluation and Demographics in the 'Counting on Results Project.' *Public Libraries* 43 (September-October): 271–279.

Steffen, Nicolle O., Keith Curry Lance, and Rochelle Logan. 2002. Time to Tell the Whole Story: Outcome-Based Evaluation and the 'Counting on Results Project.' *Public Libraries* 43 (July-August): 222–228.

Tucker, Harold W. 1963. The Access to Public Libraries Study. *ALA Bulletin* 57 (September): 742–745.

Yan, Quan Liu, and Douglas L. Zweizig. 2000. Public Library Use of Statistics: A Survey Report. *Public Libraries* 39 (March/April): 98–105.

Yan, Quan Liu, and Douglas L. Zweizig. 2001. The Use of National Public Library Statistics by Public Library Directors. *Library Quarterly* 71 (October): 467–497.

Zweizig, Douglas L. 1985. Any Number Can Play: The First National Report of Output Measures Data. *Public Libraries* 24 (Summer): 50–53.

Web Sites

American National Standards Institute. Available: www.ansi.org.

Bibliostat Connect. Available: www.informata.com.

Chief Officers of State Library Agencies (COSLA). Available: www.cosla.org.

Hennen, Thomas J., Jr. 2003. Hennen's American Public Library Ratings. Available: www.haplr-index.com/index.html.

Information Use Management and Policy Institute, John C. Bertot, and Charles R. McClure. Public Library Network Statistics: Librarian Education for the Collection, Analysis, and Use of Library Network Services and Resources Statistics. Available: www.ii.fsu.edu/getProjectDetail.cfm?pageID=8&ProjectID=4.

International Institute for Sustainable Development. Compendium of Sustainable Development Indicator Initiatives. Available: www.iisd.org/measure/compendium.

Lance, Keith Curry, et al. 2002. *Counting on Results: New Tools for Outcome-Based Evaluation for Public Libraries.* Aurora, CO: Bibliographical Center for Research. Available: www.lrs.org/documents/cor/CoRFin.pdf (accessed November 2, 2003).

National Information Standards Association. Available: www.niso.org/index.html.

National Information Standards Organization. Draft Standard for Trial Use. *Information Services and Use: Metrics and Statistics for Libraries and Information Providers-Data Dictionary,* NISO Z39.7-2002. Available: www.niso.org/emetrics/index.cfm (accessed July 8, 2004).

New York State Library. Bibliostat Connect: Easy Online Access to Public Library Statistics from your State Library. Available: www.nysl.nysed.gov/libdev/libs/biblcnct.htm.

Oregon State Library. *Reporting Public Library Statistics.* Available: www.osl.state.or.us/home/libdev/reportpublibstats.html.

U.S. National Center for Education Statistics. Public Libraries Data. Available: http://nces.ed.gov/pubsearch/ (accessed July 8, 2004).

U.S. National Center for Education Statistics. Public Library Peer Comparison Tool. Available: http://nces.ed.gov/surveys/libraries/publicpeer (accessed July 8, 2004).

U.S. National Commission on Libraries and Information Science. Library Statistics Cooperative Program. Available: www.nclis.gov/statsurv/surveys/fscs/fscs.html (accessed February 18, 2004).

U.S. National Commission on Libraries and Information Science. The Federal-State Cooperative System (FSCS) for Public Library Data: Chronology 1980–2003. Available: www.nclis.gov/statsurv/surveys/fscs/aboutFSCS/FSCS_History.pdf (accessed July 8, 2004).

5. Organization, Law, Funding, and Politics

Books and Chapters in Books

American Library Association. 1930. *American Library Laws.* Volumes and supplements published 1930, 1943, 1962 (supplements 1965–1970), 1972 (supplements 1972–1978), 1983. Chicago: American Library Association.

Buschman, John E. 2003. *Dismantling the Public Sphere: Situating and Sustaining Librarianship in the Age of the New Public Philosophy.* Westport, CT: Libraries Unlimited.

Fiels, Keith Michael, Joan Neumann, and Eva R. Brown. 1991. *Multitype Library Cooperation State Laws, Regulations and Pending Legislation*. Chicago: Association of Specialized and Cooperative Library Agencies.

Garceau, Oliver. 1949. *The Public Library in the Political Process: A Report of the Public Library Inquiry*. New York: Columbia University Press.

Halsey, Richard Sweeney. 2003. *Lobbying for Public and School Libraries: A History and Political Playbook*. Lanham, MD: Scarecrow Press.

Healey, James S. 1974. *John E. Fogarty: Political Leadership for Library Development*. Metuchen, NJ: Scarecrow Press.

Held, Ray E. 1973. *The Rise of the Public Library in California*. Chicago: American Library Association.

Himmel, Ethel E., William J. Wilson, and GraceAnne DeCandido. 2000. *The Functions and Roles of State Library Agencies*. Chicago: American Library Association.

Holley, Edward G., and Robert Schremser. 1983. *The Library Services and Construction Act: An Historical Overview from the Viewpoint of Major Participants*. Greenwich, CN: JAI Press.

Joeckel, Carleton Bruns. 1935. *The Government of the American Public Library*. Chicago: University of Chicago Press.

Josey, E. J. 1980. *Libraries and the Political Process*. New York: Neal-Schuman Publishers.

Josey, E. J. 1987. *Libraries, Coalitions and the Public Good*. New York: Neal-Schuman Publishers.

Josey, E. J. and Kenneth D. Shearer. 1990. *Politics and the Support of Libraries*. New York: Neal-Schuman Publishers.

Krane, Dale, Platon N. Rigos, and Melvin Hill, Jr. 2001. *Home Rule in America: a Fifty State Handbook*. Washington, DC: CQ Press.

Ladenson, Alex. 1982. *Library Law and Legislation in the United States*. Metuchen, NJ: Scarecrow Press.

Lipinski, Tomas A. 2002. *Libraries, Museums and Archives: Legal Issues and Ethical Challenges in the New Information Era*. Lanham, MD: Scarecrow Press.

Merrill, Julia Wright. 1942. *Regional and District Library Laws*. Chicago: American Library Association.

Mersel, Jules. 1969. *An Overview of the Library Services and Construction Act, Title 1*. New York: R. R. Bowker.

Minow, Mary, and Tomas A. Lipinski. 2003. *The Library's Legal Answer Book*. Chicago: American Library Association.

Tolman, Frank, Leland. 1937. *Digest of County Library Laws of the United States*. Chicago: American Library Association.

Turner, Anne M. 2000. *Vote Yes for Libraries: A Guide to Winning Ballot Measure Campaigns for Library Funding*. Jefferson, NC: McFarland and Co.

Wallace, Linda K. 2000. *Library Advocates Handbook*. Chicago: American Library Association.

Yust, William. F. 1911. *Library Legislation*. Chicago: American Library Association.

Articles

Advocacy Grows at Your Library. 2004. *American Libraries* 35 (February): 32–36.

Bertot, John Carlo, Charles R. McClure, and Joe Ryan. 2002. Impact of External Technology Funding Programs for Public Libraries: A Study of LSTA, E-Rate, Gates and Others. *Public Libraries* 41 (May-June): 166–171.

Brawner, Lee. 1993. The People's Choice. *Library Journal* (January): 59–62.

California State Library. *California Statewide Plan for Use of Library Services and Technology Funds 2002/03–2006–07.* Available: www.library.ca.gov/assets/ acrobat/STATE_PLAN_02-07.pdf (accessed November 6, 2003).

Coffman, Steve. 2004. Saving Ourselves: Plural Funding for Public Libraries. *American Libraries* 35 (February): 37–39.

Eberhart, George M. 2004. Referenda Roundup. *American Libraries* 35 (January): 18–23.

Fry, James W. 1975. LSA and LSCA, 1956–1973: A Legislative History. *Library Trends* 24 (July): 7–28.

Gordon, Andrew C., et al. 2003. The Gates Legacy. *Library Journal* (March 1): 44–48.

Hennen, Thomas J., Jr. 2002. Are Wider Library Units Wiser? *American Libraries* 33.6 (June/July): 65–70. (Also titled, Wider and Wiser Units.) Available: www .haplr-index.com/wider_and_wiser_units.htm.

Herrera, L. 2003. It's Our Turn. *Public Libraries* 42 (November/December): 343.

Krois, Jerome W. 2002. An Introduction to Public Library Foundations: A Members Guide. *The Unabashed Librarian* 122: 22–26.

Ladenson, Alex. 1970. Library Legislation: Some General Considerations. *Library Trends* 19 (October): 175–181.

A National Plan for Libraries. 1935. *ALA Bulletin* 29 (February): 91–98.

A National Plan for Libraries. 1939. *ALA Bulletin* 33 (February): 136–150.

Reed, Sally Gardner. 2004. FOLUSA Turns 25. *American Libraries* 35 (February): 40–41.

Schaefer, Steve W. 2001. Going for the Green: How Public Libraries get State Money. *Public Libraries* 40 (September/October): 298–304.

Schuman, Patricia. 1999. Speaking Up and Speaking Out: Ensuring Equity Through Advocacy. *American Libraries* 30 (October): 50–53.

Web Sites

Alliance for Regional Stewardship. Available: www.regionalstewardship.org.

American Library Association. Washington Office. Available: www.ala.org/washoff. Also available on the Children's Internet Protection Act (CIPA) Web site: www .ala.org/cipa.

Bill and Melinda Gates Foundation. Libraries. Available: www.gatesfoundation.org/ libraries (accessed November 2, 2003).

Chief Officers of State Library Agencies (COSLA). Available: www.cosla.org.

Community Foundations of America. Available: www.cfamerica.org/index.cfm.

Council on Foundations. Community Foundations. Available: www.cof.org.

Foundation Center. Available: http://fdncenter.org.

Friends of Libraries USA (FOLUSA). Available: www.folusa.org.

GEOLIB. Available: www.geolib.org.

Institute of Museum and Library Services. Available: www.imls.gov/index.htm. See the IMLS Web page on "Grants to State Library Agencies" at: www.imls.gov/grants/library/lib_gsla.asp.

Libraries for the Future. Community Foundations and the Public Library. Available: www.lff.org/research/community.html.

National Association of Counties. Available: www.naco.org/Template.cfm?Section=About_NACo.

National Governors Association. Available: www.nga.org/nga/1,1169,,00.html.

The Public Access to Computing Project: Legacy of Gates U.S. Library Project. Available: www.pacp.net/LJ_PAGE_1.html.

U.S. Census Bureau. Median Income of Four-Person Families By State. Available: www.census.gov/hhes/income/4person.html.

U.S. Conference of Mayors. Available: www.usmayors.org.

U.S. National Center for Education Statistics. Public Libraries Data. Available: http://nces.ed.gov/pubsearch/pubsinfo.asp?pubid=2003398 (accessed July 8, 2004).

6. Administration and Staffing

Books and Chapters in Books.

American Library Association. 1992. *Standards for Accreditation of Master's Programs in Library and Information Studies.* Chicago: American Library Association.

American Library Association. 2003. Library and Information Studies and Human Resource Utilization: Policy Statement. In *ALA Handbook of Organization, 2003–2004,* Policy 54.1. Chicago: American Library Association.

Altman, Ellen, and Roberta Bowler. 1980. *Local Public Library Administration.* Chicago: American Library Association.

Association for Library and Information Science Education. *Library and Information Science Education Statistical Report, 2003.* State College, PA: Association for Library and Information Science Education.

Avery, Elizabeth Fuseler, et al. 2001. *Staff Development: A Practical Guide.* 3rd ed. Chicago: American Library Association.

Baugham, James C. 1993. *Policymaking for Public Library Trustees.* Englewood, CO: Libraries Unlimited.

CALTAC. 1998. *Trustee Toolkit for Library Leadership.* Sacramento, CA: California State Library.

Childers, Thomas, and Nancy Van House. 1993. *What's Good? Describing Your Public Library's Effectiveness.* Chicago: American Library Association.

Dixon, Sandy. 2001. *Iowa Public Library Director's Handbook, 2001.* Des Moines, IA: State Library of Iowa.

Driggers, Preston F., and Eileen Dumas. 2002. *Managing Library Volunteers: A Practical Toolkit*. Chicago: American Library Association.

Garceau, Oliver. 1949. The Governing Authority of the Public Library. In *The Public Library in the Political Process: A Report of the Public Library Inquiry*, 53–110. New York: Columbia University Press.

Getz, Malcolm. 1980. *Public Libraries: An Economic View*. Baltimore, MD: Johns Hopkins University Press.

Hernon, Peter, Ronald R. Powell, and Arthur P. Young. 2003. *The Next Library Leadership: Attributes of Academic and Public Library Directors*. Westport, CT: Libraries Unlimited.

Joeckel, Carleton Bruns. 1935. Municipal Libraries Managed by Boards: Organization of the Library Board; Municipal Libraries: Power and Functions of the Library Board; and An Appraisal of the Library Board as a Governmental Agency. In *The Government of the American Public Library*, 170–262. Chicago: University of Chicago Press.

Kay, Linda. 2002. *New Jersey Public Libraries: A Manual for Trustees*. Trenton, NJ: New Jersey State Library.

Larson, Jeanette, and Herman Totten. 1998. *Model Policies for Small and Medium Public Libraries*. New York: Neal-Schuman Publishers.

Massis, Bruce E. 2003. *The Practical Library Manager*. New York: Haworth Information Press.

Mayo, Diane, and Jeanne Goodrich. 2002. *Staffing for Results*. Chicago: American Library Association.

Nelson, Sandra S., and June Garcia. 2003. *Creating Policies for Results: From Chaos to Clarity*. Chicago: American Library Association.

Nelson, Sandra, Ellen Altman, and Diane Mayo. 2000. Managing Your Library's Staff. In *Managing for Results: Effective Resource Allocation for Public Libraries*, 29–110. Chicago: American Library Association.

Owens, Stephen. 1996. *Public Library Structure and Organization in the United States*. Washington, DC: National Center for Education Statistics.

Pungitore, Verna L. 1989. Governance of Public Libraries. In *Public Librarianship: An Issues Oriented Approach*, 47–58. New York: Greenwood Press.

Robinson, Maureen K. 2001. *Non-Profit Boards That Work: Ending One-Size-Fits-All Governance*. New York: John Wiley and Sons.

Sager, Donald J. 1989. *Managing the Public Library*. Boston: G. K. Hall.

Sager, Donald J. 2000. *Small Libraries: Organization and Operation*. Ft. Atkinson, WI: Highsmith Press.

Saulmon, Sharon A. 1997. *Sample Evaluations of Library Directors*. Chicago: American Library Trustee Association/American Library Association.

Singer, Paula M. 2002. *Developing a Compensation Plan for Your Library*. Chicago: American Library Association.

Sullivan, Peggy, and William Ptacek. 1982. *Public Libraries: Smart Practices in Personnel*. Littleton, CO: Libraries Unlimited.

Urban Libraries Council. 1997. *Governing and Funding Metropolitan Public Libraries*. Evanston, IL: Urban Libraries Council.

Wade, Gordon S. 1991. *Working with Library Boards of Trustees: A How-To-Do-It-Manual*. New York: Neal-Schuman Publishers.

Wheeler, Joseph Lewis, Herbert Goldhor, and Carlton C. Rochell. 1981. *Wheeler and Goldhor's Practical Administration of Public Libraries*. New York: Harper and Row.

Winston, Mark. 1999. *Managing Multiculturalism and Diversity in the Library: Principles and Issues for Administrators*. New York: Haworth Press.

Wisconsin Department of Public Instruction. Division of Libraries, Technology and Community Learning. 2000. *Certification Manual for Wisconsin Public Library Directors*. Madison, WI.

Weingand, Darlene E. 2001. *The Administration of the Small Public Library*. Chicago: American Library Association.

Young, Virginia. 1995. *The Library Trustee: A Practical Handbook*. 5th ed. Chicago: American Library Association.

Articles

Auld, Hampton. 2002. The Benefits and Deficiencies of Unions in Public Libraries. *Public Libraries* 41 (May/June): 135–142.

Batson, C. Daniel, and Nadia Ahmad. 2002. Four Motives for Community Involvement. *Journal of Social Issues* 58 (Fall): 429–445.

Callen, J. L., A. Klein, and D. Tinkelman. 2003. Board Composition, Committees and Organizational Efficiency. *Nonprofit and Voluntary Sector Quarterly* 32 (December): 493–520.

Casey, James B. 2002. The 1.6% Solution. *American Libraries* 33 (April): 85–86.

Clay, Edwin S., III, and Patricia C. Bangs. 2000. Entrepreneurs in the Public Library: Reinventing an Institution. *Library Trends* 48 (Winter): 606–618.

FLA Friends and Trustees Section. 2000. Floridians Value Their Libraries. *Florida Libraries* 43 (Fall): 18.

Farmer, Leslie. 2003. Teen Library Volunteers. *Public Libraries* 42 (May/June): 141–142.

Frank, Donald G. 1997. Activity in Professional Associations: The Positive Difference in a Librarian's Career. *Library Trends,* 46 (Fall): 307–317.

Freedman, Maurice J. 2002. The Campaign for America's Librarians. *American Libraries* 33 (August): 7.

Glennon, Michael. 1997. Developing and Passing a Bond Issue: A Trustee's View. *Public Libraries* 36 (January/February): 24–28.

Hague, Rodger. 1999. A Short History of the Stevens County Rural Library District. *Alki* 15 (July): 22–23.

Hilyard, Nann Blaine. 2003. Our Trusty Trustees. *Public Libraries* 42 (July/August): 220–223.

Holley, Carroll, and Linda Klancher. 2002. Labor Unions in Public Libraries: A Perspective from Both Sides of the Issue. *Public Libraries* 41 (May/June): 138.

Johnson, Cameron. 2002. Professionalism, not Paternalism. *Public Libraries* 41 (May/June): 139–140.

Jordan, Amy. 2002. Can Unions Solve the Low-Pay Dilemma? *American Libraries* 33 (January): 65–69.

Kelley, H. Neil. 1999. Portrait of the Illinois Trustee Community. *Illinois Libraries* 81 (Fall): 222–225.

Kinnaly, Gene. 2002. Pay Equity, Support Staff, and ALA. Library *Mosaics* 13 (March/April): 8–10.

Kreamer, Jean T. 1990. The Library Trustee as a Library Activist. *Public Libraries* 29 (July/August): 220–3.

Lisker, Peter. 2001. Lifelong Learning for Librarians. *Public Libraries* 40 (May/June): 145.

Lynch, Mary Jo. 2003. Public Library Staff: How Many Is Enough? *American Libraries* 32 (May): 58–59.

McCook, Kathleen de la Peña, ed. 2000. Ethnic Diversity in Library and Information Science. *Library Trends* 49 (Summer): 1–214.

Miller, Ellen G. 2001. Advocacy ABCs for Trustees. *American Libraries* 32 (September): 56–59.

Miller, Ellen G. 2001. Getting the Most from your Boards and Advisory Councils. *Library Administration and Management* 15 (Fall): 204–212.

Musick, Marc A., John Wilson, and William B. Bynum, Jr. 2000. Race and Formal Volunteering: The Differential Effects of Class and Religion. *Social Forces* 78 (June): 1539–1570.

Nalen, James E. 2003. Union and Collective Bargaining Websites. *Journal of Business and Finance Librarianship* 8 (3/4): 223–235.

Naylor, Richard J. 2000. Core Competencies: What They Are and How to Use Them. *Public Libraries* 39 (March/April): 108–114.

Omoto, Alan. M., and Mark Snyder. 2002. Considerations of Community: The Context and Process of Volunteerism. *The American Behavioral Scientist* 45 (January): 848–867.

Recruitment of Public Librarians. 2000. *Public Libraries* 39 (May/June): 168–172.

Sager, Donald J. 1998. Public Library Trusteeship in the 21st Century. *Public Libraries* 37 (May/June): 170–174.

Sager, Donald J. 2001. Evolving Virtues: Public Library Administrative Skills. *Public Libraries* 40 (September/October): 268–272.

Scheppke, Jim. 1991. The Governance of Public Libraries: Findings of the PLA Governance of Public Libraries Committee. *Public Libraries* 30 (Sept./Oct.): 288–94.

Sparanese, Ann, C. 2002. Unions in Libraries: A Positive View. *Public Libraries* 41 (May/June): 140–141.

Winters, Sharon. 1999. Strengthening the Commitment to Staff Development. *Public Libraries*, 38 (July/August): 248–252.

Young, Virginia. 1977. Library Governance by Citizen Boards. *Library Trends* 25 (Fall): 287–297.

Web Sites

American Library Association-Allied Professional Association. *Advocating for Better Salaries and Pay Equity Toolkit.* Compiled as part of the Campaign for America's Librarians, Library Advocacy Now! Training program developed by the ALA 2002–2003 President Maurice J. (Mitch) Freedman's Better Salaries and Pay Equity for Library Workers Task Force. Available: www.ala-apa.org/toolkit.pdf.

Asian/Pacific American Library Association (APALA). Available: www.apalaweb.org.

Association for Library and Information Science Education. Available: www.alise.org.

Association for Research on Nonprofit Organizations and Voluntary Action. Available: www.arnova.org.

BoardSource (Building Effective Nonprofit Boards). Available: www.ncnb.org/default.asp?ID=1.

Black Caucus of the American Library Association (BCALA). Available: www.bcala.org.

Campaign for America's Librarians. American Library Association. 2003. Available: www.ala-apa.org/toolkit.pdf.

Chinese-American Librarians Association (CALA). Available: www.cala-web.org.

Friends of Libraries USA. Available: www.folusa.org. For examples of volunteer effort, see the Web page: www.folusa.org/html/best4.html.

Kentucky State Board for the Certification of Librarians. Certification Manual. 2001. Available: www.kdla.ky.gov/libsupport/certification/manual.PDF.

Library Support Staff Interests Round Table. American Library Association. Available: www.ala.org/lssirt.

Lynch, Mary Jo. Spending on Staff Development—2001. American Library Association. Office for Research and Statistics. Available: www.ala.org (enter "staff development" in search box).

Missouri Public Library Standards: An Implementation Plan. http://www.sos.mo.gov/library/libstan.pdf

Public Library Association. Public Librarian Recruitment. Available: www.pla.org.

REFORMA—National Association to Promote Library and Information Services to Latinos and the Spanish-Speaking. Available: www.reforma.org.

Service Employees International Union. Available: www.seiu.org.

U.S. Department of Labor. Bureau of Labor Statistics. *Occupational Outlook Handbook; Occupational Outlook Quarterly; Occupational Employment Statistics.* Available: http://stats.bls.gov/home.htm.

U.S. Institute of Museum and Library Services. Librarians for the 21st Century. Available: www.imls.gov/grants/library/lib_bdre.htm.

U.S. National Center for Education Statistics. Public Libraries. Available: http://nces.ed.gov/pubsearch/pubsinfo.asp?pubid=2003399.

Examples of State Trustee and Board Materials Developed by States

Mississippi Library Commission. Library Boards of Trustees. Available: www.mlc .lib.ms.us/advocacy/trustees/index.htm.

Nebraska Library Association, Trustee, User and Friends Section. Nebraska Library Association. Available: www.nol.org/home/NLA/TUFS/index.html.

Office of Library and Information Services. *Rhode Island Public Library Trustees Handbook*. Available: www.lori.state.ri.us/trustees/default.php.

Public Library System Directors Organization of New York. 2000. *Handbook for Library Trustees of New York State*. Millennium edition. New York: Mid-York Library System. Available: www.nysalb.org/Handbook.pdf.

Shaw, Jane Belon, et al., eds. Trustee Facts File. Available: www.cyberdriveillinois .com/library/isl/ref/readyref/trustee/index.htm.

Wisconsin Department of Public Instruction. Trustee Essentials: A Handbook for Wisconsin Public Library Trustees. Available: www.dpi.state.wi.us/dltcl/pld/ handbook.html.

7. Structure and Infrastructure

Books and Chapters in Books

American Library Association. 2003. Library Services for People with Disabilities. In *ALA Handbook of Organization, 2003–2004,* 54.3.2. Chicago: American Library Association.

American Library Association. Coordinating Committee on Revision of Public Library Standards. 1956. *Public Library Service: A Guide to Evaluation with Minimum Standards*. Chicago: American Library Association.

American Library Association. Public Library Association, Standards Committee. 1967. *Minimum Standards for Public Library Systems, 1966*. Chicago: American Library Association.

Bobinski, George S. 1969. Carnegie Library Architecture. In *Carnegie Libraries: Their History and Impact on American Library Development*, 57–75. Chicago: American Library Association.

Dahlgren, Anders C. 1996. *Planning the Small Library Facility*. 2nd ed. Chicago: American Library Association.

Feinberg, Sandra, Joan F. Kuchner, and Sari Feldman. 1998. *Learning Environments for Young Children: Rethinking Library Spaces and Services*. Chicago: American Library Association.

Joeckel, Carleton B., and Amy Winslow. 1948. *A National Plan for Public Library Service*. Chicago: American Library Association.

Jones. Theodore. 1997. *Carnegie Libraries Across America: A Public Legacy*. New York: John Wiley.

Lushington, Nolan. 2002. *Libraries Designed for Users: A 21st Century Guide*. New York: Neal-Schuman Publishers.

Mayo, Diane, and Sandra Nelson. 1999. *Wired for the Future: Developing Your Library Technology Plan*. Chicago: American Library Association.

McCabe, Gerald B. 2000. *Planning for a New Generation of Public Library Buildings*. Westport, CT: Greenwood Press.

McCook, Kathleen de la Peña. 2000. *A Place at the Table: Participating in Community Building*. Chicago: American Library Association.

McCook, Kathleen de la Peña. 2002. *Rocks in the Whirlpool: The American Library Association and Equity of Access*. ERIC ED462981. Chicago: American Library Association. Available: www.ala.org/ala/ourassociation/governingdocs/key actionareas/equityaction/rockswhirlpool.htm.

Public Library Association, Standards Committee. 1967. *Minimum Standards for Public Library Systems, 1966*. Chicago: American Library Association.

Putnam, Robert D., and Lewis M. Feldstein. 2003. Branch Libraries: The Heartbeat of the Community. In *Better Together: Restoring the American Community*, 34–54. New York: Simon and Schuster.

Rabun, J. Stanley. 2000. *Structural Analysis of Historic Buildings: Restoration, Preservation and Adaptive Reuse Applications for Architects and Engineers*. New York: Wiley.

Sannwald, William W. 2001. *Checklist of Building Design Considerations*. 4th ed. Chicago: American Library Association.

U.S. National Commission on Libraries and Information Science. 1992. Pathways to Excellence: A Report on Improving Library and Information Services for Native American Peoples. Available: www.nclis.gov/libraries/nata.html.

Van Slyck, Abigail Ayres. 1995. *Free to All: Carnegie Libraries and American Culture, 1890–1920*. Chicago: University of Chicago Press.

Articles

Bertot, John Carlo. 2001. Measuring Service Quality in the Networked Environment: Approaches and Considerations. *Library Trends* 49 (Spring): 758–775.

Bertot, John Carlo, Charles R. McClure, and Joe Ryan. 2002. Impact of External Technology Funding Programs for Public Libraries: A Study of LSTA, E-Rate, Gates and Others. *Public Libraries* 41 (May-June): 166–171.

Building for the Future. 2003. *American Libraries* 34 (April): 41–62.

Campbell, Anne L. 2003. Magical Models. *Library Journal* (February 15): 38–40.

Dorr, Jessica, and Richard Akeroyd. 2001. New Mexico Tribal Libraries: Bridging the Digital Divide. *Computers in Libraries* 21, no. 8 (October): 36–43. Available: www.infotoday.com/cilmag/oct01/dorr&akeroyd.htm.

Forrest, Charles. 2002. Building Libraries and Library Building Awards—Twenty Years of Change: An Interview with Anders C. Dahlgren. *Library Administration and Management Journal* 16 (Summer): 120–125.

Fox, Bette-Lee. 2002. The Building Buck Doesn't Stop Here: Library Buildings 2002. *Library Journal* 127.20 (December): 42–55.

Gordon, Andrew C., et al. 2003. The Gates Legacy. *Library Journal* (March 1): 44–48.

Gregory, Gwen. 1999. The Library Services and Technology Act: How Changes from LSCA are Affecting Libraries. *Public Libraries* 38 (November-December): 378–382.

Jaeger, Paul T., and Charles R. McClure. 2004. Potential Legal Challenges to the Application of the Children's Internet Protection Act (CIPA) in Public Libraries: Strategies and Issues. *First Monday* 9 (February). Available: http://firstmonday.org/issues/issue9_2/jaeger/index.html.

Kenney, Brian. 2001. Minneapolis PL to Revitalize Its Downtown. *Library Journal* 126 (June 15): 12.

Kent, Fred, and Phil Myrick. 2003. How To Become a Great Public Space. *American Libraries* 34 (April): 72–76.

Kline, Kerry A. 2002. Libraries, Schools and Wired Communities in Rural Areas and the Changing Communications Landscape. *Rural Libraries* 22 (no. 2): 13–41.

Lane, Christian K. 1989. Chicago Public Library Competition. *Chicago Architectural Journal* 7: 6–27.

Six Chicago Architects: Impressions of the Chicago Public Library Competition. 1989. *Chicago Architectural Journal* 7: 28–37.

Supreme Court Upholds CIPA. 2003. *Newsletter on Intellectual Freedom* 52 (September): 173; 187–191.

Web Sites

ALATechSource. Available: www.techsource.ala.org.

Bill and Melinda Gates Foundation. Libraries. Available: www.gatesfoundation.org/libraries (accessed July 8, 2004).

Bill and Melinda Gates Foundation. 2003. Designing for the Future. *Connections: Progress in Libraries* 1.4. Available: www.gatesfoundation.org/Libraries/RelatedInfo/Connections/ConnectionsVol14.htm#DesigningfortheFuture (accessed July 8, 2004).

Chicago Public Library. The Development of a Central Library. Available: www.chipublib.org/003cpl/cpl125/hwlc.

Crossroads. Available: www.webjunction.org/do/Navigation?category=30.

Dahlgren, Anders C. Public Library Space Needs: A Planning Outline/1998. Wisconsin Department of Public Instruction: Public Library Development. Available: www.dpi.state.wi.us/dltcl/pld/plspace.html#Introduction (accessed July 8, 2004).

Dorr, Jessica, and Richard Akeroyd. 2001. New Mexico Tribal Libraries: Bridging the Digital Divide. *Computers in Libraries* 21, no. 8 (October): 36–43. Available: www.infotoday.com/cilmag/oct01/dorr&akeroyd.htm.

Institute of Museum and Library Services. Status of Technology and Digitization in the Nation's Museums and Libraries, 2002 Report. Available: www.imls.gov/reports/techreports/intro02.htm.

Kansas City Public Library. Available: www.kclibrary.org/support/central/index.cfm.

LAMA Building Consultants List. Available: https://cs.ala.org/lbcl/search (accessed May 23, 2004).

Library of Congress. National Library Service for the Blind and Physically Handicapped. Available: www.loc.gov/nls.

Library Technology Guides: Key Resources and Content Related to Library Automation. Available: www.librarytechnology.org/index.pl?SID=20030413217346191 &UID=&auth.

Libris Design. Available: www.librisdesign.org/index.html (accessed November 1, 2003).

Minneapolis Public Library. New Central Library. Available: www.mplib.org/ncl _projectsummary102803.asp.

Oklahoma Territorial Museum and Carnegie Library. Available: www.ok-history .mus.ok.us/mus-sites/masnum21.htm.

Public Access Computing Project. Research Reports. Available: http://webjunction .org/do/DisplayContent?id=886 (accessed July 8, 2004).

Project for Public Spaces. Available: www.pps.org.

Seattle Public Library. Capital Projects. Available: www.spl.org/lfa/central/building anewcentral.html.

Tompkins County Public Library. Available: www.tcpl.org/index.html.

U.S. Access Board. Accessibility Guidelines and Standards. Available: www.access -board.gov/indexes/accessindex.htm.

U.S. Department of Education. Office of Educational Research and Improvement. Biennial Evaluation Report, 1995–1996. Public Library Construction and Technology Enhancement Grants to State Library Agencies (CFDA No. 84-154). Available: www.ed.gov/pubs/Biennial/95-96/eval/603-97.pdf (accessed November 1, 2003).

U.S. National Telecommunications and Information Administration. Technology Opportunities Program. Available: www.ntia.doc.gov/otiahome/top/index.html.

The Universal Service Administrative Company. Available: www.sl.universalservice .org (accessed July 8, 2004).

WebJunction. Available: www.webjunction.org/do/Home.

Wisconsin Public Library Standards, 2000. 3rd ed. Available: www.dpi.state.wi.us/ dltcl/pld/chapter7.html (accessed May 23, 2004).

Video

MARZ Associates, in association with WGBH, Boston. 1989. Nova: Design Wars. VHS. Boston: WGBH Educational Foundation.

8. Adult Services.

Books and Chapters in Books

American Library Association. 1926. *Libraries and Adult Education: Report of a Study made by the American Library Association.* Chicago: American Library Association.

American Library Association. (Annual). Library Services for People with Disabilities (54.3.1); Minority Concerns (60); Goals for Indian Library and Information Services (60.3); Library Services for the Poor (61). In *ALA Policy Manual.* Chicago: American Library Association.

Birge, Lynn E. 1981. *Serving Adult Learners: A Public Library Tradition.* Chicago: American Library Association.

Christensen, Karen, and David Levinson, eds. 2003. *Encyclopedia of Community.* Thousand Oaks, CA: Sage Publications. See especially the articles, Information Communities, 657–660; Public Libraries, 1114–1117; and Libraries Build Community, Appendix 2, 1533–1551.

Davies, D. W. 1974. *Public Libraries as Culture and Social Centers: The Origins of the Concept.* Metuchen: Scarecrow Press.

Freeman, Robert S., and David M. Hovde, eds. 2003. *Libraries to the People: Histories of Outreach.* Jefferson, NC: McFarland and Co.

Güereña, Salvador. 2000. *Library Services to Latinos.* Jefferson, NC: McFarland and Co.

Heim (de la Peña McCook), Kathleen M., and Danny P. Wallace. 1990. *Adult Services: An Enduring Focus for Public Libraries.* Chicago: American Library Association.

Heim (de la Peña McCook), Kathleen M., and Harry D. Nuttall. 1990. *Adult Services: A Bibliography and Index. A Component of the Adult Services in the Eighties Project.* ERIC ED320609. Baton Rouge, LA: Louisiana State University.

Herald, Diana Tixier. 2000. *Genreflecting: A Guide to Reading Interests in Genre Fiction.* 5th ed. Englewood, CO: Libraries Unlimited.

Johnson, Alvin. 1938. *The Public Library—A People's University.* New York: American Association for Adult Education.

Josey, E. J. 1994. Race Issues in Library History. In *Encyclopedia of Library History*, ed. W. A. Wiegand and D. G. Davis, 533–537. New York: Garland Publishing.

Learned, William S. 1924. *The American Public Library and the Diffusion of Knowledge.* New York: Harcourt.

Lee, Robert Ellis. 1966. *Continuing Education for Adults through the American Public Library 1833–1966.* Chicago: American Library Association.

Lyman, Helen. 1954. *Adult Education Activities in Public Libraries.* Chicago: American Library Association.

McClure, Charles R., et al. 1987. *Planning and Role Setting for Public Libraries: A Manual of Options and Procedures.* Chicago: American Library Association.

McCook, Kathleen de la Peña. 1990. Adult Services: An Enduring Focus. In *Adult Services: An Enduring Focus for Public Libraries*, ed. Kathleen M. Heim (de la Peña McCook) and Danny P. Wallace, 11–26. Chicago: American Library Association.

McCook, Kathleen de la Peña. 1991. The Developing Role of Public Libraries in Adult Education: 1966 to 1991. In *Partners for Lifelong Learning: Public Libraries and Adult Education,* 21–53. Washington, DC: U.S. Department of Education.

McCook, Kathleen de la Peña. 2002. *Rocks in the Whirlpool: The American Library Association and Equity of Access.* ERIC ED462981. Chicago: American Library Association. Available: www.ala.org/ala/ourassociation/governingdocs/key actionareas/equityaction/rockswhirlpool.htm.

Monroe, Margaret E. 1963. *Library Adult Education: The Biography of an Idea.* New York: Scarecrow Press.

Monroe, Margaret E., and Kathleen Heim (de la Peña McCook). 1979. *Emerging Patterns of Community Service. Library Trends* 28 (Fall): 129–138.

Nelson, Sandra. 2001. *The New Planning for Results: A Streamlined Approach.* Chicago: American Library Association.

Schlachter, Gail A. 1982. *The Service Imperative for Libraries: Essays in Honor of Margaret E. Monroe.* Littleton, CO: Libraries Unlimited.

Smith, Helen Lyman. 1954. Adult Education Activities in Public Libraries. Chicago: American Library Association.

Venturella, Karen M. 1998. *Poor People and Library Services.* Jefferson, NC: McFarland and Co.

Wallace, Danny P. 1990. The Character of Adult Services in the Eighties. In *Adult Services: An Enduring Focus for Public Libraries,* ed. Kathleen M. Heim (de la Peña McCook) and Danny P. Wallace, 27–165. Chicago: American Library Association.

Weibel, Kathleen. 1982. *The Evolution of Library Outreach 1960–75 and Its Effect on Reader Services: Some Considerations.* Occasional Paper Number 16. Urbana, IL: Graduate School of Library and Information Science. Also available as ERIC ED231376.

Articles

American Library Association. Board on Library and Adult Education. 1935. The Library and Adult Education: 1924–1934. *ALA Bulletin* 29 (June): 316–323.

Brown, Walter L. 1917. The Changing Public. *ALA Bulletin* 11 (July): 91–95.

Hicks, Jack Alan. 1998. Planning Successful Author Programming. *Public Libraries* 37 (July/August): 237–238.

Jensen, Leif, and Tim Slack. 2003. Underemployment in America: Measurement and Evidence. *American Journal of Community Psychology* 12 (September): 21–31.

Library Rights of Adults. 1970. *ASD Newsletter* 8 (Winter): 2–3.

McCook, Kathleen de la Peña. 1986. Adult Services as Reflective of the Changing Role of the Public Library. *RQ* 26 (Winter): 180–187.

McCook, Kathleen de la Peña. 1992. Where Would We Be Without Them? Libraries and Adult Education Activities: 1966–1991. *RQ* 32 (Winter): 245–253.

Stevenson, Grace T. 1954. The ALA Adult Education Board. *ALA Bulletin* 48b (April): 226–231.

Stone, C. Walter. 1953. Adult Education and the Public Library. *Library Trends* 1 (April): 437–453.

Wellman, Hiller C. 1915. The Library's Primary Duty. *ALA Bulletin* 9 (July): 89–93.

Web Sites

American Library Association. Office for Diversity. Available: www.ala.org/diversity.

American Library Association. Office for Public Programs. Available: www.ala.org/publicprograms.

American Library Association. Office on Literacy and Outreach Services. Outreach at your Library. Available: http://cs.ala.org/olos/outreach/participating.cfm.

Library of Congress. Center for the Book. Available: www.loc.gov/loc/cfbook.

Library of Congress. Center for the Book: State Center Affiliates. Available: www
.loc.gov/loc/cfbook/stacen.html.

Reference and User Services Association (RUSA). The ALA Division that focuses on
Adult Services. Available: www.ala.org/RUSA.

U.S. Institute of Museum and Library Services. Available: www.imls.gov/index.htm.

Specific Service Responses

Commons

Clark, Wayne. 2000. *Activism in the Public Sphere: Exploring the Discourse of Political Participation*. Burlington, VT: Aldershot.

Kranich, Nancy, ed. 2001. *Libraries and Democracy: The Cornerstones of Liberty*.
Chicago: American Library Association.

McCabe, Ronald B. 2001. *Civic Librarianship: Renewing the Social Mission of the
Public Library*. Lanham, MD: Scarecrow Press.

McCook, Kathleen de la Peña. 2001. Authentic Discourse as a Means of Connection
Between Public Library Service Responses and Community Building Initiatives. *Reference and User Services Quarterly* 40 (Winter): 127–133.

McCook, Kathleen de la Peña. 2000. *A Place at the Table: Participating in Community Building*. Chicago: American Library Association.

McCook, Kathleen de la Peña. 2003. Public Libraries and Community. In *Encyclopedia of Community,* ed. Karen Christensen and David Levinson, 1114–111.
Thousand Oaks, CA: Sage.

Molz, Redmond Kathleen, and Phyllis Dain. 1999. *Civic Space/Cyberspace: The
American Public Library in the Information Age*. Cambridge, MA: MIT Press.

Community Information and Referral

2–1–1. Get Connected. Get Answers. United Way. Alliance for Information and
Referral Services. Available: www.211.org.

Alliance of Information and Referral Services. Available: www.airs.org.

Bajjaly, Stephen T. 1999. *The Community Networking Handbook*. Chicago: ALA
Editions.

Childers, Thomas. 1984. *Information and Referral: Public Libraries*. Norwood, NJ:
Ablex.

Croneberger, Robert. 1975. *The Library as a Community Information and Referral
Center.* ERIC ED108653. Morehead State University, KY: Appalachian Adult
Education Center.

Croneberger, Robert, and Carolyn Luck. 1975. Defining Information and Referral
Service. *Library Journal* 100 (November 1): 1984–1987.

Durrance, Joan C., and Karen E. Fisher-Pettigrew. 2003. Determining How
Libraries and Librarians Help. *Library Trends* 51 (Spring): 541–570.

Durrance, Joan C., and Karen E. Pettigrew. 2002. *Online Community Information: Creating a Nexus at Your Library.* Chicago: American Library Association.

Fisher, Karen E., and Joan C. Durrance. 2003. Information Communities. In *Encyclopedia of Community*, ed. Karen Christensen and David Levinson, 657–660. Thousand Oaks, CA: Sage.

Helpseeking in an Electronic World. Available: www.si.umich.edu/helpseek/About/index.html.

Jones, Clara S. 1978. *Public Library Information and Referral Service.* Syracuse, NY: Gaylord Professional Publications.

Maas, Norman L., and Dick Manikowski. 1997. *Guidelines for Establishing Community Information and Referral Services in Public Libraries.* 4th ed. Chicago: American Library Association.

McCook, Kathleen de la Peña. 2000. Service Integration and Libraries. *Reference and User Services Quarterly* 40 (Winter): 22–25.

Owens, Major R., and Miriam Braverman. 1974. *The Public Library and Advocacy: Information for Survival.* New York: Columbia Teachers College.

Pettigrew, Karen E., Joan C. Durrance, and Kenton T. Unruh. 2002. Facilitating Community Information Seeking Using the Internet: Findings from Three Public Library-Community Network Systems. *Journal of the American Society for Information Science and Technology* 53 (September): 894–903.

U.S. National Commission on Libraries and Information Science. 1983. *Final Report to the National Commission on Libraries and Information Science from the Community Information and Referral Task Force.* ERIC ED241014. Washington, DC: National Commission on Libraries and Information Science.

Current Topics and Titles

Adult Reading Round Table. Available: www.arrtreads.org.

American Library Association. Notable Books. Available: www.ala.org/rusa/notable.html.

American Library Association. Office for Public Programs. Available: www.ala.org/publicprograms.

Appleyard, J. A. 1990. *Becoming a Reader: The Experience of Fiction from Childhood to Adulthood.* Cambridge, MA: Cambridge University Press.

Balcom, Ted. 1992. *Book Discussion for Adults: A Leader's Guide.* Chicago: American Library Association.

Balcom, Ted. 2002. The Adult Reading Round Table. *Reference and User Services Quarterly* 41 (Spring): 238–243.

Booktalking: Quick and Simple. Available: http://nancykeane.com/booktalks.

Brandehoff, Susan E. 1996. ALA's Touring Shows Spur Programs: Traveling Exhibits ALA has Developed since 1983. *American Libraries* 27 (January): 85–86.

Carpenter, Kenneth E. 1996. *Toward a History of Libraries and Culture in America.* Washington, DC: Library of Congress.

Carrier, Esther Jane. 1965. *Fiction in Public Libraries, 1876–1900.* New York: Scarecrow Press.

Carrier, Esther Jane. 1985. *Fiction in Public Libraries, 1900–1950.* Littleton, CO: Libraries Unlimited.

Goodes, Pamela A. 1998. Writers Live at the Library. *Public Libraries* 37 (July/August): 240–241.

Gray, William S., and Ruth Munroe. 1929. *The Reading Interests and Habits of Adults.* New York: Macmillan.

Haines, Helen E. 1924. Modern Fiction and the Public Library. *Library Journal* 49 (May 15): 458–460.

Haines, Helen E. 1935. *Living with Books: The Art of Book Selection.* New York: Columbia University Press.

Hawthorne, Karen, and Jane E. Gibson. 2002. *Bulletin Board Power: Bridges to Life-long Learning.* Greenwood Village, CO: Libraries Unlimited.

Herald, Diana Tixier. 2000. *Genreflecting: A Guide to Reading Interests in Genre Fiction.* 5th ed. Englewood, CO: Libraries Unlimited.

Howell, R. Patton. 1989. *Beyond Literacy: The Second Gutenberg Revolution.* San Francisco: Saybrook.

Kaplan, Paul. 1998. The Benefits of Local Author Programs. *Public Libraries* 37 (July/August): 238.

Karetzky, Stephen. 1982. *Reading Research and Librarianship: A History and Analysis.* Westport, CT: Greenwood Press.

Korda, Michael. 2001. *Making the List: A Cultural History of the American Best Seller, 1900–1999.* New York: Barnes and Noble.

Local Book Festivals and Reading Programs. Institute of Museum and Library Services. Available: www.imls.gov/pubs/bookfest.htm.

Library of Congress. Center for the Book. Available: www.loc.gov/loc/cfbook.

Library of Congress. Center for the Book: State Center Affiliates. Available: www .loc.gov/loc/cfbook/stacen.html.

Library of Congress. National Book Festival. Available: www.loc.gov/bookfest/related sites/index.html.

Library of Congress. National Library Service for the Blind and Physically Handicapped. Available: www.loc.gov/nls.

Long, Sarah Ann. 2001. Foreword. In *Civic Librarianship: Renewing the Social Mission of the Public Library*, ed. Ronald B. McCabe, vii-ix. Lanham, MD: Scarecrow Press.

McCook, Kathleen de la Peña. 1993a. Considerations of Theoretical Bases for Readers' Advisory Services. In *Developing Readers' Advisory Services: Concepts and Commitments*, ed. Kathleen de la Peña McCook and Gary O. Rolstad, 7–12. New York: Neal-Schuman Publishers.

McCook, Kathleen de la Peña. 1993b. The First Virtual Reality. *American Libraries* 24 (July/August): 626–628.

McCook, Kathleen de la Peña, and Gary O. Rolstad, eds. 1993. *Developing Readers' Advisory Services: Concepts and Commitments.* New York: Neal-Schuman Publishers.

Manguel, Alberto. 1996. *A History of Reading.* New York: Penguin.

Nell, Victor. 1988. *Lost in a Book: The Psychology of Reading for Pleasure.* New Haven, CT: Yale University Press.

Nordmeyer, Ricki. 2001. Readers' Advisory Websites. *Reference and User Services Quarterly* 41 (Winter): 139–143.

Pearl, Nancy. 2002. *Now Read This II: A Guide to Mainstream Fiction, 1990–2001.* Greenwood Village, CO: Libraries Unlimited.

Pearl, Nancy. 2003. *Book Lust: Recommended Reading for Every Mood, Moment and Reason.* Seattle, WA: Sasquatch Books.

Pearl, Nancy, Martha Knappe, and Chris Higashi. 1999. *Now Read This: A Guide to Mainstream Fiction, 1978–1998.* Englewood, CO: Libraries Unlimited.

Radway, Janice A. 1997. *A Feeling for Books: The Book-of-the-Month Club, Literary Taste, and Middle Class Desire.* Chapel Hill, NC: University of North Carolina Press.

Salwak, Dale. 1999. *A Passion for Books.* New York: St. Martin's Press.

Saricks, Joyce G. 2001. *The Readers' Advisory Guide to Genre Fiction.* Chicago: American Library Association.

Saricks, Joyce G., and Nancy Brown. 1997. *Readers' Advisory Services in the Public Library.* 2nd ed. Chicago: American Library Association.

Shearer, Kenneth D. 1996. *Guiding the Reader to the Next Book.* New York: Neal-Schuman Publishers.

Shearer, Kenneth D., and Robert Burgin. 2002. *Readers' Advisor's Companion.* Littleton, CO: Libraries Unlimited.

Shorris, Earl. 2000. Promoting the Humanities, Or How to Make the Poor Dangerous. *American Libraries* 31 (May): 46–48.

Shorris, Earl. 2000. *Riches for the Poor.* New York: W. W. Norton and Company.

Smith, Duncan. 2000. Talking with Readers: A Competency Based Approach to Readers' Advisory Services. *Reference and User Services Quarterly* 40 (Winter): 135–142.

Waples, Douglas, and Ralph W. Tyler. 1931. *What People Want to Read About: A Study of Group Interests and a Survey of Problems in Adult Reading.* Chicago: University of Chicago Press.

Weiner, Stephen. 1998. Authors are a Community's Celebrities. *Public Libraries* 37 (July/August): 240.

Wilson, Louis R. 1938. *The Geography of Reading: A Study of the Distribution and Status of Libraries in the United States.* Chicago: University of Chicago Press.

Wyatt, Neal. 2002. A Year Inside Notable Books. *Reference and User Services Quarterly* 41 (Summer): 340–343.

Lifelong Learning

American Library Association. Office for Public Programs. Available: www.ala.org/publicprograms.

Burge, Elizabeth J. 1983. Adult Learners, Learning and Public Libraries. Special issue, *Library Trends* 31 (Spring).

Carr, David. 2003. *The Promise of Cultural Institutions*. Walnut Creek, CA: AltaMira Press.

Dane, William J. 1990. John Cotton Dana: A Contemporary Appraisal of His Contributions and Lasting Influence on the Library and Museum Worlds 60 Years After His Death. *Art Libraries Journal* 15: 5–9.

Dilevko, Juris, and Lisa Gottlieb. 2003. Resurrecting a Neglected Idea: The Re-Introduction of Library-Museum Hybrids. *Library Quarterly* 73 (April): 160–198.

Falk, John H., and Lynn D. Dierking. 2000. *Learning From Museums: Visitor Experiences and the Making of Meaning*. Walnut Creek, CA: Rowman and Littlefield.

Houle, Cyril O. 1979. Seven Adult Educational Roles of the Public Library. In *As Much to Learn as to Teach: Essays in Honor of Lester Asheim*, ed. Joel M. Lee and Beth A. Hamilton, 94–116. Hamden, CT: Linnet.

Johnson, Debra Wilcox. 1999. The Library as Place: Cultural Programming for Adults. *American Libraries* 30 (June/July): 92.

Lear, Brett W. 2002. *Adult Programs in the Library*. Chicago: American Library Association.

Mates, Barbara T. 2003. *5-Star Programming and Services for your 55+ Customers*. Chicago: American Library Association.

McCook, Kathleen de la Peña, and Maria A. Jones. 2002. Cultural Heritage Institutions and Community Building. *Reference and User Services Quarterly* 41 (Summer): 326–329.

Monroe, Margaret E. 1981. The Cultural Role of the Public Library. *Advances in Librarianship* 11: 1–49.

National Endowment for the Humanities. Available: www.neh.fed.us.

National Endowment for the Humanities. State Humanities Councils. Available: www.neh.gov/whoweare/statecouncils.html.

Rubin, Rhea Joyce. 1997. *Humanities Programming: A How-To-Do-It Manual*. New York: Neal-Schuman Publishers.

U.S. Department of Education. 2000. *Lifelong Learning NCES Task Force: Final Report, Volume II, Working Paper No. 2000-16b*. Washington, DC: U.S. Department of Education.

Van Fleet, Connie. 1990. Lifelong Learning Theory and the Provision of Adult Services. In *Adult Services: An Enduring Focus for Public Libraries,* ed. Kathleen M. Heim (de la Peña McCook) and Danny P. Wallace, 166–211. Chicago: American Library Association.

Van Fleet, Connie, and Douglas Raber. 1990. The Public Library as a Social/Cultural Institution: Alternative Perspectives and Changing Contexts. In *Adult Services: An Enduring Focus for Public Libraries,* ed. Kathleen M. Heim (de la Peña McCook) and Danny P. Wallace, 456–500. Chicago: American Library Association.

Watkins, Christine. 2000. Live at the Library 2000: Building Cultural Communities. *American Libraries* 31 (June/July): 69.

Cultural Awareness

American Library Association. Ethnic and Multicultural Information Exchange Round Table. Available: http://lonestar.utsa.edu/jbarnett/emie.html.

American Library Association. Gay, Lesbian, Bisexual, and Transgendered Round Table. Available: http://calvin.usc.edu/~trimmer/ala_hp.html.

Balderrama, Sandra Ríos. 2000. This Trend Called Diversity. *Library Trends* 49 (Summer): 194–214.

Carmichael, James V., Jr. 1998. *Daring to Find Our Names: The Search Lesbigay Library History.* Westport, CT: Greenwood.

Dawson, Alma. 2000. Celebrating African-American Librarians and Librarianship. *Library Trends* 49 (Summer): 49–87.

Güereña, Salvador, and Edward Erazo. 2000. Latinos and Librarianship. *Library Trends* 49 (Summer): 139–181.

Joyce, Steven. 2000. Lesbian, Gay and Bisexual Library Service: A Review of the Literature. *Public Libraries* 39 (September/October): 270–279.

Liu, Mengxiong. 2000. The History and Status of Chinese Americans in Librarianship. *Library Trends* 49 (Summer): 109–137.

McCook, Kathleen de la Peña, ed. 2000. Ethnic Diversity in Library and Information Science. *Library Trends* 49 (Summer): 1–214.

Patterson, Lotsee. 2000. History and Status of Native Americans in Librarianship. *Library Trends* 49, no. 1 (Summer): 182–193.

Roy, Loriene. 2000. To Support and Model Native American Library Services. *Texas Library Journal* 76 (Spring): 32–35.

Yamashita, Kenneth A. 2000. Asian/Pacific American Librarians Association: A History of APALA and Its Founders. *Library Trends* 49 (Summer): 88–108.

Local History and Genealogy

American Association for State and Local History. Available: www.aaslh.org.

Archibald, Robert R. 1999. *A Place to Remember: Using History to Build Community.* Walnut Creek, CA: Rowman and Littlefield.

Reference and User Services Association (RUSA). 1993. Guidelines for Establishing Local History Collections. Available: www.ala.org/ala/rusa/rusaprotools/referenceguide/guidelinesestablishing.htm.

Reference and User Services Association (RUSA). 1999. Guidelines for Developing Beginning Genealogical Collections and Services. Available: www.ala.org/ala/rusa/rusaprotools/referenceguide/guidelinesdeveloping.htm.

Basic Literacy

American Library Association, Office for Literacy and Outreach Services. Available: www.ala.org/ala/olos.

BuildLiteracy. American Library Association. Available: www.buildliteracy.org/index.htm.

DeCandido, GraceAnne, ed. 2001. *Literacy and Libraries: Learning From Case Studies*. Chicago: American Library Association.

Lyman, Helen H. 1973. *Library Materials in Service to the Adult New Reader*. Chicago: American Library Association.

Lyman, Helen H. 1976. *Reading and the Adult New Reader*. Chicago: American Library Association.

Lyman, Helen H. 1977. *Literacy and the Nation's Libraries*. Chicago: American Library Association.

McCook, Kathleen de la Peña, and Peggy Barber. 2002a. *Chronology of Milestones for Libraries and Adult Lifelong Learning and Literacy*. ERIC ED458888. Washington, DC.

McCook, Kathleen de la Peña, and Peggy Barber. 2002b. Public Policy as a Factor Influencing Adult Lifelong Learning, Adult Literacy and Public Libraries. *Reference and User Services Quarterly* 42.1 (Fall): 66–75.

National Assessments of Adult Literacy. Available: http://nces.ed.gov/naal.

National Institute for Literacy. Available: www.nifl.gov.

Rolstad, Gary O. 1990. Literacy Services in Public Libraries. In *Adult Services: An Enduring Focus for Public Libraries*, ed. Kathleen M. Heim (de la Peña McCook) and Danny P. Wallace, 245–265. Chicago: American Library Association.

U.S. National Center for Education Statistics. 2002. *Programs for Adults in Public Library Outlets*. Washington, DC: National Center for Education Statistics.

Information Literacy

American Library Association. Presidential Commission on Information Literacy: Final Report. (Release Date: January 10, 1989). Available: www.ala.org/ala/acrl/acrlpubs/whitepapers/presidential.htm.

Association for College and Research Libraries (ACRL). Information Literacy Toolkit. Available: www.ala.org/acrl. See especially the ACRL paper, Guidelines for Distance Learning Library Services.

Breivik, Patricia Senn, Vicki Hancock, and J. A. Senn. 1998. A Progress Report on Information Literacy: An Update on the American Library Association Presidential Committee on Information Literacy: Final Report. Chicago: Association of College and Research Libraries. Available: www.ala.org/ala/acrl/acrlpubs/whitepapers/progressreport.htm.

Reference and User Services Association (RUSA). 1997. Guidelines for the Introduction of Electronic Information Resources to Users. Available: www.ala.org/ala/rusa/rusaprotools/referenceguide/guidelinesintroduction.htm.

Spitzer, Kathleen L., Michael B. Eisenberg, and Carrie A. Lowe. 1998. *Information Literacy: Essential Skills for the Information Age*. ERIC ED427780. Syracuse, NY: ERIC Clearinghouse on Information and Technology.

Formal Learning Support

Association of College and Research Libraries. Guidelines for Distance Learning Library Services. Available: www.ala.org/acrl/guides/distlrng.html.

Kleist-Tesch, Jane M. 1998. Homeschoolers and the Public Library. *Journal of Youth Services* 11 (Spring): 231–241.

General Information

Curry, Ann, and Gayle J. E. Harris. 2000. Reference Librarians' Attitudes Toward the World Wide Web. *Public Library Quarterly* 18: 25–38.

Frank, Donald G., et al. 1999. The Changing Nature of Reference and Information Services: Predictions and Realities. *Reference and User Services Quarterly* 39 (Winter): 151–157.

Janes, Joseph, and Chrystie Hill. 2002. Finger on the Pulse: Librarians Describe Evolving Reference Practice in an Increasingly Digital World. *Reference and User Services Quarterly* 42 (Fall): 54–65.

Reference and User Services Association (RUSA). 1996. Guidelines for Behavioral Performance of Reference and Information Service Providers. Available: www .ala.org/ala/rusa/rusaprotools/referenceguide/guidelinesbehavioral.htm.

Reference and User Services Association (RUSA). 2000. Guidelines for Information Services. Available: www.ala.org/ala/rusa/rusaprotools/referenceguide/guide linesinformation.htm.

Reference and User Services Association (RUSA). 2003. Professional Competencies for Reference and User Services Librarians. Available: www.ala.org/ala/rusa/ rusaprotools/referenceguide/professional.htm.

Ross, Catherine Sheldrick, and Kirsti Nilsen. 2000. Has the Internet Changed Anything in Reference?: The Library Visit Study, Phase 2. *Reference and User Services Quarterly* 40 (Winter): 147–155.

Government Information

Government Documents Round Table. Available: http://sunsite.berkeley.edu/ GODORT.

Business and Career Information; Consumer Information

Bleiweiss, Maxine. 1997. *Helping Business: the Library's Role in Community Economic Development.* New York: Neal-Schuman Publishers.

Business Reference and Services Section (BRASS). Reference and User Services Association. Available: www.ala.org/ala/rusa/rusaourassoc/rusasections/brass/ brass.htm.

Durrance, Joan C. 1993. *Serving Job Seekers and Career Changers.* Chicago: Public Library Association.

9. Youth Services

Books and Parts of Books

American Association of School Librarians and Association for Educational Communications and Technology. 1998. *Information Power: Building Partnerships for Learning*. Chicago: American Library Association.

American Library Association. 1984. *Realities: Educational Reform in a Learning Society*. Chicago: American Library Association.

American Library Association. 2003. *Young Adults Deserve the Best. Professional Development Center*. Available: www.ala.org/ala/yalsa/professsionaldev/ya competencies/competencies.htm.

Aries, Philipe. 1962. *Centuries of Childhood*. New York: Random House.

Association for Library Service to Children (ALSC). 1999. *Competencies For Librarians Serving Children in Public Libraries*. Available: www.ala.org/alsc/competencies.html.

Association for Library Service to Children (ALSC). 2000. *Intellectual Freedom for Children: The Censor is Coming*. Chicago: American Library Association.

Baker, Augusta, and Ellin Greene. 1987. *Storytelling Art and Technique*. New York: Bowker.

Bellah, Robert N., et al. 1985. *Habits of the Heart: Individualism and Commitment in American Life*. Berkeley, CA: University of California Press.

Benton Foundation. 1996. *Buildings, Books, and Bytes: Libraries and Communities in the Digital Age*. Washington, DC: Benton Foundation.

Booktalking: Quick and Simple. Available: http://nancykeane.com/booktalks.

Boyer, Ernest L. 1991. *Ready to Learn: A Mandate for the Nation*. Princeton, NJ: Princeton University Press.

Bransford, John D., Ann L. Brown, and Rodney R. Cocking, eds. 1999. *How People Learn: Brain, Mind, Experience, and School*. Washington, DC: National Academy Press.

Braverman, Miriam. 1979. *Youth, Society and the Public Library*. Chicago: American Library Association.

Bredekamp, Sue, ed. 1987. *Developmentally Appropriate Practice in Early Childhood Programs Serving Children from Birth through Age 8*. Exp. ed. Washington, DC: National Association for the Education of Young Children.

Broderick, Dorothy. 1965. *An Introduction to Children's Work in Public Libraries*. New York: H. W. Wilson.

Chelton, Mary K. 2000. *Excellence in Library Services to Young Adults: The Nation's Top Programs*. Chicago: American Library Association.

Connor, Jane Gardner. 1990. *Children's Library Services Handbook*. Phoenix, AZ: Oryx.

Council on Interracial Books for Children. 1980. *Guidelines for Selecting Bias-free Textbooks and Storybooks*. New York: Council on Interracial Books for Children.

Cross, Gary. 1997. *Kids' Stuff: Toys and the Changing World of American Childhood.* Cambridge, MA: Harvard University Press.

Day, Frances Ann. 1999. *Multicultural Voices in Contemporary Literature: A Resource for Teachers.* Rev. ed. Portsmouth, NH: Heinemann.

DeBell, Matthew, and Chris Chapman. 2003. *Computer and Internet Use by Children and Adolescents in 2001.* Washington, DC: U.S. Department of Education. Available: http://nces.ed.gov/pubsearch/pubsinfo.asp?pubid=2004014 (accessed December 4, 2003).

DeWitt Wallace-Reader's Digest Fund. 1999. *Public Libraries as Partners in Youth Development.* New York: DeWitt Wallace-Reader's Digest Fund.

Dictionary of Occupational Titles. CD-ROM. U.S. Department of Employment and Training. U.S. Employment Service, 1998.

Doyle, Christina S. 1994. *Information Literacy in an Information Society: A Concept for the Information Age.* ED372763. Syracuse, NY: ERIC Clearing House on Information and Technology, Syracuse University.

Dresang, Eliza T. 1999. *Radical Change: Books for Youth in a Digital Age.* New York: H. W. Wilson.

Dresang, Eliza T. 2000. Outstanding Literature: Pura Belpré and Américas Selections with Special Appeal in the Digital Age. In *Library Services to Youth of Hispanic Heritage*, ed. Barbara Immroth and Kathleen de la Peña McCook, 69–87. Jefferson, NC: McFarland and Co.

Evans, Sara M., and Harry C. Boyte. 1986. *Free Spaces: The Sources of Democratic Change in America.* New York: Harper and Row.

Fasick, Adele M. 1991. *Managing Children's Services in the Public Library.* Englewood, CO: Libraries Unlimited.

Federal Interagency Forum on Child and Family Statistics. 1999. *America's Children: Key National Indicators of Well-being.* Washington, DC: U.S. Government Printing Office.

Feinberg, Sandra, Joan F. Kuchner, and Sari Feldman. 1998. *Learning Environments for Young Children: Rethinking Library Spaces and Services.* Chicago: American Library Association.

Fletcher, William I. 1876. Public Libraries and the Young. In *Public Libraries in the United States: Their History, Condition and Management*, 412–418. Washington, DC: Department of the Interior, Bureau of Education.

Garbarino, James, et al. 1992. *Children in Danger: Coping with the Consequences of Community Violence.* San Francisco: Jossey-Bass.

Gleason, Eliza Atkins. 1941. *The Southern Negro and the Public Library: A Study of Government and Administration of Public Library Service to Negroes in the South.* Chicago: University of Chicago Press.

Gnehm, Kurstin Finch. 2002. *Youth Development and Public Libraries, Tools for Success.* Evanston, IL: Urban Libraries Council.

Gonzalez, Lucia M. 2000. Developing Culturally Integrated Children's Programs. In *Library Services to Youth of Hispanic Heritage*, ed. Barbara Immroth and Kathleen de la Peña McCook, 19–21. Jefferson, NC: McFarland and Co.

Gross, Elizabeth Henry. 1963. *Children's Services in Public Libraries.* Chicago: American Library Association.

Gregory, Vicki L., Marilyn Stauffer, and Thomas Keene, Jr. 1999. *Multicultural Resources on the Internet: The United States and Canada.* New York: Neal-Schuman Publishers.

Halperin, Wendy Anderson. 1998. *Once Upon a Company: A True Story.* New York: Orchard.

Hawes, Joseph M. 1991. *The Children's Rights Movement: A History of Advocacy and Protection.* Boston: Twayne.

Healy, Jane M. 1998. *Failure to Connect: How Computers Affect our Children's Minds—For Better and Worse.* New York: Simon and Schuster.

Heyns, Barbara. 1978. *Summer Learning and the Effects of Schooling.* New York: Academic Press.

Hildebrand, Janet. 1997. Is Privacy Reserved for Adults? Children's Rights at the Public Library. In *School Library Journal's Best: A Reader for Children's, Young Adult, and School Librarians,* ed. Lillian N. Gerhardt, 419–422. New York: Neal-Schuman Publishers.

Himmel, Ethel, and William James Wilson. 1998. *Planning for Results: A Public Library Transformation Process.* Chicago: American Library Association.

Immroth, Barbara, and Kathleen de la Peña McCook. 2000. *Library Services to Youth of Hispanic Heritage.* Jefferson, NC: McFarland and Co.

Jeffery, Debby Ann. 1995. *Literate Beginnings: Programs for Babies and Toddlers.* Chicago: American Library Association.

Jones, Dolores Blythe, and Anne H. Lundin. 1998. *Building a Special Collection of Children's Literature in Your Library.* Chicago: American Library Association.

Jones, Patrick. 1998. *Connecting Young Adults and Libraries: A How-To-Do-It Manual.* 2nd ed. New York: Neal-Schuman Publishers.

Jones, Patrick, and Linda L. Waddle. 2002. *New Directions for Library Service to Young Adults.* Chicago: American Library Association.

Kafai, Yasmin. 1993. *Minds in Play: Computer Game Design as a Context for Children's Learning.* Hillsdale, NJ: Erlbaum.

Kleiner, Anne, and Laurie Lewis. 2003. *Internet Access in U.S. Public Schools and Classrooms: 1994–2002.* Washington, DC: U.S. Department of Education. Available: http://nces.ed.gov/pubsearch/pubsinfo.asp?pubid=2004011.

Kohn, Alfie. 1992. *No Contest: The Case Against Competition.* Boston: Houghton Mifflin.

Kohn, Alfie. 1993. *Punished by Rewards: The Trouble with Gold Stars, Incentive Plans, A's, Praise, and Other Bribes.* Boston: Houghton Mifflin.

Kruse, Ginny Moore, and Kathleen Horning. 1991. *Multicultural Literature for Children and Young Adults.* Madison, WI: Wisconsin Department of Public Instruction.

Kuharets, Olga. R., ed. 2001. *Venture Into Cultures.* 2nd ed. Chicago: American Library Association.

Kuipers, Barbara. 1995. *American Indian Reference and Resource Books for Children and Young Adults.* 2nd ed. Englewood, CO: Libraries Unlimited.

Kuklin, Susan. 1998. *Iqbal Masih and the Crusaders Against Child Slavery.* New York: Holt.

Leslie, R., et al. 2001. *Igniting the Spark: Library Programs that Inspire High School Patrons.* Westport: CT: Libraries Unlimited.

Long, Harriet G. 1969. *Public Library Service to Children: Foundation and Development.* Metuchen, NJ: Scarecrow Press.

Lundin, Anne H., and Carol W. Cubberley. 1995. *Teaching Children's Literature: A Resource Guide with a Directory of Courses.* Jefferson, NC: McFarland and Co.

McClure, Charles R., et al. 1987. *Planning and Role Setting for Public Libraries: A Manual of Options and Procedures.* Chicago: American Library Association.

McCook, Kathleen de la Peña, ed. 2000. Ethnic Diversity in Library and Information Science. *Library Trends* 49 (Summer): 1–214.

Metoyer-Duran, Cheryl. 1993. *Gatekeepers in Ethnolinguistic Communities.* Norwood, NJ: Albex.

Minkel, Walter, and Roxanne Hsu Feldman. 1999. *Delivering Web Reference Services to Young People.* Chicago: American Library Association.

Molz, Redmond Kathleen, and Phyllis Dain. 1999. *Civic Space/Cyberspace: The American Public Library in the Information Age.* Cambridge, MA: MIT Press.

Moore, Anne Carroll. 1969. *My Roads to Childhood: Views and Reviews of Children's Books.* Boston: Horn Book.

Murnane, Richard J., and Frank Levy. 1996. *Teaching the New Basic Skills: Principles for Educating Children to Thrive in a Changing Economy.* New York: Free Press.

Muse, Daphne. ed. 1997. *The New Press Guide to Multicultural Resources for Young Readers.* New York: New Press.

National Education Association. 1899. *Report of the Committee on the Relations of Public Libraries to Public Schools.* Washington, DC: National Education Association.

National Research Council. 1998. *Starting Out Right: A Guide to Promoting Children's Reading Success,* ed. Susan M. Burns, Peg Griffin, and Catherine E. Snow. Washington, DC: National Academy Press.

Negroponte, Nicholas. 1995. *Being Digital.* New York: Knopf.

Nelson, Sandra. 2001. *The New Planning for Results: A Streamlined Approach.* Chicago: American Library Association.

Nespecca, Sue McCleaf. 1994. *Library Programming for Families with Young Children.* New York: Neal-Schuman Publishers.

New York Library Association. Task Force on Standards for Youth Services. 1984. *Standards for Youth Services in Public Libraries of New York State.* New York: Youth Services Section of NYLA.

Nichols, May Anne, and C. Allen Nichols. 1998. *Young Adults and Public Libraries.* Westport, CT: Greenwood Press.

Nilsen, Alleen, and Kenneth L. Donelson. 2001. Literature for Today's Young Adults. 6th ed. New York: Longman.

Odean, Kathleen. 2003. *Great Books for Babies and Toddlers: More than 500 Recommended Books for Your Child's First Three Years.* New York: Ballantine.

O'Dell, K. 2002. *Library Materials and Services for Teen Girls.* Greenwood Village, CO: Libraries Unlimited.

Olcott, Frances Jenkins. 1905. Rational Library Work with Children and the Preparation For It. In *Proceedings of the American Library Association Conference*, 71–75. Chicago: American Library Association.

Papert, Seymour. 1993. *The Children's Machine: Rethinking School in the Age of the Computer*. New York: Basic Books.

Reid, R. 2002. *Something Funny Happened at the Library: How to Create Humorous Programs for Children and Young Adults*. Chicago: American Library Association.

Rheingold, Howard. 1993. *The Virtual Community: Homesteading on the Electronic Frontier*. Reading, MA: Addison-Wesley.

Riechel, Rosemarie. 1991. *Reference Services for Children and Young Adults*. Hamden, CT: Library Professional Publications.

Rollock, Barbara T. 1988. *Public Library Services for Children*. Hamden, CT: Shoestring Press.

Rong, Xue Lan, and Judith Preissle. 1998. *Educating Immigrant Students: What We Need to Know to Meet the Challenges*. Thousand Oaks, CA: Corwin/Sage.

Rovenger, Judith, and Ristiina Wigg. 1986. *Libraries Serving Youth; Directions for Service in the 1990s*. New Paltz, NY: New York Library Association.

Rushkoff, Douglas. 1998. *Playing the Future: How Kids' Culture Can Teach us to Thrive in an Age of Chaos*. New York: HarperCollins.

Sanders, Rickie, and Mattson, Mark T. 1998. *Growing Up in America: An Atlas of Youth in the USA*. New York: Simon and Schuster/Macmillan.

Sayers, Frances Clarke. 1972. *Anne Carroll Moore*. New York: Atheneum.

Schall, Lucy. 2003. *Booktalks and More : Motivating Teens to Read*. Westport, CT: Libraries Unlimited.

Schall, Lucy. 2001. *Booktalks Plus: Motivating Teens to Read*. Englewood, CO: Libraries Unlimited.

Sims, Rudine. 1982. *Shadow and Substance: Afro-American Experience in Contemporary Children's Fiction*. Urbana, IL: National Council of Teachers of English.

Slapin, Beverly, and Doris Seala, ed. 1992. *Through Indian Eyes: The Native Experience in Books for Children*. 3rd ed. Philadelphia, PA: New Society Publishers.

Smith, Henrietta M. 1994. *The Coretta Scott King Awards Book: From Visions to Reality*. Chicago: American Library Association.

Smith, Henrietta M. 1999. *The Coretta Scott King Awards Book, 1970–1999*. Chicago: American Library Association.

Smith, Henrietta M. 2004. *The Coretta Scott King Awards Book, 1970–2004*. Chicago: American Library Association.

Smith, Laura. 1992. *Children's Book Awards International, 1990 through 2000*. Jefferson, NC: McFarland and Co.

Sommerville, John. 1982. *The Rise and Fall of Childhood*. Beverly Hills, CA: Sage.

Staerkel, Kathleen, Mary Fellows, and Sue McCleaf Nespecca. 1995. *Youth Services Librarians as Managers: A How-to Guide from Budgeting to Personnel*.

Chicago: American Library Association/Association for Library Service to Children.

Steiner, Stanley F. 2001. *Promoting a Global Community through Multicultural Children's Literature*. Englewood, CO: Libraries Unlimited.

Tapscott, Don. 1998. *Growing Up Digital: The Rise of the Net Generation*. New York: McGraw-Hill.

Teale, William H. 1995. Public Libraries and Emergent Literacy: Helping Set the Foundation for School Success. In *Achieving School Readiness: Public Libraries and National Education Goal No. 1*, ed. Barbara Froling Immroth and Viki Ash-Geisler. Chicago: American Library Association.

Thomas, Fannette H. 1982. The Genesis of Children's Library Services in the American Public Library, 1876–1906. PhD diss., University of Wisconsin-Madison.

Turkle, Sherry. 1995. *Life on the Screen: Identity in the Age of the Internet*. New York: Simon and Schuster.

U.S. Census Bureau. 1993. *We the American Children*. Washington, DC: U.S. Department of Commerce, Census Bureau.

U.S. National Center for Education Statistics. 1995. *Services and Resources for Children and Young Adults in Public Libraries*. Washington, DC: U.S. Department of Education.

U.S. National Center for Education Statistics. 1988. *Services and Resources for Young Adults in Public Libraries*. Washington, DC: Government Printing Office.

Walter, Virginia A. 1992. *Output Measures for Public Library Service to Children: A Manual of Standardized Procedures*. Chicago: American Library Association.

Walter, Virginia A. 1995. *Output Measures and More: Planning and Evaluating Public Library Services for Young Adults*. Chicago: American Library Association.

Walter, Virginia A. 2001. *Children and Libraries: Getting It Right*. Chicago: American Library Association.

Walter, Virginia A., and Elaine Meyers. 2003. *Teens and Libraries: Getting It Right*. Chicago: American Library Association.

Willett, Holly G. 1995. *Public Library Youth Services: A Public Policy Approach*. Norwood, NJ: Ablex.

Wishy, Bernard. 1968. *The Child and the Republic: The Dawn of Modern American Child Nurture*. Philadelphia, PA: University of Pennsylvania Press.

Yaakov, Juliette, and Anne Price. 2003. *Children's Catalog*. New York: H. W. Wilson.

Young Adult Library Services Association. 2003. *Young Adults Deserve the Best. Professional Development Center*. Available: www.ala.org/ala/yalsa/professsional dev/yacompetencies/competencies.htm.

Articles

Agosto, Denise E. 2001. Bridging the Cultural Gap: Ten Steps Toward a More Multicultural Youth Library. *Journal of Library Services in Libraries* 4 (Spring); 38–41.

Aldrich, Stacey. 1999. Sound Bytes of Possibilities. *Journal of Youth Services in Libraries* 12 (Winter): 5–9.

American Library Association. Best Books for Young Adults. *Booklist.* Available: www.ala.org/ala/booklist/booklist.htm.

American Library Association. Notable Children's Books. *Booklist.* Available: www .ala.org/ala/booklist/booklist.htm.

American Library Association. Notable Children's Media. *Booklist.* Available: www .ala.org/ala/booklist/booklist.htm.

Anderson, Sheila B. 2000. I Stink and My Feet are Too Big! Training Librarians to Work with Teens. *Voice of Youth Advocates* 22 (February): 388–390.

Anderson, Sheila. B., and John P. Bradford. 2001. State-Level Commitment to Public Library Services to Young Adults. *Journal of Youth Services in Libraries* 14 (Spring): 23–27.

Arnold, Renae. 2002. Coming Together for Children: A Guide to Early Learning Childhood Programming. *Journal of Youth Services in Libraries* 15 (Winter): 24–30.

Barban, L. 2003. More Than "May I Help You": The Assertive Children's Librarian. *Public Libraries* 42 (March/April.): 73–74.

Bingham, Anne. 2002. Goin' Someplace Special: Trends in Children's Literature. *Alki* 18 (July): 14–15.

Bird, B. 2002. Solving the Mystery: Children's Librarianship and How to Nurture It. *Australasian Public Libraries and Information Services* 15 (March): 14–23.

Bishop, Kay, et al. 2001. Responding to Developmental Stages in Reference Service to Children. *Public Libraries* 40 (November/December): 354–358.

Bishop, Kay, and Pat Bauer. 2002. Attracting Young Adults to Public Libraries: Frances Henne/YALSA/VOYA Research Grant Results. *Journal of Youth Services in Libraries* 15 (Winter): 36–44.

Bitterman, Lisa. 2002. Across Towns and Across Times: Library Service to Young People in Rural Libraries. *Rural Libraries* 22: 43–62.

Blumson, L. 2003. Libraries for Lifelong Learning in Queensland: Towards the Smart State. *Australasian Public Libraries and Information Services* 16 (March): 17–20.

Bussmann, I., et al. 2000. New Services to Develop Children's and Young People's Information Skills–The European Projects CHILIAS and VERITY. *New Review of Children's Literature and Librarianship* 6: 137–146.

Campbell, Patty. 1994. The Sand in the Oyster: White Children's Book Authors' Books on Multicultural Topics. *The Horn Book Magazine* 70 (July/August): 491.

Chelton, Mary Kay. 1997. Three in Five Public Library Users Are Youth. *Public Libraries* (March/April): 104–108.

Chernek, V. 2002. Baltimore County Students and Parents Say Yes! to Library Summer School Program Involving Online Instruction and Tutoring. *Book Report* 20 (January/February): 49.

Cheumwattana, A., et al. 2002. Small is Beautiful: The Library Train for Homeless Children. *Library Management* 23 (1/2): 88–92.

Clark, Marilyn L. 1997. The Public Library and Homework Help. *Public Libraries* 36 (January/February): 19–20.

Costello, J., et al. 2001. Promoting Public Library Partnerships with Youth Agencies. *Journal of Youth Services in Libraries* 15 (Winter): 8–15.

Cox, R. O. 2002. Lost Boys. *Voice of Youth Advocates* 25 (June): 172–173.

Cresswell, Stephen. 1996. The Last Days of Jim Crow in Southern Libraries. *Libraries and Culture* 31 (Summer/Fall): 557–573.

Crew, Hilary S. 2002. Five Foot Bookshelf: Essential Books for Professionals Who Serve Teens. *Voice of Youth Advocates* 25 (October): 260.

Curran, Charles. 1990. Information Literacy and the Public Librarian. *Public Libraries* 29 (November/December): 349–353.

YALSA Research Committee. 2001. Current Research Related to Young Adult Services. *Journal of Youth Services in Libraries* 14 (Winter): 20, 25–30.

Danley, Elizabeth. 2003. The Public Children's Librarian as Educator. *Public Libraries* 42 (March/April): 98–101.

DeMarco, P. 2003. Teens are a Work in Progress: Finding our Way in a Construction Zone. *Voice of Youth Advocates* 25 (February): 440–442.

Dresang, Eliza T. 1997. Influence of the Digital Environment on Literature for Youth: Radical Change in the Handheld Book. *Library Trends* 45 (Spring): 639–663.

Dresang, Eliza T., et al. 2003. Project CATE: Using Outcome Measures to Assess School-age Children's Use of Technology in Urban Public Libraries: A Collaborative Research Process. *Library and Information Science Research* 25 (no. 1): 19–42.

Epstein, Connie C. 2001. Create a World for Young Readers. *The Writer* 114 (June): 34.

Feinberg, Sandra, and Caryn Rogoff. 1998. Diversity Takes Children to a Friendly Family Place. *American Libraries* 29 (August): 50–52.

Fenwick, Sara Innis. 1976. Library Services to Children and Young People. *Library Trends* 25 (Summer): 329–360.

Fine, J. R. 2001. From the Field: Reaping the Benefits of Partnerships. *Journal of Youth Services in Libraries* 15 (Fall): 16–22.

Fisher, H. 2000. Children's and Young Adult Service: Like a Box of Chocolates. *Australasian Public Libraries and Information Services* 13 (May): 113–118.

Fitzgibbons, Shirley. 2001a. Libraries and Literacy: A Preliminary Survey of the Literature. *IFLA Journal* 27: 91–106.

Fitzgibbons, Shirley. 2001b. School and Public Library Relationships. *Journal of Youth Services in Libraries* 13 (Spring): 3–7.

Geloff, K., et al. 2002. Library Services to Homeless Youth. *Alki* 18 (July): 16.

Goldsmith, F. 2001. Literacy Daycamp at the Library: Collaborating with Coworkers and Teens. *Voice of Youth Advocates* 23 (February): 408–409.

Gorman, M. 2002. Wiring Teens to the Library. *Library Journal part Net Connect* (Summer): 18–20.

Gross, M. 2000. The Imposed Query and Information Services for Children. *Journal of Youth Services in Libraries* 13 (Winter): 10–17.

Hake, K. 2000. Programming and Children's Services. *Bookmobiles and Outreach Services* 3 (no. 2): 7–10.

Hamilton, Virginia. 1999. Sentinels in Long Still Rows. *American Libraries* 30 (June/July): 68–71.

Henricks, S. 2001. Reconnecting with Teens. *The Unabashed Librarian* 121: 24–28.

Hewins, Caroline. 1892. Yearly Report on Boys' and Girls' Reading. *Library Journal* 7 (July/August): 182–190.

Hilyard, N. B. 2002. Assets and Outcomes: New Directions in Young Adult Services in Public Libraries. *Public Libraries* 41 (August/September): 195–199.

Howrey, Sara P. 2003. De Colores: The Universal Language of Bilingual Storytime. *American Libraries* 34 (October): 38–40, 42–43.

Hunenberg, D. 2002. Duh!!! Seven Tips for Improving Customer Service to Teens. *The Unabashed Librarian* 125: 10–12.

Ishizuka, K. 2003. Girl Scouts Build Big Ugly Library. *School Library Journal* 49 (March): 26.

Janes, J. 2003. Digital Reference for Teens. *Voice of Youth Advocates* 25 (February): 451.

Jenkins, Christine A. 1996. Women of ALA Youth Services and Professional Jurisdiction: Of Nightingales, Newberies, Realism, and the Right Books, 1937–1945. *Library Trends* 44 (Spring): 813–839.

Jenkins, Christine A. 2000. The History of Youth Services Librarianship: A Review of the Research Literature. *Libraries and Culture* 35 (Winter): 103–139.

Jones, Patrick. 2001a. Showing You the Money: LSTA Funds and Fifty-two Resources to Find Funding for Youth Services in Libraries. *Journal of Youth Services in Libraries* 15 (Fall): 33–38.

Jones, Patrick. 2001b. Why We Are Kids Best Assets. *School Library Journal* 47 (November): 44–47.

Kinney, M. S. 2001. A Bird's (or State's) Eye View of Cooperation. *Journal of Youth Services in Libraries* 15 (Fall): 25.

Lee, R. 2000. Remember All the Nifty Children's Programs you Had? Programs Like... *American Libraries* 31 (February): 46–47.

Levine, A. 2002. Providing Information on Sexuality: Librarians Can Help Youth Become Sexually Healthy Adults. *Journal of Youth Services in Libraries* 15 (Winter): 45–48.

Locke, Jill. 1992. Summer Reading Activities—Way Back When. *Journal of Youth Services in Libraries* 6 (Fall): 72–77.

Lundin, Anne H. 1993. The Company We Keep: Advisory Services for Youth. *Collection Building* 12: 45–56.

Lundin, Anne. 1996. The Pedagogical Context of Women in Children's Services and Literature Scholarship. *Library Trends* 44 (Winter): 840–850.

Machado, Julie et al. 2000. A Survey of Best Practices in Youth Services Around the Country. *Journal of Youth Services in Libraries* 13 (Winter): 30–35.

McCook, Kathleen de la Peña. 2001. Authentic Discourse as a Means of Connection between Public Library Service Responses and Community-Building Initiatives. *Reference and User Services Quarterly* 41 (Winter): 127–133.

McCook, Kathleen de la Peña, and Rachel Meyer. 2001. Public Libraries and Comprehensive Community Initiatives for Youth Development. *Public Libraries* 40 (September/October): 282–288.

McKechnie, L. E. F. 2001. Children's Access to Services in Canadian Public Libraries. *Canadian Journal of Information and Library Science* 26 (December): 37–55.

McNeil-Nix, H. 2001. Family Friendly Libraries Are Us. *Journal of Youth Services in Libraries* 14 (Winter): 17–19.

Mediavilla, Cindy. 1998. Homework Assistance Programs in Public Libraries: Helping Johnny Read. In *Young Adults and Public Libraries: A Handbook of Materials and Services*, ed. Mary Anne Nichols and C. Allen Nichols, 181–189. Westport, CT: Greenwood.

Meyers, E. 2001. The Road to Coolness: Youth Rock the Public Library. *American Libraries* 32 (February): 46–48.

Meyers, E. 2002. Youth Development and Libraries: A Conversation with Karen Pittman. *Public Libraries* 41 (September/October): 256–260.

Minkel, Walter. 2002. When Homework is Good Politics. *School Library Journal* 48 (April): 39.

Minkel, Walter. 2003. We're Not Just a Building. *Library Journal part Net Connect* (Spring): 26–27.

Moore, Anne Carroll. 1898. Special Training for Children's Librarians. *Library Journal* 12 (August): 81.

Nesbitt, Elizabeth. 1954. Library Service to Children. *Library Trends* 3 (October): 118-128.

O'Driscoll, J. A. 2000. Recipe for Young Adult Spaces and Services. *Voice of Youth Advocates* 23 (April): 27.

Phares, C. 2001. Super Duper Program Planning. *Mississippi Libraries* 65 (Fall): 74–77.

Programs for School-Aged Youth in Public Libraries: Report of a survey conducted for the DeWitt Wallace-Reader's Digest Fund. 1999. *Teacher Librarian* 27 (October): 71–72.

Rollock, Barbara T. 1988. *Public Library Services for Children.* Hamden, CT: Shoe String Press.

Reagan, Robert. 1997. Homework Centers: Four Important Pluses. *Public Libraries* 36 (January/February): 20–21.

Reynolds, T. K. 2001. Too Dangerous and Subversive? Kids, Books, the Internet, and Libraries. *Alki* 17 (December): 26–28.

Rock, F., et al. 2002. Children are Service Users Too. *Public Library Journal* 17 (Spring): 8–10.

Ryan, S. 2000. It's Hip to be Square. *School Library Journal* 46 (March): 138–141.

Sager, Donald. 1997. Beating the Homework Blues. *Public Libraries* 36 (January/February): 19–23.

Sasse, Margo. 1973. Invisible Women: The Children's Librarian in America. *School Library Journal* 19 (January 15): 213–217.

Saunders, M. 2003. The Young Adult Outpost: A Library Just for Teens. *Public Libraries* 42 (March/April): 113–116.

Sayers, Frances Clarke. 1963. The Origins of Public Library Work with Children. *Library Trends* 12 (July): 6–13.

Scheps, Susan G. 1999. Homeschoolers in the Library. *School Library Journal* 45 (February): 38–39.

Schmitzer, Jeanne C. 2003. YOYA's Most Valuable Program for 2003: Making Personal Connections with History. *Voice of Youth Advocates* 26 (October): 276–28.

Schulte-Cooper, L. 2003. ALSC Builds a Future for Children. *American Libraries* 34 (April): 10.

Sexton, J. 2002. From Hanging Out to Homework: Teens in the Library. *OLA Quarterly* 8 (Fall): 10–12, 19.

Shoup, B. 2001. Heart, Mind, and Hands: Creating a Teen Writing Workshop. *Voice of Youth Advocates* 24 (June): 174–177.

Sloan, C., et al. 2000. The Extra Mile. *The School Librarian* 48 (Winter): 183.

St. Lifer, E. 2002. The Future of Youth Services. *School Library Journal* 48 (July): 9.

Sullivan, E. T. 2001. Teenagers are not Luggage; They Don't Need Handling. *Public Libraries* 40 (March/April): 75–77.

Carty, Natasha S. 2003. Teen Zone: C. Burr Artz Library, Frederick County Public Libraries, Frederick, Maryland. *Voice of Youth Advocates* 26 (August): 204–205.

Thomas, Fannette H. 1990. Early Appearances of Children's Reading Rooms in Public Libraries. *Journal of Youth Services* (Summer): 81–85.

Thompson, J. 2003. After School and Online. *Library Journal part Net Connect* (Winter): 35–37.

Trabucco, D., et al. 2003. Early Literacy and a Little Read Wagon. *Texas Library Journal* 79 (Spring): 8–11.

Train, B. A. 2001. Valuable Club Scene. *Public Library Journal* 16 (Summer): 44–46.

Train, B., et al. 2000. Homework Clubs: A Model for the Qualitative Evaluation of Public Library Initiatives. *New Review of Children's Literature and Librarianship* 6: 177–192.

Vaillancourt, R. J., et al. 2001. Read Any Good Movies Lately? Conducting YA Book and Movie Discussions. *Voice of Youth Advocates* 24 (July): 250–253.

Vandergrift, Kay. 1996. Female Advocacy and Harmonious Voices: A History of Public Library Services and Publishing for Children in the United States. *Library Trends* 44 (Spring): 683–718.

Viti, Thomas. 1997. The Role of the Public Library in Homework Assistance. *Public Libraries* 36 (January/February): 21–22.

Volume of Children's Work in the United States. 1913. *ALA Bulletin* 7: 287–90.

Walter, Fran K. 1941. A Poor But Respectable Relation—the Sunday School Library. *Library Quarterly* 12 (July): 734.

Walter, Virginia A. 2001. The Once and Future Library. *School Library Journal* 47 (January): 48–53.

Walter, Virginia A. 2002. Library Services to Children: Future Tense. *Journal of Youth Services in Libraries* 15 (Spring): 18–20.

Walter, Virginia A. 2003. Public Library Services to Children and Teens: A Research Agenda. *Library Trends* 51 (Spring): 571–589.

Walter, Virginia A., and Penny Markey. 1997. Parent Perceptions of a Summer Reading Program. *Journal of Youth Services* 11 (Fall): 49–65.

Watson, Dana. 1998. Multicultural Children's Literature Selection and Evaluation: Incorporating the World Wide Web. *The Acquisitions Librarian* 20: 171–83.

White, Dan R. 2002. Working Together to Build a Better World: The Importance of Youth Services in the Development and Education of Children and Their Parents. *OLA Quarterly* 8 (Fall): 15–19.

Winston, M. D., et al. 2001. Reference and Information Services for Young Adults: A Research Study of Public Libraries in New Jersey. *Reference and User Services Quarterly* 41 (Fall): 45–50.

Woolls, Blanche. 2001. Public Libraries-School Library Cooperation: A View from the Past with a Predictor for the Future. *Journal of Youth Services in Libraries* 14 (Spring): 8–10.

Wright, Lisa A. 1996. Public Library Circulation Rises along with Spending. *American Libraries* 27 (October): 57–58.

Wright, M. 2003. Adapting Library Programs for ADHD Children. *Mississippi Libraries* 67 (Spring): 3–5.

Web Sites of Youth-Related Associations

American Association of School Librarians (AASL). Available: www.ala.org/aasl/index.html.

> This is the Web site for AASL, a division of the ALA for school librarians and school library media specialists. Included are conference and event information, the new national guidelines and standards, professional materials for handling book and material challenges, resources on Internet filtering, and AASL mission and position statements.

American Library Association. Ethnic and Multicultural Information Exchange Round Table. Available: http://lonestar.utsa.edu/jbarnett/emie.html.

Association for Library Service to Children (ALSC). Available: www.ala.org/alsc.

> Supporting children's librarianship is the stated goal of the ALSC, a division of the ALA. Through the ALSC Web site, members and nonmembers can discover association news, conference information, and links to various related Web sites. School and public librarians who work with children will find this site useful and members will find a direct route to involvement in the association.

Children's Book Committee at Bank Street College. Available: www.bnkst.edu/book com.

> The Children's Book Committee at Bank Street College was formed 75 years ago with the purpose of selecting the best children's books published each year. The site provides information on the committee, its book awards and publications, and its annual list of the 600 best children's books.

The Children's Book Council (CBC). Available: www.cbcbooks.org.

> The CBC has been in existence since 1945 and provides various opportunities for encouraging reading in children. The CBC Online has links of interest to publishers, authors, teachers, librarians, booksellers, and parents. In addition, special events are highlighted and presented. The Teachers and Librarians Page features information about new books, noteworthy authors and illustrators, bibliographies, reading activities, featured topic forums, and authors. Members of the CBC will find this site useful for council news, while librarians and teachers will discover useful ideas for use in the classroom.

Children's Literature Assembly (CLA). Available: www.childrensliteratureassembly .org.

> Affiliated with the National Council of Teachers of English, the CLA promotes children's literature and its teaching. The site includes the CLA's annual list of notable children's trade books in the language arts, its annual report, and a list of the Orbis Pictus Award for Outstanding Nonfiction for Children.

Children's Literature Association. Available: http://ebbs.english.vt.edu/chla/ChLA Home.html.

> Promoting scholarship and research in children's literature, the Children's Literature Association Web page presents membership information, an overview of the association, conference information, and links to its publications, including a topical index to ChLA Quarterly. While designed to promote and support the association, this Web site will provide the general learner with information.

Society of Children's Book Writers and Illustrators (SCBWI). Available: www .scbwi.org.

> Representing the writer's side of children's literature, SCBWI is the only professional organization dedicated to the writers and illustrators of children's books. The site provides information about the children's publishing industry as well as the Golden Kite Award lists and selected SCBWI publications.

Young Adult Library Services Association (YALSA). Available: www.ala.org.yalsa.

Web Sites for Resources to Serve Youth

ALAN Review. Available: http://scholar.lib.vt.edu/ejournals/ALAN.

ALFY. Available: www.ALFY.com.

The Amazing Picture Machine. Available: www.cc.tec.org/picture.htm.

American Library Association. Banned Books. Available: www.ala.org/bbooks.

American Library Association. Best Books for Young Adults. *Booklist.* Available: www.ala.org/ala/booklist/booklist.htm.

American Library Association. Great Web Sites for Kids. Available: www.ala .org/Content/NavigationMenu/ALSC/Great_Web_Sites_for_Kids/Great_Web Sites_for_Kids.htm.

American Library Association. Notable Children's Books. *Booklist.* Available: www .ala.org/ala/booklist/booklist.htm.

American Library Association. Notable Children's Media. *Booklist*. Available: www .ala.org/ala/booklist/booklist.htm.

Anne Frank Online. Available: www.annefrank.com.

Barahona Center for the Study of Books in Spanish for Children and Adolescents. Available: www.csusm.edu/csb.

Ben's Guide to U.S. Government for Kids. Available: http://bensguide.gpo.gov.

Black Community Crusade for Children (BCCC). Available: www.childrensdefense .org/bccc.htm.

BookList Magazine. Available: www.ala.org/booklist.

Blue Web'n. Available: www.kn.pacbell.com/wired/bluewebn.

Brown v. Board of Education. Available: www.nps.gov/brvb and www.slpl.lib.mo.us/ kidzone/links/BHM2004JuvBrownvBoardofEd.htm.

Caldecott Medal Home Page. Available: www.ala.org/alsc/caldecott.html.

Celebrating Latin Americans. Available: www.nlci.org/activity/dlnsplash.htm.

Child Trends. Available: www.childtrends.org/HomePg.asp.

Children's Group Calls for Bold Initiatives to Improve Child Care Quality. Available: www.childrennow.org/newsroom/news-02/pr-3-21-02.cfm.

Children's Literature Web Guide. Available: www.acs.ucalgary.ca/~dkbrown.

Coretta Scott King Award. Available: www.ala.org/srrt/csking.

Dia de los Niños, Dia de los Libros. Available: http://reforma.org/resources/ninos/dia .html.

Discovery. Available: www.Discovery.com.

Filamentality. Available: www.kn.pacbell.com/wired/fil.

Gay and Lesbian Characters and Themes in Children's Literature. Available: www .armory.com/~web/gaybooks.html.

Grouchy Café. Available: www.grouchy.com.

Horn Book. Available: www.hbook.com.

International Reading Association. Available: www.reading.org.

The Internet and the Family. Available: www.appcpenn.org/internet/family.

The Internet Public Library. Available: www.ipl.org.

Kay E. Vandergrift's Special Interest Page. Available: www.scils.rutgers.edu/ ~kvander.

Kids Count. Available: www.aecf.org/kidscount

KidSpace@ The Internet Public Library. Available: www.ipl.org/div/kidspace.

Learning HTML. Available: www.ipl.org/div/kidspace/kidsweb.

Library of Congress. National Book Festival. Available: www.loc.gov/bookfest/related sites/index.html.

Library of Congress. National Library Service for the Blind and Physically Handicapped. Available: www.loc.gov/nls.

Media Awareness Network. Available: www.media-awareness.ca/eng/sitemap.html.

National Center for Family Literacy. Available: www.famlit.org.

Newbery Medal Home Page. Available: www.ala.org/alsc/newbery.html.

Online Children's Library. Available: www.spl.org/children/children.html.

Pura Belpré award. American Library Association. Available: www.ala.org/alsc/belpre.html.

Readers' Advisory Service. Available: www.ala.org/rusa/bestbooks.html.

Reading is Fundamental For Literacy. Available: www.rif.org.

Soon's Historical Fiction Site. Available: http://uts.cc.utexas.edu/~soon/histfiction.

Teenage Hoopla (ALA/YALSA). Available: www.ala.org/teenhoopla.

TeenSpace @ the Internet Public Library. Available: www.ipl.org/div/teen/pathways.

Virginia Hamilton Literary Award. Available: http://dept.kent.edu/virginiahamilton conf/litawd1.htm.

Voices from the Gap. Available: http://voices.cla.umn.edu.

Wired for Youth. Available: www.wiredforyouth.com (accessed December 8, 2003).

YALSA Booklists and Book Awards. Available: www.ala.org/yalsa/booklists.

10. Connections

Books and Chapters in Books

Alliance for Regional Stewardship. 2003. *Inclusive Stewardship: Emerging Collaborations Between Neighborhoods and Regions.* Denver, CO: The Alliance.

American Association of State Libraries. 1963. *Standards for Library Functions at the State Level.* Chicago: American Library Association.

American Association of State Libraries. 1970. *Standards for Library Functions at the State Level.* 2nd ed. Chicago: American Library Association.

Association of Specialized and Cooperative Library Agencies. 1985. *Standards for Library Functions at the State Level.* 3rd ed. Chicago: American Library Association.

Association of Specialized and Cooperative Library Agencies. 1990. *Standards for Cooperative Multitype Library Organizations.* Chicago: American Library Association.

Becker, Joseph. 1979. Network Functions. In *The Structure and Governance of Library Networks,* ed. Alan Kent and Thomas J. Galvin, 89. New York: Marcel Dekker.

Bundy, Alan. 2003. Joint-Use Libraries: The Ultimate Form of Cooperation. In *Planning the Modern Library Building,* ed. Gerald B. McCabe and James R. Kennedy, 129–148. Westport, CT: Libraries Unlimited.

Fiels, Keith Michael, Joan Neumann, and Eva R. Brown. 1991. *Multitype Library Cooperation State Laws, Regulations and Pending Legislation.* Chicago: Association of Specialized and Cooperative Library Agencies.

Frug, Gerald. E. 1999. *City Making: Building Communities Without Building Walls.* Princeton, NJ: Princeton University Press.

Himmel, Ethel E., William J. Wilson, and GraceAnne DeCandido. 2000. *The Functions and Roles of State Library Agencies.* Chicago: American Library Association.

Information Today. Networks, Consortia, and Other Cooperative Library Organizations. In *American Library Directory 56th Edition, 2003–2004*, 2411–2440. Medford, NJ: Information Today.

Keller, Shelly G., ed. 1997. *Proceedings of the Convocation on Providing Public Library Service to California's 21st Century Population*. ERIC ED422000. Sacramento, California, May 22–23.

Knight, Douglas M., and E. Shepley Nourse, eds. 1969. *Libraries at Large: Traditions, Innovations and the National Interest; The Resource Book Based on the Materials of the National Advisory Commission on Libraries*. New York: R. R. Bowker.

Laughlin, Sara. 2000. *Library Networks in the New Millennium: Top Ten Trends*. Chicago: American Library Association.

Long, Sarah Ann. 1995. Systems, Quo Vadis? An Examination of the History, Current Status, and Future Role of Regional Library Systems. *Advances in Librarianship* 19: 118.

McCook, Kathleen de la Peña. 2000. *A Place at the Table: Participating in Community Building*. Chicago: American Library Association.

Monypenny, Phillip. 1966. *The Library Functions of the States*. Chicago: American Library Association.

Nelson Associates, Inc. 1969. *Public Library Systems in the United States: A Survey of Multijurisdictional Systems*. Chicago: American Library Association.

Nelson Associates, Inc., in association with National Advisory Commission on Libraries. 1967. *American State Libraries and State Library Agencies: An Overview with Recommendations*. ERIC ED022486. New York: National Advisory Commission on Libraries. Repr., in *Libraries at Large: Traditions, Innovations and the National Interest*, ed. Douglas M. Knight and E. Shepley Nourse, 400–411. New York: R. R. Bowker, 1969.

Public Library Association. 1967. *Minimum Standards for Public Library Systems, 1966*. Chicago: American Library Association.

St. Angelo, Douglas. 1971. *State Library Policy, Its Legislative and Environmental Contexts*. Chicago: American Library Association.

Shavit, David. 1985. *Federal Aid and State Library Agencies: Federal Policy Implementation*. Westport, CT: Greenwood Press.

U.S. National Advisory Commission on Libraries. 1969. *Libraries at Large: Traditions, Innovations, and the National Interest*, ed. Douglas M. Knight and E. Shepley Nourse. New York: R. R. Bowker.

U.S. National Center for Education Statistics. 2004. *State Library Agencies, Fiscal Year 2002*. Washington, DC: U.S. Department of Education. Available: http://nces.ed.gov/pubs2004/2004304.pdf.

U.S. Bureau of Education. 1876. *Public Libraries in the United States of America: Their History, Condition, and Management. Special Report*. Washington, DC: U.S. Government Printing Office. Repr., as Monograph Series, no. 4, Champaign, IL: University of Illinois, Graduate School of Library Science.

Woodsworth, Anne. 1991. Governance of Library Networks: Structures and Issues. *Advances in Librarianship* 15: 155–174.

Articles

Basolo, Victoria. 2003. U.S. Regionalism and Rationality. *Urban Studies* 40 (March): 447–462.

Dornseif, Karen, and Ken Draves. 2003. The Joint-Use Library: The Ultimate Collaboration. *Colorado Libraries* 29 (Spring): 5–7.

Frug, Gerald. E. 2002. Beyond Regional Government. *Harvard Law Review* 115 (May): 1763–1836.

Helfer, Doris Small. 2002. OCLC's March into the 21st Century. *Searcher* 10 (February): 66–69.

Wheeler, Stephen M. 2002. The New Regionalism: Key Characteristics of an Emerging Movement. *Journal of the American Planning Association* 68 (Summer): 267–278.

Web Sites

Alliance for Regional Stewardship. Available: www.regionalstewardship.org.

American Library Association. Chapter Relations Office. Chapter Profile Survey, 2003, ALA Chapters Fact Sheet. Available: www.ala.org.

American Planning Association. Available: www.planning.org.

AMIGOS. Available: www.amigos.org.

BCR. Bibliographical Center for Research. Available: www.bcr.org.

Chief Officers of State Library Agencies (COSLA). Available: www.cosla.org.

Citizens Network for Sustainable Development. Available: www.citnet.org.

Colorado Digitization Program. Available: www.cdpheritage.org.

Cooperative State Research, Education, and Extension Service. Research, Education and Economics. Available: www.reeusda.gov/ecs/rrdc.htm.

Himmel, Ethel E. and William J. Wilson. Library Systems and Cooperatives. Himmel and Wilson Library Consultants. Available: www.libraryconsultant.com/LibrarySystems.htm (accessed March 27, 2003).

ILLINET. Available: www.cyberdriveillinois.com/departments/library/who_we_are/OCLC/home.html.

INCOLSA. Indiana Cooperative Library Services Authority. Available: www.incolsa.net.

Library of Congress. National Library Service for the Blind and Physically Handicapped. Available: www.loc.gov/nls.

MLC. Michigan Library Consortium. Available: www.mlnc.org.

MLNC. Missouri Library Network Corporation. Available: www.mlnc.org.

MINITEX. Available: www.minitex.umn.edu.

National Association of Regional Councils. Available: www.narc.org.

National Library Service for the Blind and Physically Handicapped. Library of Congress. Available: www.loc.gov/nls/index.html.

NEBASE. Nebraska's OCLC Connection. Available: www.nlc.state.ne.us/netserv/nebase/nebserv.html.

NELINET. Available: www.nelinet.net.

NYLINK. Available: http://nylink.suny.edu.

OCLC. Online Computer Library Center. Available: www.oclc.org.

OCLC. Regional Service Providers. Available: http://oclc.org/contacts/regional/default.htm.

OCLC CAPCON. Available: www.oclc.org/capcon.

OCLC Western Service Center. Available: www.oclc.org/western/info/contacts.htm.

OHIONET. Available: www.ohionet.org.

PALINET. Available: www.palinet.org.

Tekker Consultants, L.L.C., in association with Public Library Association. 2002. Strategic Plan, June 2002. Available: www.ala.org/ala/pla/plaorg/plastrategic plan/stratplan.pdf.

SOLINET. Southeastern Library Network. Available: www.solinet.net.

WiLS. Wisconsin Library Services. Available: www.wils.wisc.edu.

11. Global Public Library Issues

Books and Parts of Books

Black, Alistair. 1996. *A New History of the English Public Library: Social and Intellectual Contexts, 1850–1940.* London: University of Leicester Press.

Black, Alistair. 2000. *The Public Library in Britain, 1914–2000.* London: The British Library.

Caballero, Maria Cristina. 2003. *Biblored: Colombia's Innovative Library Network.* Washington, DC: Council on Library and Information Resources.

Carroll, Frances, and John Frederick Harvey. 2001. *International Librarianship: Cooperation and Collaboration.* Lanham, MD: Scarecrow Press.

Coombs, Douglas. 1988. *Spreading the Word: The Library Work of the British Council.* London: Mansell Publishing Limited.

Greenhalgh, Liz, Ken Worpole, and Charles Landry. 1995. *Libraries in a World of Cultural Change.* London: UCL Press.

Hanratty, Catherine, and John Sumsion. 1996. *International Comparison of Public Library Statistics.* Loughborough, UK: Loughborough University, Library and Information Statistics Unit.

Henry, Carol K., and Donald G. Davis, Jr. 2002. *IFLA 75th Anniversary.* The Hague: Netherlands, IFLA.

International Federation of Library Associations and Institutions and Freedom of Access to Information and Freedom of Expression. 2001. *Libraries and Intellectual Freedom: IFLA/FAIFE World Report: Denmark.* Denmark: IFLA/FAIFE Office.

International Federation of Library Associations and Institutions. 2001. *The Public Library Service: IFLA/UNESCO Guidelines for Development.* München: K. G. Saur.

Issak, Aissa. 2000. *Public Libraries in Africa: A Report and Annotated Bibliography.* Oxford: International Network for the Availability of Scientific Publications.

Koops, Willem, R. H., and Joachim Wieder. 1977. *IFLA's First Fifty Years: Achievement and Challenge in International Librarianship*. München: Verlag Dokumentation.

Laubier, Guillaume de, and Jacques Bosser. 2003. *The Most Beautiful Libraries in the World*. New York: Harry N. Abrams.

McCook, Kathleen de la Peña, Barbara J. Ford, and Kate Lippincott. 1998. *Libraries: Global Reach—Local Touch*. Chicago: American Library Association.

Stam, David H., ed. 2001. *International Dictionary of Library Histories*. Chicago: Fitzroy Dearborn Publishers.

Stringer, Roger. 2002. *The Book Chain in Anglophone Africa: A Survey and Directory*. Oxford: International Network for the Availability of Scientific Publications.

Sturges, Paul, and Richard Neill. 1998. *The Quiet Struggle: Information and Libraries for the People of Africa*. 2nd. ed. London: Mansell.

Swedish Library Association. 1999. *Library at the Centre of the World: Multicultural Library Services*. Lund, Sweden: Committee on Multicultural Library Services of the Swedish Library Association.

Thorhauge, J., G. Larsen, et al. 1997. *Public Libraries and the Information Society*. Luxembourg: European Commission.

UNESCO. 1998. *World Culture Report 1998: Culture, Creativity and Markets*. France: UNESCO.

United Nations Development Programme. 2003. *Human Development Report 2003: Millennium Development Goals: A Compact Among Nations to End Human Poverty*. New York: United Nations.

Vashishth, C. P., ed. 1995. *Libraries as Rural Community Resource Centres: Papers and Proceedings of the Workshop on Rural Community Resource Centres*. Delhi: B. R. Publishing.

Wedgeworth, Robert. 1998. Global Perspective. In *Libraries: Global Reach-Local Touch*, ed. Kathleen de la Peña McCook, Barbara J. Ford, and Kate Lippincott, 6–11. Chicago: American Library Association.

Wendell, Laura. 1998. *Libraries for All: How to Start and Run a Basic Library*. Paris: UNESCO.

Windau, Bettina, ed. 1999. *International Network of Public Libraries*. 6 vols. Lanham, MD: Scarecrow Press.

Yitai, Gong, and G. E. Gorman. 2000. *Libraries and Information Services in China*. Lanham, MD: Scarecrow Press.

Articles

Atuti, Richard M. 1999. Camel Library Service to Nomadic Pastoralists: the Kenyan Scenario. *IFLA Journal* 25: 152–158.

Auld, Hampton. 2002. Public Libraries in the Developing World. *Public Libraries* 41 (January/February): 25–33.

Campbell, Harry C. 2002. Library Universality in a Divided World. *IFLA Journal* 28: 118–135.

Clifford, Nerida. 2003. International Public Library Trends. *Australasian Public Libraries and Information Services* 16 (September): 115–122.

Davis, Donald G., Jr. 2003. Strengthening Links Between Library Associations and Their Members: The 25th Anniversary of the IFLA Section of Library and Information Science Journals. *IFLA Journal* 29: 235–244.

Erickson, Carol A., and Abbagliati Boils. 2003. Chile's Information Transformation. *American Libraries* 34 (January): 52–54.

Ford, Barbara. 2002. International Public Librarianship. *Public Libraries* 41 (January/February): 12.

Haratsis, Brian. 1995. Justifying the Economic Value of Public Libraries in a Turbulent Local Government Environment. *Australasian Public Libraries and Information Services* 8: 164–172.

Onwubiko, Chidi P. C. 1996. The Practice of Amadi's Barefoot Librarianship in African Public Libraries. *Library Review* 45: 39–47.

Payne, Beth A. 2002. Creating a Nation's First Public Library. *Public Libraries* 41 (January/February): 49–51.

Rahman, Faizur. 2000. Status of Rural and Small Libraries in Bangladesh: Directions for the Future. *Rural Libraries* 20: 52–64.

Roy, Loriene. 2000. The International Indigenous Librarians' Forum: a Professional Life-Affirming Event. *World Libraries* 10 (Spring/Fall): 19–30.

Rudolf, Málek. 1970. On the Origin of the International Organization of Librarians (IFLA): the Congress of Librarians in Prague, 1926. *Libri* 20: 222–224.

Sager, Donald. J. 2000. The Sister Libraries Program. *Public Libraries* 39 (July/August): 195–199.

Strong, Gary E. 2002. International Experiences at the Queens Borough Public Library. *Public Libraries* 41 (January/February): 41–43.

Sturges, R. P. 2001. The Poverty of Librarianship: An Historical Critique of Public Librarianship in Anglophone Africa. *Libri* 51 (March): 38–48.

Wieder, Joachim, and Harry Campbell. 2002. IFLA's First Fifty years. *IFLA Journal* 28: 107–117.

Web Sites

African Books Collective. Available: www.africanbookscollective.com/index.html.

American Library Association. International Relations Round Table. Available: www.ala.org/irrt.

Bill and Melinda Gates Foundation. International Library Initiatives. Available: www.gatesfoundation.org.

Book Aid International. Available: www.bookaid.org/cms.cgi/site/index.htm.

Canadian Organization for Development Through Education. Available: www.sabre.org/books/bookorg/bkdn_cod.htm.

Carnegie Corporation. Available: www.carnegie.org.

Carnegie United Kingdom Trust. Available: www.carnegieuktrust.org.uk.

Council on Library and Information Resources. Access to Learning Award. Available: www.clir.org/fellowships/gates/gates.html.

Danish International Development Agency. Available: www.um.dk/danida.

European Commission. Available: http://europa.eu.int/comm/index_en.htm.

International Federation of Library Associations and Institutions. Core Values. Available: www.ifla.org.

International Federation of Library Associations and Institutions. Glasgow Declaration. Available: www.ifla.org/faife/policy/iflastat/gldeclar-e.html.

International Network for the Availability of Scientific Publications. Available: www.inasp.info.

International Network of Public Libraries Available: www.public-libraries.net and www.bertelsmann-stiftung.de.

Norwegian Agency for Development Cooperation. Available: www.norad.no/default.asp?V_SITE_ID=2.

Open Society Institute, Soros Foundation. Available: www.soros.org. Examples of the Soros Foundation's support of international public libraries include the following:

Electronic Information for Libraries. Available: www.osi.hu/nlp.

Information Program. Available: www.soros.org/initiatives/information.

Soros Foundation. Open Society Institute. Available: www.soros.org.

UNESCO. Available: www.unesco.org.

UNESCO. The IFLA/UNESCO Public Library Manifesto. Available: www.ifla.org/documents/libraries/policies/unesco.htm.

UNESCO Libraries Portal. Available: www.unesco.org/webworld/portal_bib/Groups/Networks.

United Nations. Millennium Declaration. Available: www.un.org/millennium/declaration/ares552e.htm.

University of Illinois Library at Urbana-Champaign. Mortenson Center for International Library Programs. Available: www.library.uiuc.edu/mortenson.

World Library Partnership. Available: http://worldlibraries.org.

World Summit on the Information Society. Available: www.itu.int/wsis.

12. Twenty-First Century Trends in Public Librarianship

Books and Parts of Books

Baker, Timothy J. 2003. Interpolation from a Cloud of Points. In *Proceedings, 12th International Meshing Roundtable*, 55–63. Sandia National Laboratories. Available: www.andrew.cmu.edu/user/sowen/abstracts/Ba960.html.

Craft, Mary Anne. 1999. *The Funding Game: Rules for Public Library Advocacy.* Lanham, MA: Scarecrow Press.

Gould, Stephen Jay. 2003. *The Hedgehog, the Fox and the Magister's Pox: Mending the Gap Between Science and the Humanities.* New York: Harmony Books.

Healy, Tom, et al. 2001. *The Well-Being of Nations: The Role of Human and Social Capital.* Paris: Organisation for Economic Co-operation and Development.

Henton, Douglas, John Melville, and Kim Walesh. 2003. *Civic Revolutionaries: Igniting the Passion for Change in America's Communities.* San Francisco: John Wiley and Sons/Jossey-Bass.

Hesse, Hermann. 1969. *The Glass Bead Game (Magister Ludi).* Translated by Richard and Clara Winston. New York: Holt, Reinhart and Winston.

Holt, Glen E. 2001. *Public Library Benefits Valuation Study.* St. Louis Public Library. Available: www.slpl.lib.mo.us/using/valuation.htm.

McCook, Kathleen de la Peña. 2000. *A Place at the Table: Participating in Community Building.* Chicago: American Library Association.

Nelson, Sandra. 2001. *The New Planning for Results: A Streamlined Approach.* Chicago: American Library Association.

OCLC. 2003 Environmental Scan: Pattern Recognition. Available: www.oclc.org/membership/escan/default.htm.

Singer, Audrey. The Rise of Immigrant Gateways. The Brookings Institution. Available: www.brookings.edu/urban/pubs/20040301_gateways.pdf (accessed February 2004).

Swan, James. 2002. *Fund-Raising for Libraries: 25 Proven Ways to Get More Money for Your Library.* New York: Neal-Schuman Publishers.

U.S. National Center for Education Statistics. 1988. *Services and Resources for Young Adults in Public Libraries.* Washington, DC: Government Printing Office.

Articles

Allen, Bryce. 2003. Public Opinion and the Funding of Public Libraries. *Library Trends* 51 (Winter): 414–423.

Balatti, Jo, and Ian Falk. 2002. Socioeconomic Contributions of Adult Learning to Community: A Social Capital Perspective. *Adult Education Quarterly* 52 (August): 281–298.

Gornish, Stanley E. 1998. How to Apply Fund-Raising Principles in a Competitive Environment. *Library Administration and Management* (Spring): 94–103.

Hoene, Christopher, and Michael A. Pagano. 2003. Fend for Yourself Federalism: The Impact of Federal and State Deficits on American Cities. *Government Finance Review* 19 (October): 36–37.

Holt, Glen E., and Donald Elliott. 2003. Measuring Outcomes: Applying Cost-Benefit Analysis to Middle-Sized and Smaller Public Libraries. *Library Trends* 51 (Winter): 424–440.

Jensen, Leif, and Tim Slack. 2003. Underemployment in America: Measurement and Evidence. *American Journal of Community Psychology* 12 (September): 21–31.

Johnson, James H., Jr. 2002. A Conceptual Model for Enhancing Community Competitiveness in the New Economy. *Urban Affairs Review* 37 (July): 763–780.

Krapp, John. 2002. Hermann Hesse's Hegelianism: The Progress of Consciousness Towards Freedom in *The Glass Bead Game.* *Studies in Twentieth Century Literature* 26 (Summer): 256–279.

Sen, Amartya. 2003. The Social Demands of Human Rights. *New Perspective Quarterly* 20 (Fall): 83–84.

Ventriss, Curtis. 1998. Radical Democratic Thought and Contemporary American Public Administration: A Substantive Perspective. *The American Review Of Public Administration* 28: 227–245.

Warner, Mildred, and Amir Hefetz. 2002. Applying Market Solutions to Public Services: An Assessment of Efficiency, Equity, and Voice. *Urban Affairs Review* 38 (September): 70–90.

Web Sites

Center for Rural Librarianship. Rural Librarianship and Bookmobile and Outreach Services. Available: http://eagle.clarion.edu/~grads/csrl/csrlhom.htm.

Edge. Available: www.edge.org.

Global Insight. 2003. U.S. Metro Economies: Types of Jobs Lost and Gained 2001–2005. U.S. Conference of Mayors. Available: www.usmayors.org/USCM/home.asp.

Institute of Museum and Library Services (IMLS). Available: www.imls.gov (accessed December 3, 2003).

National Conference of State Legislatures. NCSL Calls Upon the Federal Government to Meet Its Responsibilities To The States—July 2003. Available: www.ncsl.org.

OCLC. 2003 Environmental Scan: Pattern Recognition. Available: www.oclc.org/membership/escan/default.htm.

WebJunction. Available: www.webjunction.org/do/Home.

Further Resources (Topically Arranged)

Sense of Place (SoP) in the Context of Regionalism

Alliance for Regional Stewardship. Available: www.regionalstewardship.org.

Brockman, John. 2003. *The New Humanists: Science at the Edge.* New York: Barnes and Noble.

The Citistates Group. Available: http://citistates.com/index.html.

Congress for the New Urbanism. Available: www.cnu.org/index.cfm.

Ford, Larry R. 2003. *America's New Downtowns: Revitalization or Reinvention?* Baltimore, MD: Johns Hopkins University Press.

Frug, Gerald. E. 2002. Beyond Regional Government. *Harvard Law Review* 115 (May): 1763–1836.

Great Public Spaces. Available: www.pps.org/gps.

Hiller, Jean, and Emma Rooksby. 2002. *Habitus: A Sense of Place.* Burlington, VT: Ashgate.

International Economic Development Council. Available: www.iedconline.org.

Lewis Mumford Center for Comparative Urban and Regional Research. Available: www.albany.edu/mumford.

Livable Communities. Available: www.lgc.org.

Low, Setha M. 2003. *Behind the Gates: Life, Security and the Pursuit of Happiness in Fortress America.* New York: Routledge.

National Association of Regional Councils. Available: www.narc.org.

Oldenburg, Ray. 2001. *Celebrating the Third Place.* New York : Marlowe & Co.

Putnam, Robert D., and Lewis M. Feldstein. 2003. Branch Libraries: The Heartbeat of the Community. In *Better Together: Restoring the American Community,* 34–54. New York: Simon and Schuster.

Smart Growth Online. Available: www.smartgrowth.org/default.asp.

Wheeler, Stephen M. 2002. The New Regionalism: Key Characteristics of an Emerging Movement. *Journal of the American Planning Association* 68 (Summer): 267–278.

Williamson, Thad, et al. 2002. *Making a Place for Community: Make a Place for Democracy in a Global Era.* New York: Routledge.

Convergence of Cultural Heritage Institutions

American Library Association. Public Programs Office. Available: www.ala.org/public programs.

Ball, David. 2003. Public Libraries and the Consortium Purchase of Electronic Resources. *Electronic Library* 21: 301–309.

Block, Marylaine. 2003. *Net Effects: How Librarians Can Manage the Unintended Consequences of the Internet.* Medford, NJ: Information Today.

CPANDA. Cultural Policy and the Arts National Data Archive. Available: www.cpanda.org.

Carr, David. 2003. *The Promise of Cultural Institutions.* Walnut Creek, CA.: AltaMira Press.

Connet, Michael, and James Fellows. 2001. Together Again? The New Case for Public Telecommunications and Education Partnerships. *Technos: Quarterly for Education and Technology* 10 (Fall): 30–34.

Corporation for Public Broadcasting. Available: www.cpb.org.

Digital Library Federation. Available: www.diglib.org/dlfhomepage.htm.

Digitization for Cultural Heritage Professionals. Available: www.ils.unc.edu/DCHP.

Dilevko, Juris, and Lisa Gottlieb. 2003. Resurrecting a Neglected Idea: The Re-Introduction of Library-Museum Hybrids. *Library Quarterly* 73 (April): 160–198.

European Library Automation Group. 2000. Archives, Libraries and Museums Convergence: 24th Library Systems Seminar, Paris (April 12–14).

Flew, Terry. 2002. Educational Media in Transition: Broadcasting, Digital Media and Lifelong Learning in the Knowledge Economy. *International Journal of Instructional Media* 29: 47–60.

Institute for Free Choice Learning. Available: www.ilinet.org/freechoicelearning.html.

Institute of Museum and Library Services (IMLS). Available: www.imls.gov (accessed December 3, 2003).

International Society for Knowledge Organization. Available: http://is.gseis.ucla.edu/orgs/isko.

Lim, Adriene. 2003. Collaborative Digitization Projects. *Information Technology and Libraries* 22 (June): 75–78.

López-Huertas, M. J. ed. 2002. *Challenges in Knowledge Representation and Organization for the 21st Century: Integration of Knowledge across Boundaries: Proceedings of the Seventh International ISKO Conference (Granada, Spain, July 10–13, 2002)*. Advances in Knowledge Organization, no. 8. Würzburg: Ergon.

Martin, Robert S. 2003. National Planning for Library and Information Services in the U.S.: the Role of the U.S. Institute of Museum and Library Services. *Alexandria* 15: 111–119.

McCabe, Ronald B. 2001. *Civic Librarianship: Renewing the Social Mission of the Public Library*. Lanham, MD: Scarecrow Press.

McCook, Kathleen de la Peña, and Maria A. Jones. 2002. Cultural Heritage Institutions and Community Building. *Reference and User Services Quarterly* 41 (Summer): 326–329.

Metcalfe, Ruth. 2001. Cultural Connections: Collaborative Partnerships between Libraries, Museums, and Educators. *Journal of Youth Services in Libraries* 15 (Fall): 26–28.

National Endowment for the Humanities. Available: www.neh.fed.us.

National Video Resources. Available: www.nvr.org.

Schuster, J. Mark Davidson. 2002. *Informing Cultural Policy*. New Brunswick, NJ: Center for Urban Policy Research.

Stille, Alexander. 2002. *The Future of the Past*. New York: Farrar, Strauss and Giroux.

UNESCO. 1995. *Our Creative Diversity: Report of the World Commission on Culture and Development*. Paris: UNESCO.

U.S. Environmental Protection Agency. Office of Water. 2002. *Community Culture and the Environment; Understanding a Sense of Place*. Washington, DC: Environmental Protection Agency.

Vollmar-Grone, Michael. 2002. Public Library Video Collections. In *Video-Collection Development in Multitype Libraries*, 15–39. Westport, CT: Greenwood.

Walker, Chris, and Carlos A. Manjarrez. 2003. *Partnerships for Free Choice Learning: Public Libraries, Museums and Public Broadcasters Working Together.* Washington, DC: Urban Institute. Evanston, IL: Urban Libraries Council.

Inclusive Service Mandates and Social Justice Commitments

2–1–1. Get Connected. Get Answers. United Way. Alliance for Information and Referral Services. Available: www.211.org.

American Library Association. American Indian Library Association (AILA). Available: www.nativeculture.com/lisamitten/aila.html.

American Library Association. Asian/Pacific American Library Association (APALA). Available: www.apalaweb.org.

American Library Association. Black Caucus of the American Library Association (BCALA). Available: www.bcala.org.

American Library Association. Chinese-American Librarians Association (CALA). Available: www.cala-web.org.

American Library Association. Ethnic and Multicultural Information Round Table. Available: http://lonestar.utsa.edu/jbarnett/emie.html.

American Library Association. Libraries Serving Special Populations Section. Available: www.ala.org/lsspsTemplate.cfm?Section=LSSPS.

Vision, mobility, hearing, and developmental differences, people who are elderly, people in prisons, health care facilities.

American Library Association. Office for Literacy and Outreach Services. Available: www.ala.org/olos.

American Library Association. Subcommittee on Service to the Poor and Homeless. Social Responsibilities Round Table. Hunger, Homelessness and Poverty Task Force. Available: http://libr.org/HHP.

Bill and Melinda Gates Foundation. 2004. Toward Equality of Access: The Role of Public Libraries in Addressing the Digital Divide. Available: www.gates foundation.org/nr/Downloads/libraries/uslibraries/reports/TowardEqualityof Access.pdf.

Bishop, Ann. 1999. Public Libraries and Networked Information Services in Low Income Communities. *Library and Information Science Research* 21.3: 361–390.

Chatman, Elfreda A. 1987. Opinion Leadership, Poverty, and Information Sharing. *RQ*. 26 (Spring): 341–353.

Deines-Jones, Courtney, and Connie Van Fleet. 1995. *Preparing Staff to Serve Patrons with Disabilities* New York: Neal Schuman Publishers.

Feinberg, Sandra, et al. 1999. *Including Families of Children with Special Needs.* New York: Neal-Schuman Publishers.

Hilyard, Nann Blaine. 2003. Disabilities in the Library. *Public Libraries* 42 (January/February): 14–19.

Information for Social Change. Available: www.libr.org/ISC/who.html.

McCook, Kathleen de la Peña. 2001. Poverty, Democracy, and Public Libraries. In *Libraries and Democracy: The Cornerstones of Liberty*. ed. Nancy Kranich, 28–46. Chicago: American Library Association.

McCook, Kathleen de la Peña. 2002. *Rocks in the Whirlpool: The American Library Association and Equity of Access*. ERIC ED462981. Chicago: American Library Association. Available: www.ala.org/ala/ourassociation/governingdocs/key actionareas/equityaction/rockswhirlpool.htm.

Mickelson, Kristin D., and Laura D. Kubzansky. 2003. Social Distribution of Social Support. *American Journal of Community Psychology* 32: 265–281.

Murphy, Patricia Watkins, and James C. 2003. Cunningham. *Organizing for Community Controlled Development: Renewing Civil Society*. Thousand Oaks, CA: Sage Publications.

Osborne, Robin, ed. 2004. *From Outreach to Equity: Innovative Models of Library Policy and Practice*. Chicago: American Library Association.

Petter, John, et al. 2002. Dimensions and Patterns in Employee Empowerment. *Journal of Public Administration Research and Theory* 12 (July): 337–400.

Poland, Nancy L. 2002. Making Service Integration a Reality. *Policy and Practice of Public Human Services* 60 (September): 24–27.

Progressive Librarian. Available: www.libr.org/PL/index.html.

REFORMA—National Association to Promote Library and Information Services to Latinos and the Spanish-Speaking. Available: www.reforma.org.

Rubin, Rhea Joyce. 2001. *Planning for Library Services to People with Disabilities. ASCLA Changing Horizons Ser. 5.* Chicago: American Library Association.

Social Responsibilities Round Table. Available: http://libr.org/SRRT.

Sennett, Richard. 2003. *Respect in a World of Inequality.* New York: W. W. Norton.

Shin, Hyon B., and Rosalind Bruno. 2003. *Language Use and English-Speaking Ability: 2000. Census 2000 Brief.* Washington, DC: U.S. Census Bureau.

Shorris, Earl. 2000. Promoting the Humanities, or: How to Make the Poor Dangerous. *American Libraries* 31 (May): 46–49.

Tirimanne, Nimo. 2001. The Ethics of Information Provision: A Case for Refugees. *Journal of Information Ethics* 10 (Fall): 67–73.

Urban Library Council. 2003. *Public Library Services to New Americans: Speeding Transition to Learning, Work and Life in the U.S.* Evanston, IL: Urban Libraries Council.

U.S. Census Bureau. 2002. Coming to America: A Profile of the Nation's Foreign-Born (2000 update). Washington, DC: U.S. Census Bureau. Available: www .census.gov/prod/2002pubs/cenbr01-1.pdf (accessed November 13, 2003).

U.S. Census Bureau. 2003. Disability. Available: www.census.gov/hhes/-www/ disability.html.

Venturella, Karen M. 1998. *Poor People and Library Services.* Jefferson, NC: McFarland and Co.

Sustaining of the Public Sphere

ALA, ACLU Challenge CIPA with Dual Federal Lawsuits. 2001. *American Libraries.* 32 (May): 20–21.

American Civil Liberties Union. Keep America Safe and Free. Available: www.aclu .org/SafeandFree/SafeandFree.cfm?ID=12126&c=207.

American Civil Liberties Union, et al. v. Ashcroft. U.S. Court for Eastern District of PA, 2003. *Ashcroft v. American Civil Liberties Union, et al.,* 535 U.S. 234, 252, 2002.

American Library Association. Office for Intellectual Freedom. 2002. *Intellectual Freedom Manual.* 6th ed. Chicago: American Library Association.

American Library Association. Public Programs Office. Available: www.ala.org/ publicprograms.

Bollier, David. 2001. *Public Assets, Private Profits: Reclaiming the American Commons in an Age of Market Enclosure.* Washington, DC: New America Foundation.

Buschman, John E. 2003. *Dismantling the Public Sphere: Situating and Sustaining Librarianship in the Age of the New Public Philosophy.* Westport, CT: Libraries Unlimited/Greenwood.

Budd, John M. 2003. The Library, Praxis and Symbolic Power. *Library Quarterly* 73 (January): 19–32.

Budd, John M., and Cynthia Wyatt. 2002. Do You Have Any Books On—: An Examination of Public Library Holdings. *Public Libraries* 41 (March/April): 107–112.

Crawford, Walt. 2003. Coping with CIPA: A Censorware Special. *Cities and Insights* 3.9.

Creative Commons. Available: http://creativecommons.org.

Durrance, Joan, et al. 2001. Libraries and Civil Society. In *Libraries and Democracy: The Cornerstones of Liberty,* ed. Nancy Kranich, 49–59. Chicago: American Library Association.

First Amendment Center. Available: www.firstamendmentcenter.org/default.aspx.

Free Press: Media Reform. Available: www.mediareform.net.

Habermas, Jürgen. 1996. *Between Facts and Norms: Contributions to a Discourse Theory of Law and Democracy.* Translated by William Rehg. Cambridge, MA: The MIT Press.

Jaeger, Paul T., and Charles R. McClure. 2004. Potential Legal Challenges to the Application of the Children's Internet Protection Act (CIPA) in Public Libraries: Strategies and Issues. *First Monday* 9 (February). Available: www .firstmonday.org/issues/issue9_2/jaeger.

Jaeger, Paul T., et al. 2004. The Effects of the Children's Internet Protection Act (CIPA) in Public Libraries and Its Implications for Research: A Statistical, Policy, and Legal Analysis. *Journal of the American Society for Information Science and Technology* (n.p.).

Kranich, Nancy. 2001. Libraries Create Social Capital. *Library Journal* 126 (November 15): 40–41.

Kranich, Nancy. 2003. Staking a Claim in the Information Commons. *Knowledge Quest* 31 (March/April): 22–25.

Lichtblau, Eric. 2003. Ashcroft Mocks Librarians and Others Who Oppose Parts of Counterterrorism Law. *New York Times* (September 16, Section A, p. 23.)

McChesney, Robert, and John Nichols. 2002. *Our Media, Not Theirs: The Democratic Struggle Against Corporate Media.* New York: Seven Stories Press.

McCook, Kathleen de la Peña. 2001. Authentic Discourse as a Means of Connection Between Public Library Service Responses and Community Building Initiatives. *Reference and User Services Quarterly* 40 (Winter): 127–133.

McCook, Kathleen de la Peña. 2003. Suppressing the Commons: Misconstrued Patriotism vs. A Psychology of Liberation. *Reference and User Services Quarterly* (Fall): 14–17.

Martín-Baró, Ignacio. 1994. Toward a Liberation Psychology. In *Writings for a Liberation Psychology,* 17–31. Cambridge, MA: Harvard University Press.

Misztal, Barbara. 2001. Trust and Cooperation: The Democratic Public Sphere. *Journal of Sociology* 37 (December): 371–388.

National Endowment for the Humanities. Available: www.neh.fed.us.

National Issues Forum. Available: www.nifi.org.

National Video Resources. Available: www.nvr.org.

Post, Robert C. 1998. *Censorship and Silencing: Practices of Cultural Regulation.* Los Angeles: The Getty Research Institute for the History of Art and the Humanities.

Robbins, Louise S. 1996. *Censorship and the American Library: The American Library Association's Response to Threats to Intellectual Freedom: 1939–1969.* Westport, CT: Greenwood Press.

Sobel, David. L. Net Filters and Libraries. First Amendment Center. Available: www .firstamendmentcenter.org/default.aspx (accessed November 2003).

Watts, Roderick J., et al. 2003. Sociopolitical Development. *American Journal of Community Psychology* 31 (March): 185–194.

Appendix B
Bibliography of National Statistics on Public Libraries

1850 to 1900

Government Publications

Jewett, Charles Coffin. 1851. Report on the Public Libraries of the United States of America, January 1, 1850. In *Report of the Board of Regents of the Smithsonian Institution*. Washington, DC: Smithsonian Institution.

Rhees, William Jones. 1859. *List of public libraries, institutions and societies in the United States and British provinces of North America*. Washington, DC: Smithsonian Institution.

U.S. Bureau of Education. 1870. *Report of the Commissioner of Education made to the Secretary of the Interior for the Year 1870, with Accompanying Papers*. Includes table, "Principal Libraries of the United States, Exclusive of those connected with Colleges, etc." Washington, DC: U.S. Government Printing Office.

U.S. Office of Education. 1876. *Public Libraries in the United States of America; Their History, Condition, and Management. Special Report*. Washington, DC: U.S. Government Printing Office.

U.S. Office of Education. 1886. *Statistics of Public Libraries in the United States. From the Report of the Commissioner of Education for the Year 1884–85. With Additions*. Washington, DC: U.S. Government Printing Office.

Flint, Weston. 1893. *Statistics of Public Libraries in the United States and Canada.* Washington, DC: U.S. Government Printing Office.

U.S. Bureau of Education. 1897. *Public, Society and School Libraries in the United States, with Library Statistics and Legislation of the Various States.* Washington, DC: U.S. Government Printing Office.

Nongovernment Publications

Trübner, Nicholas, Benjamin Moore, and Edward Edwards. 1859. *Trübner's Bibliographical Guide to American Literature. A Classed List of Books Published in the United States of American During the Last Forty Years. With Bibliographical Introduction, Notes and Alphabetical Index.* Includes Public Libraries in the United States. London: Trübner and Co.

1901–1950

Government Publications

U.S. Office of Education. 1901. *Public, Society, and School Libraries.* Washington, DC: U.S. Government Printing Office.

U.S. Office of Education. 1903. *Public, Society and School Libraries in the United States, with Library Statistics and Legislation of the Various States.* Washington, DC: U.S. Government Printing Office.

U.S. Bureau of Education. 1904. *Public, Society, and School Libraries.* Washington, DC: U.S. Government Printing Office.

U.S. Bureau of Education. 1909. *Statistics of Public, Society, and School Libraries Having 5,000 Volumes and Over in 1908.* Washington, DC: U.S. Government Printing Office.

U.S. Bureau of Education. 1913. *Public, Society, and School Libraries.* Washington, DC: U.S. Government Printing Office.

U.S. Bureau of Education. 1915. *Public, Society, and School Libraries.* Washington, DC: U.S. Government Printing Office.

U.S. Bureau of Education. 1926. *Statistics of Public, Society, and School Libraries, 1923.* Washington, DC: U.S. Government Printing Office.

U.S. Office of Education. 1931. *Statistics of Public, Society, and School Libraries, 1929.* Washington, DC: U.S. Government Printing Office.

U.S. Office of Education. 1939. *Public Library Statistics, 1938/39.* Washington, DC: U.S. Government Printing Office.

U.S. Office of Education. 1947. *Public Library Statistics, 1944–45.* Washington, DC: U.S. Government Printing Office.

U.S. Office of Education. 1947. *Statistics of Public Libraries in Cities with Populations of 100,000 or More.* Washington, DC: U.S. Government Printing Office.

Nongovernment Publications

American Library Association. 1916. *Statistics of libraries*. Chicago: American Library Association.

1950–1988

Government Publications

Willhoite, Mary M. 1952. *Statistics of Public Libraries in Cities with Populations of 50,000 to 99,999, 1950*. Washington, DC: Education Office, Federal Security Agency.

Willhoite, Mary M. 1952. *Statistics of Public Libraries in Cities with Populations of 100,000 or More, 1951*. Washington, DC: Education Office, Federal Security Agency.

Willhoite, Mary M. 1953. *Statistics of 50 Large County and Regional Libraries for 1952*. Washington, DC: Education Office, Health, Education, and Welfare Dept.

Willhoite, Mary M. 1953. *Statistics of Public Libraries in Cities with Populations of 50,000 to 99,999, 1952*. Washington, DC: Education Office, Health, Education, and Welfare Dept.

Willhoite, Mary M. 1953. *Statistics of Public Libraries in Cities with Populations of 100,000 or More, 1952*. Washington, DC: Education Office, Health, Education, and Welfare Dept.

Dunbar, Ralph M. 1954. *Public Library Statistics, 1950*. Washington, DC: Education Office, Health, Education, and Welfare Dept.

Willhoite, Mary M. 1954. *Statistics of County and Regional Libraries Serving Populations of 50,000 or More, Fiscal Year 1953*. Washington, DC: Education Office, Health, Education, and Welfare Dept.

Willhoite, Mary M. 1954. *Statistics of Public Libraries in Cities with Populations of 100,000 or More, Fiscal Year 1953*. Washington, DC: Education Office, Health, Education, and Welfare Dept.

Willhoite, Mary M. 1954. *Statistics of Public Library Systems in Cities with Populations of 50,000 to 99,999, Fiscal Year 1953*. Washington, DC: Education Office, Health, Education, and Welfare Dept.

Willhoite, Mary M. 1955. *Statistics of County and Regional Libraries Serving Populations of 50,000 or More, Fiscal Year 1954*. Washington, DC: Education Office, Health, Education, and Welfare Dept.

Willhoite, Mary M. 1955. *Statistics of Public Libraries in cities with Populations of 100,000 or More, Fiscal Year 1954*. Washington, DC: Education Office, Health, Education, and Welfare Dept.

Willhoite, Mary M. 1956. *Statistics of County and Regional Libraries Serving Populations of 50,000 or More, Fiscal Year 1955*. Washington, DC: Education Office, Health, Education, and Welfare Dept.

Willhoite, Mary M. 1956. *Statistics of Public Libraries in Cities with Populations of 50,000 to 99,999, Fiscal Year 1955*. Washington, DC: Education Office, Health, Education, and Welfare Dept.

Willhoite, Mary M. 1956. *Statistics of Public Libraries in Cities with Populations of 100,000 or More, Fiscal Year 1955.* Washington, DC: Education Office, Health, Education, and Welfare Dept.

Willhoite, Mary M. 1957. *Statistics of County and Regional Libraries Serving Populations of 50,000 or More, Fiscal Year 1956.* Washington, DC: Education Office, Health, Education, and Welfare Dept.

Willhoite, Mary M. 1957. *Statistics of Public Libraries in Cities with Populations of 50,000 to 99,999, Fiscal Year 1956.* Washington, DC: Education Office, Health, Education, and Welfare Dept.

Willhoite, Mary M. 1957. *Statistics of Public Libraries in Cities with Populations of 100,000 or More, Fiscal Year 1956.* Washington, DC: Education Office, Health, Education, and Welfare Dept.

Vainstein, Rose, and Mary M. Willhoite. 1958. *Statistics of Public Libraries in Cities with Populations of 50,000 to 99,999, Fiscal Year 1957.* Washington, DC: Education Office, Health, Education, and Welfare Dept.

Vainstein, Rose, and Mary M. Willhoite. 1958. *Statistics of Public Libraries in Cities with Populations of 100,000 or More, Fiscal Year 1957.* Washington, DC: Education Office, Health, Education, and Welfare Dept.

Vainstein, Rose, Mary M. Willhoite, and Doris C. Holladay. 1958. *Statistics of Public Libraries in Cities with Populations of 35,000 to 49,999, Fiscal Year 1957.* Washington, DC: U.S. Department of Health, Education, and Welfare.

Willhoite, Mary M. 1958. *Statistics of County and Regional Libraries Serving Populations of 50,000 or More, Fiscal Year 1957.* Washington, DC: Education Office, Health, Education, and Welfare Dept.

U.S. Office of Education. 1959. *Statistics of Public Libraries: 1955–56.* Washington, DC: U.S. Government Printing Office.

Vainstein, Rose. 1959. Statistics of Public Libraries, 1955–56. In *Biennial survey of education in the United States, 1954–56.* Washington, DC: U.S. Office of Education.

Vainstein, Rose, and Doris C. Holladay. 1959. *Statistics of Public Libraries in Cities with Populations of 100,000 or More, Fiscal Year 1958.* Washington, DC: Education Office, Health, Education, and Welfare Dept.

Vainstein, Rose, and Doris C. Holladay. 1960. *Statistics of County and Regional Library Systems Serving Populations of 50,000 or More, Fiscal Year 1959.* Washington, DC: Education Office, Health, Education, and Welfare Dept.

Willhoite, Mary M. 1960. *Statistics of County and Regional Libraries Serving Populations of 50,000 or More, Fiscal Year 1959.* Washington, DC: Education Office, Health, Education, and Welfare Dept.

Rather, John Carson, and Nathan Marshall Cohen. 1961. *Statistics of Libraries, Annotated Bibliography of Recurring Surveys.* Washington, DC: Education Office, Health, Education, and Welfare Dept.

Schick, Frank Leopold, and Doris C. Holladay. 1961. *Statistics of Public Library Systems Serving Populations of 100,000 or More: Fiscal Year 1960.* Washington, DC: Education Office, Health, Education, and Welfare Dept.

Drennan, Henry T., and Doris C. Holladay. 1962. *Statistics of Public Library Systems Serving Populations of 35,000 to 49,999: Fiscal Year 1960.* Washington, DC: Education Office, Health, Education, and Welfare Dept.

Schick, Frank Leopold, Henry T. Drennan, and Doris C. Holladay. 1962. *Statistics of Public Library Systems Serving Populations of 50,000 to 99,999: Fiscal Year 1960.* Washington, DC: Education Office, Health, Education, and Welfare Dept.

Drennan, Henry T., Doris C. Holladay, and United States Office of Education. 1965. *Statistics of Public Libraries, 1962. Part I: Selected Statistics of Public Libraries Serving Populations of 35,000 and Above: Institutional Data.* Washington, DC: U.S. Government Printing Office.

U.S. Office of Education. Division of Library Services, and Educational Facilities and National Center for Educational Statistics. 1965. *Statistics of Public Libraries Serving Communities with at least 25,000 Inhabitants.* Washington, DC: Education Office, Health, Education, and Welfare Dept.

U.S. Office of Education. Library Services Branch. 1966. *1962 Statistics of Public Libraries Serving Populations of Less Than 35,000.* Champaign, IL: Illini Union Book Store.

U.S. Office of Education. National Center for Educational Statistics. 1968. *Statistics of Public Libraries Serving Communities with at Least 25,000 Inhabitants, 1965.* Washington, DC: U.S. Government Printing Office.

Boaz, Ruth L., and National Center for Educational Statistics. 1970. *Statistics of Public Libraries Serving Areas with at Least 25,000 Inhabitants, 1968.* Washington, DC: U.S. Dept. of Health, Education, and Welfare, Office of Education, National Center for Educational Statistics.

Eckard, Helen M., and National Center for Educational Statistics. 1978. *Survey of Public Libraries: LIBGIS I, 1974.* Washington, DC: U.S. Dept. of Health, Education, and Welfare, Education Division.

National Center for Education Statistics. 1978. *Library Statistics Publications, 1960–1977.* Washington, DC: National Center for Education Statistics.

Eckard, Helen M., and National Center for Educational Statistics. 1982. *Statistics of Public Libraries, 1977–1978.* Washington, DC: National Center for Education Statistics.

U.S. Department of Education. *Patron use of Computers in Public Libraries.* 1986. Washington, DC: U.S. Department of Education.

U.S. Office of Educational Research and Improvement Center for Statistics. 1986. *Statistics of Public Libraries, 1982.* Washington, DC: Center for Statistics, U.S. Department of Education.

U.S. Department of Education. 1988. *National Center for Education Statistics Survey Report: Services and Resources for Young Adults in Public Libraries.* Washington, DC: Office of Educational Research and Improvement, U.S. Department of Education.

Nongovernment Publications

Ulshafer, Anne. 1963. *Selected Statistics of Public Libraries in the United States and Canada Serving 100,000 Population or More*. Fort Wayne, IN: Fort Wayne Public Library.

Carpenter, Beth E., and Abla M. Shaheen. 1971. *Selected Statistics of Public Libraries in the United States and Canada Serving 100,000 Population or More*. Fort Wayne, IN: Fort Wayne Public Library.

Statistics of Public Libraries in the United States and Canada Serving 100,000 Population or More. 1977. Fort Wayne, IN: Fort Wayne Public Library.

Statistics of Public Libraries in the United States and Canada Serving 100,000 Population or More. 1979. Fort Wayne, IN: Fort Wayne Public Library.

Allen County Public Library. 1981. *Statistics of Public Libraries in the United States and Canada Serving 100,000 Population or More*. Fort Wayne, IN: Allen County Public Library.

Goldhor, Herbert. 1981. *Fact Book of the American Public Library*. Champaign, IL: University of Illinois, Graduate School of Library and Information Science.

Allen County Public Library. 1983. *Statistics of Public Libraries in the United States and Canada Serving 100,000 Population or More*. Fort Wayne, IN: Allen County Public Library.

Public Library Association and American Library Association. 1985. *Statistics of Public Libraries, 1981–82: Data Gathered by the National Center for Education Statistics, U.S. Department of Education*. Chicago: Public Library Association.

Lynch, Mary Jo. 1987. *Libraries in an Information Society: A Statistical Summary*. Chicago: American Library Association.

1988–Present

Government Publications

Podolsky, Arthur. 1989. *FSCS: An NCES Working Paper: Public Libraries in Forty-Four States and the District of Columbia, 1988*. Washington, DC: U.S. Department of Education.

Lewis, Laurie, and Elizabeth Farris. 1990. *Services and Resources for Children in Public Libraries, 1988–89*. Available: http://nces.ed.gov/pubs90/90098.pdf (accessed November 25, 2002).

National Center for Education Statistics. 1991. *Public Library Data*. Washington, DC: U.S. Department of Education.

Podolsky, Arthur, and National Center for Education Statistics. 1991. *Public Libraries in 50 States and the District of Columbia, 1989*. Washington, DC: U.S. Department of Education.

Chute, Adrienne. 1992. *Public Libraries in the United States: 1990*. Washington, DC: U.S. Department of Education.

National Center for Education Statistics. 1992. *Public Library Data*. Washington, DC: U.S. Department of Education.

Chute, Adrienne. 1993. *Public Libraries in the United States: 1991*. Washington, DC: U.S. Department of Education.

Kindel, Carrol B. 1994. *Report on Coverage Evaluations of the Public Library Statistics Program*. E. D. TAB. NCES Number: 94430. Washington, DC: U.S. Department of Education. (Release Date: June 14, 1994).

Chute, Adrienne. National Center for Education Statistics. 1994. *Public Libraries in the United States, 1992*. E.D. TAB. Washington, DC: U.S. Department of Education.

Data Comparability and Public Policy New Interest in Public Library Data: Papers Presented at Meetings of the American Statistical Association. 1994. Washington, DC: U.S. Department of Education.

U.S. Census Bureau, Governments Division. 1994. *Report on Coverage Evaluation of the Public Library Statistics Program: A Report*. Washington, DC: U.S. Department of Education.

U.S. Department of Education. National Center for Education Statistics. 1995. *Public Libraries in the United States: 1993*. E.D. TAB, ed. Adrienne Chute, et al. (Release Date: September 30, 1995). Available: http://nces.ed.gov/pub search/pubsinfo.asp?pubid=95129 (accessed 25 November 2002).

National Center for Education Statistics. 1995. *Finance Data in the Public Library Statistics Program: Definitions, Internal Consistency, and Comparisons to Secondary Sources: A Report*. Washington, DC: National Center for Education Statistics.

Heaviside, Sheila, et al. 1995. Services and Resources for Children and Young Adults in Public Libraries. (Release Date: September 13, 1995). Available: http://nces.ed.gov/pubs95/95357.pdf (accessed November 25, 2002).

Kindel, Carrol B. 1995. *Finance Data in the Public Library Statistics Program: Definitions, Internal Consistency, and Comparisons to Secondary Sources: A Report*. Washington, DC: National Center for Education Statistics.

Kindel, Carrol B. 1995. *Report on Evaluation of Definitions Used in the Public Library Statistics Program*. NCES 95430. Washington, DC: National Center for Education Statistics.

Kindel, Carrol B. 1995. *Staffing Data in the Public Library Statistics Program: Definitions, Internal Consistency, and Comparisons to Secondary Sources: A Report*. Washington, DC: U.S. Department of Education.

National Center for Education Statistics. 1995. *Public Libraries in the United States, 1993*. Washington, DC: U.S. Department of Education.

Collins, Mary A. and Kathryn Chandler. Use of Public Library Services by Households in the United States: 1996. (Release Date: March 3, 1997). Available: http://nces.ed.gov/pubs/97446.pdf (accessed November, 25 2002).

Kindel, Carrol B. 1996. Public Library Structure and Organization in the United States.(Release Date: April 1, 1996). Available: http://nces.ed.gov/pubs/96229.pdf (accessed 25 November 2002).

National Center for Education Statistics. 1997. *Public Libraries in the United States, 1994*. Washington, DC: U.S. Department of Education.

U.S. Census Bureau. *Public Libraries in the United States, FY 1994*. NCES 97-418. E.D. TAB. Washington, DC: U.S. Department of Education. (Release Date:

March 3, 1997). Available: http://nces.ed.gov/pubs97/97418.pdf (accessed November 25, 2002).

Bassman, Keri, et al. 1998. *How Does Your Public Library Compare? Service Performance of Peer Groups.* Washington, DC: National Center for Education Statistics. (Release Date: October 27, 1998). Available: http://nces.ed.gov/pubs98/98310.pdf (accessed November 25, 2002).

National Center for Education Statistics. 1998. *Public Libraries in the United States, FY 1995.* Washington, DC: U.S. Department of Education.

Chute, Adrienne and P. Elaine Kroe. 1999. *Public Libraries in the United States, FY 1996.* Washington, DC: U.S. Department of Education.

U.S. Department of Education. 1999. *Public Libraries in the United States: FY 1996.* E.D. TAB, ed. Adrienne Chute, et al. Washington, DC: U.S. Department of Education. (Release Date: February 23, 1999). Available: http://nces.ed.gov/pubs99/1999306.pdf (accessed November 25, 2002).

U.S. Department of Education. 2000. *Public Libraries in the United States: FY 1997.* E.D. TAB, ed. Adrienne Chute, et al. Washington, DC: U.S. Department of Education. (Release Date: June 22, 2000). Available: http://nces.ed.gov/pubs2000/2000316.pdf (accessed November 25, 2002).

U.S. Department of Education. 2001. *Public Libraries in the United States: Fiscal Year 1998.* E.D. TAB, ed. Adrienne Chute, et al. Washington, DC: U.S. Department of Education. (Release Date: July 9, 2001). Available: http://nces.ed.gov/pubs2001/2001307.pdf (accessed November 25, 2002).

Glover, Denise. 2001. *Public Library Trends Analysis Fiscal Years 1992–1996.* Washington, DC: U.S. Department of Education.(Release Date: June 21, 2001). Available: http://nces.ed.gov/pubs2001/2001324.pdf (accessed November 25, 2002).

National Center for Education Statistics. 2002. *Public Libraries in the United States, 1989–2000.* Washington, DC: U.S. Department of Education. Available: at http://purl.access.gpo.gov/GPO/LPS17333.

U.S. Department of Education. 2002. *Public Libraries in the United States: Fiscal Year 1999.* E.D. TAB, ed. Adrienne Chute, et al. Washington, DC: U.S. Department of Education. (Release Date: February 11, 2002). Available: http://nces.ed.gov/pubs2002/2002308.pdf (accessed November 25, 2002).

U.S. Department of Education. 2002. *Public Libraries in the United States, Fiscal Year 2000.* E.D. TAB, ed. Adrienne Chute, et al. Washington, DC: U.S. Department of Education. (Release Date: July 2, 2002). Available: http://nces.ed.gov/pubs2002/2002344.pdf (accessed November 25, 2002).

National Center for Education Statistics. *Public Libraries.* Available: http://nces.ed.gov/pubsearch/pubsinfo.asp?pubid=2003398 (accessed November 2, 2003).

Kroe, Elaine. 2003. *Data File, Restricted Use: Public Libraries Survey: Fiscal Year 2001.* U.S. Department of Education. (Release Date: June 30, 2003). Available: http://nces.ed.gov/pubsearch/pubsinfo.asp?pubid=2003397.

Nongovernment Publications

Public Library Association Statistical Series

The Public Library Data Service (PLDS) Statistical Report is published annually. It presents exclusive, timely data from 1,000 public libraries across the country on finances, library resources, annual use figures, and technology. In addition to these topics, recent editions contains a "special survey."

Public Library Association. 1988. *Public Library Data Service Statistical Report '88.* Chicago: American Library Association.

Public Library Association. 1989. *Public Library Data Service Statistical Report '89.* Chicago: American Library Association.

Public Library Association. 1990. *Public Library Data Service Statistical Report '90.* Chicago: American Library Association.

Public Library Association. 1991. *Public Library Data Service Statistical Report '91.* Chicago: American Library Association.

Public Library Association. 1992. *Public Library Data Service Statistical Report '92.* Chicago: American Library Association.

Public Library Association. 1993. *Public Library Data Service Statistical Report '93.* Chicago: American Library Association.

Public Library Association. 1994. *Public Library Data Service Statistical Report '94: Special Section–Children's Services Survey.* Chicago: American Library Association.

Public Library Association. 1995. *Statistical Report '95: Public Library Data Service; Special Section, Technology Survey.* Chicago: American Library Association.

Public Library Association. 1996. *Statistical Report '96: Public Library Data Service; Special Section, Business Services Survey.* Chicago: American Library Association.

Public Library Association. 1997. *Statistical Report '97: Public Library Data Service; Special Section, Children's Services Survey.* Chicago: American Library Association.

Public Library Association. 1998. *Statistical Report '98: Public Library Data Service. Special Section: Finance Survey.* Chicago: American Library Association.

Public Library Association. 1999. *Statistical Report '99: Public Library Data Service; Special Section: Public Library Facilities Survey.* Chicago: American Library Association.

Public Library Association. 2000. *Statistical Report 2000: Public Library Data Service; Special Section: Children's Services Survey.* Chicago: American Library Association.

Public Library Association. 2001. *Statistical Report 2001: Public Library Data Service; Special Section: Finance Survey.* Chicago: American Library Association.

Public Library Association. 2002. *Statistical Report 2002: Public Library Data Service; Special Section: Public Library Facilities Survey.* Chicago: American Library Association.

Public Library Association. 2003. *Statistical Report 2003: Public Library Data Service; Special Section: Children's Services Survey.* Chicago: American Library Association.

Index

About the Authors

Primary Author

Kathleen de la Peña McCook is Distinguished University Professor, School of Library and Information Science, University of South Florida, Tampa. She is a past president of the Association for Library and Information Science Education and was the 2002 Latino Librarian of the Year (Trejo Award). She has also received the Beta Phi Mu Award for distinguished service to education for librarianship, the ALA-Elizabeth Futas Catalyst for Change Award, the ALA-RUSA-Margaret E. Monroe Adult Services Award and the ALA Equality Award. She was the inaugural recipient of the Achievement in Library Diversity Research Award from the ALA Office for Diversity in 2004. The Chicago Public Library honored her as its Scholar in Residence in 2003. Other books include *A Place at the Table: Participating in Community Building* (ALA Editions, 2000); *Ethnic Diversity in Library and Information Science* (*Library Trends*, 2000); and *Women of Color in Librarianship* (ALA, 1998).

Coauthors of Chapter 9

Linda Alexander is Assistant Professor, School of Library and Information Science, University of South Florida, Tampa. One of her

405

specialties is teaching courses in young adult materials online, and she has also taught children's literature.

Barbara Immroth is Professor, School of Information, University of Texas at Austin. She is a past president of the Association for Library Services to Children, a Trustee of the Freedom to Read Foundation, former president of the Texas Library Association, and past national president of Beta Phi Mu, LIS honorary society.

Author of Chapter 11

Barbara J. Ford is Mortenson Distinguished Professor, Mortenson Center for International Library Programs, University of Illinois at Urbana-Champaign. She is a past president of the American Library Association and former Assistant Commissioner of the Chicago Public Library.